ECOTAXATION

ECOTAXATION

edited by Tim O'Riordan
CSERGE
University of East Anglia and
University College London

St. Martin's Press
New York

Scholarly and Reference Division
St. Martin's Press
175 Fifth Avenue
New York, NY 10010

First published in the United Kingdom in 1997

First published in the United States of America in 1997

Printed and bound in Great Britain by
Biddles Limited, Guildford and King's Lynn

ISBN 0-312-17343-1

Library of Congress Cataloging in Publication Data applied for.

CONTENTS

PART I: SETTING THE SCENE

PART II: THE DOUBLE DIVIDEND DEBATE

PART III: ECOTAXATION IN PRACTICE

LIST OF CONTRIBUTORS

Giles Atkinson is Senior Research Associate, CSERGE, Department of Economics, University College London, Gower Street, London WC1E 6BT

Jean-Philippe Barde is Principal Administrator in the Environment Directorate, OECD, 2 rue Pascal, 75775 Paris, Cedex 16

Terry Barker is Chairman of Cambridge Econometrics, Covent Garden, Cambridge CB1 2HS

Peter Bohm is Professor of Economics, Department of Economics, University of Stockholm, S-106 91 Stockholm, Sweden

Amelia Craighill is a Research Associate, CSERGE, School of Environmental Sciences, University of East Anglia, Norwich NR4 7TJ

Paul Ekins is Senior Lecturer in the Environmental Policy Unit of the Department of Economics, University of Keele, Keele, Staffordshire ST5 5BG and is Director of the Sustainable Economy Unit of Forum for the Future

David Gee works on Information Strategy and Special Projects at the European Environment Agency, Kongens Nytorv 6, DK-1050, Copenhagen, Denmark

Kirk Hamilton is a Senior Research Fellow at the World Bank, 1818 H Street NW, Washington, DC 20433, USA, and Visiting Research Fellow, CSERGE, Department of Economics, University College London, Gower Street, London WC1E 6BT

Paul Herrington is a Senior Lecturer in Economics, University of Leicester, Leicester LE1 7RH

Daniel McCoy is a lecturer in Economics and a researcher in CSERGE, Department of Economics, University College London, Gower Street, London WC1E 6BT

Geoff Mulgan is Director of DEMOS, 9 Bridewell Place, London EC4 6AP

Jon O'Riordan is Assistant Deputy Minister, Operations, Ministry of the Environment, Parliament Buildings, Victoria, BC, Canada

Tim O'Riordan is Associate Director, CSERGE, School of Environmental Sciences, University of East Anglia, Norwich NR4 7TJ

Jane Powell is a Senior Research Associate, CSERGE, School of Environmental Sciences, University of East Anglia, Norwich NR4 7TJ

Judith Rees is Professor of Geography, London School of Economics, Houghton Street, London WC2A 2AE

Stephen Smith is Deputy Director, Institute for Fiscal Studies, and Reader in Economics, Department of Economics, University College, London WC1E 6BT

Michael Spackman is an Under Secretary in HM Treasury, currently on secondment to Nuffield College, Oxford OX1 1NF

Hans Vos is Head of the Environmental Policy Department in DHV Environment and Infrastructure (a private consultancy firm), Laan 1914, nr 35, PO Box 1076, 3800 Amersfoort, The Netherlands.

LIST OF FIGURES

LIST OF TABLES

LIST OF BOXES

ACRONYMS AND ABBREVIATIONS

ACBE	Advisory Committee on Business and the Environment
ADEME	French Environment Protection Agency
CAP	Common Agricultural Policy
CBI	Confederation of British Industry
CBS	Central Bureau of Statistics
CEPU	Centre for Environmental Policy and Understanding
CFC	chloro-fluorocarbon
CGE	computable general equilibrium
CIC	Construction Industry Council
CSERGE	Centre for Social and Economic Research on the Global Environment
CSO	Central Statistical Office, now the ONS
CZM	coastal zone management
DoE	Department of the Environment
EEA	European Environment Agency
EFTEC	Economics for the Environment Consultancy
EI	economic instrument
EMF	Energy Modelling Forum
EPA	Danish Environmental Protection Agency
EPA	UK Environmental Protection Act
ESRC	Economic and Social Research Council
ETR	Economic Tax Reform
EU	European Union
FGD	flue gas desulphurization
FoE	Friends of the Earth
GATT	General Agreement on Tariffs and Trade
GDP	gross domestic product
GEM	general equilibrium model
GFC	General Fuel Charge
GHG	greenhouse gas
GNP	gross national product
GWP	global warming potential
IE	interdependency effect
INT	Integrated scenario
I/O	input/output
IPC	Integrated Pollution Control

LA 21	Local Agenda 21
LARAC	Local Authority Recycling Advisory Committee
LETS	Local Employment Trading Scheme
LRMC	long-run marginal cost
MAC	marginal-abatement cost
MDM	Cambridge Multisectoral Dynamic Model
MEB	marginal-excess burden
MFWM	Modernization Fund for Waste Management
NAWDC	National Association of Waste Disposal Contractors
NDP	net domestic product
NEPP	National Environmental Policy Plan
NGO	non-governmental organization
NHS	National Health Service
NIC	National Insurance Contributions
NRA	National Rivers Authority
ODCs	ozone-depleting chemicals
OECD	Organization for Economic Cooperation and Development
ONS	Office of National Statistics, formerly the CSO
PIP	Policy-in-the-Pipeline
PSBR	public-sector borrowing requirement
RCEP	Royal Commission on Environmental Pollution
RE	recycling effect
REF	Reference scenario
RV	rateable value
SEEA	System of Environmental and Economic Accounting
SME	small- to medium-sized enterprise
SNA	System of National Accounts
SSC	Social Security Contributions
SST	social security tax
TPR	tax-plus-rebate
UGR	Federal Statistical Office (Germany)
VAT	value added tax
VOC	volatile organic compounds
WTO	World Trade Organization

ACKNOWLEDGEMENTS

This book has taken double the time of an elephant calf to gestate. Originally conceived in a lively seminar in Green College, Oxford, the kicking foetus was fed by new ideas, new contributors and new political developments. The result is a far more mature offspring than would have been delivered in 1994. I am grateful to the Economic and Social Research Council for providing the core funding for the Centre for Social and Economic Research on the Global Environment from which the original seminar was financed. Sir Crispin Tickell, the Warden of Green College, and his two able assistants, Casper Henderson and Rachel Duncan, provided hospitality and good cheer, plus a number of contributors. Pauline Blanch, Ann Dixon and Elaine Bennett created a work of art out of my drafting and redrafting. I am always grateful to them. My colleagues at CSERGE provided the perfect mix of fun and intellect that makes this sort of prolonged endeavour worthwhile. And the contributors, all of them, remained cheerful and obliging even in the face of a request for a third redraft. To all of you, my sincere thanks.

Tim O'Riordan
Norwich
September 1996

Part I

SETTING THE SCENE

EDITORIAL INTRODUCTION

The stimulus for this book arose out of the final chapter of the white paper published by the European Commission in December 1993. This document is covered in some detail by David Gee in Chapter 6 of this volume, as he was asked by the Commission to conduct an awareness-raising programme on the practicability of a progressive shift in the source of taxation from income and savings towards environmental damage and depletion of non-renewable resources. The superficial logic of the Commission's proposals was attractive. Taxation was becoming politically very difficult to sustain, a point stressed by Geoff Mulgan in Chapter 4, so any new taxation 'take' might look more tolerable if it were to become attached to the promotion of sustainable development, and through that route, towards the apparently benign objectives of retaining or promoting jobs and enabling local communities to prosper in the pursuit of social and ecological harmony.

Ecotaxation is increasingly taking on the mantle of a social policy rather than an environmental one, a switch in bias that reflects the judicial and ethical components of sustainable development. In Chapter 11, Jean-Philippe Barde points out that unemployment in the European Union exceeds 35 million, with a majority of the longer-term unemployed among poor and under-educated groups. Apart from the obvious wastage of talent, the social malaise and community frustration that such widespread inactivity potentially creates could result in higher social costs of crime, drugs, out-migration and ethnic tension, and family breakdown. There is a point where these costs, irrespective of the very personal hardships involved, become greater than the burden on the uncorrected economy of switching the basis of taxation. One purpose of this book is to explore how close we are to that zone of fundamental tax policy shift.

These distressing outcomes become an economic drag in their own right, for they result in the untimely deployment of social payments towards insurance premiums, crime prevention, rehabilitation of offenders and the disenchanted, and the growing burden of a dispirited non-democracy. After all, social malaise and growing inequality cannot provide a stable basis for any recognizable sustainability transition. That process is going to prove testing enough for social cohesion and economic productivity without the added burdens of alienation and non-compliance. Uncared-for people are unlikely to care for each other, let alone for the planet. Such conditions, therefore, cannot promote the cause of sustainable development.

There were other factors that stimulated this book. The Centre for Social and Economic Research on the Global Environment (CSERGE) cooperated with the Centre for Environmental Policy and Understanding at Green College, Oxford, to explore why environmental taxes and other economic instruments did not appear to be politically endorsed for so long a time, despite the many and repeated claims by a host of economists that such instruments could be designed to be efficient, socially fairer and effective. Paul Ekins in Chapter 8 summarizes the literature on this point.

This inertia led to a search for the causes of the resistance. One such cause is the difficulty of putting into effective practice many of these mechanisms in a world of almost chaotic economic interrelationships and very incomplete knowledge of, for example, what polluting waste streams contain, where they come from and where they go, and what damage in the immediate and more distant future such emissions create. Hans Vos, in Chapter 12, shows that the Dutch Parliament prevaricated for many years over the tough implementation of environmental taxes, for these very reasons. It was not that successive Dutch governments were not keen on the idea. It was largely because the political and administrative dilemma of trying to target such taxes correctly, in a very imperfect market economy, proved daunting. The best hope was to phase in such mechanisms gradually, with plenty of debate and warning, and to set up reasonably reliable programmes of monitoring and publicity.

Even then, such schemes are not always easy to do well, even with the most thoughtful and sincere preparation. Jon O'Riordan in Chapter 16 tells how the British Columbia Government, in which he is a senior policy analyst and adviser, launched a series of monetary charges against undesirable waste products (disposable nappies, used car batteries, tyres of all descriptions) to redirect that waste stream into usable products through secondary markets that thereby created new jobs. He shows how an initial pilot project is developing progressively into something more like an environmental tax with less opposition than anticipated. He suggests that waste creators have begun to recognize that such payments provide an opportun-ity for new business ventures to re-examine old approaches that uncritically led to 'wastes'. These new 'taxes' may not be the most efficient in terms of economic theory, but they have begun to alter both behaviour and attitudes.

The UK landfill levy is ambiguously called a tax. However, it is increasingly characterized as a levy in the sensitive political vocabulary around taxation that will cast its shadow over British party political rhetoric for many years to come. Jane Powell and Amelia Craighill point out that the creation of this levy was a matter of intense consultation over, and adjudicative juggling of, tactics and proposed charges. Their Chapter 15 reveals very clearly just how difficult it will be to impose such a levy in an arena of many different players and regulatory motives, and where the actual waste streams are very difficult to follow. This suggests that the cost of administrating the levy will not be cheap, and that there can be no guarantees against miscalculation, plain error and fraud – not to mention the temptation to discard waste in any out-of-the-way nook and cranny on the landscape. But, to its credit, the government has held its nerve, and a fascinating experiment in ecotaxation is about to begin as this book is published.

The final stimulus was the growing economic and political debate over the so called 'double dividend'. In this case the revenue generated from a specific environmental tax could be applied to a social or economic benefit, while damage to the ecology or to people, or to both, could be reduced progressively. In a time of very tight public spending rounds and the ever-present fear of rising interest rates, such a windfall of income could be politically potent for a serving government, especially if it could be directed at jobs and training. This may be the longer-term objective of the landfill levy – we shall see. Certainly its promise has already created a welter of waste recycling and reduction measures that arguably would not otherwise have been stimulated.

The landfill levy is the first example in the UK of a tax that is specifically earmarked for a sustainability objective. This is a fascinating innovation, even though the actual economic effects will be small. More significant still is the scope for passing the tax through a series of environment trusts. Technically speaking, these are charities that combine the funds of the private sector, in this case the waste-collecting and disposing industry, with additional public funds to create investment pools for the promotion of clean technology, for the remediation of landfill sites and contaminated locations, and, possibly, for research and education into waste-avoiding economic behaviour. This may all seem modest: after all, the UK Treasury still wants to avoid the dreaded word 'hypothecation', or advance allocation of predetermined funds. But, as Mulgan indicates in Chapter 4, hypothecation should be a joy to experiment with in a sustainable age, while in Chapter 3, Michael Spackman, a Treasury official writing in a personal capacity, reveals that hypothecation can and increasingly does come in various guises. Jon O'Riordan describes in Chapter 16 how a modest pilot scheme in hypothecation has become quite acceptable to public opinion.

This leaves us with the economic theorists who remain uneasy over both the practice of earmarking and the principle of double dividend. Stephen Smith in Chapter 2 looks at how the tax system is passing through a series of reformations as the political objectives of taxation are refashioned to apply to morals as well as economics. If you, the reader, are not a trained economic theorist, then you are advised at this point to turn to Chapter 10. There, Daniel McCoy will help you to understand in lay language just what are the arguments for and against the double dividend debate. The answer lies in the way any new tax can be deployed to offset inefficiencies and distortions in existing taxation, as well as how far it actually cuts the social costs of environmental deterioration. Frankly, that combination is extremely difficult to determine in actual practice. Models help, as Terry Barker reveals in Chapter 9 in his calculations of the stimuli provided for jobs and for the economy generally, following a series of different taxes geared to reduce carbon dioxide emissions. But these models depend enormously on assumptions about responses in the economy that cannot be guaranteed, since so many other dependent factors are neither predictable nor incorporated fully in the models. So both the theory, well covered by Peter Bohm in Chapter 7 and Paul Ekins in Chapter 8, and the models explored by Terry Barker in Chapter 9, do not really tell us any more than that we ought to be very careful about reaching premature cost decisions on the economic efficiency of such taxes.

This means that ecotaxation is more likely to be a political and social measure than an economic one in the coming decades. The deployment of economic instruments to reduce the need for burdensome regulation is partly politically motivated: it gives the gloss, at least, of a deregulatory measure, highly popular among political champions of the right. In the brave new world of market testing, quasi-independent public agencies run on corporatist lines and value-for-money audits, any advance in the application of charges will be politically welcomed, irrespective of their more subtle economic or distributional consequences. So Jean-Philippe Barde is right in assuming that greater opportunism, with respect to a myriad of cost-recovering charges and penalizing taxes against environmental sins, should grow in political popularity. This is a lively time for such regulatory innovation, spurred on by the greater sensitivity of industry to sustainability principles and practices, and by the increasingly effective campaigning of environmental and consumer groups.

In addition, the privatization of the big energy and water utilities brings with it a host of opportunities for more environmentally targeted charging, as pointed out for the water resource case by Paul Herrington and Judith Rees in Chapters 13 and 14 respectively. In an age of economic advance, global warming, climate change and greater ecological integration into land-use planning and *in situ* surface and groundwater management, the water resource cannot sustain all the many demands expected of it without a radical approach to charging and the application of the precautionary principle. So ecotaxation becomes attractive partly because the business climate is more favourably inclined, the regulatory envelope more accommodating, the environmental protective lobby more openly aggressive, and the consumer more conscious of a sustainability responsibility.

Finally, there is the spate of recent work on sustainability indicators and 'green' national accounting. The former are connected to national and local strategies for sustainable development, as well as to the emerging regulatory practice of quasi-voluntaristic, industry-wide, environmental agreements. The latter relate to widening the basis of national income accounts. Atkinson and Hamilton address these issues in Chapter 5.

Ecotaxation is becoming a deeply political issue. The Labour Party think tank, known as the Institute for Public Policy Research, published a pamphlet on *Green Taxes* in October 1996 as part of a drive to encourage all political parties to look at taxing environmental 'bads' to boost employment and to create a pool of public sector cash for local sustainability initiatives. This theme is now on the agenda.

This, then, is the context of this book. Ecotaxation is a loose term for a host of motivations, tactics and opportunities. The world of environmental politics is no longer confined to nature conservation, waste reduction and pollution control. It has moved into the mainstream political arenas of fiscal strategy, constitutional reform, social welfare, democratic rehabilitation, corporate ethics and community activism. Into this rapidly expanding world of new policy alliances and interest-group realignments, ecotaxation is pushing its transformational practices into a host of ideologies and behaviours. Ecotaxation may not achieve its original objectives of decoupling economy from environmental disruption. Nevertheless, it could achieve a more imaginative objective of bonding social justice to democratic reincarnation to economic innovation without bringing the habitable world to a halt. That, in other guises, is sustainable development, and if sustainable development is the ultimate goal, then ecotaxation could become one of the catalysts for its successful implementation. If that really is the case, then it would be unwise to rely on economic theory as its ultimate judge. Alternative approaches for evaluating the sustainability transition are offered in Chapter 1 and in the overall conclusions to this volume.

C   h   a   p   t   e   r   1

ECOTAXATION AND THE SUSTAINABILITY TRANSITION

Tim O'Riordan

What on earth is the sustainability transition? It is a wonderfully 'flakey' phrase covering how any society and economy move from a present, non-sustainable state to a future, less unsustainable state. It is a phrase that covers any conceivable topic and pathway. It is a term of art rather than an actual routeway. Willy-nilly we are embarked on it, so we might as well try to get to grips with what it would look like and what it will involve.

Looking across the formidably treacherous terrain of the early phases of this transition, the more distant prospect does not appear very inviting to many late 20th-century citizens. Most, if not all, are embalmed by a predominant outlook and way of life that are at cross purposes with that vision. Citizens will be expected to act like socially responsible citizens, not individually self-gratifying consumers, and to for their neigh-bours near and far. The amount of waste created to produce any useful item should be cut by at least half and preferably more. Energy and mate-rials usage will be reduced by almost as much per unit of value used in the pursuit of happiness. Prices will reflect the full ecological and social 'foot-print' of economic activity and the precautionary principle will become the bible of management and science. Equity issues – notably, the well-being of critically endangered ecosystems and human populations threatened by unmanageable catastrophe – will come to dominate effi-ciency rules in the determination of valuation, risk avoidance and cost-benefit analysis. Citizens will be expected to 'get involved' in the process of communal governance, providing guidance, evaluating scenar-ios and giving their assent to the next phase of the transition. There will not be an opportunity to hide away or to cop out. The fatalist and the non-cooperative will be encouraged to adopt their communal stewardship mantle. The sustainable polity will be a collectivist polity, indentured to tend the global commons.

This last paragraph has been peppered with the futuristic and deterministic 'will' before every verb. Of course the middle horizon may not look like that. Obviously, it depends enormously on what the near horizon pathways create. In any case, outlooks may change in the process. What may appear alienating and uninviting today may become a part of the civic culture tomorrow, just as computer-game playing might have been viewed as awesome by 19th-century youngsters had they envisioned it without social and technological preparation. Until we embark on the journey, we will not know how we may become transformed by our experience. But transformed we must inevitably be if we are to explore a less non-sustainable age.

ENVISIONING SUSTAINABLE DEVELOPMENT

There are almost as many definitions of sustainable development as there are writers who contemplate it. That may be as it should. The very ambiguity of the term allows interests from many different walks of life to debate and seek to achieve it. Because sustainable development is seen as a 'good thing', so it is stretched to accommodate almost any unrequited social goal. As Lele (1991, p 613) wryly remarked:

> Sustainable development is a 'metafix' that will unite everybody from the profit-minded industrialist and risk minimising subsistence farmer to the equity seeking social worker, the pollution-concerned or wildlife loving First Worlder, the growth maximising policy maker, the goal orientated bureaucrat, and, therefore, the vote counting politician.

This is a neo-renaissance idea that covers the whole of human endeavour and planetary survival. Who could possibly oppose it? The round tables that have sprung up in a number of countries survive because members have a wish to reach some form of consensus, no matter how unsatisfactory that may be from their starting point. The very continuation of such round tables is a form of institutional commitment to a process that is seen as good and worthwhile, even when progress is painful and the language unintelligible. As this book will reveal, experiments in tax reform and in adjustments to market prices continue to evolve, despite the tremendous difficulties of fair implementation and the shake-out of gainers and losers. The record of achievement is understandably unsatisfactory, but that does not stop the analysts and the experimenters. Sustainable development is a socially energizing force that may come to have the same momentum as creative evolution itself. We are not at all sure where we will end up but we keep on trying, almost as if a greater force is propelling us. That may prove to be the most important driver towards envisioning sustainable futures.

In an interesting experiment, Nagpal and Foltz (1995) solicited the imaginings of 52 people from 34 countries in 5 languages on how they envisioned the future. What they picked up was an enormous energy of social concern for the future of their children as well as for the plight of present generations less fortunate than they were. Equally interesting was the apparent psychological difficulty of jumping too far from the here and now into a world where the main strands of personal identity appear too disconnected and chaotic. Thus Nagpal and Foltz (1995, p 159) observe:

> People's visions for the future are frequently coloured by their nostalgia for the past. People mourn the passing of former days, but simultaneously express longing for a future free of restrictive cultural traditions. Thus, visions often reflect a struggle between shrugging off the burden of custom and the effort to keep traditions alive as an anchor against the tides of change.

The essays also reveal a deep contradiction in the role of the state. Those who advocate localism, community empowerment and collective responsibility through individual enlightenment see the state as a facilitator and as a protector of the peace. Those who favour ecoefficiency seek international frameworks that will guide competitiveness into socially constructive and cooperative ways, yet will still unleash all the best in innovation and enterprise. It may be possible to reconcile the two by adjusting the role of the state into international 'broker' for global agreements on trade, competitiveness and regulation, and local 'facilitator' for communal self-reliance and consensus building. Such a combination would mean the reconciliation of the two great forces that may prove to be the most important influences on the sustainability transition over the next generation – namely, globalism and localism. Globalism is being unleashed by the almost unrestrainable tendencies of technological and managerial advance, information ordering, and the ubiquitousness of knowledge, capital flight and capital investment. Localism is the antidote: the call for greater control over local lives and natural worlds. The result is the uneasy relationship between the invisible process of homogeneity and the do-it-yourself politics of heterogeneity.

Nagpal and Foltz (1995, p 168) sum up this dilemma in a very perceptive quote:

> The paradox we face is: How do we help the poor if their survival is repeatedly put at risk by those who say they wish to help them, but whose primary concern is capital accumulation and exploitation of raw materials? There exists a far reaching force of importing alien models of consumption and behaviour – in sum, changing indigenous cultures – with no purpose other than foisting the western market model on these peoples ... or to make these people useful tools for enriching others.

There we have it: what is sustainable development actually for? If it is for the gradual victory of capitalism in some eco-moderated form, then the equity and cultural identity goals get short shrift. If the objective is greater social justice, more effective sharing of the global life-support commons, and the respect for community identity at a local level, then much of the case for ecoefficiency based on quasi-market principles will be treated with circumspection.

Envisioning sustainable futures will mean, at the very least, clarifying these underlying value premises. It will also entail discovering even more than we do at present, why such value premises are formed and through what revelations they may be accommodated into larger and more coherent wholes. That, in turn, opens up the dilemma that sustainable development has to be visualized at various scales of space and time, culture and economy, ecosystem and biogeochemical flux. We do not have ready institutional or psychological means of coordinating these scales of envisioning. We appear to be temperamentally and constitutionally capable of connecting only a small number of these scales at a time. If it is to progress, the sustainability transition will have to help us all to connect up scales of perception and consequence that are almost unnatural to us now.

DEFINING SUSTAINABLE DEVELOPMENTS

Despite the huge literature on definitions of sustainable development, it is possible and representative to characterize sustainable development in three ways: *economistic*, *developmental* and *radical*. Yet, in doing so, one must bear in mind Sachs's view that:

> ...definitions tacitly shape the definition of the problem, highlight certain solutions and consign others to oblivion, therefore it features certain types of social actors, marginalising others, and certain types of transformation, degrading others.
>
> *(Sachs, 1993, p 9)*

The economistic view favours a discourse around terms such as carrying capacity, critical load, resource depletion, economic efficiency, natural capital, valuation and cost-benefit analysis. The underlying logic is that there is nothing inherently wrong with the economic system that cannot be righted by appropriate adjustments based on 'good science and ecological principles'. Precaution is acceptable but only within this narrowly conceived domain. Acting ahead of scientific proof is only justified if the likely threat is so severe that the consequences are worth avoiding by premature action. The risk has to be real and the consequences of present inaction have to be alarmingly worrying. This is still a form of cost-benefit analysis, where the costs can be justified on a no-regret basis. In this light, ecological tax reform has no great purpose. Environmental taxes to correct market imperfections are quite another matter, although the use of the revenue is generally not discussed.

The second outlook, or developmental view, discusses sustainable development in the language of overcoming the North–South divide, of redirecting Northern patterns of consumption, of burden sharing, debt removal, making fairer terms of trade, and addressing population stabilization as a civil rights and poverty-eliminating issue. In this sense, the economistic term 'critical natural capital' applied to the vital life-support services that keep the planet habitable suggests that for the North to enjoy its comforts, the South must be helped to avoid damaging the well-being of all future generations. The government in its first, post-Brundtland foray into this debate (Department of the Environment, 1989, pp 1–2) summarized the dilemma thus :

As populations increase they make additional demands on natural resources for their basic necessities, as do demands for resources to be exported to other countries. The environmental pressures which these demands create can be particularly severe in developing countries that are often less well equipped to address them... The result is further decline into poverty, leading to even greater pressures on the environment.

This comes from a government that cut the aid budget by 40 per cent in 1996–97 so that only 16 of the poorest 40 countries are now given direct assistance. It also comes from a government that is making no systematic attempt to calculate what consumption at trading demands the UK economy is making on developing countries that may exacerbate their materials export dependency and undermine further vital global processes.

Yet such unhelpful policies come in the wake of this rhetoric, as announced in the first white paper on a UK sustainable development strategy (HM Government, 1990, p 10):

The starting point for this Government is the ethical imperative of stewardship, which must underlie all environmental policies. We have a moral duty to look after our planet and to hand it over to good order to future generations. That is what experts mean when they talk of 'sustainable development'.

The third perspective, or radical view, takes the planet as the focus of attention, and justice as the guiding metaphor. Ecojustice means treating the life-support systems of the earth with a degree of care and respect that can only emerge if society also treats itself and its offspring similarly. As we shall see, here are very different approaches to valuation, social order and quality of life. Sustainable development becomes the guiding beacon for power transfer and decentralization. None of this is new: the deep green philosophy has been arguing along these lines since the early 1970s. What is different is the more socially relevant framework for this imperative. Saving the planet comes after we save each other. Human welfare, and policies to ensure that the disadvantaged and alienated are brought into meaningful participatory democracies at the local level, become the normative objectives of this vision of sustainable development.

The rhetoric of sustainable development is loosely anchored in the ideologies of development, the roles of government and the *locus* for action over social change. The fact that the concept has persevered and that it is enabling something of a dialogue between environmentalists and social reformers is a step forward. The formation of a coalition of 44 non-governmental groups under the title 'Real World' is an example of this positioning. Created by the energetic Jonathon Porritt, Real World brings together environmental non-governmental organizations (NGOs), developmental charities, anti-poverty campaigners and constitutional reformers. As Porritt explains:

The immediate intention is to force our collective concerns onto the agenda for the next general election... we will be lobbying the parties about their manifestos, briefing journalists, undertaking surveys of public opinion, encouraging the formation of *local* Real World coalitions, and preparing for a major publicity campaign during the general election itself.

(Porritt, 1996, p 34)

This particular election may come too early for Real World to be more than a side-show, but the issues it espouses are embedded in the sustainability transition. Whatever happens in the forthcoming election, the conditions for Real World to be active will likely be far more favourable in the next election. For a fuller explanation, see Jacobs (1996).

Any move towards market reform or tax reconstruction has to take into account the objectives and positioning of the sustainability transition. The economistic view will look to least cost, more socially efficient outcomes and procedures – as is illustrated by the hypothecation and double dividend debates that follow. The developmental-evolutionary perspective looks for more North–South sharing and capacity-building as an outcome of any redirected revenue. The radicals look to human and ecological well-being as the basis of valuation and democratic institutions. Taxes as they see them should be redesigned to correct market imperfections that create inequality and the inability to live according to ecological norms, particularly for those poor who would genuinely like to do so. Thus the purpose of tax reform in the sustainability transition is very much a matter of perspective. There is no agreement on the matter. Tax reform would be difficult enough to achieve even if there were consensus about its purpose. The chapters that follow indicate that there is no agreement either as to objective or to method. One has to sense that even a modest shift towards ecological tax reform will be a long time coming.

CALCULATING ECOLOGICAL FOOTPRINTS

One way forward is to gain a better understanding of what we do when we tread on the earth. The verb 'tread' is a metaphor for economic activity that creates ecological disturbance and social disruption. When a stone is thrown into a pond, the ripples can be seen and their pathways predicted, because the initiating event and the boundary of the consequences are visible and calculable. But when a national economy uses wood, for example, it is by no means easy to estimate the complete disturbance that a wood-consuming society creates for the various scales of distance, time, economy and culture. Yet any sustainability audit ought to take such estimates into account. It does not help to complain about the level of ignorance over the nature of the effects, the various consequences for physical, biological and social parameters, and the appropriate application of precaution in the face of anxiety. These limitations are actually part of the audit and indicator assessment process. That process is a coupling of unknowingness, guesswork, social weighting and good faith. It is also part of the mechanism of valuation. Valuation is not handed down from expert task forces. Ideally, it should be the outcome of popular involvement through citizens' task forces operating on the basis of trust, where the finally agreed package incorporates the effort of reaching conciliation. Those involved will value the final product all the more because they have struggled to listen to, and to accommodate, the values of others in order to reach a consensual outcome that contains their commitment. That process is now referred to as stakeholding; the resolution of different perspectives into a social consensus is one aspect of valuation.

The work of analysts in developing a set of environmental indicators deserves recognition. Giles Atkinson and Kirk Hamilton summarize the best of the output in Chapter 5. Hammond and his colleagues (1995) provide a readable review of actual casework. They point out that good indicators are based on a great deal of good monitoring and data collection, and that the very best are designed to communicate aggregated information effectively and in comparable form. Coupled with targets, indicators have powerful political and policy relevance.

So the final calculation of the ecological footprint depends entirely on who was involved in estimating it and by what means. Wackernagel and Rees (1995, p 9) define the ecological footprint more narrowly as:

> ...an accounting tool that enables us to estimate the resource consumption and waste assimilation requirements of a defined human population or economy in terms of a corresponding productive land area.

Thus it is possible to calculate the land and water area necessary for a city both to 'feed' its economy and to 'dispose' of its wastes. This involves land- and life-support processes that are globally dispersed, or the expropriated carrying capacity per inhabitant. The authors calculate the average land/water equivalent for a typical Canadian as 4.3 hectares. But in practice, the 'footprint' will vary according to the energy and material content of all the goods and services any typical resident consumes. In general, the 'invisible' materials, energy and biogeochemical 'fields' required to support a Western citizen extend far and wide in space and time. For the US citizen, this amounts to the equivalent of the natural productivity of 5.1 hectares; for the Indian citizen the equivalent is 0.4 hectares (see Table 1.1), (ibid, p 85). The footprint of London is 120 times its geographical size (ibid, p 91). For the wood industry:

> ... the results show that 6.4 million hectares of forest land throughout the world are taken up 'more or less permanently' [to supply Britain annually with its wood needs] and that an additional 67000 ha are deforested... Britain's total forest products footprint is three times the area of the country's non productive forest... UK per capita consumption of timber products is 66 per cent higher than the 'permissible' global average.
>
> (Wackernagel and Rees, 1995, p 92)

Sustainable futures will somehow have to come to grips with the calculation of ecological footprints, no matter how crudely to begin with, otherwise the burden of human evolution will threaten many of the species. If humanity were free from morals and a sense of perspective, we would probably follow the Darwinian route of the dinosaurs and the dodo, and evolve into a smaller, leaner population of *homo ecologicus*. But we have the

Table 1.1 Ecological footprints for Canada, USA and India

Consumption per Person in 1991	Canada	US	India	World
CO_2 emission (tonnes per year)	15.2	19.5	0.81	4.2
Purchasing power ($1000 per person)	19.3	22.1	1.0	3.8
Vehicles per 100 persons	46.0	57.0	0.2	10.0
Paper consumption (kg per year)	247.0	317.0	2.0	44.0
Fossil energy use (gigajoules per year)	250.0	287.0	5.0	86.0
Freshwater withdrawal (m^3 per year)	1688.0	1868.0	612.0	644.0
Ecological footprint (ha per person)	4.3	5.1	0.4	1.8

Source: Wackernagel and Rees, 1995, p 85

burden of conscience and hence the travail of ecological responsibility. The protection of that conscience and its practical expression in a more ethically weighted, ecologically biased economics is part of the sustainability transition. This is why the technological advance of vast data-storage and retrieval arrangements allows us to develop both numerical and socially constructed indicators of ecological disruption and livability, which in turn will influence national and local accounts.

It is the very facility of complex data handling that permits a more socially activated process of quality-of-life valuation through which more sophisticated and response-demanding assessments of footprints will emerge. It would make sense if any ecological tax reform was able to have access to these calculations. This is not just because they are necessary for any repricing: it is also necessary because the valuation processes themselves should alert the populace into an acceptance of the tax reform. The sustainability transition has to create the revelatory outcomes that make its progress politically tolerable.

ONE MAJOR DRIVER: AVOIDABLE UNEMPLOYMENT

Unemployment afflicts over a quarter of employable people in the UK at present, but in the more deprived pockets of inner-city high ethnicity, the figure is three times that (Leadbetter and Mulgan, 1994, p 7). Since 1950, over five million jobs have disappeared from the goods-producing industries. Although eight million new jobs were created in the service sector during the same time, the labour force has expanded by additional births and larger numbers of women seeking employment. The information revolution has removed, and continues to remove, millions of jobs that used to be done by anybody with relatively minimal training. During the 1990s, employment will continue to fall by 24 per cent in the primary sector, by 12 per cent in manufacturing and by 3 per cent in construction (Department of Employment, 1993). Any jobs that will be created will require a high degree of skills, notably in computer literacy. The pace of technological change also means that job flexibility and continuous retraining will be essential if employees are not to be made redundant because they are out of phase.

The unskilled are seriously in danger of being permanently unemployed or confined to the black economy. According to Dickenson (1994), there is a close association between perceived permanent unemployment and crime, a conclusion hotly disputed by the government.

As matters stand, this dismal picture for up to 30 per cent of the future UK work-force is not helped by undirected training, part-time low wage conditions, the poverty trap of tax-take biting at too early a wage rate, tight restrictions on voluntarism for work experience while volunteers are receiving social security payments, deregulation of the labour markets, and a collective failure to find any realistic alternative to constructive employment outside the market place. Globalization and industrial restructuring have made managerial classes just as vulnerable to redundancy as the lower skilled, while up to 40 per cent of undergraduates with excellent talent cannot get into the labour-force without some form of practical experience. Should they fail to obtain appropriate employment, then they would be faced with expensive retraining after five years.

A related factor, and one that is yet to focus seriously in contemporary economic and taxation debates, is that of the likely shift in the demographic balance from young to old. The European Commission reports that by 2025, nearly 30 per cent of the population will be over 60 years' old, while only 20 per cent will be under 20. More and more people will be requiring social services long after they have ceased productive work. The shift in the burden of preparing for old age is likely to move increasingly to taxation in work. Ecotaxation, therefore, may play its part in what must become a fundamental tax revolution.

So far this potential social time-bomb remains ticking in the cupboard. Part-time working, contracting out and relatively generous early retirement schemes have held off the worst of the social damage, but the serious phase of structural underemployment is now almost upon us. If the link between social malaise, poverty, crime and alienation from authority is proven by more case evidence, then the conditions for any meaningful sustainability transition are unlikely to be fulfilled. The potential significance for democratic institutions, for community cohesiveness, and for the social cost burden of care, crime prevention and health promotion could be awesome in terms either of public expenditure to individual pain and suffering, or, most likely, both.

Mulgan and Murray (1993) favour a package of shifting taxes towards consumption, to land and property – especially where capital gains are made as a result of social expenditures – and by environmental damage and depletion levies. The added income would be geared to training, to tax rebates encouraging in-job employment skills development, and to adjust the various social costs of acquiring labour. The UK Liberal Democratic Party (1993) has adopted this line as a key plank in its sustainability strategy. So far this is the only UK political party formally to embrace ecological tax reform, although the Labour Party (1994) are flirting with adjustments to the costs of hiring labour, reached out of reallocated tax revenues. The Liberal Democrats see social-fairness compensation payments as a key aspect of hypothecation, partly because many of their electoral supporters are rural and family forming. Accordingly they tend to be dependent on the car (and hence sensitive to any significant petrol tax increase) but because they are more educated than is the average, they tend to favour redistribution as a political objective. Labour, on the other hand, is no longer in a political position to discuss changes in taxation without stirring up an often misguided hue and cry. Tony Blair's speech on 27 February 1996 toned down any talk of tax reform and muted the calls from his more radical, non-Treasury spokespeople for a more decisive shift towards social payments and poverty alleviation.

Intriguingly the US President's Council on Sustainable Development (1996, Chapter 2) has recognized more explicitly than UK politicians the relationship between shifting the tax burden, reallocating income for social justice reasons, and improving environmental well-being. Council members favoured the establishment of a Tax Commission to investigate the implications of a shift in taxation towards inefficiency, waste and pollution through revenue neutral arrangements. The criteria such a Commission should follow, argued the Council, would include the following:

- Social equity must be improved to meet the goals of sustainable development. Therefore the burden of taxation should fall on the higher paid.
- The tax regime should encourage savings, private investment and job creation.
- Any shift should be gradual, it should not obviate high environmental protection standards, and it should enhance the efficiency of meeting quality-of-life objectives. Since federal and state environmental regulatory measures cost on average 55 units in the dollar in administration and in cost-ineffective response measures (see the coverage in Ekins, Chapter 8), there is a strong case for switching to pollution taxes as part of a move towards ecological tax reform.
- There should be a critical review of existing tax subsidies that run counter to the implementation of sustainable development, particularly those subsidies in water, forestry and land-management programmes that positively promote wastage.

The report of the President's Council is significant because it was designed to produce consensus across a broad sweep of policy communities, most particularly business and the voluntary environmental sectors, as well as government representatives. The fact that tax reform received a prominent billing – in a report that stressed new public-private partnerships and a wide variety of social agencies leading towards community self-advancement – suggests that the President's Council sought to look at tax reform as a basis for social renaissance as much as for environmental improvement and economic efficiency. This is the kind of triple alliance that should help to make Agenda 21 become a reality.

A SECOND DRIVING FORCE: LOCAL AGENDA 21

Local Agenda 21 (LA 21) is the encapsulation of the Rio message at the household and neighbourhood level. To get action there, individuals have to feel that they can and should change things for the betterment of their locality. One of the factors to cause this reaction is the unease over the seemingly uncontrollable forces of globalization. Globalization is just as elusive matter as is sustainable development. It is essentially defined in terms of what is not perceived to be controllable by central governments, who think of themselves as accountable. It is the sense of a loss of control over forces that could be devastating to the well-being of 'ordinary' people, that gives rise to so much misgiving over the apparently dangerous forces of globalization. It refers to patterns of change that cannot be altered by national governments, let alone local governments. These include such matters as the introduction of biotechnology, the spread of capital accumulation and deficit, the growing homogenization of the media that is beginning to swamp cultural identity, and the loss of language and custom that maintain a sense of continuity with the everyday.

The Commission on Global Governance (1995, p 49) addresses the five main challenges to global governance as poverty, nuclear proliferation, debt, war and environmental degradation. The Commission argued for a civic ethic that should guide individual response to those forces, as 'a respect for life, liberty, justice, equality, mutual respect, caring and integrity'. Globalization creates a desire for locality in the form of a democratic entity that gives meaning to global action with local effects. This in turn enables individual local actions to feel connected to invisible networks of like-minded but unobserved behaviour that, in accumulation, will make a difference on the planetary stage.

The Rio Agenda 21 contained Chapter 28, entitled Local Authorities' Initiatives, in support of Agenda 21. This reflected the agreement that local authorities are designated as one of nine stakeholders to A 21 whose participation is vital for the success of any sustainability transition. For the record, the other stakeholders, all of whom received a separate chapter, were indigenous peoples, women, youth, science, business, trades unions, agriculture and NGOs. The text of Agenda 21, Chapter 28, argued for the following two principles:

1. Sustainability must be defined locally and be accepted locally by people who are participating freely to reach outcomes that they feel duty bound to support by virtue of their participation in creating these futures. This means that LA 21 must resonate with the aspirations of all strands of local opinion in such a way as to carry conviction, hope and involvement.

2. Sustainability means empowerment, sharing and effective democracy at the local level as a means of ensuring that people trust the process and have respect for the views of those communally involved. Any transition to a less non-sustainable state, no matter how uncertain and ill-directed, will create a host of different gainers or losers compared with those who benefit or suffer in the conventional growth process. LA 21 has to find a mechanism for identifying these interests, and hence to devise meaningful mechanisms to ensure that everyone sees a common purpose in sharing each other's burden and appreciating each other's advantage.

Understandably, local authorities are approaching this process in a tentative fashion. To begin with, there is no concept of these two ideals operating in any organized way at local neighbourhood level. In any case, many residents feel that the local authority is either too impoverished or too neutered by the lack of power, or too bereft of money, staff, trained competence or technology to broker meaningful partnerships which would create the critical mass for a momentum. For the most part, if local authorities are involved at all, it is primarily at the level of gathering data, building networks, looking for policy alliances, evaluating cost-saving strategies that cut energy and waste, and activating community action in schools and neighbourhood programmes. The bigger issues of creating alternative economies through informal job-trading schemes (Local Employment Trading Schemes – LETS), or via the imaginative use of local taxation revenue to pump public-private charitable trusts, remain, for the most part, background gossip fodder and the stuff of visionary ideologies.

In a study of five LETS in the UK, Sefang (1996, pp 44–5) found that all were small, most had fewer than 100 members, and industry was rarely involved. About 40 per cent of the activities were domestic services, such as computer use, accounting and child-minding. Most of the trading was transferred from the cash economy, with no new money in circulation. The majority could have paid for all their LETS services in cash. Their primary motivation was social and political. Any meaningful move towards a radical interpretation of the sustainability transition, therefore, would suggest that the poor and the unemployed should be targeted. It might be difficult to get them interested, however, for fear of exciting the ever-watchful attentions of the tax inspectors.

LA 21 is tapping two important nerve centres for its momentum (if there is a momentum). One is the yearning for more do-it-yourself politics of the kind that springs up almost against the political grain, simply to enable groups to get things done. The other is a strong sense of grievance that the local authority has been sacrificed for too long to meet the greater glory of a centralizing, elected 'parliamentary dictatorship', and that it is time to call a halt. LA 21 provides the perfect vehicle for doing just that.

Networking channels between local authorities, and between local goevrnments and other actors, are creating opportunities to share the experience of success and failure. The Local Government Management Board, a LA pressure group, has the backing of the local authorities' associations and a National LA 21 Coordination Forum. Policy entrepreneurs and local political parties also appear to be a factor in pushing a slightly more focused effort towards the sustainability transition. Local authorities, faced with the crisis over clear democratic legitimacy – as electoral votes fall to alarmingly low levels in some areas (Hambleton, 1993) – are forced more and more into contracting out their services and undertaking internal management reorganizations. These are not conducive conditions for any sustainability transition. Job insecurity hardly encourages a concern for the distant less privileged, nor for the more distant future. Yet local governments really do want a greater say in their political lives. The sustainability transition has given local government a new enabling role which, if handled sensitively, could return to them some of that lost democratic legitimacy.

There are many innovative activities that local authorities might initiate, requiring only modest injections of cash:

1. Coordinated information in the form of helplines for environmental action, for opening up new networking opportunities among small businesses in particular, but also across different interest groups. Green telephone lines could be used for (anonymous) calls over evidence of environmental or social misbehaviour (but not legally defined crime).

2. Various community partnerships that create the synergy to achieve a range of objectives but which no single partner feels sufficiently motivated to initiate on their own. For example, local woodland fuel-burning schemes might involve partnerships of landowners, conservation groups, banks, the local power company, haulage contractors, and job-creation and training schemes. A modest diversion of the proceeds of any future carbon levy (although there would be some carbon levy imposed on the wood burning) would act as a catalyst to support the financing of a project facilitator, and this individual would in turn show each of the parties how they would gain for their modest investment. This should generate confidence in collective commitment and crystallize what would otherwise be a languishing idea into a practical solution. Similar partnerships, sponsored by charitable ecotaxation revenue, could be applied to local taxi schemes or the provision of safe urban cycle routes, or waste-composting schemes.

3. 'Action' days could highlight new ways of looking at a problem. Locally redirected taxation might help to finance the preparation and publicity necessary to make such days work.

4. Supplier-distributor sustainability claims could help to purchase local produce and set up local consumer outlets. True there may be a premium, but if that premium protected jobs and maintained communal enterprise, maybe that is how local economics might work for the future.

These initiatives are beginning to happen. In the UK the LA 21 newsletter is a model of information on such activities. But we should not be misled. The money is not really there yet. For many local authorities the sheer size of the task in the face of competing pressures is stopping anything more imaginative than a built-in approach to existing policy. Very few local councils have got beyond the narrow state of environment reporting and internal environmental audits (Tuxworth and Carpenter, 1995). The expansion of LA 21 into the more tricky areas of health care, poverty alleviation, housing, crime prevention, drug-abuse rehabilitation and employment-training schemes, any or all of which could promote the radical agenda for the sustainable transition, awaits the kind of pump-priming, public-private charitable trusts that are beginning to emerge out of the landfill levy. This is where ecotaxation, if packaged and made locally accountable, could play an enormously modest but effective role in the elusive sustainability transition.

REFERENCES

Blair, T (1996) *Sustainable Development: The Labour Party View*, The Labour Party, London

Commission on Global Governance (1995) *Our Global Neighbourhood*, Oxford University Press, Oxford

Department of the Environment (1989) *Sustaining our Common Future*, Department of the Environment, London

Dickenson, D (1994) *Crime and Unemployment*, Department of Applied Economics, University of Cambridge, Cambridge

Hambleton, R (1993) *Reinventing Local Government*, Parliamentary Brief, 4–7 July

Hammond, P, Adriaanse, A, Rodenburg, E, Bryant, D and Woodward, R (1995) *Environmental Indicators*, World Resources Institute, Washington, DC

HM Government (1990) *This Common Inheritance: Britain's Environmental Strategy*, HMSO, London

Jacobs, M (1996) *The Politics of the Real World*, Earthscan Publications, London

Labour Party (1994) *In Trust for Tomorrow: Report of a Study Group*, Labour Party, London

Leadbetter, C and Mulgan, G (1994) *The End of Unemployment: Bringing Work to Life*, Demos, pp 2–21, London

Lele, S (1991) 'Sustainable Development: A Critical Review', *World Development* Vol 19, No 6, pp 607–21

Liberal Democratic Party (1993) *Taxing Pollution not People*, Liberal Democratic Party, London

Mulgan, G and Murray, R (1993) *Reconnecting Taxation*, Demos, London

Nagpal, T and Foltz, C (eds) (1995) *Choosing Our Future: Unions of a Sustainable World*, World Resources Institute, Washington, DC

Owen, G (1955) *Energy Policy: The Government and the Energy Regulators. A Case Study of Energy Saving Trust*, GEC 95-35, CSERGE, University of East Anglia, Norwich

Porritt, J (1996) 'Real World Politics' *Town and Country Planning*, Vol 65, No 2, p 34

Sachs, W (ed) (1993) *Global Ecology*, Zed Books, London

Seyfang, G (1996) 'Local Exchange Trading System and Sustainable Development', *Environment*, Vol 36, No 10, p 5, pp 44–5

Tuxworth, B and Carpenter, C (1995) 'Local Agenda Survey 1994–95', Local Government Management Board, Luton

US President's Council on Sustainable Development (1996) *Sustainable America: A New Consensus for Prosperity, Opportunity and a Healthy Environment*, US Government Printing Office, Washington, DC

C h a p t e r 2

ENVIRONMENTAL TAX DESIGN

Stephen Smith

INTRODUCTION

A common theme in the major fiscal reforms introduced by many OECD countries over the past decade has been a move towards simplification and uniformity, as a way of allowing market forces to guide the pattern of economic activity. Such reforms, for example, have sought to cut direct tax rates, while at the same time broadening the tax base through the removal of exemptions and special allowances. There has been a growing tendency to argue that the role of taxation should be confined to raising revenue in an efficient and equitable manner, and not to induce people or businesses to make different decisions from those they would make in the absence of taxation. Any wider policy goals should be achieved through other, non-fiscal, policy instruments.

This trend towards uniformity and simplification has been given a conceptual expression through the somewhat imprecise notion of 'fiscal neutrality' as a desirable property of a tax system. In a restricted sense, neutrality is often simply equated with uniformity in taxation – for example, the tax system should not apply different rates of tax to different goods and services, or to different financial assets.

Often, this interpretation coincides with the more fundamental notion of economic efficiency in taxation. This would require that tax revenue should be raised in a way which imposes the least possible cost on the economy as a whole. The relevant costs include not only administrative costs

The research on which this paper draws has been supported by the ESRC Research Centre at IFS (Grant M544285001) and by the European Community Environment Programme (Grant EV5VCT94-0370). The opinions expressed are those of the author alone, and not of the funders, nor of the IFS which has no corporate views.

and taxpayer compliance costs, but also the economic welfare costs of induced changes in taxpayer emissions. These economic welfare costs generally arise where taxation regimes induce individuals or firms to make different choices about such things as labour supply, saving and spending from those that they would otherwise have made in the absence of taxation. Nevertheless, uniformity in the tax treatment of all goods and services does not necessarily imply economic efficiency. Certainly, if the tax system involves arbitrary and large differences in the taxation of similar activities or similar commodities, this will often increase the costs of raising revenues. However, under some conditions, a non-uniform pattern of commodity taxes may reduce the welfare costs of raising revenues (although it will generally increase the administrative costs). There are also wholly familiar arguments in favour of 'sin' taxes – for example, on alcohol and tobacco – where targeted heavy taxation may be justified by the social costs that excessive alcohol consumption or tobacco use tend to cause.

This trend towards simplification and uniformity in general tax policy collides with a movement in the opposite direction which has originated from various aspects of environmental policy. Increasingly it is recognized that there are strong arguments for greater use of 'economic instruments', such as taxes, charges and emissions trading in environmental policy. Economic instruments, which seek to influence polluter behaviour through financial incentives, have potential advantages over conventional regulatory policy, in terms of permitting greater flexibility in the way polluters achieve compliance with an aggregate pollution requirement, and/or in terms of a reduced need for the regulatory authorities to have detailed information on the circumstances of individual polluters. The economic gains from using economic instruments mean that a higher standard of environmental protection can be achieved for a given economic sacrifice, or, viewed from a different angle, that the current standard of environmental protection could be achieved with a lower economic sacrifice.

Superficially, the use of the tax system to achieve environmental objectives would appear to be a reversal of the trend to greater fiscal neutrality. Environmental taxes would be used with the specific intention of altering patterns of behaviour, in a direction that would reduce damage to the environment.

From the economic point of view, there is no fundamental contradiction between these two trends. 'Neutrality', in the sense of a uniform tax treatment of different commodities or economic activities, is justified where it contributes to economic efficiency. This will often be the case where there are no externalities involved. However, uniformity will not promote economic efficiency if production and consumption activities are accompanied by externalities – in other words, costs or benefits imposed on others, as a result of an individual or firm's activities. If a tax regime does not alter the pattern of externalities, the apparently level playing-field of a uniform tax system will contain biases – and even gaping pot-holes – which fundamentally will distort economic activity away from the social optimum. Policy intervention, possibly in the form of differential taxation of externality-generating activities, is required to deal with these cases. In these circumstances, using taxes to discourage activities associated with environmental damage would, in fact, promote economic efficiency. This would be the case because such targeted taxes should ensure that decision-makers take into account all relevant costs and benefits from their actions. David Gee takes this position further in Chapter 6.

The key to achieving the potential gains from the use of taxation as an instrument of environmental policy does not lie in the indiscriminate introduction of taxes with a vaguely defined environmental justification. Rather, it lies in the effective targeting of incentives to the pollution or other environmental problems which policy seeks to influence. Poorly targeted environmental taxes may increase the economic costs of taxation, while offering little in the way of compensating environmental gains. Indeed, badly designed environmental taxes may be much worse than no environmental taxes at all.

This chapter addresses some issues in the efficient design of environmental taxes. It aims to set out general criteria which will be helpful in designing environmental taxes, so that they can contribute most effectively to a more efficient environmental policy. A number of different types of environmental taxes are identified; each may be appropriate in particular circumstances. The choice between types, it is argued below, will need to take account both of the administrative costs of different tax options, and the extent to which different tax designs can achieve effective targeting of the environmental incentive. The institutional assignment of responsibility for tax-setting, and the allocation of the revenues, may also affect efficiency in environmental taxation.

The chapter is organized around a distinction between environmental taxes of three different basic types:

1. *Measured emission taxes.* This group of market-based instruments includes those which involve tax payments which are directly related to metered or measured quantities of polluting effluent.
2. *Use of other taxes to approximate a tax on emissions.* Changes in the rates of indirect taxes (excise duties, sales taxes or value-added taxes) may be used as an indirect alternative to the explicit taxation of measured emissions. Goods and services which are associated with environmental damage in production or consumption may be taxed more heavily – for example, carbon taxes and taxes on batteries and fertilizers – while goods which are believed to benefit the environment may be taxed less heavily than their substitutes – for example, reduced taxes on lead-free petrol.
3. *Non-incentive taxes.* In many cases, environmental taxes have been used principally for the purposes of revenue-raising, rather than to provide incentives to reduce polluting emissions (Opschoor and Vos, 1989). Where environmental taxes have been employed in this way, it has generally been to raise earmarked revenues for particular public expenditures related to environmental protection – for example, to recover the costs of administering a system of environmental monitoring or regulation, or to pay for public or private expenditures on pollution abatement measures.

Sections 1 and 2 of the chapter consider the choice between the first two types of environmental tax identified above. These both employ the tax principally as an incentive instrument, but achieve this in different ways. In the first case, tax payments are directly related to polluting emissions; in the second, the environmental incentive is based on an indirect relationship between the tax base and emissions. Both, in appropriate circumstances, may have a role to play as a substitute for conventional regulation in environmental policy.

The second half of the chapter considers 'revenue' aspects of environmental taxes. Section 3 considers the third type of 'environmental tax', as an earmarked revenue source for particular categories of public or collective expenditure. Section 4 discusses wider questions concerning the assignment of ecotax revenues and rate-setting responsibility.

MEASURED-EMISSIONS TAXATION

The choice between a tax that is directly related to emission quantities and a tax that is more indirectly linked to the pollution it aims to control will depend on considerations of two sorts: administrative cost and 'linkage' (meaning efficient targeting of the incentive). Often there will be a trade-off between lower administrative cost and better linkage. In many cases, environmental taxes based on measured emissions will have higher administrative costs than taxes which are levied on some other base, but will be better linked to the amount of pollution caused, and will thus provide a more precisely targeted incentive to reduce pollution. The balance between these two considerations is, however, likely to differ from case to case.

New environmental taxes based on measured emissions quantities will require, as a minimum, the additional costs to be borne of a system for the assessment or measurement of the emission quantities on which the tax is levied. These costs will depend on:

1. *Measurement costs per source.* This will vary, depending on the technical characteristics of the emissions (flow, concentration, stability, etc), the substances involved, and the range of currently available measurement technologies. Recent scientific and commercial developments in measurement and control are likely to have substantially widened the range of technologies available for monitoring the concentrations and flows of particular substances in effluent discharges, and hence to have increased the range of pollution problems for which charging on the basis of direct measurement is likely to be a feasible and cost-effective option. It is also probable that the future pace of development and commercialization of such technologies will be stimulated in part by a greater use of direct emissions charging.

2. *The number of emissions sources.* Direct charging for measured emissions quantities will be less worthwhile the more separate emission sources there are. An extreme example of this is the case

of non-point-source pollution – in other words, where no identifiable pipe, outlet or chimney provides a 'point source' at which emissions can be measured. The leaching of agricultural fertilizers and pesticides into the water system are examples of non-point-source pollution; for such pollution problems, direct measurement is likely to be costly and/or highly imprecise.

3. *Scope for integration with normal commercial activities.* The costs of a system of emissions measurement will generally be reduced if the measurement of emissions can be integrated with activities that would naturally take place for normal commercial reasons. Not only does this reduce the additional costs of measurement for tax purposes, it also tends to reduce the risk of false or misleading information being provided, since there are non-tax reasons for accurate measurement.

The administrative costs involved in new taxes on measured emissions affect the optimal environmental tax policy in three ways. First, if these costs are high, they may rule this option out entirely. Secondly, even where the additional administrative costs of new emissions taxes are sufficiently low to be acceptable, they may still affect the efficient design of a system of environmental taxes. Taking account of the administrative costs of taxation would be likely to mean that the range of tax instruments employed will be more restricted than would be the case if tax administration were costless; policy-makers will need to weigh up the costs and benefits, at the margin, of adding an extra emissions tax which may improve efficiency, but at the cost of higher administration 'dead-weight'. If different emissions are in any way correlated, an emissions tax that would be worthwhile on its own may not be worthwhile if a number of taxes on 'similar' emissions already exist. Thirdly, in some circumstances it will be desirable to take administrative costs into account in choosing the appropriate rate at which emission taxes should be levied. Polinsky and Shavell (1982) demonstrate that the relevance of administrative costs to the efficient emissions tax rate depends on the relationship between administrative costs and the number of polluters, and on where the costs of administration are borne. For example, where the administrative costs are a fixed amount per polluter and are borne by government, it may be appropriate to set the emissions tax rate above the level of the external cost, so as to reduce the administrative cost; but this rule will not be appropriate where the costs of administration are borne by the polluters themselves.

As far as the issue of 'linkage' is concerned, environmental taxes based directly on measured emissions, in principle, can be very precisely targeted to the environmental objectives underlying policy. When polluting emissions rise, the polluter's tax base rises, and the polluter pays additional tax directly in proportion to the rise in emissions. Likewise, the only actions which the polluter can take to reduce their tax liability are actions which also reduce emissions.

Even where the marginal pollution damage from individual emissions sources varies, each source could be faced, in principle, with an appropriate schedule of tax rates, reflecting the precise marginal damage from the source's emissions. This is possible, ultimately, because the location of the emissions is known, fixed, and given by the location of the emissions measurement.

However, such cases may not always be amenable to environmental tax measures. In particular, there may be difficulties of various sorts in drawing up tailor-made emissions tax schedules for each individual source of emissions. Knowledge of the marginal damage costs of pollution, even at an aggregate level, is inevitably limited, and the information on which to base the tax schedules for each emitter may be very weak indeed. In these circumstances, it could be argued that emission tax schedules for each source would have the character of arbitrary taxation, not grounded adequately in the basic legislation and in the objective characteristics of the taxpayer. Also, where there is little good evidence on which to base emissions schedules for each source, it would be rather easy for polluters to influence, through lobbying efforts, the tax schedule drawn up for their emissions. Without strong evidence to justify any particular pattern of rates, the authorities would be particularly vulnerable to lobbying, or to appeals against their initial decisions. In these circumstances, the highest tax rates might be applied, not to the polluters causing the most damage, but to the polluters making the most vigorous and effective lobbying efforts.

RESTRUCTURING EXISTING TAXES

The administrative costs of any new tax will depend normally on how much scope there is for the tax to be incorporated in existing systems of administration and control. Where the additional administrative costs of an environmental tax system based on direct charging for measured emissions are high, restructuring of the existing tax system may provide an alternative way of introducing fiscal incentives to reduce environmental damage. If the assessment, collection or enforcement of environmental taxes can be 'piggy-backed' on to corresponding operations already undertaken for existing taxes, the costs of environmental tax measures may be significantly less than where wholly new administrative apparatus and procedures are required.

The vast majority of existing taxes are levied on transactions – for instance, the value of goods and services sold, the value of incomes paid or received. The scale economies that can be achieved from the administrative integration of environmental taxes are likely to be greatest where environmental taxes, too, are levied in a form based on transaction values. Thus, the differentiation of existing tax rates (which may be seen as the limiting case of a tax reform closely compatible with existing tax administration) may gain considerably from combined administration. On the other hand, there are likely to be few gains from combining the administration of a tax on measured emission quantities with existing transaction-based taxes.

It is necessary to bear in mind that even the most sophisticated administrative piggy-backing is unlikely to be wholly costless from the point of view of the administration of existing taxes. Greater complexity is likely to increase administrative costs in all areas, although the extent of this will depend on the existing degree of complexity in the tax structure. This point is taken further in the discussion of ecotaxation in British Columbia (Chapter 16), and in the early stages of the application of the landfill levy in the UK (Chapter 15).

Linkage

How effective changes in the existing tax system are in achieving an efficient pattern of pollution abatement will depend on the degree to which the taxation is closely linked to the pollution it aims to control. If the tax rises, does it encourage taxpayers to reduce their tax burden by reducing the processes or activities which give rise to polluting emissions, or are they, instead, just as likely to find ways of reducing their tax payments without changing their level of pollution?

This issue of linkage is central to any case for or against fiscal instruments, other than those based on direct charging for measured emissions. Where the linkage between tax base and pollution is weak, the tax may fail to have the desired impact on pollution, and, at the same time, may introduce unnecessary and costly distortions into production and consumption decisions.

'Indirect' environmental tax policies depend on the existence of a stable relationship between the tax base and pollution, but relationships which appear stable in the absence of policy measures can turn out to be unstable once a tax is introduced. A good illustration of this phenomenon is given by Sandmo's (1976) account of Norway's attempt to introduce a system of charging for domestic refuse collection by charging for the special refuse sacks which householders were required to use. The logic for the system was that the number of sacks used would be a rough proxy for the quantity of refuse collected from each household. Unfortunately, the charging scheme, once implemented, changed the relationship between sacks used and refuse collected. Some households tended to economize on sacks rather than to economize on refuse, and responded to the tax by over-filling the sacks, or by dumping refuse, causing environmental problems elsewhere. In the UK landfill tax case, serious fears have been expressed that fly-tipping will be encouraged following the imposition of the tax.

Where there is a wide range of available techniques which differ widely from one another in the relationship between tax base and pollution, linkage is likely to be more of a problem than where the range of technologies is small, and the tax base pollution relationship is broadly stable across production techniques. Technical data about the range of available production techniques and their environmental attributes will thus help to assess the practical relevance of linkage problems for any particular environmental tax.

McKay, Pearson and Smith (1990) observe that a particularly severe problem of linkage arises where it is sought to influence pollution emissions from a production process through taxes on inputs, and where significant scope exists for pollution abatement through effluent 'cleaning' at the end of the production process. One case in point is the scope for cleaning the sulphur dioxide emissions of coal-fired power stations by fitting 'scrubbers' (flue-gas desulphurization equipment (FGDs)). Where effluents can be cleaned in this way, taxes on production inputs will not be an effective way of encouraging an efficient pattern of pollution abatement. Such a tax – for example, a tax on sulphurous coal – may discourage the use of polluting materials in production, but will provide no incentive to clean up effluents from the process. Although pollution may be reduced, the way in which pollution reductions are achieved will not necessarily be the most efficient.

Environmental taxes on fuel inputs may be more appropriate to control carbon dioxide emissions, where effluent cleaning is not currently a commercially viable option, than with sulphur emissions, where important effluent-cleaning technologies are available. A number of countries, including Sweden and Finland, have already introduced carbon taxes on fuels (Hoeller and Wallin, 1991). In Chapter 11, Jean-Philippe Barde reviews the record. However, it should be noted that what is at issue is not merely the existence of (commercially viable) alternative technologies, but also the potential for them to be developed, since an efficient pollution tax will create an incentive for new technologies, involving less pollution, to be developed. The acceptability of a carbon tax on fuel inputs instead of a tax on measured carbon emission quantities depends, in part, on a judgement of how rapidly such technological developments are likely to take place, and how far their future development might be inhibited by the choice of a tax on inputs rather than on measured emissions.

A number of authors have considered the efficient pattern of tax rates where the only administratively feasible policies involve some degree of approximation in the linkage between tax base and pollution damage. One group has considered models where administrative limitations require that all individuals causing externalities are taxed at the same rate, but where the externalities from some are more damaging than from others. In the context of taxing measured emissions, taxing different polluters at different rates, according to the damage from their emissions, may require a large element of judgement, which thus tends to expose the system to lobbying or regulatory capture. In the case of conventional product taxes, an example might be the use of a tax on coal to encourage smoke abatement; although smoky chimneys may be more damaging in densely populated areas, it would be impracticable to tax coal at different rates in different areas, since it is almost impossible to prevent urban dwellers from buying their coal from rural suppliers. (In practice, of course, market instruments in this case are likely to be easily dominated by a simple regulatory rule: forbidding the use of smoky fuels in urban areas.)

Diamond (1973) shows that the rate at which such a uniform tax should be levied depends on the relationship between the externality and individual consumption. If there is separability between the externality and consumption, the appropriate tax rate is simply the weighted average of the marginal contributions to the externality, where the weights are given by the sensitivities of demand for the good which generates the externality. Where the separability assumption is relaxed, so that externalities affect demand as well as utility, calculation of the optimal tax rate is more complex, and 'perverse' cases cannot be ruled out, in which it would be appropriate to subsidize the good causing the externality.

Where linkage is poor, it may be possible to improve matters by going beyond taxation of the good associated with the externality; complements or substitutes to the externality-causing good may be taxed or subsidized. Sandmo (1976), Green and Sheshinksi (1976) and Balcer (1980) consider cases where individual externality effects differ, and where the optimal tax on the good causing the externality would therefore be at different rates. Where goods exist that are complements (or substitutes) to the externality-generating good, this may allow a better package of tax measures to be designed, including changes to the taxation of these related goods. Depending on the interaction between demand for the complement (or substitute) and the externality, it may be possible to improve on the taxation of the externality-causing good alone, by taxing or subsidizing the complementary or substitute good. For example, if the objective is to deal with urban congestion, high petrol taxes might be supplemented by subsidies to urban public transport and taxes on urban parking spaces. Sometimes the appropriate policy rules will appear counter-intuitive. Balcer shows a simple case where a subsidy to a complementary good would be appropriate, and Wijkander (1985) discusses cases where the policy rule is complicated by the cross-effects between various complements or substitutes to the externality-causing good.

REVENUE EARMARKING

Current interest in environmental taxes principally concerns incentive applications, rather than the choice of earmarked revenue sources for particular functions. Many environmental taxes in European countries, however, have, been assigned as revenue sources to particular agencies or earmarked to particular categories of expenditure, and there is considerably greater enthusiasm for earmarking among the advocates of environmental taxes than in other areas of policy. What function might the earmarking of environmental taxes serve, and are there stronger reasons for earmarking environmental taxes than other revenue instruments?

First, it is necessary to clarify what is meant by 'earmarking'. In what follows, earmarking is taken to refer to a situation where the revenues from a tax are pre-assigned, in some sense, to certain public expenditures, or to a particular agency or department. The implication is that, while the level of spending on other areas of government policy might be the subject of an annual budgetary process in which the government could choose, in principle, freely to increase or reduce the level of spending, spending on the earmarked category is governed by the revenues from the earmarked tax – at least in the sense that these revenues cannot be used for any other purpose. The notion of earmarking thus includes an element of pre-commitment, or of 'tying the government's hands' in the use of the revenues from the environmental tax. The two chapters that follow take these points further.

Earmarking in this sense goes further than simply linking the introduction of a new tax to certain accompanying tax or expenditure measures. Often there will be good reasons for the introduction of environmental tax measures to be accompanied by other tax or expenditure measures, which may offset undesirable social, distributional or sectoral effects of the tax. For example, a carbon tax might need to be accompanied by spending on assistance for poor or elderly energy consumers who would otherwise be disproportionately harmed by higher energy costs, or by measures to stimulate more efficient operation of the market for insulation and other energy-efficient products. More generally, any policy measure which increases taxation will be accompanied, as a matter of principle, by an offsetting tax or spending measures, as a consequence of the government's budget constraint. If any new tax is introduced, then sooner or later the money it raises must be spent on something, or other taxes must be reduced. It may be good public-relations for the government to stress the expenditures or tax cuts that the environmental tax will permit, so that taxpayers do not dismiss the environmental tax as simply another excuse for a profligate government to raise the tax burden. As noted in Chapter 15, the UK government's recent proposal for a landfill levy includes a well-advertised link with a reduction in employer National Insurance contributions. This is designed to make clear to business taxpayers that the overall burden of tax on business would remain unaltered.

None of this, however, involves the degree of pre-commitment that is implied by earmarking. Many tax changes, in the sense set out in the previous paragraph, are accompanied by other policy measures that are designed to make the change in taxation palatable, or to offset certain side-effects of the tax. The UK Government's annual Budget statement involves a whole package of tax and spending measures, some of which are designed to interact, or to offset undesirable features of other elements in the package. For earmarking to be a term with any real content, it needs to involve a tighter link between environmental tax revenues and other tax or spending measures than simply the construction of a coordinated package of measures.

The key sense in which earmarking differs from normal tax and spending decision-making is, we have argued, the element of pre-commitment in certain spending choices. For this to be meaningful, it must constrain spending choices in a dynamic, multi-period context, so that the evolution over time of certain spending items will be governed by the evolution over time by the revenues from the earmarked tax. However, in this sense, earmarking is liable to lead to inefficiency in budgeting and expenditures. There is no reason to wish expenditures on particular items to be governed by the revenues raised by a particular tax or charge. Likewise, it is unlikely to be the case that the efficient level of an environmental tax will coincide exactly with the revenue needed for a particular expenditure heading. If one constrains the other, in either direction, both cannot be set at the right level, except by rare coincidence.

If, therefore, earmarking genuinely constrains the level and evolution of expenditures by the level and evolution of the earmarked tax base, or dictates the tax rate by the level and evolution of certain expenditure headings, it should be avoided. Earmarking, if it involves pre-commitment to a particular time-path for revenues or expenditures, does not allow policy to react to changing circumstances or changing priorities. On the other hand, earmarking in this sense would be remarkably hard to achieve. It might be possible to make the necessary pre-commitment in those countries where public finance is regulated in detail by a formal constitution, if the earmarking could be enshrined in the provisions of the constitution. But without this kind of constraint on future government decisions, what governments decide to do, they can often as easily undo. In the UK, for example, a commitment to increase expenditures in line with revenues from an environmental tax could easily be abandoned if circumstances changed.

The practical content of earmarking is further undermined where the budget heading receiving earmarked revenues also receives additional revenues from general tax revenues. Then, the earmarking no longer determines the level of spending on the functions concerned. Changes at the margin in the allocation of general revenues can offset, and 'undo', all of the effects of the earmarking, except to the extent that the revenues from the earmarked tax set a 'floor' below which the level of expenditures cannot fall. A claim to earmark revenues would then amount to little more than a presentational fiction, with no real practical effect, masking the real motives and processes in public revenue raising and budgetary allocation.

In general, therefore, with environmental taxes as with other areas of government fiscal policy, there are powerful reasons to avoid the earmarking of taxes to particular government agencies, departments or expenditure heading. Are there ever circumstances in which a respectable case could be mounted for earmarking in this 'commitment' sense? Two cases, with certain similarities, might be suggested.

One is the case of an environmental tax which applies to only part of an industry. For example, this may be an appropriate response to high unit costs of emissions measurement; measurement may then only be worthwhile for a subgroup of polluters, such as large emitters, or with the greatest need for emissions flexibility. Other sources may be regulated completely differently – for example, through direct 'command-and-control'. Partial coverage by the emissions tax would be liable to distort the pattern of competition between the firms subject to the tax (which would face an additional tax burden for each unit of residual emissions) and those firms which are not covered by the system. In practical examples of taxes with partial coverage, two approaches have been adopted to limit the extent of the distortion between the two groups of firms. One, adopted in the case of the water pollution charges in The Netherlands, is to impose a non-measured charge on the firms which are not subject to the measured-emission tax, of approximately the same level they would face if they were subject to the tax on measured emissions. This point is developed further by Hans Vos in Chapter 12, where he observes that only partial success can be claimed. The second approach, employed in the Swedish tax on NO_x emissions, is to return the revenues from the measured emission tax to the taxpaying firms, as a group, choosing a basis for the revenue return which does not 'undo' the initial incentive effect of the charge. Thus, for example, the Swedish NO_x tax returns the revenues to the taxpaying firms in proportion to their output level. The environmental incentive is preserved, because firms with high emissions per unit of output lose overall, while those with low emissions in relation to output gain overall. At the same time, the overall net burden of the environmental tax (after taking account of the revenue return) on the taxpaying firms as a group is zero, and distortion between the firms subject to the tax and other competing firms in the industry is thus avoided.

A second case is that of the common funding of facilities (mutualization) which are used by, or confer benefits on, a number of firms (or, conceivably, individuals) in a particular area. An example would be where a water purification plant cleans up a waterway into which a group of firms all discharge. In some cases, such a collective treatment facility may be one of a number of possible ways of reducing the environmental damage from emissions. It would be desirable for the collective treatment of this form to be chosen by firms where it is cheaper (perhaps due to economies of scale) than the other available options for pollution abatement, such as individual treatment by each source or switching to an alternative 'clean' production technology which does not generate the emissions. Equally, it would be undesirable for it to be selected where it is more costly than the alternatives. To ensure that firms face the right incentives to choose appropriately between the 'collective' option or the alternatives, it is desirable that firms face the real costs of each option. The collective option should not be advantaged or disadvantaged in its fiscal treatment relative to the others. A system of emissions charges, from which the revenues are earmarked for expenditure on the collective facility, may provide an efficient basis both for dividing the financial contributions of polluters to the collective treatment facility and for determining the overall fiscal burden on polluters. The earmarked revenue source in this case might be an environmental tax, but it need not be. Alternative taxes might better reflect the demands placed on the collective facility.

In this type of arrangement, it is desirable that the earmarking should group together the tax payments of those polluters placing demands on an individual facility, and should use the revenues for expenditures affecting the group. Earmarking of national aggregate expenditures to aggregate expenditures in general will achieve little gain in efficiency. In particular, one of the most important decision-margins which the system may affect is the location decision, ensuring that firms group themselves efficiently, where there are economies-of-scale gains from collective provision. This issue is essentially one of optional club formation. Revenue earmarking will only ensure that this decision is made without fiscal distortion if the revenue contribution of an additional polluter in an area corresponds to the demands that that polluter will place on the collective facility.

REVENUE ASSIGNMENT AND RATE-SETTING INCENTIVES

A second aspect of the assignment of revenues from environmental taxation is that it may affect the institutional process by which the environmental tax rates are determined. The agency or government department to which the tax revenues are assigned will have an interest in choosing revenue-maximizing tax rates, and this may conflict with using the tax to meet environmental objectives. Are there revenue assignments which would reduce the risk of this undesirable outcome?

Oates (1991) poses this question in the context of a choice between assigning responsibility for environmental tax rate determination and assigning the resultant tax revenues, to either 'economic' or 'environmental' departments of government – for example, the choice between the Ministry of Finance or the Environment Ministry. He observes that the assignment of responsibility for environmental tax policy clearly needs to reflect decisions about assignment of taxes in other policy areas.

In principle, for environmental tax policies to be designed efficiently, they need to be coordinated both with other environmental policies, and with other fiscal policies. In an ideal world, the level of environmental taxes would be set with regard to the economic costs and environmental benefits of a particular tax level, and with regard to the marginal excess burden of raising revenue through other fiscal instruments. However, perfect coordination of environmental taxes with both environmental and fiscal policies may not be feasible. Where government institutions already separate decision-making responsibility for environmental and fiscal policies, by allocating responsibility to specialized departments, efficient environmental tax policy will require cross-departmental coordination.

Regardless of whether responsibility for environmental taxation is assigned to the environmental department or the economic department, it will be inevitable that the assignment of its responsibility will result in better coordination with one of these related areas of government policy but poorer coordination with the other. A choice then has to be made, either of poor coordination between environmental taxes and other environmental policy, or between environmental taxes and other fiscal policy.

In recommending a solution to the allocation of responsibilities between governmental departments, Oates (1991) points out that there is no need for the same part of government to be responsible for determining the rate of the environmental tax and to receive its revenues. Indeed, in some circumstances this may be positively undesirable. He recommends a split assignment in which the determination of the structure and rate of environmental taxes should be under the control of environmental policy-makers, while the revenue should accrue to the general exchequer rather than to the environmental agency's budget.

The reason for assigning rate-setting responsibility to the environmental ministry is that there may be little loss in rate-setting efficiency if fiscal policy-makers are not able to integrate the choice of environmental and non-environmental tax rates. The range of instruments available to fiscal policy-makers for revenue-raising is wide, so that setting environmental taxes without regard to efficient revenue-raising is unlikely to increase significantly the aggregate excess burden of taxation. On the other hand, the range of alternative environmental policy instruments is smaller, and setting the level of environmental taxes with principal regard to their revenue rather than to environmental effects is likely to lead to appreciably sub-optimal environmental policy outcomes.

Nevertheless, while it may be more efficient to locate responsibility for setting the rate of environmental taxes with the environmental policy authorities, there would be a risk of inefficiency if they derived budget revenues from the environmental tax. The agency's budgetary needs might encourage it to 'milk' the environmental tax for revenue rather than to set it at the efficient level from the environmental point of view.

This line of argument might also be used to suggest the level of government, in a multi-tier system, which should be in charge of rate-setting and which should receive the revenues (Smith, 1995). Priority should be give to assigning policy responsibility for the rates of environmental taxes to the same level of government as has responsibility for related aspects of environmental policy, so that an efficient balance can be drawn between environmental taxes and other environmental policy instruments. Coordination with fiscal policies is less critical.

As with the choice between government departments, however, the assignment of revenues need not follow the assignment of rate-setting. In general, it is desirable that the revenue from environmental taxes should accrue to levels of government with many other potential revenue sources, since they are less likely to drive environmental tax levels beyond the level which is efficient from the point of view of environmental policy (and general revenue-raising efficiency). On the other hand, a tier of government which is highly constrained in terms of budgetary resources might well be inclined to increase environmental tax revenues above the efficient level, even at the cost of sub-optimality from the environmental point of view. This could involve either the environmental tax rate being set too low or too high, depending on whether the revenue-maximizing tax rate is lower or higher than the optimal externality tax.

CONCLUSION

Many of the recent tax system reforms in industrialized countries have aimed to simplify the tax system and to reduce the extent to which it is directed at any objectives other than efficient revenue-raising. However, in the field of environmental policy, there has been considerable enthusiasm for a move in the opposite direction – to use taxes as environmental incentive mechanisms. The two trends, while apparently conflicting, have quite similar underlying motivations in terms of increased efficiency. Greater simplicity and 'neutrality' in taxation has been seen as a way of reducing the distortionary and administrative costs associated with taxation, while the use of 'green' taxes has been part of a trend towards using 'market mechanisms' to cut the economic costs of achieving a given level of pollution control.

Where, however, the fiscal policy concern with efficiency in revenue-raising, and with minimizing the distortionary impact of taxation, has implications for environmental tax policy is in highlighting the importance of the administrative costs and possible distortionary effects associated with environmental taxes. The administrative costs of 'green' taxes, like any other taxes, are a dead-weight cost which should be minimized where possible. On the other hand, efficient targeting, so that the tax incentive is clearly linked to the polluting behaviour which the tax aims to affect, is needed to ensure that the tax secures the desired changes in polluting behaviour, while not leading to unnecessary distortions in other aspects of economic behaviour. The balance between low administrative costs and efficient targeting is likely to point in the direction of different types of environmental tax instrument, depending on individual circumstances. In particular, there is a central choice between 'direct' externality taxation and 'proxy' taxation, through the restructuring of existing components of the tax system.

Direct taxation of measured emissions can target an environmental incentive more efficiently than changes to the structure of existing taxes on commodities, but may have the drawback of higher costs of administration and taxpayer (administrative) compliance. Nevertheless, technological changes in flow measurement and instrumentation are reducing the administrative cost disadvantage of direct emissions taxation, and this option should be given wider consideration than it has so far achieved.

Much of the current policy interest in environmental taxes, and many of the practical measures implemented in European countries, has concerned the use of existing tax bases to deliver incentives for reduced pollution or other environmentally desirable changes in behaviour. In these cases, by contrast with measured-emissions taxes, the linkage between tax base and pollution is usually imprecise; what can be taxed in the existing system usually does not correspond exactly to a polluter's level of emissions. In assessing the case for such tax reform it is important to consider how far it matters that the incentive is not precisely targeted. Perhaps the most important question to consider is how the externalities are generated and how this relates to the proposed tax base. What is the technological relationship between the taxed commodity and the externality, and is this relationship likely to be stable?

Although the earmarking of environmental tax revenues is in practice a feature of many of the systems introduced in European countries, the arguments for earmarking are, in the main, presentational in the sense that a suspicious public may be more willing to pay a tax if they see that the revenues are clearly assigned to a socially just policy measure. Where it influences significantly the evolution over time of tax-rate decisions, or the expenditures to which the revenues are hypothecated, it may have damaging effects on the efficient attainment of environmental objectives or on the efficiency of public expenditures. Where it does not have any significant influence on how revenues or spending evolve over time, it weakens, rather than strengthens, the transparency of public decision-making. However, there may be circumstances where earmarking may be more respectable; the chief of these is where, perhaps for reasons of administrative feasibility or cost, an environmental tax applies to only part of an industry. As in the case of the Swedish NO_x tax, earmarked return of the revenues to the taxpayers as a group may minimize the distortionary impact on industrial structure of the partial tax coverage.

Finally, efficiency may be affected not only by the design of the tax itself, but also by the assignment of responsibility and control over the tax. If efficiency is the aim of environmental taxation, the rates of environmental taxes should reflect primarily environmental rather than fiscal considerations; this may be better achieved if the primary responsibility for rate-setting is assigned to environmental agencies or ministries. It does not follow, however, that the revenues should also be assigned to these agencies as well. Indeed, it will generally be better if revenue and rate-setting assignments are split, with revenues accruing to the general public budget.

REFERENCES

Balcer, Y (1980) 'Taxation of externalities: Direct versus indirect', *Journal of Public Economics*, 13, pp 121-29

Diamond, P A (1973) 'Consumption externalities and imperfect corrective pricing', *Bell Journal of Economics and Management Science*, pp 526–38

Green, J and Sheshinski, E (1976) 'Direct versus indirect remedies for externalities', *Journal of Political Economy*, 83, pp 797–808

Hoeller, P and Wallin, M (1991) *Energy Prices, Taxes and Carbon Dioxide Emissions*, OECD Economics and Statistics Department Working Papers, No 106, OECD, Paris

Johnson, P, McKay, S and Smith, S (1990) *The Distributional Consequences of Environmental Taxes*, IFS Commentary No 23, The Institute for Fiscal Studies, London

McKay, S, Pearson, M and Smith, S (1990) 'Fiscal Instruments in Environmental Policy', *Fiscal Studies*, 11 (4), pp 1–20

Oates, W E (1991) *Pollution Charges as a Source of Public Revenues*, Working Paper No 91-2, Department of Economics, University of Maryland, Silver Springs, Maryland

Opschoor, J B and Vos, H B (1989) *Economic Instruments for Environmental Protection*, OECD, Paris

Polinsky, A M and Shavell, S (1982) 'Pigouvian Taxation with Administrative Costs', *Journal of Public Economics*, 19, pp 385–394

Sandmo, A (1976) 'Direct versus indirect Pigovian taxation', *European Economic Review*, 7, pp 337–49

Smith, S (1995) 'The role of the European Union in environmental taxation', *International Tax and Public Finance*, 2, pp 375–87

Wijkander, H (1985), 'Correcting externalities through taxes on/subsidies to related goods', *Journal of Public Economics*, pp 111–25

EDITORIAL INTRODUCTION TO THE HYPOTHECATION DEBATE

The Green College Seminar that sparked this book was held in March 1994. At that seminar was Sir Crispin Tickell, Warden of Green College, recently appointed by the Prime Minister, John Major, as Chair of the British Government Panel on Sustainable Development in January 1994. This Panel is one of a series of initiatives established by the government as part of the British national audit of its progress towards sustainable development, as laid down in the Rio Agenda 21 in June 1992. Through international agreement, Britain has to submit an annual report of its progress to the UN Commission on Sustainable Development. Britain has an enviable reputation of taking seriously such responsibilities, at least in terms of formal reporting and national discussion. One can always quibble as to whether the performance meets the expectations, and generally it falls very far short even of the modest promises set down. But at least a process is under way and criticism can be targeted at various quarters, including ministers and opposition during general elections, and local council members at local authority polls. That may seem far fetched and even whimsical to the hardened cynic, but a form of societal transformation is taking place in Britain these days; within the adjustment process, institutions designed to promote the cause of sustainable development are being promoted.

The British Government Panel is one such innovation. Its role is to direct the Prime Minister and Cabinet's attention to issues on the 'middle and further horizons' (Tickell, 1995, p 9) which it considers 'need higher priority or renewed attention', or which require detailed and protracted consideration and experimentation, so as to prepare the British people for the challenging new world of sustainable development.

The Panel is flanked by a round table representing a range of interests; all are expected to reach consensus on major issues so that the government and non-governmental organizations can move forward on matters where there is inevitably a great deal of unease over interpretation and progress. Since the round table was only formed in 1995, it is still too early to assess its performance and policy significance. This is written at a time when it is apparent that the round table is undergoing serious teething problems of identity, protocol and political accommodation. It will take at least another year before the tensions shake out, but the signs are that the round table will survive and will mature into a serious consensus-seeking mechanism capable of informing the public debate and resonating with its external and internal criticisms.

The round table is part of a wider series of investigatory institutions, including the Royal Commission on Environmental Pollution which advises the government directly; the Advisory Committee on Business and the Environment which reports to the Department of the Environment but, in effect, also to the Department of Trade and Industry; the Biodiversity Action Plan Steering Group which directs its energies to the environment and planning departments, but which has a powerful educational remit; the Scottish Advisory Group on Sustainable Development which is geared to the Scottish Office; and the House of Lords' Select Committee on Sustainable Development which was created in March 1994 to promote parliamentary oversight to the Agenda 21 strategy.

Not by any means will all of these bodies look at ecotaxation in a serious way in the foreseeable future, but undoubtedly all will in time. To start the ball rolling the Tickell Panel, possibly stimulated by the Green College seminar and the interest among opposition parties in the matter, expressed the view that it would:

> ...support a gradual move away from taxes on labour, income, profits and capital towards taxes on pollution and the use of resources. Currently we tax people on the value they add rather than the value they subtract. *In some cases it might be wise and assist public understanding if part of the revenue raised from economic instruments were used for demonstrably environmental purposes* (italics added).
>
> (Tickell, 1995, p 12)

This was a challenge to the Treasury to reconsider its well-established and even doctrinaire opposition to earmarking, or hypothecation. The House of Lords' Select Committee (1995, pp 38–9) recognized that hypothecation, taken too far too quickly, would introduce rigidities into taxation revenue and expenditures that could prove both economically wasteful and politically embarrassing. However, the Committee also recognized that a degree of directional expenditure already takes place, as Michael Spackman illustrates in Chapter 3. For example, the BBC licence fee is in reality an hypothecated charge, as is the road vehicle licence tax. Both the electricity and the gas regulators can and do charge a small fee on sales to stimulate fuel conservation, although the matter is highly controversial because the gas regulator has balked at funding this to any significant extent and the electricity regulator is also playing down the future significance of this measure (see Owen, 1995, for an extended review). The landfill levy is cleverly masked from its real role as hypothecation. This is why the levy receives such detailed treatment in Chapter 15. Despite its misgivings over full-blooded hypothecation, the Lords' Committee was clearly on the side of the Tickell Panel on the matter:

> The case for a fundamental reconsideration of the sources of environmental expenditure, and an objective review of the potential role of hypothecation, is difficult to resist... We believe that there are compelling arguments to support a degree of revenue hypothecation within some environmental programmes.
>
> (House of Lords' Select Committee on Sustainable Development, 1995, p 39)

Hypothecation is clearly a mid-horizon theme. Much will depend on how far fiscal analysts will pursue seemingly obvious cases where the Treasury may be persuaded. This is not an arena where environmental lobbies have much expertise. At the Green College Seminar the Treasury representatives welcomed further dialogue with all groups on both the use of economic instruments in such aspects as road pricing, petrol taxes and company car taxation. There is a willingness within the Treasury to be more open on this matter, so such an invitation ought to encourage environmental groups seriously interested in the transition towards more sustainable development to address the technical world of fiscal reform.

The Lords' Select Committee on Sustainable Development (1995, p 37) was rather miffed at the Treasury, castigating it for its 'essentially reactive approach' to proposals for changes in fiscal policy which could 'slow progress towards the wider use of economic instruments'. 'The Treasury', concluded the Committee, 'should be actively looking for ways to shift the burden of taxation onto pollution and the use of resources, and away from income and capital in particular'.

In an interesting commentary, given to the editor off the record, a former senior Treasury official noted that the culture of the Treasury official was unreconstructed compared with the outlook of the typical environmentalist. The Treasury official was cautious, topical, dispassionate, quantitative and inclined to seek evidence before forming a final view, rather than to operate on instinct. When environmental issues came up, the informant noted, 'the Treasury response was to belittle the problem and resist the investment needed to tackle it'.

On tax matters, the traditional Treasury view was to regard any tax as distortionary on enterprise and wealth creation, so the instinct was to seek low tax rates, with minimal exceptions and no special deals. This tends to obstruct the environmentalists' preferences for directed spend. Hence, on the surface at least, the Treasury is no special friend of green thinking.

Michael Spackman, although writing in a personal capacity, points out that any notable shift towards large-scale hypothecation is simply not likely even on the middle horizon. This is because, as Stephen Smith illustrates, the tax system is so hugely distorting and complicated, in any case, that even with the best will in the world hypothecation as an objective of tax policy would, in all probability, simply not meet its objectives. But Michael Spackman hints that the Treasury would be amenable to more deployment of 'policy packaging' reforms, where revenue is recycled within tightly defined schemes. This is because government departments are willing to seize opportunities for new programmes, ministers like presentationally attractive initiatives, and directional spending in targeted areas can meet a short-term public expenditure shortfall with an element of social acceptance. Hence the use of the value added tax (VAT) revenue to offset the additional income burdens on the poor, and especially pensioners. Although this move was belatedly and blatantly applied in a vain attempt to obtain a tight House of Commons vote in favour of increasing VAT on domestic fuel, nevertheless it is an example of this packaging.

So, too, is the landfill trust idea, introduced in Chapter 15. This is a piece of remarkable innovation within the Department of the Environment (DoE) to create a charitable pool of money from the private sector element of the levy, supported by the DoE, enabling job-creating and technology-forcing experiments to be funded at no real extra cost to the public purse. In effect, 10 per cent of the money allocated comes from the levy, so with a 90 per cent core investment, the DoE obtains an element of private sector 'gearing' for a public interest sustainability outcome. One suspects that this will be the first of a number of clever ruses to accommodate the 'sustainability reality' of quasi-hypothecation to the 'other world' reality of Treasury-speak that hypothecation has not taken place. Possibly, the difference between the two 'realities' is not as great as that sentence makes out.

Meanwhile, don't expect too much of a switch towards any form of earmarking of tax revenue from HM Treasury. The anonymous former Treasury adviser points out that the Treasury will continue to resist broad-based hypothecation for two very practical political reasons.

1. Tax-based programmes of public spend never relate to tax payments by citizens. To do so would undermine the whole system of taxation.
2. Environmental gains are cause enough for ecotaxes. To add another layer of social justification requires extra political support.

However, he points out that the Treasury is much more favourably disposed to economic instruments because they are seen as more effective and an essential offset to public expenditures that have to be cut for over-riding political reasons.

It is tempting to believe that the British Government, faced with an almost impossible conundrum of ever-rising public expenditures in real terms (though marginally falling in terms of proportion of gross domestic product (GDP)) and the political unpopularity of new taxes, should be attracted by the application of a 'sin' tax on energy use, car travel, and vehicle congestion at a time when the real prices of energy are falling (Department of Trade and Industry, 1995). Yet the opportunity arose to increase the vehicle fuel tax by a 5 per cent escalator. This was imposed by the Chancellor in 1994, as advocated by the Royal Commission on Environmental Pollution (1994). And that chance was lost: because of falling petrol prices, the actual price at the pump was barely higher. In his November 1995 Budget speech the Chancellor proclaimed proudly that despite the imposition of the fuel-tax escalator, 'petrol prices in this country should remain lower than in any other major European country (quoted in ENDS, No 250, 1995, p 5). Opportunities to raise the duty on diesel (because of PM_{10} polluting particulates) or to lower the duty on less polluting refor-mulated diesel fuels were also not taken up (ENDS, No 250, 1955, p 5).

This suggests that there is something of an ideological battleground in the Cabinet between those who favour deregulation and the unfettering of enterprise, on the one hand, and those, on the other hand, who feel that the state can direct innovation and human imagination in constructive ways that meet a wider public interest. This distinction also plagues the debate on sustainable development. The economic core of free enterprises believes that enlightened self-interest will lead to a wealthier economy which subse-quently can be redirected to meet social ends. The more radical free enterprises believe that a combination of regulation and taxation can unleash a new era of technologically and managerially driven investments in efficiency practices and innovative clean-technology industries. The latter should propel forward a more eco-orientated economy and create jobs.

In a widely analysed speech to the Royal Society on 27 February 1996, Tony Blair, the leader of the Labour Party, captured this theme:

> There are tremendous opportunities for job creation in new environmental technologies. The global market is thought to be worth some $200 billion in 1990 and growing to $300 billion in the year 2000... we aim to encourage investment in our industries and infrastructure, to develop and upgrade the skills of our people and to promote the use of new technology. As well as economic modernisation we need environmental modernisation, to equip us for the demanding circumstances of the 21st century.
>
> *(Blair, 1996, p 7)*

It is possible that the Blair speech may propel the general theme of the sustainability transition. However, it will be popularly termed in the general election debate of 1996–97.

In his contribution, Stephen Smith distinguishes between the policy-packaging interpretation cautiously favoured by Spackman, and the predetermined earmarking allocations that full-blown hypothecation implies. He is not in favour of the latter for three reasons:

1. Hypothecation results in potentially long-term commitments of expenditure to programmes that may not meet a public need or justify the pre-set level of spend over the time period of the allocation. This results in a tax distortion and, possibly, a political difficulty because policy may not be flexible enough to meet changing priorities that cannot be foreseen at the outset.
2. Hypothecation will rarely raise revenue at precisely the amount that a given environmental expenditure will merit at it margins of investment.
3. Hypothecation can be undone by governments adjusting general taxation elsewhere to offset the earmarked revenue effect. For example, a shift in the imposition of value added tax could be used to counteract a particular subsidy.

All this suggests that hypothecation as a formal tax objective is neither likely nor necessary for the so-called sustainability transition. More likely, it will be subtle and, at times, fairly obvious measures to redirect expenditures into socially popular policy arenas as a result of specific taxation measures, but allocated to spending departments through various auditing devices, such as cost-effectiveness scrutinies and coordinated programme planning. Raising the excise tax on motor fuel on a graduated basis, for example, could release funds for innovative communal transport ventures, possibly run as public-private partnerships – though, for the foreseeable future, it may be difficult to find a direct revenue link.

This is the line adopted by Geoff Mulgan in Chapter 4. Mulghan favours a shift towards functional hypothecation, where revenue is raised from environmental 'sins', such as the private car's exhaust fumes in favour of a more integrated investment in mobility. He believes that such packaged revenue collection would help to bring about one of the more elusive objectives of the sustainability transition – namely, the encouragement of lateral multi-level governmental coordination and policy integration to assess ministries. This approach could further be stimulated by user charges – for example, small fees on container bins for waste collection – and/or by public-private mechanisms, such as the environment trusts mentioned earlier. There seems to be enormous scope for innovation here, and there is every sign that in the 'middle horizon' much of this will take place.

The other half of the hypothecation debate is the rise of the green account, or a fuller audit of environmental and social gains and losses within an economy and society in transition towards sustainability. The Tickell Panel (Tickell, 1996, p 6) in its second report urged greater innovation and experimentation in this area.

Doubtless both the round table and the Environment Select Committee will pronounce on that. In Chapter 5, Giles Atkinson and Kirk Hamilton summarize recent developments in this rapidly evolving arena of research. They point to a number of very imaginative studies in prestigious organizations where conventional economic indicators normally hold sway.

These include the World Bank, the UN Statistical Office, various government statistics agencies, and, most recently, the European Environment Agency (EEA) (1995). In the last example, the EEA has produced an imaginative report, based on the Dutch approach outlined by Atkinson and Hamilton, which sets out target indicators for a series of objectives laid down in the Fifth Environmental Action Programme. Then the report reaches three conclusions:

1. The following targets should be met by 2000:
   – SO_2 emissions
   – reduction in ozone-depleting substances
   – CO_2 emissions
2. The following will not be met to the point where extra action is needed:
   – acidification
   – volatile organic compounds (VOCs)
   – nitrates
   – solid waste
   – urban air pollution from motor vehicles
   – conservation and protection of biodiversity
3. Current policies are not sufficient to tackle:
   – CO_2 removal beyond 2000
   – traffic congestion and pollution
   – water abstraction
   – noise abatement
   – coastal zone management (CZM) in vulnerable areas
   – erosion and desertification.

This approach to policy targeting may prove useful for encouraging fresh lobbying over the proposed Sixth Environmental Action Plan, which is due to begin in 1997. Again, sadly, one must be cautious. European Commission bureaucracies do not like to be pushed around and told to mix their budgets any more than do national departments of state. Bullying by fancy statistical devices may well prove counterproductive. Much as 'green accounting' is seen as attractive and desirable, it is still too young a technique to be pushed too hard too quickly. As the Commission itself noted (European Commission, 1995, p 27): 'what is lacking is a genuine change in attitude, the desire to step resolutely down the path of sustainability'.

The rise of more formal auditing of resource flows – for example, soil erosion, water depletion, groundwater contamination – and environmental protection expenditures (stimulated in the European Union by the rise in influence of the European Environment Agency), as well as better measures of health costs, have all contributed to a greater disaggregation of expenditures set against socially derived measures of environmental capital and quality-of-life indicators. No matter how imperfect, these calculations are having some effect on long-established auditing procedures. In addition, as they become more intelligible through imaginative computerized displays, such accounts will give a better image of the well-being of social and economic progress.

At all kinds of levels of government, such devices, to a point, are bound to help the debate over what constitutes a positive or negative move towards sustainable development.

The UK Government has always taken its international obligations seriously. Often criticized for its environmental illiteracy, the government has at least published an annual report of its environmental performance under the general heading of *This Common Inheritance*. The latest version of a series of documents that have appeared since 1990 is a combination of the UK strategy and the official response to the Rio Agenda 21 (HM Government, 1995). For the first time their paper set out a number of agreed and quantifiable targets for global atmospheric protection, air and water quality, landfill and biodiversity. Admittedly, many of the targets are vague, few are met, and all are fudged in one way or another. One gets the impression that this is an attempt by the Department of the Environment, not the most popular body in Whitehall, to nurse along its sister departments towards a greater commitment to sustainability. So the strategy is more a tool for policy maintenance than policy change. But at least it has numbers, programmes, indicators and auditing mechanisms in place. In Whitehall terms, that is a minor revolution.

That revolution has been backed up by the first attempt to list indicators of sustainable development for the UK (Department of the Environment, 1996). It would be easy to carp on the narrowness and technical bias of the statistics, but the political significance is far greater, as the data generate debate among interested parties and allow the DoE to observe the squirming of its colleague ministries.

As is generally the case in environmental politics nowadays, the success or failure of these accounts will not lie in the accounts themselves. They will emerge in a wider arena over priority setting, focusing attention on disadvantage and injustice, emphasizing the need for citizen awareness and appreciation of various measures for defining changes in the quality of life, and in the widening of the democratic remit to more 'do-it-yourself' community politics.

REFERENCES

Blair, T (1996) *Sustainable Development; The Labour Party View*, The Labour Party, London

Department of the Environment (1996) *Indicators of Sustainable Development in the United Kingdom*, HMSO, London

Department of Trade and Industry (1995) *Energy Trends*, HMSO, London

Environmental Data Services (1995) *Energy efficiency, air quality lose out in 'green budget'*, The ENDS Report, No 250, pp 4–5

European Commission (1995) *Second Progress Report on the EU's Fifth Environmental Action Programme: Points to Integrating Environmental Policy*, COM(95), European Commission, Brussels, p 624

European Environment Agency (1995) *Environment in the European Union 1995*, European Environment Agency, Copenhagen

HM Government (1995) *This Common Inheritance: UK Annual Report*, Cm 2822, HMSO, London

House of Lords (1995) *Select Committee on Sustainable Development, Report*, HMSO, London

Owen, G (1955) *Energy Policy: The Government and the Energy Regulators. A Case Study of Energy Saving Trust*, GEC 95-35, CSERGE, University of East Anglia, Norwich

Tickell, C (Chair) (1995) *First Report of the British Government Panel on Sustainable Development*, Department of the Environment, London

Tickell, C (Chair) (1996) *Second Report of the British Government Panel on Sustainable Development*, Department of the Environment, London

HYPOTHECATION: A VIEW FROM THE TREASURY

Michael Spackman

BACKGROUND

Government finance departments around the world are well known for wanting to restrain government expenditure and taxation. They are also, usually, opposed to earmarking specific tax revenues for hypothecation to specific expenditures. This can seem contradictory. People might be more content, or less content, to pay taxes in this way. They might therefore press in some cases for more taxation and spending, and in other cases for less, so injecting consumer choice more directly into tax and spending policy. If revenues and expenditures can even be so arranged that a tax can be reclassified as a charge to pay for a particular service, the accounting figures for both taxation and public expenditure are reduced at a stroke.

In the UK the Treasury's view of strict hypothecation, as distinct from the pragmatic packaging of changes in taxes and spending, remains very cautious. This was set out in the Department's evidence to the House of Lords' Select Committee on Sustainable Development (1995a), the key concern being that tax and spending priorities should be set on their own merits, rather than driven by hypothecation. The Committee, in its Report, still saw a case for review of the potential role of hypothecation to environmental expenditure (1995b).

GENERAL PRINCIPLES

The hypothecation of taxes has a long history in academic debate. It emphasises the 'benefit" approach to taxation, of placing the cost of public provision on those who benefit from those services. It has become more popular in political debate worldwide, parallel with the greater interest, dating broadly from the 1980s, in charging for services. A good review from a UK perspective is provided by Margaret Wilkinson (1994). A more general theoretical and institutional overview, from a US perspective, can be found in Wagner (1991).

Types of Hypothecation

Wilkinson distinguishes between earmarking which is strict, or strong, and that which is weak, with only a loose financial link between the earmarked revenue and the associated spending; and she distinguishes between wide and narrow earmarking, according to whether the target spending is a general programme, such as health care, or a more specific area, such as nursery education. A third important distinction is that between the hypothecation of general taxes and of specific taxes.

An example of wide hypothecation would be the earmarking of blocks of general taxation – say, of income tax or of VAT – for particular expenditure programmes. It is sometimes suggested in public debate that part of a general tax should be described as, say, a health tax, or perhaps an environment tax, to pay for all of a particular programme. The tax might be strictly determined by the expenditure, or vice versa. There might be public referendums on whether the tax and expenditure should be increased or decreased.

Changes of this kind might help to make people more aware of the cost of a particular programme. On the other hand, some people might wish to opt out of the hypothecated tax. More seriously, such changes would influence priorities, especially over the longer term, for or against the chosen programme relative to other programmes. There is no perfect way of optimizing the level and distribution of public expenditure, but there is much to be said for procedures which are based for the most part on well-informed argument and negotiation. Public opinion – especially informed opinion – is an important element in this debate, but it is far from clear that the strong and direct impact of majority opinion implied by hypothecation of this kind would be to the national benefit. It would certainly be a new complication. It is for governments to judge whether and to what extent they might wish to present or manage parts of taxation in this way.

A simpler alternative sometimes proposed is that a general tax should be increased to provide some specific increase in expenditure on a particular programme. This too could have presentational attractions, but it would be unlikely to have much effect on behaviour, largely because there would be no fixed baseline, for more than a year or two, to define what spending on the programme would otherwise have been.

Some way removed from the hypothecation of general taxes to whole programmes is the hypothecation of special taxes to expenditures which specially benefit those who pay the taxes. Often quoted as an example in the UK are National Insurance Contributions (NICs), paid as a charge on employment and earmarked to help pay for certain benefits for which only employees or ex-employees will be eligible. However, this is not strict hypothecation. There is a fund into which NICs are paid, but there is no fixed linkage between total contributions and total benefits paid, or between total benefits paid and total contributions. A still weaker example of the same general principle in the UK is the imposition of motoring taxes, on fuel and vehicles, in part because of public spending on roads.

Another form of hypothecation is the use of special taxes or levies for particular groups of individuals or institutions to pay for services which they collectively want, but which they do not feel able to provide as a wholly private enterprise. This may be because of the problem of free-riders: some bodies would not contribute to a non-statutory scheme, but would still gain from the service. Examples from public debate in the UK are a training levy on employers, an infrastructure levy on local businesses, and a packaging levy on producers to fund recycling.

In the environmental context it is often suggested that certain environmental taxes should be hypothecated to related environmental subsidies.

Taxes versus Charges

The debate about strict hypothecation can be seen in terms of taxes versus charges. Arguments for strict hypothecation generally amount to saying that those taxes ought to be seen as payments made by the public to particular environmental or other benefits. This distinction between payment for a service (to be treated as revenue to the service provider) and taxation (to be treated as general revenue to the government) has to be formally defined by governments for the purposes of national accounting, and for the planning and control of public expenditure.

The formal boundary is defined by international convention. In general terms, a compulsory payment which does not directly purchase a benefit is classified as a tax. A charge, in contrast, purchases a specific service and will generally vary with usage; the transaction should be a market exchange of a kind which the private sector could supply (as a principal rather than as an agent); and the charge should merely cover the cost of providing the service. In practice, many charges are as compulsory as taxes. People and institutions can reduce most tax liabilities by modifying their behaviour; and many taxes give access to benefits, with a few being tied to specific services. Any definition will therefore leave a grey area. In borderline cases, the intent of the government in levying the payment can be important in practice.

Recent or current examples of payments classified as taxes in the United Kingdom include local authority rates, the Community Charge and the Council Tax, even though these may include or have included specific precepts to pay for the costs of, for example, police authorities. However, water charges, despite their *ad hoc* linkage in many cases to property taxes, have long been classified as charges. National Health Service prescription charges are more obviously charges, not taxes; so too is the TV licence fee, collected as a charge to pay for the services of the BBC, although there is no opting out of this for those who have a television set but do not view BBC programmes.

Several examples of this boundary lie in areas of environmental interest. Vehicle excise duty could be seen as a payment for access to the road system, but it is not a payment of the cost of providing a specific service and is therefore a tax. (Fees for driving tests, in contrast, are paying for this specific service and are therefore charges.) Motorway tolls could be set up as a trading activity, with tolls recovering costs and being treated as charges; but the revenue from urban congestion pricing would much exceed the physical cost of road provision and would be expected to be a tax. (Congestion charges, nonetheless, being charges for scarce space, have features in common with land rents: if the right to collect such charges were sold to, say, a private-sector urban road-management company, the classification might need to be re-examined.)

The recovery from firms of the administration cost of environmental regulation is classified as taxation, levied to recover equitably this element of the costs imposed by the firms' activities. It covers the cost of a service to the general public, not to the firms themselves. Levies on pollution at present also fall clearly on the side of taxes rather than on charges.

These classification decisions in the UK are made not by the Treasury but by the Office of National Statistics (ONS), formerley the Central Statistical Office (CSO). The ONS in turn rely increasingly on the international 'System of National Accounts' and will also be obliged to follow the European System of Accounts to ensure consistency of determination of deficits and contributions across member states. Borderline cases are in practice rare, but where they arise, they are considered on their merits. Occasionally, decisions have to balance a wide range of factors in deciding just where the line should most sensibly be drawn. Some of these points are covered in the introductory sections to Chapter 5.

Of course, formal classification rules do not rule out hypothecation of taxes. But they do serve to define taxes as a class of payment which, in the eyes of those responsible for making these classification decisions, cannot reasonably be seen as purchasing specific services.

HYPOTHECATION IN PRACTICE

No UK government, at least in recent years, has seriously entertained the strict hypothecation of blocks of general taxation to specific expenditures; and this has attracted only limited public debate. There has been more debate about the use of specific taxes for specific expenditures.

One such example is the idea of a statutory packaging levy as a tax hypothecated to pay for recycling facilities. As a policy measure it should be compared with the effects of alternative legislation which simply requires certain levels of recycling. To meet such a requirement many producers would still probably cooperate to share the economies of scale. Different groups of companies might form a number of consortiums; and very large producers would be free to go it alone. This market freedom could be a better way of increasing recycling than a statutory levy used to finance government-approved schemes.

A training levy is at first sight attractive, but the balance of argument is again not clear cut. Different institutions' needs for training vary widely in level and in kind. There are problems in defining training. It is a matter for analysis and judgement whether regulated funding of this kind would bring more or less benefits than costs. (In the past, some industry-specific training levies have been classified as income to training boards, providing another illustration of the grey area between taxes and charges. Any future levy of this kind, if clearly imposed by the government, might well be classified as tax.)

A local infrastructure levy raises questions of how widespread the demand really is among those who would be charged and about where the cost would ultimately fall. Property taxes, for example, may ultimately fall mainly on landowners. It also raises questions, if some of the proposed extra spending is sought from other government funds, of priorities in public expenditure and wider questions of the distribution between local and central government authority.

For fairness, and for the related objective of political acceptability, there can often be a good case for packaging any new or increased tax with, for example, reductions in other taxes, or increases in benefits, so as to reduce sudden redistributions of income from those who are paying the new tax to those who are not. For example, the UK Government has undertaken to use revenue from the proposed landfill tax to cut other taxes on business, such as employers' National Insurance Contributions. This point, and the many complications that arise as a result, is covered in Chapter 15. The government will also allow landfill operators to claim a 90 per cent rebate on payments to environmental trusts set up for certain defined purposes. The proposal to increase VAT on domestic fuel to the standard rate was tied to proposals to increase benefits for the poor and elderly, and to provide grants for home insulation.

Even strict hypothecation of payments for environmental damage may be sensible in some narrow circumstances, which do not distort public spending priorities. For example, a tradable permit system in which the initial allocation of permits was made to existing producers would have this effect. The payments for permits would be wholly recycled among one set of producers. A very similar arrangement would be to charge the producers a levy on the particular pollutant, the proceeds of which were paid back to them in proportion to their output of the final product. Such repayments, or the initial allocation of tradable permits to existing producers, are not – of course – as efficient, in principle, as retaining the levy payments by the Exchequer or auctioning the initial issue of permits. They confine the incentive to change to the producers alone, without providing a further incentive for consumers to switch their expenditures to more environmentally friendly products; and they give a relative advantage to incumbent producers over potential new competitors. None the less, this may be a tolerable price to pay to make a scheme acceptable.

These examples of policy packaging, or of recycling money within tightly defined schemes, are different in kind from the proposals sometimes made for the strict earmarking and hypothecation of taxes to environmental expenditure.

It is sometimes suggested that revenues from the landfill tax, for example, should be hypothecated to environmental expenditure. This comes up against the strongest objection to strict hypothecation: that it weakens the sensible management of expenditure priorities. If a government wants stronger environmental policies, there may be a place for more taxing and more spending, but there is little logic in saying that one should be strictly hypothecated to the other. There is no reason that expenditure on environmental policy should generally increase or decrease in line with the level of environmental taxes. If anything, the linkage might be expected to go the other way: the more that polluters are charged for their environmental impacts, the less need there will be for public expenditure on environmental protection and improvement.

The general hypothecation of environmental revenues to environmental spending might be appropriate in a quite different structure, where one arm of government has total responsibility for managing the environment, including the sale of rights to exploit it, and for subsidizing environmental improvements. However, this is far removed from the present structure and would not be automatically more effective. Even in such a structure, it would be surprising if the optimal levels of environmental receipts and expenditures were even very roughly equal.

Again, if in some quite new structure much of the road system were operated as a regulated commercial network, it is possible that the charging system might include, in addition to electronic tolls on some roads, levies on fuel and on vehicles. However, such levies, if they were approved, would not be hypothecation of tax; they would be simply a practical approach to charging.

A more interesting hypothecation issue in road use could arise with urban-congestion charging. As the revenue from an urban-congestion charge would probably greatly exceed the financial cost of local road provision and maintenance, it is often suggested that it should be partly or wholly hypothecated to local public transport. In one way this would be fair. Since the charge, in contrast to a conventional pollution tax, is a charge for costs which road users are imposing mainly on themselves, and which in any case are almost wholly local, there are good arguments for at least most of the revenue collected from urban road users being retained locally. A local authority may also find it both efficient and expedient to introduce such a charge in parallel with more subsidised investment in other transport measures. More public transport subsidies generally could be a reinforcing measure to reduce the costs of congestion, and could also ease the impact of the new congestion tax on the income of urban travellers. Taking a longer view however, road congestion charging *reduces* the case for public transport subsidies. More generally it would be a serious constraint to tie congestion-charge revenue strictly to expenditure of this kind, to the exclusion of other expenditure or of reductions in taxes.

Congestion-charge revenues illustrate the danger of letting hypothecation language get in the way of carefully considered debate. Arguments good or bad can be found for using these revenues for public transport subsidies, as just noted; or to reduce taxation of the rural motorist so that motorists as a whole are little or no worse off; or to reduce general taxes on employment and elsewhere to lessen market distortions; or to reduce other local (eg, property) taxes so that the local community as a whole is no worse off. The process of choosing or distributing between these or other uses, and their subsequent management, should be governed by concerns for fairness and political acceptability, and for efficiency in the use of resources in both the short and the long term. Debate about strict earmarking can do more to hinder than to help this process, by narrowing horizons and imposing lasting rigidities.

CONCLUSION

Where it is equitable and efficient for consumers to pay directly for services provided by the public sector, this should obviously be encouraged. However, this is charging, not hypothecation of taxation. Although the boundary between taxes and charges is not absolutely sharp, taxes are essentially, by definition, payments which cannot reasonably be seen as purchasing specific services.

The main arguments in favour of hypothecating taxes are that it can make people more aware of the costs of what the public sector is providing, that it can sometimes be equitable, where special taxes are imposed on those who benefit from particular services, and that it can make new taxes more acceptable. All of these three potential benefits can be very largely met by informal or weak hypothecation, as with NICs, or by suitable packaging of sets of new policy measures. The arguments against strict hypothecation are that it is a rigidity and complication which can distort the distribution and efficiency of public expenditure.

These arguments apply to environmental taxes in much the same way as to other taxes. Every case should be approached on its merits, and there is often a persuasive case, in terms of presentation and of fairness, for explicitly packaging new environmental taxes with new benefits or lowering other taxes on the groups most affected. However, it is not easy to construct cases where the strict hypothecation of receipts from particular environmental taxes to particular expenditures would be expected to lead, in practice, to better public policy. It would be especially wrong to see hypothecation as a way of avoiding, for any one kind of expenditure, the level of scrutiny required of public expenditure proposals in general.

REFERENCES

House of Lords (1995a) *Select Committee on Sustainable Development, Minutes of Evidence*, HL Paper 31-xiii, HMSO, London

House of Lords (1995b) *Select Committee on Sustainable Development, Report*, HMSO, London

Wagner, R E (ed) (1991) *Charging for Government: User Charges and Earmarked Taxes in Principle and Practice*, Routledge, London and New York

Wilkinson, M (1994) 'Paying for public spending: is there a role for earmarked taxes?', *Fiscal Studies*, Vol 15, No 4, pp 119–35

C h a p t e r 4

FUNCTIONAL HYPOTHECATION AS A POTENTIAL SOLUTION

Geoff Mulgan

CONSTRAINTS ON TAX

Environmental tax policy is usually discussed in terms of creating a new economic rationality that can encompass the environment. Powerful arguments support the idea that tax should be shifted away from 'goods' like work and onto 'bads' such as environmentally damaging activities and waste. David Gee summarises these arguments in Chapter 6.

But in democracies tax is not just a technical issue: it is also a profoundly political relationship. Although for long periods the public will accept pretty much any tax that is taken from them, at other times questions of legitimacy rise to the top of the agenda. By assuming the benign nature of their proposals, those on the forefront of environmental tax reform have underplayed these questions of legitimacy and fairness.

Politics in this sense is now one of the two overwhelming constraints on any tax policy in the 1990s. Is a tax – like VAT on fuel – seen as inherently unfair and wasteful, or is it seen as a legitimate contribution to a common need? Is a tax, such as a carbon tax in the European Union or Australia, sufficiently widely and deeply supported to overcome the political opposition of vested interests? This is particularly pertinent if a threat to competitive advantage is envisaged.

This leads to the second constraint, namely the relationship between a tax and the global system within which any new economic tax will operate. Here the feedback loops are far faster than those of raised emissions, which may only mobilize affected interests over decades. An ill-considered tax policy quickly undermines the performance of an economy in global markets, especially if it penalizes more mobile factors of production, such as the location of new plant.

These two constraints have been given relatively little weight in the environmental taxation literature. The analysis to date remains largely informed by an economistic, technical view of taxation. It is concerned primarily with economically justifiable levels of tax, and the practical implementation of options. Some of this literature is surveyed by Paul Ekins in Chapter 8. But as recent UK experience shows, attempts to put an ecotax into practice can cause problems, and can even reverse and disrupt the patient arguments built up over many years. Arguably, this is the case with the carbon/energy tax proposals of the EU.

THE HISTORICAL CONTEXT OF TAXATION

This problem of legitimacy can only be understood in the context of tax history. Tax is the focus of the relationship between states and citizens. Each major shift in the forms of governance has been accompanied by a crisis in taxation and a move to new forms.

Today, there are some signs that we may be in the midst of such a crisis, parallel in form to those of the 1880s and 1890s, and before that the 1790s. The first set of symptoms were the tax revolts, beginning with Proposition 13 in California and gaining momentum with the rise of the neoconservative right in the 1980s. Today tax is a central issue in the electoral politics of most Western societies – in the US, the UK and Australia certainly, but also now in Germany and in Italy.

In the UK the problem has become more not less intense because, despite the reduction in rates of personal income tax during this period, public spending was not cut. Even with the closures and the privatizations – measures which became common in the West, irrespective of which party was in power – overall tax rates continued to go up. In Britain it rose from 34.1 per cent of GDP in 1980 to 35.6 per cent in 1990. In Italy the rise was from 20–29 per cent, in Canada from 30–37 per cent, in Ireland from 34–43 per cent, and in Sweden from 55–67 per cent. All but three OECD countries shared in this apparently relentless historical trend.

Part of the reason is that the demands on government are increasing. In Britain the NHS needs an annual real growth of 2 per cent to survive even at current levels. Personal social services require 2.5 per cent, and education will need an extra 0.5–1 per cent of GDP to bring post-school education up to European standards (Glennister, 1992). As a result governments have found it extremely hard to cut spending; in the UK there seems to be an almost iron rule that prevents spending falling below 40 per cent of GDP, and an almost equally iron political rule that makes it impossible to raise taxes to, or above, 40 per cent. Hence the endemic fiscal crises of both Labour and Conservative governments.

Everywhere there has been a steady increase in the number of people dependent on those in work – those staying on longer at school, living longer as pensioners, and above all those who are unemployed. In the

OECD area there are now five workers to every old age pensioner. By the year 2000 this will have fallen to 4.5, by 2040 to less than three, and in Switzerland and Germany it will be down to two. Nor is there any sign, even in boom times, that full employment will return, removing one of the main burdens on public finance.

The long-term trends of the more prosperous societies are not in dispute – greater spending on soft, 'caring' goods and services: a shift in public concern from quantity to quality, to some extent reflected in the changing politics of economic valuation; a greater concern for relativities; and greater political weight for the elderly and for the disabled. Each in their different ways exacerbates the public spending pressure on government.

Part of the reason that governments have found it so hard to legitimate taxes and spending is due to their organisational structure. This structural problem is termed disconnection: the separation of the tax bill from the benefits it finances. Traditionally, taxes were largely raised for specific ends, above all for warfare. In the 18th century, war and the costs of war debts accounted for 85 per cent of state spending in Britain. The connection between tax and spending was evident to all. But with the growth in the size and complexity of the state this link was lost, principally because of the centralization of tax collection and disbursement. The vast multiple-service system of the modern state is still organized largely on the models established in the 19th century. In the UK, tax money is pooled into the central Treasury and distributed to spending departments according to a budget and subject to approval by Parliament. Local government has adopted a similar model. Where once local services were financed through separate rates, by the 1930s these had been combined into a single rate to cover all services.

When there was a consensus on state spending, such as in wartime or in the post-war period of rebuilding and funding the welfare state, central pooling was not problematic. The shared sense of purpose helped to legitimize higher taxes: the end justified the means. In the early years of this century central pooling also fitted well with prevailing administrative wisdoms: it enabled government to plan and to prioritize.

But as the welfare consensus started to break down in the 1970s, the political foundations of pooling cracked. Cuts provoked a widespread, and often divisive, debate about priorities. A more confident consumerism demanded greater transparency and accountability in the use of state finances, particularly as the sheer complexity of modern government was making it far harder for the average citizen to understand. And a generation more sensitive to choice and identity was becoming less deferential towards government and more suspicious of handing over blank cheques.

The administrative centralization that once seemed so eminently sensible has lost much of its authority. The separation of tax collection from service provision has meant that links are made through cost budgeting by senior civil servants and politicians in invisible procedures, according to scarcely visible criteria. Levels of finance are shaped by departmental and ministerial rivalries rather than by popular support. Although experts still analyze centralized tax and spending decisions as rational processes to maximize efficiency and minimize distortions, to the outsider government appears as a black hole into which resources disappear.

By and large environmental taxes have followed in this history. They have taken for granted the model of fiscal centralization, and done little to address the issue of public trust and accountability. Certainly when VAT on fuel was discussed and introduced in the UK, no one in government proposed that the resources raised should go anywhere other than into the central pool, to contribute to everything from financing the PSBR to paying for new prisons.

Nor has there been much party political debate about the two sides of the environmental tax equation: on the one hand, the behavioural benefits to be gained from raising the costs of environmentally damaging activities, and on the other the benefits to be gained from greater public spending on such things as home insulation, beach cleaning or decommissioning old power stations.

THE POTENTIAL OF HYPOTHECATION

How then could this disconnection be addressed? The best way is through an array of different types of hypothecation which restore the connection between taxing and spending.

It is generally assumed that hypothecation is a primitive form of tax. As a principle it is fiercely opposed by most orthodox economists. And it is true that earmarking is most common in the early stages of tax development. In developing countries it is common to find airport and hotel bed taxes used to finance tourist development. Petrol tax is often used to finance road building. Just as winding country roads reflect strong local property rights and a weak state, so hypothecated taxes reflect the need for emerging and strengthening states to win popular consent. As winding roads are replaced by the motorways of strong states, so hypothecated taxes are replaced by pooled collection and the assertion of treasury control over administration.

This view applies both to strong and to weak hypothecation. Strong hypothecation is where spending is directly determined by a particular revenue source. Weak hypothecation is primarily presentational, a way of informing citizens about where their money goes. Both have their limitations. But because of the problems of legitimation of large government, we need to look again at their virtues. There are many simple examples where a tax is earmarked to a specific purpose, as in the case of the BBC licence fee (which incidentally has enabled the BBC to be one of the few public services to effectively compete with the private sector). Many such examples exist around the world. The Netherlands uses taxes on aircraft noise to help pay for noise insulation when building new airports. Sweden taxes pesticides and fertilizers to finance environmental research and improvements, and battery taxes are earmarked for the costs of disposal. The US Superfund (whatever its many problems) does at least have the same clarity of getting those responsible to pay directly for the public good. One could imagine many parallel uses of the notion in the UK. Part of the proceeds of VAT on fuel could have been explicitly earmarked to finance a programme of home insulation and energy-efficiency measures, helping to raise taxes, improve efficiency and create jobs all at once. Indeed, this was subsequently the case with £25 million allocated to the Home Energy Efficiency Scheme in 1995/96.

There is some theoretical support for these kinds of approaches. Musgrave and Musgrave (1989) support earmarked taxes that are like charges, such as US gasoline taxes. Some libertarians (notably James Buchanan) have supported earmarking as a means of cutting public spending, while some progressives support it as a way of winning public support for higher spending. All agree that earmarking only makes sense for purposes which have general benefits, such as policing, education or health. Environmental purposes fall within this group. However, these narrowly earmarked taxes have limits. They are primarily about presentation. They do not in themselves influence behaviour, or lead to a more farsighted use of public resources. Nor do they improve the quality of public accountability.

This is usually where discussions of hypothecation end. On the one side there are the politicians to whom some presentation-influenced hypothecation is attractive. Against them are the economists who point to all of the distortions that may result: funds that rise when the need for them falls; irrational distributional effects; and constraints on overall planning of public activities. These points are summarized by Daniel McCoy in Chapter 10.

Functional Hypothecation

If, however, we go a step further, the notion of hypothecation can actually bring improvements in the functioning of whole systems. This can be termed functional hypothecation, addressed to a whole system of activity (such as transport) rather than a particular component (such as car petrol).

With functional hypothecation, a tax is used to finance another part of the same functional system in order to meet some policy objective. Transport is a good example of how this could work. There is a widely acknowledged imbalance between road and rail transport, and a lack of integration between different transport modes which has been exacerbated by misconceived models of funding and accountability. Hypothecation could put things right by imposing more appropriate incentives and signals. The simplest approach would simply be to pay a proportion of the road fund licence, or of the revenue derived from urban road pricing, or specialized taxes like the US gas-guzzler taxes (cars under 23 mpg), directly into rail.

But a more promising approach, which demonstrates the wider potential of hypothecation, would be to introduce an annual public transport fee, similar in principle but not in form to the BBC licence fee. This public transport levy, with usage-based fees, would fund a public transport agency which would in turn finance railways, buses, cycle-hire groups, franchised taxis and other transport providers. It could be financed out of a range of sources, the most appropriate of which might be taxes on fuel. The important issue is that its level should be clearly visible to the public so that, as with the BBC, the level of finance would become a matter of public debate, dependent less on the decisions of cabinet committees and more on transport operators' ability to generate popular support through the quality and extent of services. Each operator would therefore have an incentive to maximize usage or, perhaps, to reduce journey times, within the overall budget constraint, just as the BBC has an incentive to keep its ratings high. The key indicator for the railways, for example, would not be the financial deficit but rather the cost of each passenger mile.

Hypothecated funding, dependent on public support and directed to an agency responsible for the overall system of transport, would then lead to a very different approach to transport provision. By giving a new incentive to maximize usage it could encourage transport integration, the re-opening of stations, the return of free carriage for bicycles on trains, the adoption of the French system of cheap bicycle hire at stations, the integration of taxis into through-ticketing arrangements, and the use of railway property for transport-intensive activities like supermarket shopping or leisure. It could encourage more systemic thinking, such as improved containerization and luggage handling to encourage the integration of driving and long-distance rail travel. And it could foster integrated ticketing and an expansion of information systems, such as electronic bus-availability data at stations and bus stops. Forced to justify a transport fee, the transport agency, and those seeking its funds, would have to consider the interests of all potential users. Financial efficiency would still count, because a higher fee would reduce public support. But finance would no longer be the sole criterion.

This is just one example of functional hypothecation. There are many others in the environmental field: pollution taxes to fund environmental programmes, energy taxes for agencies responsible for the whole gamut of energy usage (taking a few steps further the principles of least-cost planning with utilities) or the 'club' type hypothecation of the Swedish approach to NO_x. The point in each of these cases is not merely that there is an explicit spotlight thrown on systems of provision and how well they interconnect, but that the recipients of funds are required to justify themselves publicly rather than just to ministers. In the future such principles of using tax and spending to shape the management of whole systems could be extended in ways that break right across existing departmental boundaries.

Another example would be the home: taxes on domestic property directed back to the various things needed to protect home life, ranging from security to open spaces. A second would be the world of work, using national insurance payments to contribute to the quality of work environments, training and so on. A third would be an agency responsible for the whole of waste disposal and given incentives to encourage waste reduction. The proposed landfill tax discussed in Chapter 15 is a step in this direction. These remain virgin territory as far as the tax debate is concerned. Their point is to provide correct incentives to agencies, not in the narrow sense of some of the executive agencies (where efficiency is conceived predominantly in terms of throughput) but rather in terms of the qualitative performance of more complex systems.

Whether it is functional or traditional hypothecation that is used the general point is that there is a need to make more comprehensible a tax and spend system that has become far more complex and thus incomprehensible to the typical taxpayer and voter.

Globalization

Mulgan and Murray (1993) also tackle the other side of the equation, the question of globalization. We suggest that if national governments are to regain some control over taxation they will not only need to collaborate more effectively but also to develop new forms of tax on new forms of rent. Some of these have already played a part in the environmental tax debate, for example taxes on oil or mineral exploitation. More generally, there is a renewed interest in the importance of taxes on land in an era of more mobile resources. But our main proposals concern taxes on such things as copyright and patents – the key resources of the information age. These are mainly justified in terms of their political and economic impacts. But they are important too for the environmental tax argument, because unless these can be framed within broader packages that meet the objections of those who point to the pressures of globalization, they are unlikely to be fully implemented.

CONCLUSION

These two broad areas of development – the first on new forms of presentation of environmental taxes to make clear their benefits to citizens, and new forms of functional taxation to improve the working of systems; and the second concerned with avoiding the barriers that globalization places in the way of environmental taxes – are important additions to the current debate.

There is growing understanding of the need for far better presentation of tax connections, although such a move remains fiercely resisted by most tax experts, schooled in technical economics rather than in politics. Sweden is often cited as a good example of a reform package which included reductions in income tax and broadening of VAT, which helped to neutralize some potential special interest enemies. By contrast, as David Gee shows in Chapter 6, taxes that are introduced on their own tend to fail or cause controversy. Bill Clinton discovered this when he tried to impose a form of energy tax on petrol.

The confusions (or disagreements) over whether environmental taxes are primarily means of changing behaviour, or primarily means of raising funds for governments under pressure, are not likely to go away. In the short run the primary concerns about hypothecation will be to ensure that tax packages properly compensate key loser groups, particularly some other materials, energy-intensive industries, and those on low incomes. But this is just a small part of the potential and significance of a new way of thinking about tax and spending.

Hypothecation of this kind seems to fit better with public attitudes than pooled taxation. Contrary to the assumptions of the majority of economists who have influenced tax theory, most people see different goods and services such as transport, land, water, justice or schooling as different in kind, and consequently believe that it is quite appropriate to reflect these differences in tax policy. This is one reason why there is far stronger support for a more equal distribution of healthcare, justice and education than there is for an egalitarian distribution of money. In this respect Michael Walzer's (1983) approach and Jon Elster's (1992) important arguments about 'local justice' – that is to say, the very different perceptions of what counts as a just distribution in different fields – are considerably more useful than those of more abstract political philosophers and economists.

In the short run forms of hypothecation that redistribute resources within industries, from more resource-intensive and high-emission plants to less polluting and material-intensive plants, may prove the best tool for accelerating the shift to a new industrial paradigm. This ultimate form would be based on zero waste, widespread disassembly and recycling, and 'factories without pipes'. Looking further ahead, in an era of low trust in governments and in experts, we will need to take seriously models for building legitimacy so as to introduce politics into the evolving mix of environmental understanding and economic tools.

REFERENCES

Elster, J (1992) *Local Justice*, Cambridge University Press, Cambridge

Glennister, H (1992) *Paying for Welfare: Issues for the Nineties*, Discussion Paper No 2, LSE Welfare State Programme, London School of Economics, London

Mulgan, G and Murray I R (1993) *Reconnecting Taxation*, Demos, London

Musgrave, R A and Musgrave, P B (1989) *Public Finance in Theory and Practice*, McGraw-Hill, New York

Walzer, M (1983) *Spheres of Justice*, Harvard University Press, Cambridge, MA

C h a p t e r 5

GREEN ACCOUNTING: MONITORING AND POLICY IMPLICATIONS

Giles Atkinson and Kirk Hamilton

INTRODUCTION

Few aspects of the environmental debate have received so much attention in recent years as that of green accounting. This has reflected the need to develop environmental indicators to demonstrate the size of environmental change, to indicate the required level of policy intervention, and to monitor progress towards environmental goals. In the latter respect, performance-based indicators have been proposed. These measures are essentially independent of the national accounting systems which are currently used to measure economic progress. Yet, at the heart of the indicator debate is the issue of how we should measure human well-being and economic progress. For example, many of us have probably come across some reference to the short-comings of existing measures of income such as gross domestic product (GDP). In practice, calls to 'green' our measures of national income (eg, GDP) have been translated into actions to green the national accounts, or at least to provide green adjuncts (or satellites) to the core accounts. The impression often conveyed is that overhauling the way in which we record 'economic progress' will in turn alter policy towards the environment. In this chapter, we argue that this will occur only if green

Acknowledgements
CSERGE is a designated research centre of the UK Economic and Social Research Council (ESRC). This paper is part of a research programme on 'The Measurement and Achievement of Sustainable Development' funded by Directorate-General XII of the European Commission. The views expressed in this paper are those of the authors alone and should not be taken to represent the position of either the European Commission or the World Bank.

accounts are developed in a policy-relevant way. Hence, we suggest that green national accounts are a more useful response to the development of indicators than, say, are measures based on environmental indicators which are not integrated with economic data.

THE RATIONALE FOR GREEN ACCOUNTING

The growth rate of GDP is regarded as the single most important economic indicator. It is not surprising, then, that much of the green accounting debate has rallied behind the criticism of GDP. GDP mainly consists of the total value of goods and services exchanged in markets together with government expenditures on, say, education and health-care. The United Nations System of National Accounts (SNA) sets the international standard for national accounting, including the definitions and methods of measuring GDP. The key elements of the System of National Accounts are the income and expenditure accounts, measuring current flows of economic activity (eg, GDP), and the national balance-sheet accounts measuring opening and closing stocks of assets (both financial and tangible) over the accounting period.

For short-term economic decision-making, GDP is used in conjunction with other important economic indices in economic modelling and the forecasting of short-term economic activity. These include, for example, the inflation rate, which measures changes in prices of some of the key goods that are included in GDP, and the unemployment rate, which measures the amount of labour which is not currently used in the generation of GDP. Long-term policy concerns surround the explanation of long-run changes in GDP – for instance, improvements in the quality of labour, and capital and technological progress. But what about broader quality-of-life questions? GDP measures only economic activity and so does not directly account for the social aspects of well-being such as health and literacy. In response to this there is a large literature on the social indicators and the regular presentation of such indicators alongside economic data (for a discussion see World Bank, 1995, Munasinghe *et al*, 1996). Nevertheless, it is economic data in the national accounts that predominate.

Environmental concerns also show up in the conventional accounts but are seldom identified. Hence, while commercial natural resources are measured directly in the accounts, in the sense that the value added associated with their exploitation is measured in national income, the economic value of these resources as assets appears only implicitly. Environmental resources are measured more indirectly in the accounts. To the extent that there is a commercial activity associated with an environmental asset, such as tourism or hunting, then the value added in this activity appears as part of the national product. But the underlying asset, the pristine lake or wilderness, is not valued explicitly. Some environmental policies, on the other hand, show up more directly in the accounts. The values associated with market-based instruments will show up in the accounts as indirect taxes, in the case of pollution taxes, or as investments (and corresponding assets in the balance-sheet accounts), in the case of emissions permits. Because they are assets with market values, tradable emission permits would be measured as intangible assets in the balance-sheet accounts. However, the economic and social effects of broader environmental policies appear only indirectly.

Thus, in general, it is not possible to address environmental concerns using the economic indicators that are currently central to decision-making. What is required are environmental indicators that can be considered side-by-side with the economic measures that we currently rely on. This is crucial if decision-making is not to be systematically biased towards environmental degradation and the over-extraction of resources. Reaction to this measurement challenge has resulted in a proliferation of environmental data, such as air quality indices and water quality classifications (see, for example, Department of the Environment, 1992; OECD, 1994; World Resources Institute, 1994).

However, policy-makers cannot make direct use of typical environmental data that are voluminous, difficult to aggregate and not connected to other policy variables. Thus, there exists an additional task of boiling down the mass of existing environmental data into a more useful form. This is where green accounting comes in. Although lacking an actual definition it is useful to think of green accounting as encompassing not only the search for indicators but also the provision of a consistent organizing framework to analyse these data.

AGGREGATE PHYSICAL ENVIRONMENTAL INDICATORS

The OECD's 'pressure-state-response' framework has been one of the most influential means to select environment indicators. This work has been crucial in focusing attention on key descriptive indicators that reflect:

1. Pressures on the environment – eg, underlying pressures, such as population change, economic growth, structural change and public concern; and proximate pressures, such as land-use changes and waste emissions.
2. The state of the environment itself – eg, ambient pollution concentrations, amounts and concentrations of waste in the environment.
3. The response of society in terms of government policies, ameliorative measures undertaken by individuals and business, social response in terms of environmental activism, etc.

Indicators of the state of the environment have been reported for some time in developed countries, in the form of air quality indices, water quality classifications, and so on. The current emphasis has shifted, however, from these *descriptive* indicators to *performance* indicators. Performance indicators measure, in effect, the percentage deviation of current environmental conditions from some threshold or goal set by environmental policy. This provides both the means to aggregate individual measures with respect to a given theme – such as total toxic load – and the means to aggregate within and across themes by adding up the percentage deviations.

The pre-eminent example of highly aggregated environmental indicators is provided by the work of Adriaanse (1993) of The Netherlands Ministry of Housing, Physical Planning and Environment, and by Hammond *et al* (1995). This work has concentrated on the development of environmental-policy performance indicators, specifically designed to measure progress towards meeting targets set by Dutch environmental policy. Indicators are developed around a number of themes and it is these that provide the basis for weighting and combining disparate physical measures into an integrated indicator. Dutch policy sets sustainability targets for each theme, which are based typically on the assimilative capacity of the environment.

The themes that have been developed in The Netherlands are: climate change, acidification, eutrophication, dispersion (of pesticides, toxins such as cadmium and mercury, and radioactive substances), disposal (of solid waste), and disturbance (caused by odour and noise). For each theme, a number of physical measurements are combined according to their contribution to the particular environmental problem. This is best explained with an example.

Carbon dioxide is one of many greenhouse gases that contribute to global warming. Each gas can be assigned a 'global warming potential' (GWP) in relation to the predominant gas, carbon dioxide (CO_2). This global warming potential is a function of the particular physical properties of the gases concerned, in terms of their effectiveness in trapping long-wave radiation and thus warming the earth, and of their residency time in the atmosphere. The GWPs of the main greenhouse gases relative to CO_2 are shown in Table 5.1.

Table 5.1 *GWP factors of greenhouse gases*

Substance	GWP Factor
CO_2	1
CH_4	12
N_2O	290
CFC-11	3500
CFC-12	7300
CFC-113	4200
CFC-114	6900
CFC-115	6900
Halon-1211	5800
Halon-1301	5800

Source: Adriaanse, 1993

These global warming potentials are the basis for an integrated greenhouse gas emission indicator in 'carbon equivalents' (Ceq). Quantities of emissions for each gas are weighted by their GWP and the result summed to produce the results in Table 5.2 for The Netherlands in the 1980s and early

Table 5.2 *Emissions of greenhouse gases in The Netherlands (M tonnes Ceq)*

Year	CO_2	CH_4	N_2O	CFC + Halons	Total
1980	172.000	10.320	11.600	92.369	286
1981	165.000	10.423	11.600	92.000	279
1982	152.000	10.527	11.600	91.500	266
1983	152.000	10.633	11.600	89.500	264
1984	161.000	10.739	11.600	85.800	270
1985	166.000	10.846	11.600	82.000	271
1986	170.000	10.955	11.600	72.760	265
1987	177.000	11.064	11.600	59.792	260
1988	180.000	11.175	11.600	49.141	252
1989	182.000	11.287	11.600	40.816	246
1990	186.000	11.400	11.600	34.811	244
1991	185.000	11.514	11.600	31.132	239

Source: Adriaanse, 1993

1990s. This indicator becomes a performance indicator when these emissions in Ceq are compared with policy targets for The Netherlands in terms of the stabilization of greenhouse gas emissions.

Figure 5.1 shows the integrated environmental pressure index for The Netherlands over the period 1980–91. The cumulative index had reached a level of 1195 by 1991, falling from a peak value of 1346 in 1985. Because there are six component themes, the target for the cumulative index is 600. The obvious implication is that the index must fall by one half over the period 1992–2000. Eutrophication and the disposal of solid waste are the themes which are farthest from their target values in 1991.

Constructing aggregate environmental indicators in this manner involves one weighting scheme, based on contributions to particular problems such as acidification, out of many possible schemes. While criticism can be made of this weighting scheme, a greater concern is that these indicators tend not to be closely coupled to economic phenomena. Gale and Berg (1995) argue that environmental policies are more likely to be supported if they are backed up by sound economic judgement and the analysis of distributional impacts. Furthermore, they argue that a core requirement of linking environment and development is the government's annual budget. Of course, this is intimately tied up with the national accounts and the projections of finance ministries. Such arguments suggest that benefits should be associated with linking environmental indicators to the existing national accounts.

Economic data, with which to facilitate this link, are currently compiled by national statistical offices. It is not surprising that the compilation of 'official' green national accounts is largely the responsibility of these offices. What this indicator work attempts to do is to develop environmental ('green') accounts that are explicitly linked to the economic (national) accounts. However, many forms of these accounts have been proposed. This reflects the needs of countries to select and tailor various approaches

Environmental pressure index, The Netherlands,
relative to goals in the year 2000

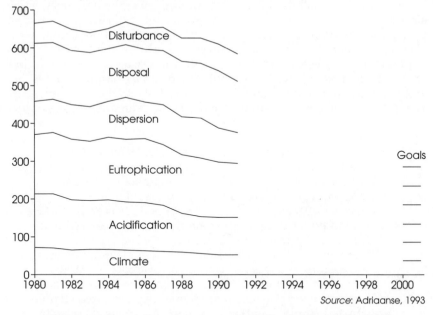

Source: Adriaanse, 1993

Figure 5.1 *An environmental pressure index for The Netherlands*

to their own environmental priorities. However, it does raise questions concerning international comparability. The first step towards standardizing the multitude of accounting approaches is provided by the UN Integrated System of Environmental and Economic Accounting (SEEA), (United Nations, 1993). While the guidelines for the balance-sheet accounts in the SNA call for the valuation of subsoil or standing natural resources, the change in value of these assets from year to year is recorded as a reconciliation item, and so again does not alter net product estimates. The SEEA is designed to be a satellite account to the System of National Accounts, in that it is an adjunct to, but not a modification of, the core accounts. The SEEA is highly complex, involving disaggregation of the standard accounts to highlight environmental relationships, linked physical and monetary accounting, imputations of environmental costs, and extensions of the production boundary of the SNA (Smith, 1994). In what follows we highlight the policy implications of four aspects of greened satellite accounts: resource and pollution flows; environmental expenditures; natural resource balances; and green accounting aggregates.

RESOURCE AND POLLUTANT FLOW ACCOUNTS

Resource and pollutant flow accounts have links to the widest variety of policy issues including those relating to environmental taxation. These linkages to economic policy domains should engender the simultaneous consideration of environmental policy options. It is worthwhile examining such policy applications in some detail.

Resource and pollutant flow accounts are generally conceived as physical extensions to the (monetary) input/output (I/O) accounts. For each production and final demand sector in the I/O tables these accounts associate a physical flow of natural resources, typically as inputs such as energy to production processes, and a physical flow of wastes and emissions in the form of carbon dioxide (CO_2), sulphur dioxide (SO_2), nitrogen oxides (NO_x) and biological oxygen demand (BOD). With links to the I/O tables, these accounts lend themselves naturally to policy modelling. Examples of policy uses include:

1. *Measuring the incidence of environmental regulations and taxes.*
    Models based on flow accounts can be used to estimate the impact (on output and profits, for example) of existing and prospective regulations and taxes with regard to the environment. Measuring the burden of policies is an important element of policy design. For example, it is often argued that environmental protection will decrease the rates of growth of GDP and increase unemployment. Policy modelling exercises can also be used to evaluate this claim. The evidence is that well-designed and well-implemented environmental policies can lead to beneficial effects on actual economies (eg, increased GDP growth and employment) as discussed in various chapters of this book. Hence, green accounting can be used as an empirical tool to respond to a potentially key obstacle to increased environmental protection.

2. *Estimating emission tax rates.* Where market-based instruments are considered as a policy option, computable general equilibrium models using pollutant flow accounts can estimate the approximate level and incidence of a tax.

    Statistics Canada has found this line of enquiry in linking measures of the physical flows of energy by I/O sector and the measures of GHG output by I/O sector ('the greenhouse gas emissions accounts'). These have contributed to the construction of a computable general equilibrium model by the Department of Finance to examine the levels of carbon taxation required to achieve the target emission levels (with regard to Canada's commitments under the Climate Change Convention at Rio). This modelling approach allows a variety of related questions to be answered – for example, the distributional consequences of this hypothetical Canadian carbon tax.

    The work of the German Federal Statistical Office (UGR, to give the German acronym) accounting system has been given a number of possible applications identified by the Federal Environment Ministry. Waste issues, including regulations on recycling and the possibility of a waste tax, are important in Germany and will have an impact on competitiveness and income distribution - UGR could have a role to play in analysing these issues.

3   *International trade.* Both resource use and pollution emissions can be linked to the level and structure of international trade through I/O based models (see, for example Pedersen, 1993; Atkinson and Hamilton, 1996). This provides the link between trade policies and the pollution burden associated with a particular structure of trade; for instance, countries that export raw and semi-finished materials will typically incur a large burden of air emissions associated with energy use. The Dutch Central Bureau of Statistics has placed particular emphasis on the connection between domestic economic activity and the use of the environment in countries supplying imports for the domestic market. Specifically, the Dutch work has examined the degree to which pollution is embodied in the import of goods to The Netherlands. Similar estimates have emerged in Denmark for pollutants embodied in exports and imports. These approaches can be used for both current analysis and prospective modelling.

4. *Macro models.* Tying resource and pollutant flow accounts to the standard macro-economic models that governments use for projections would permit the reporting of environmental effects (in terms of resource throughput and pollution emissions) as a standard component of the output from such models. Consideration of the environmental effects could then become as routine as the consideration of the balance-of-payments effects when policy analysts produce projections. Clearly, this would be an important development, given the predominance of headline economic indicators in the reporting of the state of the national economy.

5. *Dispersion and impact models.* Whichever modelling approach described above is employed, the calculation of pollution emissions is the required input for 'downstream' models of dispersion and impact. As soon as impacts on health, living resources, produced assets and natural ecosystems have been estimated, valuation of these impacts becomes possible. This implies that the *net* benefits of policies with regard to trade and development, for instance, can be estimated – which may lead to adjustments of these policies in order to maximize benefits.

NATURAL RESOURCE ACCOUNTS

Along with Canada, several other countries have begun the process of measuring the extent of their natural resources. Accounting in physical terms is the prerequisite to monetary presentation of resource wealth. This process is akin to preparing a balance sheet, with an opening stock at the beginning of the accounting period (say in terms of barrels of oil or cubic metres of timber), with flows during the accounting period - extraction, discoveries (for non-renewables), natural growth (for living resources). Adding these changes to the opening stock, we derive the closing stock at the end of the accounting period.

While countries such as Sweden and Finland have been satisfied to measure these magnitudes in purely physical terms, statistical offices in Canada and Australia have also concerned themselves with the construction of natural resource accounts in monetary terms. This leads to problems in itself. The volatility of world resource prices appear to indicate wildly changing fortunes in the national balance sheets as closing stocks are revalued at the end of each accounting period. Hence, it is difficult to infer much from green accounting given these large year-to-year oscillations. In part, however, these are due to methodological problems that presumably will be resolved in time via some combination of theoretical rigour and practical experience. In the case of Canada, the motivation for this work is provided by the desire to have some consistent basis to evaluate different components of wealth; solving these problems, therefore, is of particular importance. This is especially so where one goal of a nation's indicators programme is the derivation of consistent measures of sustainable development (see below).

Valuing the flow of resource depletion is important for one particular aspect of policy, namely, the setting of resource royalties. Since commercial resources are frequently government-owned, with the right to exploitation being leased, governments attempt to capture revenues through royalty levies. Where data are reliable, the calculation of this rent can give the government information concerning the appropriate level of taxes and royalties, given policy objectives. Cruz and Repetto (1992) argue that, in the context of the Philippines, the levying of resource rent taxes is a way of raising revenues without inflicting 'pain' on the national economy. In practice, what the government actually does with these taxes is of considerable importance to the achievement of sustainable development, as we indicate below.

THE CREATION OF MONETARY ACCOUNTS

Resource and pollution flow accounts are conceived in physical terms. Natural resource accounts contain a mixture of physical and monetary data. Considerable attention has been devoted to the construction of green satellite accounts in monetary terms. The simplest of these efforts are environmental expenditure accounts. These generally consist of detailed data on capital and operating expenditures by economic sectors for the protection and enhancement of the environment. Examples include flue gas desulphurization (FGD) to control emissions of SO_2. The United States, Canada and the United Kingdom are compiling such information as part of their green accounting programmes. Table 5.3 illustrates data for the US. The prospective uses of these accounts are fairly straightforward and consist of measuring the total economic burden of environmental protection (ie, costs and benefits of regulation) and the distribution of sectoral and unit abatement costs.

Table 5.3 *Expenditure on pollution abatement and control in the United States ($ million, 1987)*

Category of Expenditure	Expenditure ($m, 1987)		Per Annum % Change from 1987 to 1992
	1987	1992	
Pollution abatement and control	77,649	87,594	2.4
Pollution abatement	74,349	84,328	2.5
Personal consumption	11,075	7,019	−9.1
Business	45,432	55,994	4.1
Government	17,842	21,315	3.6
Regulation and monitoring	1,519	1,619	1.3
Research and development	1,781	1,648	1.6

Source: Rutledge and Vogan, 1994

Green Measures of Income

If GDP is the key economic indicator, then the quest for a green GDP can be seen as the flagship of green accounting. Indeed, its measurement provided the impetus for the pioneering green accounting studies (see, for example, Repetto *et al*, 1989). Many would like to see GDP replaced with some alternative measure of income. However, this pressure has come mostly from outside official statistical circles. In fact, few countries have signed up to this goal. One of the reasons is that this green income aggregate is seen as having limited policy relevance.

Nevertheless, some suggest that the construction of a green GDP is in itself a policy for improving the environment – ie, the creation of a 'truer' measure of the quality of life that can either replace or be directly compared to GDP. This is assuming, of course, that the messages provided are unambiguous. For example, what inferences for sustainable development can we draw when green net domestic product (NDP) growth is lower than the growth rate of GDP but is still positive as Repetto *et al* (1989), Solórzano *et al* (1991) and Cruz and Repetto (1992) all found? While the concept of green NDP has provided an important focus behind which calls for greening national accounts have rallied, we have to look elsewhere for indicators that inform policy-makers of progress towards sustainable development.

Accounting for National Wealth

The Canadian Government was one of the first to embrace sustainability as an explicit goal in its environmental policy framework. Canada's 'Green Plan' emphasizes that this is an extremely complex concept to measure, but concludes that expanding wealth accounts to measure natural resources would be a useful step in this direction. The idea behind this conclusion is that if a country is liquidating its wealth, then it is not sustainable – ie, it is eroding its ability to generate future well-being. Currently, wealth accounts consist of the stock of produced assets in monetary terms, so that extending the wealth accounts was also viewed as filling a major gap in the statistical system facilitating improved analysis of economic performance and sector productivity.

Wealth accounting is very much in its infancy, although the concept has been adopted recently by the World Bank in its own green accounting programme. The World Bank has released data on wealth for 192 countries. Some of these data are presented in Table 5.4 and include not only the value of a nation's produced assets (buildings, machines) but also tentative estimates of the value of natural resources (including agricultural land) and human capital (ie, the stock of knowledge). Australia is the wealthiest country in the world (with some $835,000 per person). Ethiopia is the poorest. The UK is 171st with $324,000.

Table 5.4 *Wealth accounting*

Global Wealth Rank	Country	Sources of Wealth (% total)			Estimated Wealth per Capita ($)
		Human Resources	Produced Assets	Natural Assets	
1	Ethiopia	40	21	39	1,400
20	India	64	25	11	4,300
31	China	77	15	8	6,600
161	Saudi Arabia	28	18	55	184,000
171	United Kingdom	83	14	3	324,000
181	USA	59	16	25	421,000
192	Australia	21	7	71	835,000

Source: World Bank, 1995

While these rankings make for good press coverage (as was indeed the case when they were issued in autumn 1995), the data remain very limited and subject to significant margins of error. None the less, refinements of the data will undoubtedly provide useful inputs for portfolio analysis and management. Measuring natural resources in the national balance-sheet implies that governments can work with a measure of total wealth in examining policies for sustainable development. The balance of natural, human versus produced assets in this measure of total wealth then becomes an important indicator as governments consider development options.

A complementary indicator that reflects the same policy concerns is that of genuine savings. The basic difference between the value of wealth in one period and the next is the amount that society has saved (the creation of wealth) and the value of the assets that it has liquidated (the destruction of wealth). This is what genuine savings are intended to measure (see Pearce and Atkinson, 1993; Hamilton, 1994; World Bank, 1995).

An illustration for the United Kingdom is provided in Figure 5.2 and involves four steps and four measures of saving. First, we need to know the level of gross savings in an economy, something which is easily estimated

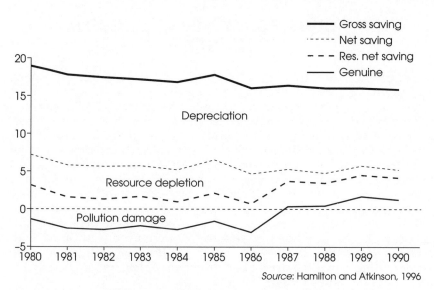

Figure 5.2 *United Kingdom savings rates*

from the existing national accounts. Secondly, deduct from gross savings the value of depreciation of produced assets (conventional net saving). Thirdly, deduct the value of the depletion of oil and natural gas extracted (resource net saving). Lastly, make a deduction for the value of air pollution (genuine saving). It would also be desirable to net out water pollution costs. However, at the national level such estimates have proved extremely difficult to derive. For sustainability, genuine savings must not be persistently negative over time. Figure 5.2 suggests that the UK performed very poorly on this basic sustainability rule during the Thatcher years, such that genuine savings were negative until the end of the 1980s.

Of course, many additional factors complicate any conclusion that 'the United Kingdom is behaving unsustainably'. Among these is technological progress. So it would be wrong to assert that the measure of genuine savings is accurate to the last fraction of a per cent, but where genuine savings measures are less than 1–2 per cent of GDP – or, even worse, when they are negative – this should be cause for concern for governments that are committed to achieving sustainable development and should suggest the need for appropriate policy responses. These include the 'correct' levying of resource royalties and environmental taxes, as has been discussed in previous sections. The government's overall fiscal stance is also of direct relevance via the broader issues of macro- and micro-economic policy that play important roles in establishing gross savings levels. However, indiscriminate cutting of government expenditures – for instance, on primary health-care and education – is likely to be harmful to the formation of human capital and social well-being. It is important to recognize that investment in human capital is one of the surest ways to increase future well-being (see, for instance, World Bank, 1995, Chapter 8).

THE ACTUAL POLICY IMPACT OF GREEN ACCOUNTING

In the preceding discussion, we have highlighted the numerous policy implications of green national accounting. Early studies, such as those presented by the World Resources Institute (Repetto *et al*, 1989; Solórzano *et al*, 1991) proceeded without clear reference to policy usefulness. Greening national income was seen to be an end in itself. Similarly, in terms of the wider environmental indicator debate, the early focus was on the development of descriptive indicators of environmental change. All this has clearly evolved. Physical performance indicators have adapted these descriptive data, tying them to clear reference points based on policy targets. These indicators can raise the profile of environmental issues and help to monitor progress on environmental policy. More detailed policy questions can be addressed by linking environmental indicators with economic data in the core national accounts. This is an additional task to that of boiling down the mass of environmental data into a form that is more useful for policy-makers.

Hence, the satellite accounting techniques, especially construction of pollution emissions accounts – but including resource flow and environmental protection expenditure accounts – appear to have the most direct policy relevance. Regarding the issue of the need for environmental taxation, this is clearly a question that lies outside the accounts. However, given a policy commitment on behalf of a government regarding the reduction of emissions, green satellite accounts, by augmenting existing macro, general equilibrium and input/output models, can be used to estimate the appropriate level of the environmental tax and its possible impacts. This explicit linkage between account development and policy modelling is most striking in Norway. There, the active role of the Central Bureau of Statistics (CBS) in economic analysis, research and modelling, makes the CBS a natural bridge between the Ministry of Finance and the Ministry of Environment in analysing environment-economy linkages. This non-adversarial relationship between data providers and policy analysts is a definite strength. The integration of environment into standard models offers the intriguing possibility of reporting environmental effects as a component of the output from such models. Consideration of environmental effects could then become a routine aspect of economic forecasting.

The direct policy uses of adjusted national accounts aggregates appear to be limited. It would be a mistake, however, to underestimate the political usefulness of the measures of sustainability that can be derived from these new aggregates, such as genuine savings and measures of national wealth. These indicators of sustainability could have a powerful influence on national and international public opinion, thereby indirectly influencing policy. The savings approach may also appeal to the Ministries of Environment and Finance as it uses a concept of sustainability which is familiar to both.

It must be remembered that green accounting is still in its relative infancy. Dramatic progress has been made in compiling reliable data and in condensing these data into policy relevant indicators in well-defined frameworks such as the national accounts. However, it is too early to draw lessons from the actual use of these accounts by governments as there is still a large element of research in much of this work, with inherently uncertain pay-offs. National and international organizations are nowadays exploring this new area, with the United Nations taking the first steps towards standardizing definitions and methods. Similarly, although the World Bank has adopted the genuine savings and national wealth approaches, there is no official line on how these indicators might be used to shape the future of bank-lending policies to developing countries. We might speculate that these approaches will provide fresh justification for public programmes to increase education and health-care provision, thereby increasing national wealth by augmenting human capital. For example, the whole area of the economic cost of environment-linked health damage may provide a powerful policy-relevant focus for green accounting efforts. The past five years have to be seen as a process of refining methodology and increasing the policy usefulness of the numbers that are emerging. Although this process is still incomplete, the challenge of the next five or so years will be using green accounts in the actual construction and monitoring of environmental policies.

REFERENCES

Adriaanse, A (1993) *Essential Environmental Information: The Netherlands*, Ministry of Housing, Physical Planning and Environment, The Hague

Atkinson, G and Hamilton, K (1996) *Measuring Global Resource Consumption: Direct and Indirect Asset Flows in International Trade*, Centre for Social and Economic Research on the Global Environment (CSERGE), University College London and University of East Anglia, London and Norwich

Cruz, W and Repetto, R (1992) *The Environmental Effects of Stabilization and Adjustment Programs: The Philippines Case*, World Resources Institute, Washington, DC

Department of the Environment (1992) *The UK Environment*, HMSO, London

Gale, R and Berg, S (eds) (1995) *Green Budget Reform*, Earthscan, London

Hamilton, K (1994) 'Green adjustments to GDP', *Resources Policy*, 20, pp 155–68

Hamilton, K and Atkinson, G (1996) 'Air Pollution and Green Accounts', *Energy Policy*, 24 (7), pp 675–684

Hammond, A, Adriaanse, A, Rodenburg, E, Bryant, D and Woodward, R (1995) *Environmental Indicators*, World Resources Institute, Washington, DC

Hueting R, Bosch, P R and de Boer, B (1992) 'Methodology for the Calculation of Sustainable National Income', Statistical Essays M44, Central Bureau of Statistics, Voorburg, The Netherlands

Munasinghe, M, Hamilton, K, Atkinson, G, Dubourg, W R and Pearce, D W (1996) 'Measuring Sustainable Development: Macroeconomy and Environment', unpublished manuscript, CSERGE, Department of Economics, University College London, London

Organization for Economic Cooperation and Development (1994) *Environmental Indicators*, OECD, Paris

Pearce, D W and Atkinson, G (1993) 'Capital theory and the measurement of sustainable development: an indicator of weak sustainability', *Ecological Economics*, 8, pp 103–8

Pedersen, O G (1993) 'Input-Output Analysis and Emissions of CO_2, SO_2 and NO_x – the linkage of physical and monetary data', paper presented to the Tenth International Conference on Input-Output Techniques, Seville, Spain

Repetto, R, Magrath, W, Wells, M, Beer, C and Rossini, F (1989) *Wasting Assets: Natural Resources in the National Accounts*, World Resources Institute, Washington, DC

Rutledge, G L and Vogan, C R (1994) 'Pollution abatement and control expenditures, 1972–1992', *Survey of Current Business*, May, pp 36–49

Smith, P (1994) 'The Canadian National Accounts Environmental Component', A Status Report, London Group Meeting on National Accounts and the Environment, London: CSERGE, Department of Economics, University College London, London

Solórzano, R, de Camino, R, Woodward, R, Tosi, J, Watson, V, Vásquez, A, Villalobos, C, Jiménez, J, Repetto, R and Cruz, W (1991) *Accounts Overdue: Natural Resource Depreciation in Costa Rica*, World Resources Institute, Washington, DC

United Nations (1993) *Integrated Environmental and Economic Accounting*, Series F, No 61, United Nations, New York

World Bank (1995) *Monitoring Environmental Progress*, Environment Department, The World Bank, Washington, DC

World Resources Institute (1994) *World Resources 1994–5*, World Resources Institute, Washington, DC

Part II

THE DOUBLE DIVIDEND DEBATE

EDITORIAL INTRODUCTION TO THE DOUBLE DIVIDEND DEBATE

The five chapters that follow grapple with a much discussed area of economic theory – namely, whether environmental taxes create a double benefit of removing inefficient pre-existing tax distortions (by creating new and more environmentally targeted price signals), and also by improving environmental quality. The ideal combination should generate the kinds of conditions suitable for sustainable development.

What emerges from this analysis is that the double dividend by no means can be guaranteed. To begin with, the existing tax regime creates a host of distortions for any sustainability pathway, as well as distortions even for more conventional measures of social and economic welfare. But these distortions are so numerous, so interconnected and so embedded in political expectations that any serious attempt to remove them by another series of tax measures could create chaotically unpredictable outcomes, both for the economy and for society generally. It is rarely known just what would be the marginal deficiencies of successive removals of even one area of distortion, let alone an interconnected set of distortions. In any case, the models of the economy rely on measures of economic and social responsiveness that may not be mirrored in actual behaviour. Thus, in the Treasury evidence to the House of Lords' Select Committee on Sustainable Development (1995, p 33) officials accepted that they 'were not 100 per cent confident' about the elasticities they assumed for the response in car driving behaviour which arose out of the petrol excise-tax escalator. This in turn means that any estimates of the 'actual' environmental improvement will also be problematic, even if the science is better understood regarding the health gains from lower exhaust emissions. Then there are the uncertainties of how the car manufacturers would behave in the face of rising petrol prices, but where there is an absence of firm regulatory measures geared to alternative fuels or to lighter and more fuel-efficient cars, and so on. One can readily see that both the theory and the models cannot help except to provide insight into what ought to be known better, what ought to be monitored closely if pilot schemes are tried out, and what ought to be re-examined in terms of consumer behaviour or voting intentions when courageous governments impose progressive ecotaxes and stand back when the fuse is lit.

The point of departure should be Chapter 10 in which Daniel McCoy reviews all the evidence. He points out that the criteria for defining success need to be debated and agreed beforehand. He also comments that economists tend to divide into two camps over those criteria. One group looks to environmental dividends in the shape of real gains to environmental well-being. For them, the tax rate may well be higher than the standard rate which was designed to remove an externality, depending on the degree of responsiveness to the tax. Here is where the uncertainty over petrol price and, say, water use, elasticities, means that a precautionary policy might favour a tougher tax, but also a more aggravated consumer and voter response.

The other view is that of the public expenditure auditor who searches for a more fiscally neutral formula – namely, one that does not add to the tax burden on the economy. Here is where the complications of the inter-connectedness of tax regimes make life difficult for the implementor. In practice, fiscal neutrality is all but impossible to achieve, at least if the costs of monitoring and post-tax auditing are not to become excessive. This suggests, from the theoretical viewpoint anyway, that ecotaxes will only be remotely optimal if the target arena is clearly environmentally damaging, and the distorting taxes that can be removed obviously favour the minority at the expense of the majority. Reducing the favourable tax advantages on company cars would be one such area.

Peter Bohm sets out to review the recent literature by economists who claim the double dividend argument is a false one. In his analysis, presented in Chapter 7, he does not attempt to look at all the relevant liter-ature, only the material which is critical of the double dividend gains. Bohm concludes from his assessment that the double dividend is likely when removable distortions are obvious and readily targetable, and where tax packages are on offer to ensure consistency in the new arrangements after environmental taxes are put in place. But where such measures are not consciously applied, then Bohm believes that an environmental tax could increase pre-existing tax distortions, leading to greater inefficiencies. He stresses that this would be a narrow interpretation of the evidence, because inventive adjustments to tax arrangements should be capable of being implemented.

These are broadly the same conclusions offered by Paul Ekins in a more detailed analysis of the issues in Chapter 8. He supports the role of ecotaxes as 'first' dividends, irrespective of the advantages of reinvesting the revenues. This is because there should be gains to environmental quality, and equally there should be the spending of revenues to offset immediate social consequences, notably for the poor. But when revenues are specifi-cally recycled to create new job opportunities, or to improve resource use efficiencies elsewhere, he believes that – potentially at least – multiple divid-ends are on offer. The employment dividend, in his view, is suffi-ciently great for policy-makers not to ignore.

This view is endorsed by the UK Liberal Democratic Party (1993) which has specifically supported the thesis of taxing pollution, not income. The Liberal Democrats are unlikely to form a government in the UK, but it is conceivable that their policies may be very influential on a future Labour government, should it be elected with Liberal Democrat support.

In this context, the kinds of calculations made by Terry Barker in Chapter 9 would become of great interest to a Labour-Liberal Democrat axis which was interested in job creation and environmental improvement through community action programmes. Barker's models are inevitably dependent on a host of arguable assumptions, but his central conclusions – namely that up to one million jobs could be created by a double dividend arising out of a higher petrol exercise tax escalator and a carbon-energy tax – are becoming attractive to the Liberal Democrats and, to a much more cautious extent, to the Labour Party. In addition, his analysis that more jobs and investment might find their way to the north of England and Scotland would find much favour in such a coalition. Add to that the justification that a 20 per cent additional reduction in CO_2 emissions would result, meeting the Toronto target by 2005, and there is scope for a great deal of party political interest in this approach.

As will be the case generally in this book, one should be cautious of excessive optimism. In his only speach on sustainable development to date, the Labour Party leader, Tony Blair (1996, p 7), sounded almost like his Tory counterpart, John Gummer (although far less eloquent), when he said that new environmental regulations operate in a cost-effective way and that environmental measures 'have been criticized in the past for raising the cost of goods for those least able to afford them'. So, for an incoming Labour administration, there would be no new taxes, only better efficiency measures.

We shall have to await the settling of the political dust. Intriguingly, a Labour-Liberal Democratic political axis might be more disposed to a European Commission which is still feverishly working away on a procrastinated carbon-energy tax, with the dividends targeted to job creation and the improvement of livability in cities. This combination of Europolicy and environmental enhancement via social measures of training, employment and health programmes suggests that the fine detail of economic analysis may give way in the next decade to a more populist political analysis which favours a more aggressive approach to ecotaxation.

In Chapter 6, David Gee looks more closely at the European Commission's proposals for ecological tax reform. He touches on the likelihood that public opinion could favour the introduction of a slow switch to more socially and environmentally directed spend from specific new taxes on external nuisances that are not paid for by producers and consumers alike. He cites the recent set of polls from the 1995 Eurobarometer survey (European Commission, 1995) as encouraging in this regard. In this survey green taxes were characterized as making goods that are favourable to the environment less expensive, and goods that are harmful to the environment more expensive. To this proposition, 73 per cent agreed or tended to agree and 87 per cent felt that such taxes should be introduced (31 per cent said that green taxes should be introduced quickly, 56 per cent said they should be introduced more slowly). Over 4 in 10 people were willing to accept such taxes even if the economy might be slowed, and 13 per cent would tolerate such taxes even if growth was slowed significantly. This book suggests that such a distinction may actually pose a false dichotomy, and that jobs should be created and retained by the targeted redeployment of ecotax revenue.

The American economist Robert Repetto (1995) expands these arguments. He picks on a lively debate in contemporary US politics – namely, how far should environmental regulation go as a target-driven bureaucratic activity, compared with a market-driven, voluntaristic agent? The dominant mood in the US, across the political spectrum, is that market incentives aimed at removing materials and energy-use inefficiencies would be far better in terms of cost effectiveness and business adaptability terms than old-style regulation. So the ecotax argument is beginning to resonate in a deeper political debate in the US, a debate that is beginning to bridge social justice and economic efficiency.

This point is developed by Terry Barker in Chapter 9 and reviewed more extensively by Mors (1995, pp 127–28). Mors is an economic analyst in DGII of the European Commission – namely, the bureau concerned with tax and revenue matters. He concludes that a shift towards cutting labour social security payments arising from a carbon/energy tax would result in a 0.5 per cent increase in employment for each 1 per cent of GDP equivalent which is contained in reductions for such payments. However, should the same effort be directed at the lowest paid, then the job increase for that group would be 12 per cent, with an overall job increase of 2 per cent, or 2.7 million otherwise underemployed or unemployed people. Such simulations depend on the social willingness to see the purpose of such taxation, a point that Ekins explicitly examines in his Chapter 8.

All this suggests that the double dividend cannot be taken for granted, and that any introduction of ecological tax reform will require painstaking presentation and opinion support and a great deal of careful monitoring of who exactly is gaining and losing in the process.

REFERENCES

Blair, T (1996) *Sustainable Development: the View of the Labour Party,* The Labour Party, London

European Commission (1995) *Europe and the Environment in 1995,* DGXI, European Commission, Brussels

House of Lords (1995) *Select Committee on Sustainable Development Report,* HMSO, London

Liberal Democratic Party (1993) *Taxing Pollution, Not Jobs,* The Liberal Democratic Party, London

Mors, M (1995) 'Environmental taxation: employment, revenues and resource taxes: genuine links or spurious coalition?', *International Journal of Environment and Pollution,* Vol 5, Nos 2–3, pp 118–34

Repetto, R (1995) *Jobs, Competitiveness and Environmental Regulation: What are the Real Issues?,* World Resources Institute, Washington, DC

C h a p t e r   6

ECONOMIC TAX REFORM IN EUROPE: OPPORTUNITIES AND OBSTACLES

David Gee

INTRODUCTION

One of the most radical observations that Jacques Delors, ex-President of the European Commission, made was: 'if the double challenge of unemployment and pollution is to be addressed, a swap can be envisaged between reducing labour costs through increased pollution charges'. That idea came right at the end of the French Socialist's last and otherwise conventional European Union (EU) white paper on 'Growth, Competitiveness and Employment' in 1993, but it was the key part of a 'new model of economic development' that Delors thought was needed. Current models, he said, tended to 'over consume' nature and 'under consume' people, causing both unemployment and eco crisis. Not surprisingly, the radical part of his paper was ignored by the EU Council of Ministers, but the UK Treasury was listening. In early 1995 it announced a landfill tax with the slogan 'Taxing Waste not Jobs', and declared that by raising revenue from waste disposal so as to make cuts in employers' National Insurance Contributions, more jobs would be retained or created, while wastes were cut down. At least, that is the intention. The practical difficulties are addressed in Chapter 15.

Environmentalists have long advocated a switch of taxes from economic 'goods', such as employment, enterprise and savings, on to environmental 'bads', such as pollution and the inefficient use of energy and resources, but the possibility of achieving multiple gains from such an 'Economic Tax Reform' (ETR) (WBMG, 1994) is of more recent origin.

This chapter summarizes the reasons why ETR is attractive to diverse groups in society and analyses the obstacles that need to be overcome for ETR to succeed.

THREE VIEWS ON TAXATION

Jacques Delors's view on taxes clearly goes beyond a few individual green taxes such as energy or landfill taxes. He took a comprehensive look at the way that many separate tax decisions, over many decades, have resulted in an overall tax system that appears to be designed to squeeze people out of the economy and to suck resources in. But designed it was not, as illustrated in Figure 6.1.

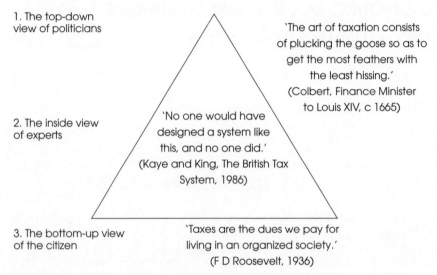

1. The top-down view of politicians

'The art of taxation consists of plucking the goose so as to get the most feathers with the least hissing.' (Colbert, Finance Minister to Louis XIV, c 1665)

2. The inside view of experts

'No one would have designed a system like this, and no one did.' (Kaye and King, The British Tax System, 1986)

3. The bottom-up view of the citizen

'Taxes are the dues we pay for living in an organized society.' (F D Roosevelt, 1936)

Figure 6.1 *Three views on taxation*

Most tax systems have evolved from the top-down view of politicians which is driven by 'What can we get away with?' This was best articulated by Colbert, Finance Minister to Louis XIV: 'The art of taxation consists of plucking the goose so as to get the most feathers with the least hissing'. 'Plucking feathers' artfully may be the short-term secret of success for chancellors, but it means that the overall tax system can end up pointing the market in the wrong direction, encouraging the overuse of nature and the underuse of people. And the 'top down' approach inhibits the development of consensus in society over the purpose and nature of the taxes which are, after all, merely 'the dues we pay for living in an organized society', as Roosevelt noted.

Although most people dislike paying taxes, they also prefer to live in an organized and civilized society rather than in a disorganized and uncivilized one. Therefore they need to agree on at least the key features of the tax systems they will support – and at a somewhat deeper level than that of media headlines. The legitimacy of tax systems in many OECD countries is currently being challenged, as seen in popular 'tax revolts', and by right-wing politicians wishing to see the 'melt-down' of the state. There is, there-fore, a need to restate the case for sensible and fair taxation. As we shall see below, ETR has a role to play in reasserting the citizen's view of taxation.

In a survey of public opinion on environmental matters, the European Commission instructed its consultants to include for the first time ques-tions on attitudes to ecotaxation. The survey itself was part of the three yearly Eurobarometer (European Commission, 1995) which taps a range of responses over a long time-frame. Nearly three-quarters of the sample surveyed from all EU countries favoured the introduction of 'green' taxes as a means of slowing down the adverse effects of humans on the natural environment. This view is most strongly held among those who express a concern for environmental degradation generally, among younger people and by women. A little over half wished for such rates to be phased in grad-ually in order to allow consumption patterns to adjust, although a third favoured rapid implementation. Citizens in Germany and Austria in partic-ular supported this view.

If green taxes were to slow down the economy, respondents became more circumspect, only 13 per cent supporting such taxes if the economy was significantly affected, with 16 per cent not sure. However, 44 per cent were prepared to support such taxes if the economy was only slightly affected. On the key issue for ETR, namely the reformulation of taxes away from income and savings towards environmental damage, 73 per cent supported this approach totally or very favourably. Their views were not affected either by age or by income, a matter of political noteworthiness. The implication of all this is that ecotaxes could be packaged for public support in Europe, given some careful preparation and a number of useful trial schemes.

ECONOMIC TAX REFORM

In order to clarify and ease the discussion on ETR, the following working definition has been produced as part of a European-wide programme of awareness raising on ETR that has been supported by DGXI of the European Commission (WBMG, 1995).

> Economic tax reform involves shifting a large proportion of taxation off the value-adding activities of people (employment, enterprise and saving) and onto the value-subtracting use of energy and resources and associated creation of wastes and pollution. The shift would involve *gradual* changes to tax and other incentives over a period of 2–20 years, following *extensive consultation* with industry, interest groups and the public. An ETR package would include *complementary measures* such as the removal of subsidies on unsustainable activities; *regulations* on energy efficiency; *investment incentives* to encourage eco-efficiency; *adjustment measures* for energy intensive sectors; and information campaigns. It would be based on *revenue recycling* and *budget neutrality*, resulting in the wiser use of nature and the wider use of people (emphasis added).

Key features of this definition are its comprehensive nature; the complementary measures, such as subsidy removal, investment incentives and regulation; the need for gradual change over long time periods; extensive consultation; and revenue recycling. An 'illustrative ETR package' is presented in Box 6.1. No country has yet advocated reform along quite such comprehensive lines, although there are an increasing number of cases where 'partial ETR' is being proposed or even implemented. Meanwhile, support for the central idea of shifting taxes from 'goods' to 'bads' is increasing, as illustrated in Box 6.2.

BOX 6.1 AN ILLUSTRATIVE *ECONOMIC* TAX REFORM PACKAGE

Fiscal Incentives:
1. The removal of subsidies and taxes that encourage unsustainable patterns of production/consumption, especially in the energy, transport and agricultural sectors.
2. A carbon/energy tax designed to achieve an average 5 per cent of annual increase in energy prices, including motor and aircraft fuels, over 10–20 years, with longer lead in times for energy-intensive sectors.
3. Reductions in taxes on labour, income, profits and capital.
4. Tax incentives for environmental investments, particularly in the energy-intensive and agricultural sectors.
5. Investment in rail and waterway freight transport.
6. Road pricing in certain cities and, later, motorway tolls.
7. Reductions in VAT for 'greener' products such as insulation and recycled goods.
8. Taxes on pesticides, nitrates and ozone depleters.
9. A land rent tax.
10. Provision for local authorities to levy taxes on domestic waste and other provisions for local taxes.
11. Landfill and incinerator taxes.
12. Taxes on primary/virgin materials, including aggregates, backed by regulations on recycling.
13. Noise taxes on planes, motorbikes and lorries.
14. Lower car taxes for rural areas.
15. A home-insulation conservation and efficiency programme targeted on the energy inefficient/poor households.
16. Temporary increases on cold weather payments and other Social Security benefits for those unable to adjust quickly to higher energy prices.
17. Higher central government grants for rural areas.
18. Investment in public transport, especially in rural areas and targeted cities.
19. Tradable permits for CO_2, water and SO_2.
20. Regulations on the energy efficiency of vehicles, domestic appliances, heating systems and buildings designed to treble their efficiency over 10–20 years.

BOX 6.2 GROWING SUPPORT FOR ETR

- The European Commission statement on 'Economic Growth and the Environment' declared:

  It seems that a review of existing tax and social security schemes is needed for broader economic and employment reasons (eg, in view of the contribution these systems might make to existing inflexibilities on goods and labour markets). The coincidence between this situation and the need to introduce corrective taxes for environmental reasons should be exploited with a view to realising possible synergies. (October 1994)

- The Business Council for Sustainable Development has recommended that governments should shift taxes away from 'value-adding activities such as labour and capital' and on to 'value depleting activities such as overuse of environmental resources'. (December 1994)
- The British Government's Advisory Panel on Sustainable Development has recently said that it 'would support a gradual move away from taxes on labour, income, profits and capital towards taxes on pollution and the use of resources'. (January 1995)
- The Ministerial Round Table Conference on Sustainable Production and Consumption in Oslo recommended several actions for achieving more sustainable economies, including: 'Removing subsidies that generate unsustainable patterns of consumption and production (eg, transport, energy and agriculture); and shifting the tax burden from labour to the use of resources and damage to the environment, to promote greater efficiency, reduce pollution, strengthen the market for cleaner technologies and create new jobs'. (6–10 February, 1995)
- The Italian White Paper on proposals for comprehensive fiscal reform, include shifting a proportion of taxes 'from people to things'. (December 1994)

Such support is not confined to OECD countries:

- The President of Costa Rica, at the Central American Environmental Summit in October 1994, said: 'we have the responsibility to review fiscal policies so that gradually today's taxes on employment, income and savings can be shifted to taxes that curb consumerism and the depletion of natural resources without ultimately diminishing total fiscal revenues'.
- Agenda 21 for Slovenia by non-governmental organizations stated:

  Traditional taxation systems that tax labour while leaving the use of natural resources untaxed have forced developed countries (Slovenia included) into a contradictory situation...generating a permanently growing level of unemployment...[with] natural resources remaining unreasonably under-priced, yielding wasteful use and worsening levels of environmental pollution. The solution to both problems can be found through a fiscally neutral shift of taxes from labour to natural resources and pollution.

Why Is ETR Attractive?

There are several reasons why ETR is beginning to attract the attention of politicians and the public. First, tax reform is in the air, as the accretions of decades of 'feather plucking' have produced complex, opaque and often overly centralized tax systems that appear to be increasingly inappropriate for the 'lean' organizational and political ideologies of the 1990s. Furthermore, the combination of ballooning budget deficits, tax revolts, and declining conventional tax bases is further concentrating the minds of politicians and policy-makers on tax reform.

Figure 6. 2 summarizes these motives for tax reform and illustrates how the three main 'drivers' of ETR – the need for environmental improvement, employment and 'eco-efficiency' – can be used to contribute to a more acceptable tax system.

Figure 6.2 *The role of ETR in tax reform*

For example, the most comprehensive tax-reform package that has been proposed in Europe recently, by the Italian Government in 1994, tried to address three main issues: a shift from national to local taxation; a shift from 'people to things', with energy and transport taxes replacing some income tax; and a shift from complexity to simplicity, as 100 separate taxes become replaced by eight (Italian Finance Ministry). However, little progress has been achieved with these proposals as they require a measure of political stability and consensus that is currently not a feature of Italian political society.

Secondly, the distortionary effects of current taxes are receiving greater attention. For example, US studies indicate that taxes on labour and capital 'cost' the economy some 40–90 cents for every dollar of tax collected owing to the disincentive effects of marginal tax rates (Repetto *et al*, 1992). There is controversy among economists on this issue, particularly over income tax (Brown and Sandford, 1991). There is much less disagreement about the distortions caused by subsidizing economic activities that cause environmental losses, such as subsidies on coal or agriculture, or taxes which encourage unsustainable behaviour, such as company car use. The European Commission is presently studying the environmental distortions of current taxes in member countries (Moret, Ernst and Young, 1996).

Thirdly, the failure of market prices to capture the full costs of production, use and disposal was noted over 70 years ago by the economist Pigou (1920). The market prices for energy, transport, food, water and chemicals do not include the real costs of pollution, ill health, and natural resource damage and depletion that their extraction, production and use entails. (There are also 'positive externalities', where economic activity contributes more than their purchased products – for instance, the CO_2 absorption, air-cleansing and water-retention benefits of sustainable forestry.)

However, little has been done in practice (Skou Andersen, 1994) to implement Pigou's recommendation for 'extraordinary constraints', in the form of taxes, to help internalize the environmental 'externalities of pollution' that he observed. One reason for the poor take-up of pollution taxes is the problem of valuing environmental assets, such as clean air and water, which worries those economists who want to set the 'correct' tax. Pigou was less bothered by this than many modern economists, although he did cite an inquiry in Manchester that proved an annual loss of £290,000 from 'the extra laundry costs, artificial light and damage to buildings as a result of heavy air pollution'.

More recent evaluations of 'externalities' show that perhaps 10 per cent of GNP (Weizsacker, 1994) is wasted on such costs, with transport externalities alone costing 2–3 per cent of GNP (Royal Commission on Environmental Pollution (RCEP), 1994), owing to air pollution, noise, accidents, etc. Pigou (1947) noted the obvious welfare loss from pollution; the failure of the market to deal with these costs as they were 'external' to the accounts of the businesses which caused them; and concluded that, where such 'maladjustments' in resource use had come about, then:

> it is always possible...to correct them by imposing appropriate rates of tax
> on resources employed in ways that tend to be pushed too far and
> employing the proceeds to provide bounties, at appropriate rates, on uses
> of the opposite class.

The under-consumption of people and the over-consumption of natural resources noted by Jacques Delors is a classic case of such 'maladjustments', and the role of taxes in encouraging this waste of both people and nature provides the fourth reason for the increasing popularity of ETR.

Since 1960, the burden of taxation on employment (mainly income tax and Social Security Contributions) has increased from 28 per cent of tax revenues, on average in Europe, to 50 per cent. Meanwhile, taxes on the environment (the use of energy, resources and the creation of pollution and wastes) have been small and stable at around 7–9 per cent of revenues, as

Per cent

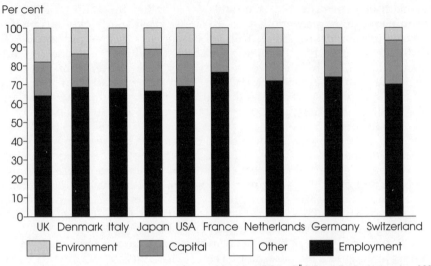

Source: Memo on ETR by FÖS, Bonn/Berlin, November 1994

Figure 6.3 *Sources of tax revenues: an international comparison, 1990*

illustrated in Figure 6.3. European economies have duly responded to these price signals and have squeezed out people, contributing to unemployment, and sucked in energy and resources, contributing to environmental decline.

The combined costs of such wastage could be as much as 15–20 per cent of GNP in EU countries, when unemployment costs are added to environmental costs – a powerful incentive to consider the tax shifts that Pigou and Delors have recommended. The 'sordidness of mean streets and the joylessness of withered lives', which Pigou saw as the inspiration of economic science, and which is a moving metaphor for pollution and unemployment, may not motivate everybody, but wasting up to a fifth of GNP is a gross inefficiency that cannot be ignored.

Fifthly, the desire for new sources of revenue that are likely to be more popular than direct taxes, are more difficult to evade and which have low administrative costs is causing finance ministers to look favourably on environmental taxes.

Finally, ETR is seen as providing the catalyst for moving OECD economies on to new growth trajectories based on the innovation, new products and processes that will come from concentrating more on resource productivity than on labour productivity (Porter and van der Linde, 1995). Labour productivity has increased some 20-fold since the Industrial Revolution began (Weizsacker, 1994), whereas resource productivity overall has grown much more slowly.

Today, globalization means that 'increasingly, the nations and companies that are the most competitive are not those with access to the lowest cost inputs but those that employ the most advanced technology and methods in using their inputs' (Porter and van der Linde, 1995). Rapid innovation is what global competition demands, and such innovation will come from a concentration on resource productivity, an objective that has been relatively neglected (Repetto,1990; Cararro, 1994). A challenge facing OECD economies is to meet the 10-fold improvement in resource productivity (or 'eco-efficiency') called for by 'The Factor Ten Club' promoted by economists and environmentalists. The Carnoules Declaration, 1994, as presented in Box 6.3 is a challenge that will stimulate enormous innovation. However, as we have seen, the prevailing tax and subsidy structures have focused the economies on labour efficiency and resource profligacy. ETR is therefore seen as one of the main ways of refocusing companies and economies on 'eco-efficiency' and employment.

BOX 6.3 FACTOR 10

In industrialised countries, the current resource productivity must be increased by an average of a FACTOR of 10 during the next 30 to 50 years. This is technically feasible if we mobilise our know-how to generate new products, services, as well as new methods of manufacturing.

Source: Carnoules Declaration of the Factor 10 Club, 1994

ETR is often presented as offering the possibility of a 'double dividend' of an improved environment and increased employment. In fact, there is an additional 'double dividend' from a more efficient tax system and from the spur to innovation and eco-efficiency that ETR could provide, particularly if the taxes are aimed at improving pollution prevention rather than pollution control.

WILL ETR WORK?

Since 1992 there have been over a dozen studies on the likely effects of shifting parts of the tax burden from 'people to things'. These usually have been confined to various forms of energy taxes, with revenues being recycled into reduced labour charges, payments to cushion the effect of energy price rises on poor households, and into tax incentives for energy-efficiency investments. These studies, which have addressed the 'double dividend' hypothesis, have been reviewed recently by de Wit, 1995, and Ekins, 1995. In addition, the three chapters that follow cover the important issue in more depth. The conclusions of de Wit are reproduced in Box 6.4.

MODELLING ETR

The comprehensive reform package implied by the 'working definition' of ETR described earlier would be extremely difficult to model, but the EU has published a large study which goes much further than the usual energy tax studies. The DRI (1994) study, based on analysis for the six biggest EU countries (France, Germany, Italy, The Netherlands, the UK and Spain),

■

BOX 6.4 A DOUBLE DIVIDEND FROM ETR? EMPLOYMENT EFFECTS OF ECOLOGICAL TAX REFORM: A REVIEW OF THE EVIDENCE

1. All evidence suggests that a tax shift has positive employment effects *in the short and medium term*, on the condition that 'dirty businesses' are prevented from moving abroad on a large scale.
2. In the *long term* it is less clear, although in any case negative employment effects seem to be unlikely. The extent to which the production factors are mobile in the long run is crucial. This is difficult to predict and subject to changing circumstances.
3. These conclusions hold true, even for implementation of ETR in a single country. However, implementation in a broader international context makes a tax shift more effective, because in such a case the opportunities for business to move abroad and/or capital flight become less.
4. Positive employment effects can be improved substantially by recycling the revenues in such a way that the labour costs of low-skilled, lower-paid jobs are particularly reduced. Such a policy would also have an effect on income distribution.
5. In the present models some factors (technological development, first-mover advantage, productivity gains by a cleaner environment, reduced market imperfections because of an energy tax) remain underdeveloped. Such factors could improve the working of ETR.
6. In the present models employment effects are exclusively compared with respect to a situation with no alternative environmental policy (and thus no alternative costs). With an evaluation with respect to a situation with an alternative form of environmental policy, it seems likely that a tax shift is the best alternative for employment, since the inclusion of environmental costs in market prices can be one of the most efficient forms of environmental policy.
7. A tax shift improves welfare *irrespective of the employment effects*, as long as this shift leads to a situation in which market prices better reflect environmental costs.

tried to model the effects of integrating environmental and economic policies (the 'INT' scenario'), and to compare these to both a 'business as usual', or 'REF', scenario, and to a 'policies in the pipeline' scenario ('PIP'), which included the proposed EU carbon/energy tax (DRI/McGraw Hill, 1994). The results for the INT scenario were much better than for REF or PIP, with both the environment (Table 6.1) and the economy (Table 6.2) gaining most from the integrated approach.

The INT scenario incorporated additional taxes on energy, congestion charges, and tradable permits for emissions by stationary sources and vehicles. It also included charges on water effluents; a doubling of water prices;

Table 6.1 *Modelling ETR: the DRI study: changes in environmental pressures between 1990 and 2010 – three scenarios.*

Theme	Reference 'BAU' or 'REF'	'Pipeline' Policies 'PIP'	Integrated Policies 'INT'
Climate change	●●●	●	=
Regional air quality			
* acid deposition	◊	◊◊◊◊	◊◊◊◊◊◊◊
* photochemical	●	◊◊	◊◊◊◊◊◊
Urban environment			
* air pollution	◊	◊◊◊	◊◊◊◊◊◊◊◊
* other	●●●●●●●	●●●●	●●
Toxic substances	◊◊	◊◊	◊◊◊
Nature and biodiversity[1]	●●	●	◊
Water quality	●●	◊◊◊	◊◊◊◊◊
Water resources	●●	●	●
Waste			
* hazardous	●●●●●●	=	◊◊◊◊◊
* non-hazardous	●●●	●	◊◊◊◊
Oil in coastal zone	●●	◊	◊◊◊

◊: improvement of 10 per cent (ie, decrease of 10 per cent in environmental pressure)

●: deterioration of 10 per cent (ie, increase of 10 per cent in environmental pressure)

=: no change

[1] The EU-6 average changes in the four adopted indicators would suggest a more optimistic future under all scenarios. However, on a regional basis there would be potential for significantly greater environmental damage, representing a loss to the EU as a whole, not just the region in question. We have, therefore, qualified the overall result for the EU-6 through consideration of regional variation in the impact of land-use changes.

Source: 'Potential Benefits of Integration of Environmental and Economic Policies', European Communities Environmental Policy Series, 1994

tradable permits for water rights in agriculture; demand-side management measures to overcome market barriers to the penetration of more efficient technologies; full reform of the Common Agricultural Policy; information campaigns to encourage changes in consumers' behaviour; and research and development programmes and investment support to encourage the rapid penetration of clean technologies.

The tax and charge levels were set at a level which is consistent with the damages imposed by environmental degradation on the economy, and the revenue obtained from such charges (some 130 billion ECU, or 1.7 per cent of GNP) was recycled in the form of reduced non-wage labour costs (the 'INT +' scenario); or to government expenditure on waste manage-

Table 6.2 *Modelling ETR: the DRI study: key macroeconomic results for the EU-6 difference in annual percentage growth between 1992 and 2010 PIP, INT and INT+ Versus REF*

	PIP	INT	INT+
Real GDP at factor costs	-0.03	+0.05	+0.06
Producer prices	+0.09	+0.20	+0.16
Wholesale prices	+0.05	+0.18	+0.14
Nominal wages	+0.07	+0.16	+0.14
Employment	0.00	+0.07	+0.15
(Salaried employment			
levels, in 000)	−63	+1,091	+2,187

Source: 'Potential Benefits of Integration of Environmental Economic Policies', European Communities Environmental Policy Series, 1994

ment and water purification (20 per cent of revenues) and reductions in personal income taxes (80 per cent), in the 'INT' scenario.

Although overall gains are larger in the 'INT' scenario (and overall employment gains greater in the 'INT +' scenario) there will be losers, at least in the short run, in particular sectors and regions. In agriculture, for example, where a comprehensive reform of the CAP is assumed (Box 6.5), although both taxpayers and consumers gain (through lower subsidies and food prices), some farmers and farm workers would lose. However, in comparison to the 'REF' and 'PIP' scenarios, major agricultural problems of pollution, biodiversity loss and water shortages would be improved most significantly under the 'INT' scenario.

BOX 6.5 INTEGRATING ENVIRONMENTAL AND ECONOMIC POLICY OBJECTIVES FOR AGRICULTURE

- To reduce the volume of agricultural nitrates leaching into watercourses and groundwater, concentrating efforts on those regions where problems are already most severe.
- To reduce the overall levels of pesticide residues deposited in the soil and in water.
- To bring long-term abstraction of water into line with supply, by improving the efficiency with which water resources are allocated and used.
- To promote biodiversity by avoiding further loss of habitat, and – where appropriate – by restoring and recreating habitats as part of a coherent ecological network.
- To move away from supporting farm incomes primarily through production subsidies, emphasising instead an alternative system of support which internalises environmental costs as far as possible.

For tourism, only the INT scenario contained the growth in environmental damage which was likely from the projected growth rates in this rapidly expanding sector, producing considerable savings (over 329 billion ECU) in solid-waste treatment and water consumption, as well as reduced land take. These results were achieved by adopting a definition of 'carrying capacity' at the EU level, and applying it at the local level. Although some price and tax tools were suggested – for example, tourism land-use taxes and tradable permits, user and entrance fees, price differentiation towards public transport and subsidies for out-of-season holidays – the main mechanism for integrating environmental and economic policies were visitor management, land-use planning, education, and a common approach to the sectors problems.

The DRI results are in line with other studies and indicate the direction and nature of the change that will be required to implement the 'new economic model' envisaged in Chapter 10 of the Delors White Paper on 'Growth, Competitiveness and Employment' (EC, 1993). But although the theoretical modelling of ETR looks favourable, what about the practice?

ETR IN PRACTICE

There are many examples of individual environmental taxes, and these have been extensively reviewed (OECD, 1989–1994; Nordic Council, 1994; IISD, 1994; Skou Andersen, 1994; and Gale, Barg and Gillies, 1995). It is clear from these reviews that well-designed and presented environmental taxes and charges, particularly if they are supplemented with complementary regulations and support for innovation, can be very successful at achieving cost-effective environmental gains. Box 6.6 provides some examples.

The lessons and 'success factors' that emerge from these reviews of specific environmental taxes are:

- They can be very effective at both changing behaviour and generating revenue, particularly if they involve predictable increases over several years.
- Reform packages with complementary elements are much more successful than isolated taxes.
- New markets and innovations can be stimulated by appropriate price signals and other incentives.
- For particular pollutants, the combination of charges and subsides can be cost-effective and politically acceptable to industry.
- Institutional cultures and policy styles will strongly affect the design and political fate of tax reforms.
- Achieving political and public support by informed discussion and consultation seems essential for reforms which tax goods that have been perceived as 'free' or 'cheap'.
- Policy creation through decentralized experimentation can lead to better results.

BOX 6.6 EXAMPLES OF EFFECTIVE ENVIRONMENTAL TAXES/CHARGES

1. Ozone-depleting chemicals tax in the USA
A tax of $1.37 per pound in 1989 has been increased to $5.35 in 1995 and applied to eight, then 20 ozone-depleting chemicals (ODCs). It generated revenues of over $1bn a year by 1994, and is set to increase by $0.45 per year. ODCs used as feedstock and consumed and/or recycled in manufacture are exempt. International competitiveness is preserved through import taxes and expert rebates on both ODCs and products containing them. Both caps on production, via regulation implementing the Montreal Protocol, and government support for research on alternative chemicals, helped to achieve ODCs production reductions that were two-thirds of those allowed under the production caps. The technology-forcing role of the tax package was also significant, with the CFC substitutes likely to be cheaper than CFCs by 2000 (IISD, 1994, pp 28–9).

2. Tax differentials for catalytic converters and unleaded petrol in Germany
This revenue neutral scheme, regulated at federal but administered at regional level, involved tax differentials for unleaded petrol, tax incentives to promote catalytic converters and low emission vehicles, and cash payments to retrofit older cars with converters. Up to DM3000 per car in tax exemptions were available in 1988, reducing to zero in 1992 when 97 per cent of all new cars had catalytic converters. Over 90 per cent of petrol for passenger vehicles is now unleaded and Germany leads Europe in emission standards for vehicles (IISD, 1994, pp 12–13). In the meantime, a black market in smuggled CFCs is causing a huge worry.

3. Water pollution charges/rebates in France, The Netherlands, Germany and Denmark
A comprehensive review concluded that The Netherlands' system of earmarked revenues for pollution-control incentives, administered by specialized water agencies, produced the most cost-effective reduction in water pollution. The size of the water charges was less important than the subsidy part of the scheme: the lower-charge French system achieved better pollution control results with the aid of its levy/bounty scheme than did the higher charges system in Germany. In contrast to Denmark, which invested heavily in sewage plants, The Netherlands targeted their subsidies on the polluting factories, encouraging them to install cleaner production methods (Skou Andersen, 1994).

4. Nitrogen oxides charge/refund system in Sweden
A charge of EK40 per kilogram of NOx emitted from large plants (the capacity of 10 MW + annual production over 50 GWh) was announced in 1990 and introduced in 1992, while the revenues were returned to plants in proportion to their energy production. 'Eco-efficient' plants that generate much energy with low emissions receive net benefits, and less-efficient plants paid net charges. The average cost of reducing 1kg of NO_x is SEK10; accordingly, many NO_x-reducing investments have proved profitable. By 1993 NOx emissions were 44 per cent lower than in 1990 (IISD, 1994).

A final lesson from UK experience and not covered in the above review, is:

- A radical reform can be introduced behind the row created by another, unpopular, reform.

The 5 per cent per year road-fuel duty 'escalator', which is to continue 'indefinitely', originally announced at 3 per cent in the November 1993 budget (but subsequently raised to 5 per cent per year in 1994), is on paper one of the greenest taxes in Europe, providing just the kind of gradual, long-term price signal recommended by Wiezsacker and Jessinghaus (1992). Figure 6.4 shows how real fuel prices will be 30 per cent above the level expected in 2000 without the 'escalator', reaching their highest level over the last 40 years. Figure 6.5 indicates how estimated CO_2 emissions will be some 2.5 million tons less than expected in 2000, as a result of the tax.

Real fuel price index (1990=100)

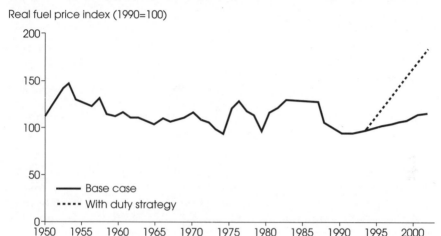

Source: Environmental Appraisal in Government Departments, Department of Environment, 1994

Figure 6.4 *UK real fuel price index, 1950–2000*

The road-fuel duty was introduced with virtually no public debate or opposition, mainly because it was overshadowed by the simultaneous introduction of VAT on domestic fuel, from 0 to 8 per cent in 1994, with a proposal to reach 17.5 per cent in 1995. However, the poor state of the UK's housing stock, which is the worst insulated in Northern Europe, has resulted in some seven million households suffering from 'fuel poverty' – the combination of low incomes and poor insulation means that people cannot afford to keep warm (Boardman, 1995). The VAT proposal hit these households badly and the resulting political storm caused the government to be defeated on the second tranche of VAT, despite belatedly promising £2.5 billion per year in welfare payments to offset the energy price increases. Had the government won, much of this money would merely have gone to heat the streets outside the fuel-poverty households.

An alternative approach would be to use a carbon/energy tax, accompanied by a £1 billion insulation and energy-efficiency programme, targeted at priority households, which would leave poor households better off than before the tax and price changes. (This point is well illustrated by Terry Barker in Chapter 9.) Meanwhile, the VAT controversy, which has

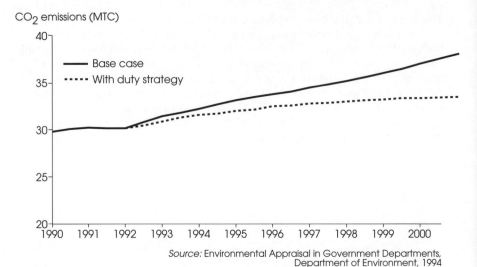

CO$_2$ emissions (MTC)

Source: Environmental Appraisal in Government Departments, Department of Environment, 1994

Figure 6.5 *UK CO$_2$ emissions, 1990–2000*

been revived by the Labour Party's 1995 announcement that it will reduce the VAT on domestic energy to the lowest permissible under EU rules – namely, 5 per cent – has closed off the option of further increases in domestic energy prices, at least until the targeted insulation programme, possibly financed through the energy-supply companies, is well under way.

THE OBSTACLES TO ETR

From the discussions and experiences of ETR and environmental taxes, the following major obstacles to ETR can be identified:

1. Taxing 'cheap' or 'essential' goods is difficult:
If the perception that, say, water is both 'cheap' and 'essential' is strong, then any attempt to raise prices to capture the full costs of extraction and treatment will be difficult to achieve. Similarly, if there is political debate about how the prices of electricity or gas should be lowered through privatization, etc, then raising its price in real terms to reflect more fully environmental costs is not going to be easy. On the other hand, if energy prices are falling because of production efficiencies, then this provides an opportunity to increase taxes without imposing immediate price increases. Within agriculture, a reform of the CAP away from price supports should lead to lower food prices which could be offset by the introduction of taxes on energy and chemicals inputs.

2. Equity: indirect taxes are regressive, direct taxes are progressive:
In general, this statement is true, particularly for energy, where the poor spend a proportionately bigger share of their income on energy than do the rich. However, for petrol taxes this is not true, as many poor people do not

own cars and the rich consume proportionately more motor fuel than the poor car-users, as they travel further in larger cars. However, it is clear that both tax and expenditure flows have to be considered before judgements on 'progression' or 'regression' can be made. For example, Table 6.3 shows that while direct taxes do have a small effect on reducing income inequalities and indirect taxes have a similar impact on increasing inequalities, the impact of the expenditure flow is much more significant in reducing inequalities than direct taxes.

An ETR package can therefore be designed to be progressive overall whilst still involving a shift of taxes from people to things (DIW, 1994; Barker, 1993). Direct expenditure on home insulation, raising income tax thresholds, increased Social Security payments and improved public transport, are some of the ways in which the progressivity of the ETR package would be achieved. However, politicians would have to be trusted to deliver these expenditures.

Table 6.3 *The importance of benefits in kind in redistribution, 1993 (Annual household income (£))*

	Original income	+ cash bens = gross income	- direct tax = disposable income	- indir tax = post tax income	+ benefits in kind = final income
Bottom 20%	1,920	6,280	5,590	3,870	7,480
Bottom 10%	1,471	5,639	4,825	3,036	7,055
Top 20%	39,370	40,420	31,100	26,200	28,270
Top 10%	48,754	49,665	38,003	32,614	34,456
Bottom 20% as percentage of top 20%	4.9%	15.8%	18.0%	14.8%	26.5%
Bottom 10% as percentage of top 10%	3.0%	11.4%	12.7%	9.3%	20.5%

Source: Economic Trends, December 1994, Table D and 3A (Appendix 1). Figures refer to all households ranked by equivalent income; Dan Corry, IPPR

3. Trust:
The trust in politicians is low, yet ETR requires considerable faith in politicians to lower people's taxes, provide investment incentives and direct public expenditure in ways that make the ETR package effective and equitable. Similarly, if trade unions are not to press for increases in wages in order to offset price increases, and not to share in the reduction in employers' National Insurance Contributions, then they have to trust employers to invest and to recruit labour in response to the new taxes and incentives, rather than to increase profits and/or dividends.

Building trust in a climate of free-market individualism is not easy. If ETR is to be successful, it needs to involve key groups in society, achieving consensus on the main features of the reforms needed, and then securing strong, cross-party support for them, particularly as they will involve long-term tax changes that go beyond the normal life-times of parliaments. Multi-stakeholder planning and conflict resolution, pioneered in Canada (Environment Canada, 1994), needs to be used in the process of designing and implementing ETR.

4. Competitiveness:
The many studies of ETR show that overall competitiveness will be increased, owing to the lowering of non-wage labour costs, and to the impetus given to innovations and technological change by the new price signals. For example, the DRI study showed that there would be a 'reduction in net imports from the rest of the world, as demand within the EU-6 shifts towards higher value-added products which have a greater domestic content and which are subject to less competition on the world market'. Intra-EU trade would increase owing to higher activity and investments, while there would also be an improvement in the net energy trade balance (DRI, 1994, p 57). Studies of individual countries, such as the UK, Germany, Switzerland, Denmark and Austria, have shown similar results.

However, within economies, some sectors gain and some lose competitiveness, depending on how energy intensive they are and how easily their goods are traded. Key 'loser' groups are fossil-fuel energy-supply industries, iron and steel, basic chemicals, paper, cement, and non-ferrous metals. Measures are needed to deal with these sectoral and, usually, regional losers, such as border tax adjustments (although GATT compatibility is not clear cut, despite the success of the CFC border tax adjustments in the USA); delayed and gradual implementation of taxes on energy-intensive sectors; investment incentives; and regional employment programmes. These measures would enable single countries to introduce ETR, but obviously the greater the international harmonization, the less there will be of competitiveness pressures and associated 'leakage' of polluting production abroad. Such harmonization is likely to be achieved in the EU only after several member states have already introduced elements of ETR unilaterally – which is slowly beginning to happen.

5. The need for integration:
ETR cannot be successful without integrating the policies, and reconciling the different interests, of the Departments of Finance, Environment, Energy, Transport, Agriculture and Employment. Despite the recognition of this in the Fifth Environmental Action Programme of the EU in 1992, it is proving difficult to achieve. Related problems arise from the desire of Finance Ministries to collect and disburse taxation and their resistance to the earmarking of revenues for specific programmes. This conflicts with the business need for as much 'within industry' recycling of revenues as possible. Some specific earmarking for particular pollutants such as NO_x, and increased 'presentational' earmarking (where the direction of expenditure is indicated without specific sums being earmarked), can help to increase political support for ETR but without losing the flexibility of general revenues.

PAYING FOR POLLUTION – THE POLLUTER, OR THE USER, OR SOMEONE ELSE?

The costs of pollution are often diffused throughout society in the form of acid rain damage, poor air quality and contaminated groundwater. As we have seen, they are hard to quantify and evaluate. Nevertheless, they are real costs that are distributed unevenly in society, with some people bearing more of the burden in terms of damaged lungs, lands, buildings or other natural assets, such as peace and quiet, clean air and a pleasant view.

Dealing with pollution by regulations or taxes and charges also has 'distributional' effects, as they affect particular groups (some industries and consumers) more than others. Analysing these distributional effects is not easy, but the OECD (1994) has concluded that:

> ...generally, pollution control *costs* tend to be regressive (ie, a higher percentage burden for low income households) and pollution control *benefits* tend to be progressively distributed when measured on physical units, but less so when measured in value terms, because lower income households appear to value environmental benefits less than upper income households.

The report concludes that measures to mitigate or compensate for unacceptable distributional impacts are available, but that much more research is needed because: 'relatively few empirical analyses have been done on the distributional effects of environmental programmes, and even fewer have been done for economic instruments'.

However, although the 'polluter pays' principle has been discussed for years, its application in the marketplace is not clear cut, with some pollution control costs being passed on to customers and others. Users of scarce resources such as land and water are increasingly expected to bear the full social costs of using the resource, and consumers are beginning to take an interest in taxes that bear mostly on them, or which are based on an 'end-of-pipe', or pollution-control approach, rather than a more integrated pollution-prevention approach (ESP, 1995).

There is more potential to change behaviour at the concept/design, resource acquisition/extraction and manufacturing stages of a product's life cycle than there is at the consumption stage. Taxes and charges should be directed at these 'upstream' parts of the economy, rather than at the 'downstream' end of consumption. This view is endorsed by the OECD (1995): 'instruments should be designed so that waste minimization can be implemented as far back in the life of the product as possible'. A sample list of economic instruments that focus on the pre-consumer stage is provided in Box 6.7.

Of course, elements of these taxes would be passed on to consumers, but the focus of the tax is on changing producer, rather than consumer, behaviour. Any costs passed through which raised prices would encourage consumers to choose more environmentally friendly products, if they are available. Consumers do generate waste, but the volumes that are created and the scope for reducing them are very small in comparison to

---

BOX 6.7 POTENTIAL ECONOMIC INSTRUMENTS FOR POLLUTION PREVENTION

- Removal of subsidies on virgin materials.
- Product design tax.
- Deposit/refund system (multi-tier/variable rates).
- Hazardous waste tax.
- Carbon content tax on fossil fuels (natural gas, coal, petroleum).
- Virgin materials input tax.
- Severance tax on cutting old growth trees.
- Excise tax on manufacturers and importers of paper and paperboard products and other materials which do not contain specified percentage of recycled content.
- Tax on ozone-depleting substances.
- Government procurement policy/requirements.
- User fees for resource extraction.

Source: ESP, 1995

those for industry (2 per cent of solid wastes for the US economy, for example (ESP, 1995)).

TWO PARTIAL ETR PROGRAMMES: DENMARK AND SWEDEN

Although comprehensive ETR has not been implemented, two 'partial' ETR packages have been put into use in Denmark and Sweden (Boxes 6.8 and 6.9), though the motives for both were mainly the desire to reduce high marginal tax rates.

Small firms continue to bear most of the industrial energy taxes; however, the Danish example does contain elements of successful ETR, such as the initial reduction of income taxes, and the steadily rising environmental tax rates over several years (1994–98).

Both examples illustrate the difficulty of achieving significant taxes on industrial energy when competing countries do not impose similar taxes. These examples, the experience of the EU carbon/energy tax (Ikwue and Skea, 1995), and attempts in Switzerland to introduce a pure carbon tax (Box 6.10), illustrate the power of small minorities of 'loser' industries to mobilize against reforming the tax system in a more sustainable direction.

CONCLUSION

At a private seminar in Zurich in September 1995, leaders of German, Swiss and Austrian big business, hosted by a major reinsurance company, concluded that ETR was essential for the long-term viability of their industries, which included car manufacturing and chemicals. Representatives

BOX 6.8 THE DANISH EXPERIENCE

The Danish 1993 tax reform introduced new or increased green taxes of 12 billion Dkr, while at the same time it lowered income taxes from an average of 52 per cent to 44 per cent, and reduced marginal tax rates. Most of the taxes introduced applied only to households, but in June 1995 it was decided to increase the CO_2 tax on energy use in manufacturing industries and to remove some of the existing exemptions with regard to energy taxes. The revenue from the CO_2 tax was used partly for targeted energy-efficiency measures and partly for neutralizing the income effects.

Despite the neutral economic impacts of a CO_2 tax expected on the basis of macroeconomic analysis, Danish industries lobbied vigorously against its intro-duction. In particular, Denmark's few cement and steel industries were vociferous in their opposition, while smaller and middle-sized companies only became active as the larger firms had obtained concessions, which shifted a larger share of the relative tax burden to the SMEs. Trade unions did not involve themselves too actively in the debate, but did lend support to the argument that voluntary agreements would be preferable to a tax. However, the Labour Movement's Business Council, an independent think-tank, was among the most active advocates of the increase in CO_2 tax. Also the large Union of Unskilled Workers was active in its support for the CO_2 and other environmental taxes, in anticipation of the jobs to be created for its members in the energy sector.

As a result of the CO_2 package passed in the Danish Folketing in June 1995, Danish industry will pay 600 Dkr per ton CO_2 (or US $100) for energy used for ordinary purposes, such as heating, while the level for energy use in produc-tion processes will be 200 Dkr per ton CO_2 (about US $33). For particularly energy-intensive production processes, the CO_2 tax can be exempted if the firm agrees to undertake the best available technology savings. The tax is being phased in gradually until 1998. The top rate of Dkr 600 is equivalent to the tax level of households, and will assure a more efficient approach to energy saving in the future. After almost 20 years of energy saving targeted at households, the marginal costs of savings had become unreasonably high compared to what could be obtained in industries. The new tax is expected to trigger substantial investment in energy saving and in fuel substitution, such as the exchange of coal with natural gas.

Source: Skou Andersen, 1994

from small family firms agreed, as they too saw the next few decades as being dependent on the resource productivity gains that would be stimu-lated by ETR. The main voices of dissent came from the official German employers federation who defended the *status quo* on behalf, largely, of their small minority of energy-intensive members.

However, an analysis of the EU carbon/energy tax proposal (Ikwue and Skea, 1995) concluded with some observations about the conditions under which 'older style antagonistic modes of operation are likely to apply', as they did with the CO_2 tax. These included political urgency and pressures; large negative effects on a few stakeholders; unclear public policy objectives owing to cross-departmental issues; little consultation with stakeholders; the perception that many would lose and a few would

BOX 6.9 THE SWEDISH EXPERIENCE

Sweden has used several environmental taxes and charges since the mid 1970s, including a charge on new cars to finance premiums on properly scrapped old cars; taxes on fertilizers and pesticides; differential taxes on petrol and diesel to encourage the development of cleaner fuels; taxes on domestic aviation fuel; charges on batteries; and taxes on CO_2, NO_x and SO_2. Most have had significant effects on behaviour and technological development, according to recent evaluation (Ministry of the Environment and Natural Resources, 1994). The taxes are set to rise in line with inflation in 1994–98.

In 1990–91 the first 'partial' ETR programme was initiated, involving reductions in income taxes and increases in environmental taxes . However, the CO_2 tax was opposed by industry on competitiveness grounds and it was reduced from SEK0.25/kg CO_2 to SEK0.08/kg for manufacturing industry, but raised to SEK0.32/kg for households, transport and services. And energy-intensive sectors had reductions until 1995. The employment effects of the reform have not yet been evaluated, but there has been a move away from fossil fuels towards biofuels in energy production and district heating, and the CO_2 tax was the decisive factor. However, 'the opportunity for increased environmental taxes provided by the general tax reform and the desire to finance lower income taxes has not really been fully used'.

Source: Sterner, 1994

BOX 6.10 SWITZERLAND'S CARBON TAX PROPOSAL

In 1994, following four years of evaluation and discussion, the government proposed a pure carbon tax, rising from £6 per ton CO_2 in 1996 to £18 per ton in 2000, which was similar to the EU proposal; rebates for energy-intensive sectors; partial earmarking of one-third of the revenues for environmental and energy-efficiency measures for ten years only; recycling the rest of the revenue to employers in the form of reductions in non-wage labour costs (one-quarter), and to households (three-quarters). Although Switzerland has few fossil-fuel industries, generating most of its power from hydro and nuclear energy, industry successfully opposed the measure because not all revenue was recycled and other competitors were not imposing a similar tax. Lessons to be learnt, according to involved Swiss observers, are:

- the positive economic advantages of the measure on both employment and growth were not relevant to the political debate because the industries directly affected, employing 2–3 per cent of the Swiss work-force, lobbied effectively, whereas the much larger group of winners was not involved;
- the fear of loss of competitiveness in a small open economy is dominant;
- the complete recycling of revenues is an essential part of any reform for industry;
- although there is now a compromise on voluntary agreements for reducing CO_2, informed actors in the debate recognize that marked increases in the prices of energy and resources, compared to labour, are essential.

Source: INFRAS, Zurich,1995

BOX 6.11 ILLUSTRATIVE* LIST OF THE SHORT-TERM 'WINNERS' AND 'LOSERS'** FROM ETR

'Winners'	'Losers'
Most manufacturing	Coal, lignite
Small/medium enterprises	Oil, gas
Construction	Base chemicals
Local authorities	Iron and steel
Education	Metals
Telecommunications	Paper
Retail	Cement
Energy efficiency	Intensive agriculture
Renewable energy	
Health services	
Social services	
Financial services	

* The detail depends on the ETR package design.

** Could benefit in long term from early move to 'resource-productivity' growth path.

gain; and lukewarm support from politicians. It follows that for ETR to succeed, 'consensus generating' conditions need to be created, such as:

- round-table discussions with major stakeholders over long-term change;
- an ETR package with gradual, positive effects for many stakeholders, and transitional measures for 'losers';
- an integrated departmental approach;
- strong backing for reform from politicians.

But, as we have seen, 'losers' mobilize and 'winners' do not. The future of ETR therefore lies with those who, operating within consensus conditions, can mobilize the winners in Box 6.11, while mollifying the losers with adjustment measures which they help to design. Sustainability, as well as the competitiveness of European industry, depends in large measure on successful ETR. But who will pick up the challenge left by Jacques Delors?

REFERENCES

Barker, T (1993) *The interdependence of equity and efficiency objectives in fiscal policies to reduce carbon emissions in the domestic sector*, Department of Applied Economics, Cambridge

BCSD (1994) *Internalising Environmental Costs to Promote Eco-efficiency*, Business Council on Sustainable Development, Geneva

Boardman, B (1995) 'Freezing out the poor', *New Economy*, Vol 2, No 3, pp 7, 11

Brown, C V and Sandford, G T (1991) *Tax and incentives: the effects of the 1988 cuts in high income taxes*, Institute for Public Policy Research, London

Cararro, C (ed) (1994) *Trade Innovation, Environment*, Fondazione Eni Enrico Mattei, Kluwer Academic Publishers, Dordrecht, The Netherlands

Carnoules Declaration (1994) *Factor 10 Club*, Wuppertal Institute, Wuppertal

De Wit, G (1995) *Employment effects of ecological tax reform*, Centre for Energy Conservation and Environmental Technology, The Hague

DIW (1994) *The economic effects of ecological tax reform*, German Economic Research Institute, Bonn

DRI/McGraw Hill (1994) *Potential benefits of integration of environmental and economic policies: an incentive based approach to policy integration*, Graham and Trotman, Office for Official Publications of the EU, London and Brussels

EC (European Commission) 1993 *Growth, Competitiveness, Employment: the Challenges and Way Forward into the 21st Century*, white paper, Bulletin of the European Communities Supplement 6/93, European Commission, Brussels

Ekins, P (1995) *Mimeograph on the Dividends from Economic Tax Reform*, Birkbeck College, London

Environment Canada (1994) 'Working in multi-stakeholder processes', manuscript by Carole Donaldson, Environment Canada, Ottawa

ESP (1995) *Putting consumers first; green and fair economic instruments*, The Environmentally Sound Packaging Coalition of Canada, Vancouver

European Commission, FGE (1995) *Europeans and the Environment in 1995*, Directorate General on Environment, Nuclear Safety and Environmental Protection, Brussels

Gale, R, Barg, S, and Gillies, A (1995) *Green Budget Reform: An International Casebook on Leading Practices*, Earthscan Publications, London

Hess, S and Mauch, S (1995) *Swiss climate change policy and ecological tax reform (ETR) in the 1990s*, INFRAS, Zurich

IISD (1994) *Making Budgets Green: Leading Practices in Taxation and Subsidy Reform*, International Institute for Sustainable Development, Winnipeg

Ikwue T and Skea J (1995) *Business and the Genesis of the European Community Carbon Tax Proposal*, Business Strategy and the Environment, European Research Press, Bradford

Italian Finance Ministry (1994) *La Riforma Fiscale: Il Libro Blanco del NUOVO Fisco – Come Passare dal vecchio al nuovo attraverso federalismo, tassaione ambientale e semplificazione*, Italian Finance Ministry, Rome

Ministry of Environment and Natural Resources (1994) *The Swedish experience – taxes and charges in environmental policy*, Ministry of Environment, Stockholm

Moret, Ernst and Young (1996) title undecided; report for DGXI of the EU DG XI, Brussels

Nordic Council (1994) *The use of economic instruments in Nordic environmental policy*, TemaNord, Copenhagen

OECD (1994) *The Distributive Effects of Economic Instruments for Environmental Policy*, Harrison, Paris

OECD (1994) *Managing the Environment: The Role of Economic Instruments*, Organization of Economic Cooperation and Development, Paris

OECD (1995) *Instruments Available to Waste Managers to Encourage Waste Minimilization*, Organization of Economic Cooperation and Development, Paris

Pigou, A C (1920) *The Economics of Welfare*, Macmillan, London

Pigou, A C (1947) *A Study in Public Finance*, Macmillan, London

Porter, M E and van der Linde, C (1995) 'Green and competitive: ending the stalemate', *Harvard Business Review*, September–October, pp 120–34

RCEP (1994) *Transport and the Environment*, 18th Report of the Royal Commission on Environmental Pollution, HMSO, London

Repetto, R (1990) 'Environmental productivity and why it is so important', *Challenge*, October–November, pp 13–19

Repetto, R *et al* (1992) *Green Fees – How a Tax Shift Can Work for the Environment and the Economy*, World Resources Institute, Washington, DC

Skou Andersen, M (1994a) *Governance by Green Taxes: Making Pollution Prevention Pay*, Manchester University Press, Manchester

Skou Andersen, M (1994b) 'The green tax reform in Denmark: shifting the focus of tax liability', *Environmental Liability*, Vol 2, No 2, pp 29–41

Sterner, T (1994) *Environmental tax reform: the Swedish experience*, Studies in Environmental and Development Working Papers, Department of Economics, Göteburg University, Sweden

WBMG, (1994) *Economic Tax Reform: Proceedings from the International Briefing*, WBMG, Environmental Communications; London

WBMG, (1995) *Tax Reform for Sustainable Development: Roundtable Discussions*, WMBG Environmental Communications, London

Weizsacker, Ernst von (1994) *Earth Politics*, Earthscan, London

Weizsacker, Ernst von and Jessinghaus, J (1992) *Ecological Tax Reform*, Zed Press, London

C h a p t e r 7

ENVIRONMENTAL TAXATION AND THE DOUBLE DIVIDEND: FACT OR FALLACY?

Peter Bohm

The observation that environmental taxes have a 'double dividend' seems to be the pro-environmental tax message that eventually made an impression on politicians, at least in some North European countries. The observation says that environmental taxes could not only correct for the enviromental effects (which command-and-control instruments also could do) but, in addition, produce extra government revenue that could be used to reduce pre-existing distortionary taxes. In recent years, the existence of this second dividend has been questioned, in particular in connection with proposals to introduce carbon taxes. The new arguments – that the double dividend may be negative, that carbon taxes are distortionary and environmental taxes typically exacerbate pre-existing tax distortions – are examined here.

At the outset of the environmental policy debate some 25 years ago, an environmental tax was seen as a corrective tax – ie, a tax which improves resource allocation (but typically reduces GDP). This view was held mainly by economists, given a limited interest in environmental policy from politicians in general and an opposition to economic-incentive instruments from environmentalists (see Bohm and Russell, 1985 and Hahn, 1989). Two changes may help to explain why the interest in such instruments has now

Acknowledgement
This is a revised version of the first section of my paper 'Government Revenue Implications of Carbon Taxes and Tradeable Carbon Permits: Efficiency Aspects', presented at the International Institute of Public Finance 50th Congress, Cambridge, MA, 22–25 August 1994. An earlier version has been circulated under the title 'Environmental Taxes, Carbon Taxes, Tax Recycling and Tax Distortions', Department of Economics, Stockholm University, 1995. Helpful comments by Per-Ove Hesselborn, Donald Katzner, David Pearce, Astri Muren and Karl-Göran Mäler are gratefully acknowledged.

increased. One seems to be a growing dissatisfaction among environmentalists concerning the capability of 'command and control', the dominating environmental policy instrument so far. Another is the increased insight among politicians, in general, that revenue from environmental taxes may help to reduce the excess burden of the taxes needed to finance a given level of government expenditure.

Thus, the interests of environmentalists and politicians seem to have coincided once again, but now in the opposite direction and in favour of environmental taxes. Hence, environmentalists now have an interest in the political support that can be gained from the side-effect – or 'second dividend' – of environmental taxes represented by the feasibility of a reduction in pre-existing distortionary taxes. Moreover, midstream politicians, who in this particular context may be interested primarily in making the tax system more efficient, rely on the view, now held also by a large number of environmentalists, that environmental taxes are (can be) 'corrective' and hence are non-distortionary. A problem for this alliance, however, is that the revenue-generating capacity of environmental taxes may be small, and hence the 'double dividend' feature of such taxes may fail to play any significant role. Part of the reason is that the tax elasticity of polluting activities may often be quite high – for instance, where the tax base of the environmental tax declines at a high rate, especially in a long-run perspective.

A carbon tax may be an exception to this rule. Since the tax elasticity of fossil fuel can be expected to remain small, revenue from this tax would be significant, if the issue of global warming is deemed important enough to call for high rates of carbon taxes. Thus, the primary case where the 'second dividend' of environmental taxes could play an important role is probably a carbon tax – or tradable carbon permits auctioned off by the government, which in this context amounts to the same thing.

In recent contributions to the literature it has been argued that (1) there are side-effects of carbon taxes that increase the distortions of pre-existing taxes (see Bovenberg and de Mooij, 1994); (2) carbon taxes themselves are distortionary (see Poterba,1993, Goulder 1994a, and Bovenberg and Goulder, 1994); and (3) the 'double dividend' of carbon taxes may well be negative – (Parry, 1994, and Proost and van Regemorter, 1995). To the extent that these arguments are correct, the attractiveness of carbon taxes and other relevant environmental taxes will be reduced, of course. These arguments are examined here. In particular, we address the following questions: To what extent do environmental taxes increase the excess burden of other taxes? In what sense are carbon taxes distortionary (or corrective)? Is the second dividend of a Pareto-efficient carbon (or other environmental) tax certain to be positive?

The arguments in the literature reviews now alluded to are presented and commented on below. Initially the focus is primarily on environmental taxes designed with respect to effects on the domestic environment of a country. The perspective is then shifted to global environmental problems. The main conclusions follow.

THE DOUBLE DIVIDEND DISCUSSION

A. Conventional wisdom concerning the welfare implications of an environmental tax, at least until a few years ago, can be illustrated by the following quotation from Pearce (1991, p 940):

> While most taxes distort incentives, an environmental tax [such as a carbon tax] corrects a distortion, namely the externalities arising from the excessive use of environmental services ... Governments may ... adopt a fiscally neutral stance on the carbon tax, using revenues to finance reductions in incentive-distorting taxes such as income tax, or corporation tax. This 'double dividend' feature of a pollution tax is of critical importance [from the point of view of] corporate and public acceptability of such a tax ... From a *social* standpoint the double dividend feature is also important. Estimates suggest that every £1 of tax raised by taxes on effort and enterprise gives rise to deadweight losses of 20–50 pence (Ballard *et al*, 1985). Thus a fiscally neutral £1 carbon tax would amount to an effective tax of 50–80 pence.

In practical application of these ideas, Sweden introduced a carbon tax in 1991 as part of a tax reform package to reduce marginal income taxes, which had risen to about 80 per cent (Bohm, 1994).

B. The addition of a 'second dividend' to the 'first dividend' of environmental improvement, hence creating the double dividend of environmental taxes, would seem potentially quite important in the case of a tax on carbon emissions. The reason is that a (global) carbon tax 'large enough to significantly slow carbon dioxide emissions would collect revenues equal to several per cent of world GDP' (Poterba,1991) or would 'well account for 10 per cent of global income' (Whalley and Wigle, 1991). Thus, using carbon-tax revenue for tax recycling would allow a possibly significant reduction in pre-existing distortionary taxes. The potential importance of this argument would seem particularly large when considering models where it has been shown that the carbon-abatement costs of a carbon tax 'can be *more* than offset if the revenues are used to cut distortionary pre-existing taxes on new capital formation', in contrast to certain other taxes; this particular result refers to the US (Shackleton *et al*, 1992; emphasis added).

C. Findings of the type just quoted seem to have led some proponents of a carbon tax to argue that an environmental reason, strictly speaking, is not needed to introduce a carbon tax, if the revenue from the tax is used to reduce the most distortionary pre-existing taxes. A similar perspective has been adopted by Goulder (1994a), who noted that the environmental benefits from a carbon tax are:

> ...highly uncertain. At the same time that efforts are undertaken to reduce these uncertainties it is useful to assess the gross economic costs of the carbon tax – that is, the economic costs exclusive of the (highly uncertain) economic benefits associated with avoided environmental damages.

Goulder (1994b) goes on to say that:

...much of the debate about the second dividend is in terms of whether environmental taxes can be introduced in a way that is costless ... [If] one cannot be assured that the costs are zero, then before one can recommend an environmental tax swap on efficiency grounds one has to be involved in the messy business of comparing (uncertain) environmental benefits with abatement costs ... Thus the debate about the double dividend reflects the desire to be able to make safe judgments about environmental reforms in the presence of uncertainty.

It is in this context that there has been talk about the 'distortionary costs of the carbon tax' (eg, Goulder, 1994a). Poterba (1993), referring to earlier work by Goulder as well as Bovenberg and de Mooij, argues that:

...since carbon taxes are indirect taxes, they reduce the real after-tax wage. (The after-tax wage is $(1-t)w/p(1+s)$, where w denotes the nominal wage, p the producer price level, t the marginal income tax rate, and s the average indirect tax rate. Carbon taxes raise s. This distorts labour supply. The cost of this distortion depends on the pre-existing level of $(1-t)/(1+s)$, the initial tax wedge. (p 55; emphasis added);

D. Bovenberg and de Mooij (1994) state as their main contribution that 'environmental taxes typically exacerbate, rather than alleviate, pre-existing tax distortions – even if revenues are employed to cut pre-existing distortionary taxes'. Using a linear general-equilibrium model with labour inputs only, fixed government expenditure, weakly separable utility functions, a tax on labour and a tax on domestic pollution, they show that an environmental tax, the revenue of which is used to reduce the labour tax, erodes both tax bases – labour and pollution. The reason is that the tax reduces labour supply (given a positive uncompensated wage elasticity) and shifts private consumption from 'dirty' to 'clean' products. A reasoning along similar lines is presented in Parry (1994).

ON THE INTERPRETATION OF 'DOUBLE DIVIDENDS' AND 'DISTORTIONARY' ENVIRONMENTAL TAXES

Where do these contributions to the literature leave us when it comes to evaluating whether the appropriate level of an environmental tax has a double dividend in (a) being corrective – ie, non-distortionary – and (b) yielding revenue that can be utilized to reduce pre-existing tax distortions? Unless otherwise stated, we concentrate in this section on a tax related to effects on the domestic environment only. (The subsections listed as A, B, C, D refer to the arguments in the corresponding subsections above.)

A. The Origin and Definitions of a 'Second Dividend'

First, we should clarify exactly what comparison or baseline is intended when saying (as in the above quotation from Pearce (1991)) that there are benefits – a second dividend – from an environmental tax in addition to environmental improvements.

Tax recycling benefits as compared to lump-sum redistribution.

To begin with, recall the following version of the standard argument for environmental taxes. Given a market economy, where firms or households use an input that now is found to have a negative effect on the domestic environment, the economy can be said to operate with a missing market for the use of environmental services (see Arrow, 1970). If this market economy were otherwise perfect, a tax equal to the marginal external effect could replace the market price of the missing market to reach a Pareto-efficient equilibrium, provided that the tax revenue is redistributed by lump-sum transfers. Introducing public goods and a second-best Pareto-efficient set of distortionary taxes to finance public provision of these goods (keeping marginal excess burdens equal across taxes), the argument for introducing an environmental tax remains the same, with two qualifications:

1. Estimating an optimal environmental tax to reflect the externality would be more complicated in this second-best optimal economy and the optimal tax rate would typically deviate from its first-best optimal level (Sandmo, 1975).
2. The most efficient use of the revenue from this tax would now be to reduce pre-existing distortionary taxes.

Note that computing the optimal environmental tax rate would have to reflect also the marginal effect of tax recycling on the excess burden of the pre-existing tax system. In this connection, it should be observed that, depending on the tax elasticity, an increase in the environmental tax rate may increase or decrease the revenue from this tax. For that reason alone, the optimal tax rate could be higher or lower than that reflecting only the marginal externality; see, for example, Lee and Misiolek (1986) and Oates (1993). However, it should also be taken into account – as is highlighted in Bovenberg and de Mooij (1994) – that the revenue from pre-existing taxes at pre-existing rates may be affected by the introduction of the environmental tax, as a result of induced changes in their tax bases. One definition of a second dividend currently used refers to the benefits that could be obtained from this form of tax recycling as compared to redistribution by lump-sum transfers.

In the absence of income-redistribution policy and barring political constraints on policy parameters, there would not be any reason for pre-existing taxes to be distortionary as was assumed in the preceding paragraph. Government expenditures for public goods could then be financed by non-distortionary (lump-sum) taxes. Thus, for pre-existing optimal-feasible taxes to be distortionary there must be more policy goals than efficiency, a natural candidate being a distribution policy goal.

Assume, for simplicity, that distribution policy amounts to redistributions from high-income to low-income groups and that the pre-existing optimal-feasible tax system is a linear income tax, $0 < t < 1$, to finance a guaranteed income or general lump-sum transfer G (> 0), maximizing a social welfare function with individual disposable incomes (y^D_i) as arguments and disregarding other government expenditure than NG for N individuals. Thus we have:

$$y^D_i = G + y_i(1 - t), \qquad t\Sigma y_i = NG$$

Introducing an environmental tax, t_e, for a newly observed externality, a 'windfall' government revenue is obtained from this tax. Assuming no other policy parameters than G, t and t_e, the revenue from t_e can now be used for lump-sum transfers, ie increasing G, or for reducing t. As argued in Proost and van Regemorter (1995), the distribution-policy objectives may be such that the option of lump-sum transfers, which are proportionally more favourable to low-income groups, is preferred to a reduction of the tax rate. If so, the second dividend from reducing the tax rate, hence reducing tax distortions, would be negative, as compared to redistribution by lump-sum transfers. But since the latter option is available, it seems more appropriate to say that there would be no benefits from the recycling of environmental taxes to replace pre-existing distortionary taxes in this case, and thus that the (minimum) second dividend would be zero. However, in this particular case, there are more than the two policy options highlighted – namely, the option of an optimal-feasible *combination* of an increase in G and a reduction in t. Moreover, since $t < 1$ reflects the implicit assumption that it is not optimal to equalize disposable incomes, it may well be that optimal increases in disposable incomes would not all be in terms of an increase in G. Hence, part of the redistribution could be to reduce t, thus increasing disposable incomes in proportion to the higher the income y. If so, the option of keeping t constant and redistributing all the environmental tax revenue by an increase in G would be dominated by some reduction in t and a lower increase in G. In other words, part of the revenue from the environmental tax could be used to reduce tax distortions and hence the second dividend would be positive.

Tax recycling benefits of environmental taxes compared to alternative environmental policies.

Shifting the perspective, assume that there are environmental effects of the production x_m of product m and that a command-and-control instrument, hitherto the 'political favourite' in real-world environmental policy, was (or would be) used to reach a certain known long-term optimal output level, x_m^1. (For simplicity, assume the environmental effects to be of the threshold type with the marginal environmental effect rising steeply at x_m^1.) Regardless of whether the consumer price, p_m, is adjusted to make demand equal to x_m^1 or only the shadow price of product m is increased to that level, the consumer price index p relevant for estimating the real wage rate will go up. With, say, a model of the Bovenberg–de Mooij type mentioned above (see also the above quotation from Poterba), employment and hence labour tax revenue would fall. Furthermore, with the optimal output level x_m^1 (the estimate of which had to take this side-effect of environmental regulation on pre-existing taxes into account), we end up with a reduced second-best optimal correction of x_m, as well as an increase in the total excess burden of the tax system when the labour tax is increased to keep government revenue unchanged. Replacing command-and-control policy with a second-best optimal environmental tax, we obtain additional government revenue which can now be used to replace parts of the distortionary labour tax. In fact, with a social welfare function including more than an efficiency objective – for instance, distributional targets – even a lump-sum redistribution of the environmental tax revenue could constitute a 'welfare improvement', compared to what could have been achieved by using a command-and-control option of environmental policy.

In this case, a second dividend is defined by the tax recycling benefits of an environmental policy, using a tax instead of direct regulation. (In fact, this comparison seems to be the origin of the 'double dividend' argument.) In general, as was illustrated when discussing the first case – namely, tax recycling benefits compared with lump-sum redistribution – the size of the second dividend now defined would be given by recycling the revenue of the environmental tax so as to maximize the relevant objective function. When the objective is efficiency alone – which is what most of the recent literature on the double dividend has focused on and also what we henceforth will assume – the second dividend is given by the efficiency gains achieved by using environmental-tax revenue to replace pre-existing distortionary taxes, compared to the baseline of an environmental policy from which no extra net government revenue would arise.

This comparison between a specific revenue-neutral tax and an alternative policy instrument is, of course, the relevant approach to identifying which policy is efficient, when both options are preferable to doing nothing. A concrete illustration is given by a country that has committed itself to the Framework Convention on Climate Change target of keeping carbon emissions in the year 2000 on the 1990 level. If a carbon tax is not introduced for this purpose, some other policy will. For example, the actual substitute may be some form of direct regulation. If, instead, the tax were compared to doing nothing – which is the approach taken in most of the literature discussed here (see Bovenberg and Goulder, 1994; Bovenberg and de Mooij, 1994; Goulder, 1994a; Goulder, 1994b and Parry, 1994) – no conclusion can be drawn on whether it is environmentally efficient or not to introduce the tax. One particular reason is that the relevant size of the tax recycling benefits, net of all effects on pre-existing tax bases, could not be determined by analysing the case where the baseline is doing nothing, when in fact the true baseline is to use another policy option which (also) may affect pre-existing tax bases. Comparing a particular (revenue neutral) tax with no such tax, *ceteris paribus*, would be relevant for the issue, whether or not introducing the tax is a worthwhile *tax reform*. Given that issue, whatever environmental improvements might arise from the introduction of the new tax would be a side-effect of the tax reform, a new type of 'second dividend'.

B. Can Environmental Policy be Costless?

In an economy where there is more than one distortionary tax prior to the introduction of the environmental tax, either of two situations can arise:

1. *The pre-existing tax structure is second-best efficient* in the sense that marginal excess burdens of the various pre-existing taxes are equalized. (For simplicity, assume that there are no significant fixed administrative costs of any of the taxes.) Thus, no benefits

would accrue from a redistribution among the set of *feasible* taxes, one of which would be an excise tax on product m. If such a tax, t_m, were actually included in the efficient set of taxes before any environmental effects of x_m had been observed, it would be a distortionary tax, which, at the selected level, t_m^*, would have an optimal marginal-excess burden equal to that of the other taxes used. In this situation, additional revenue from the introduction of an efficiently designed environmental tax on x_m, where $t_m > t_m^*$, would in principle have to be used to reduce all pre-existing taxes in order to keep marginal-excess burdens equal.

2. *The pre-existing tax structure is characterized by unequal marginal-excess burdens* of the various pre-existing taxes. An example of such a tax system was given by Shackleton *et al* (1992), as quoted above, where the marginal-excess burden was estimated to be particularly high for pre-existing taxes on new capital formation. If this situation is the result of an efficient policy in the presence of binding political constraints on specific taxes, or the existence of other policy goals in addition to an efficiency goal, it would still be second-best optimal. Moreover, the marginal-excess burdens, according to the definition relevant for this situation, would in fact be equalized. This is also likely to be the case in an economy where efficiency, in fact, is among the policy goals guiding policy design. If, however, a government has an efficiency objective, which the present discussion presupposes, but in practical policy does not implement it, the pre-existing tax structure would be inefficient. Hence, there would be room for an efficiency-improving tax reform where less distortionary taxes are substituted for more distortionary ones, regardless of whether or not there is an environmental tax under consideration and the tax base for that tax is called upon (also) in connection with a tax reform. It could still happen, of course, that an environmental tax is actually introduced – ie, an act of environmental policy is carried out – in combination with a tax reform. Nevertheless, that part of the benefits from introducing an environmental tax, which arise from reducing taxes with high marginal-excess burdens instead of some average marginal-excess burden, cannot be ascribed to the tax as an *environmental* tax.

To sum up, a particular tax may be called upon for two separate reasons: as part of a tax reform and as part of an implementation of environmental policy. Analytically speaking, these two reasons represent separate issues, implying that the additional benefits, which might accrue to the introduction of an environmental tax and which arise from a feasible tax reform not yet carried out, are not part of the tax recycling benefits, or second dividend, of that tax as an environmental policy instrument. (As noted above, if pre-existing more-than-average marginal tax distortions could not be reduced, given the total set of policy goals and constraints, there would not be any such benefits from a feasible tax reform.) For simplicity, we deal solely with the general case, where marginal-excess burdens are equal across pre-existing taxes or can be equalized prior to the introduction of an environmental tax. In this case, a tax which originates in a newly observed environmental concern and is efficiently tailored to that concern – an *environmental* tax, for short – cannot have a second dividend that exceeds the costs of abating the externality. When a particular revenue-neutral tax has such benefits, it would have been called upon already for reasons of a needed tax reform.[*]

C. 'Distortionary' Environmental Taxes

We may distinguish the following three effects of introducing a tax for environmental policy purposes: (1) effects on the environment, (2) gross abatement costs, disregarding (3) the implications of the tax repercussions on the rest of the economy, given a set of policy targets (eg, given government expenditure on public goods). The third effect includes: (i) the effect of using the tax revenue to replace other tax revenues and (ii) the effect on pre-existing tax distortions (what Parry (1994) calls the revenue effect and the interdependency effect, respectively).

As long as all three effects are taken into account, it does not matter in what order they are observed. As was shown above, Goulder (1994a, 1994b) maintains that the environmental effect (here: the effect of reduced carbon emissions) is significantly more uncertain than effects (2) and (3) as a reason for assessing separately 'the economic costs exclusive of the (highly uncertain) economic benefits associated with avoided environmental damages' – ie, effects (2) and (3). This assessment, it is argued, could then be used as the required minimum environmental benefits for introducing the tax. It should be noted, first, that this approach can be used, of course, for any environmental tax, especially since most or all (marginal) environmental effects, also those related only to the domestic economy, are highly uncertain. Secondly, it is doubtful whether the notoriously uncertain estimates of excess burdens of various taxes in complex real-world economies, hence estimates of effect (3), allow much safer judgements than estimates of environmental effects.

As was shown in the preceding section, the approach now referred to led Goulder and Poterba to classify the abatement costs (2) as 'distortionary', which presupposes that the tax is not corrective – ie, that its environmental effect is zero. To label as 'distortionary' an environmental tax which at, or up to, some (uncertain) level is indeed non-distortionary, is

---

[*] In parts of the literature the expression a 'strong double dividend' has been used for the case where the second dividend exceeds abatement costs (a general-equilibrium 'no regrets' policy). This has not helped to clarify the debate. (As an example, noted above, Parry (1994) seems to refer to this term when stating that only if the environmentally taxed commodity is 'a sufficiently weaker than average substitute for leisure ... could ... the double dividend hypothesis be correct'.) Since the second dividend from an environmental tax as such cannot exceed abatement costs, the term 'strong double dividend' is redundant. As quoted above, it is argued in Goulder (1994b) that 'much of the debate about the second dividend is in terms of whether environmental taxes can be introduced in a way that is costless'. Regardless of whether or not this is a fair characterization of the debate as it is known in the literature in the US as well as elsewhere, an (at least) costless tax would not require any additional, environmental or other reason for its introduction, since such a tax would already be called for by (other) efficiency considerations as part of a tax reform.

liable to cause confusion, at least among those who do not have full command of the theoretical underpinnings of the economics of tax and environmental policy. Given the significant role of terminology for efficient communication, in particular with laymen-economists among policy-makers, it seems important to 'call a spade a spade'. The fact that some aspect – eg, the effect of reduced tax distortions – is uncertain does not make it meaningful to take it to be zero. Similarly, it is hardly meaningful to discuss an *environmental* tax in terms that presuppose that its environmental benefits are zero, on the grounds that these benefits can take an uncertain value from zero and upwards.

D. Do Environmental Taxes Typically Exacerbate Pre-existing Tax Distortions?

To illustrate the concept of the double dividend against the background of what has been said so far, take first the perspective of a partial-equilibrium analysis where the effects of type (3) are assumed to be negligible – eg, supported by a formal assumption that the revenue from an environmental tax is redistributed by lump-sum transfers. Without any environmental policy, emissions are represented by x_m°. The optimal environmental tax – possible to determine once the marginal environmental benefits of reduced emissions (*MB*) are known or, more realistically, 'guesstimated' – is given by t_m' (see Figure 7.1).[*] The first and only dividend here is given by the cross-hatched area.

Now, shifting to a general-equilibrium perspective and using the tax revenue to the extent possible to reduce pre-existing distortionary taxes, the minimum *net* marginal abatement costs (effects (2) and (3)) are also 'guesstimated' to be those shown by the net marginal abatement cost (*MAC*) curve. This curve will eventually hit the gross *MAC* curve, partly because at some point the environmental tax volume will start decreasing. Because of the second dividend, the net *MAC* curve sets out below the gross *MAC* curve. Depending on the magnitude and the sign of the general equilibrium effects when the environmental-tax revenue is now used to replace distortionary taxes, the optimal tax may end up above or below t_m' (as t_m'' or t_m''' in Figures 7.1 and 7.2). With the gross *MAC* curve indicating the reaction of the (competitive) industry producing x_m, the tax levels indicated lead to the second-best optimal output volumes, x_m'' and x_m''', respectively. The double dividend is given by the area between the net *MAC* and the *MB* curves down to the second-best optimal volume, where areas *a* and *b–c* may be identified as the second dividend in the first case and the second case, respectively.

A comment on the main conclusions in Bovenberg and de Mooij (1994) – BdeM – quoted above can be made with reference to our illustrations. As already noted, BdeM use a simple model in which they show that the introduction of an environmental tax raises consumer prices, reduces the real

---

[*] Since we assume, as before, that distortionary taxes are used for financing given public expenditure on public goods, the optimal environmental tax in the second-best optimum need not equal the marginal external effect (= – *MB*). The illustration in Figure 7.1 assumes that the second-best and the first-best environmental taxes coincide.

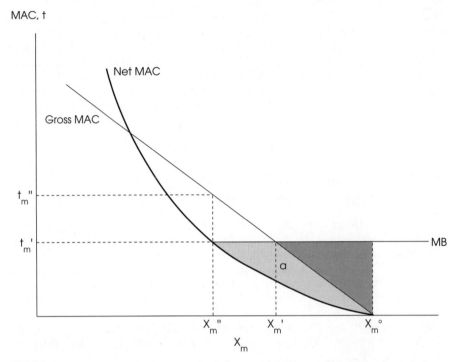

Figure 7.1 *Optimum environmental tax under conditions of imperfect knowledge*

(after-labour-tax) wage even after tax recycling, and hence – with employment as an increasing function of the real wage – reduces the labour-tax base.[*] This also explains why the second-best optimal environmental tax falls below the marginal benefits of emission reductions (a situation which is illustrated in Figure 7.2). As a less reasonable but still possible case, where the effect of the falling real wage on employment is insignificant in the relevant interval (or even positive in the case of a locally backward-bending supply curve), the effect on the labour tax base is at most negligible and the result is changed. Then, the environmental tax definitely yields a net addition to the tax volume and hence additional benefits by allowing a (further) reduction in the distortionary labour tax. At least as long as the environmental-tax revenue increases with the tax rate, the second-best optimal environmental-tax rate would then exceed the marginal externality (a case shown in Figure 7.1).

To make this argument somewhat more precise, assume that labour

---

[*] BdeM state, as a general property of their model, that 'the drop in the real after-tax wage comes about because the *lower* tax rate on labour income does not fully compensate workers for the adverse effect of the pollution levy on their real after-tax wage' (p 1087; italics added). In this connection, it can be questioned whether this statement, even if true for the BdeM model, remains so for more general models. In other words, it can be questioned whether it would remain true for all realistic cases, even in the presence of an upward sloping labour-supply curve, that the lower labour-tax rate from recycling could not in any realistic case compensate for the effect on the real after-tax wage via the increase in consumer prices.

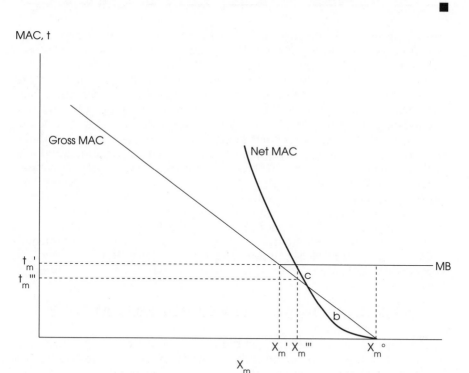

Figure 7.2 *Second-best environmental tax, case 2*

supply is independent of the real after-tax wage in the relevant interval. This means that the income and substitution effects of changes in the wage rate cancel each other out over this real-after-tax-wage interval. With reference to the presentation used by Parry (1994), it should be noted that this is equivalent to assuming that leisure and the commodity-producing environmental effects are independent – ie, they are neither substitutes nor complements. Then, while the environmental tax reduces the real after-tax wage, the tax has no effect on labour-tax revenue. The labour-tax rate (the only pre-existing tax thus far) is now reduced by recycling the environment-tax revenue. Again, the change in the real after-tax wage has no effect on employment. In this case, there is no interdependence between the two tax bases, and the second-best optimal environmental tax is determined by the marginal-environmental effect and the marginal reduction in the excess burden of the labour tax. The crucial question, then, is whether it is generally true, as assumed by Goulder, BdeM and Parry, that the uncompensated wage elasticity of labour supply is (significantly) positive (polluting commodities and leisure are (strong) substitutes) or whether, and to what extent, there are cases where this elasticity is approximately zero (polluting commodities and leisure are approximately independent).

In a more general case than that considered by BdeM, there may exist other taxes, some of which are levied on substitutes to the environmentally taxed commodity. If we were considering a carbon tax, taxes on capital goods could be an example. If so, there would exist other tax bases which grow with the environmental tax rate and which contribute to keeping the net effects on the volume of pre-existing taxes close to zero, even if revenue from the labour tax falls with increases in the environmental tax.

Against this background, we may now question the general validity of BdeM's conclusion that 'environmental taxes *typically exacerbate, rather than alleviate*, pre-existing tax distortions – even if revenues are employed to cut pre-existing distortionary taxes' (italics added). Although it is stated as generally true for their particular model that the excess burden per dollar of labour-tax revenue is increased, it seems less clear that, in general – ie, with any set of pre-existing taxes and/or with a near-zero uncompensated wage elasticity of labour supply – environmental taxes typically exacerbate pre-existing tax distortions with a reduction of the double dividend as a result. Recall, also, the observation made above that, in general – ie, even for the case of net decreases in real after-tax wage rates and hence in employment – the fundamental difference between the two environmental-policy options (direct regulation and taxes) is that it is the latter, in comparison with the former, which yields an extra – second – dividend.

IS A CARBON TAX AN ENVIRONMENTAL TAX?

The option of taxing carbon – ie, the carbon content of fossil fuel – has existed all along, of course, but did not surface except as an instrument for environmental policy purposes. If a carbon tax were found to be potentially second-best efficient on non-environmental grounds, other tax specifications, such as a tax on fossil fuel per cubic metre, or some chemical component in fossil fuel other than the carbon content, might be found equally attractive. Quite likely, the optimal, or 'natural', specification might be the energy content of fossil fuel, which is also widely used in actual tax practice. If, on the other hand, there were environmental reasons for a carbon tax, its double dividend properties would appear attractive, given that its tax base is large and cannot be expected to decrease sharply with increases in the tax rate.

The following question can now be raised: in what sense can a carbon tax, at the present time, be seen as an environmental tax? When asking this question, it should be remembered that the implications of carbon emissions for global warming are highly uncertain, a point highlighted in one of the arguments discussed above. In the presence of the uncertainty of environmental catastrophes – sea-level rise, changes in ocean currents, increased frequency of hurricanes – as a result of such emissions, the UN Framework Convention on Climate Change, as well as an increasing number of governments, have voiced a 'precautionary' motive for reducing the emissions of carbon into the atmosphere. A carbon tax therefore – which would have a significant effect on global emissions only if it were applied internationally – would appear as a specific environmental insurance policy.

Prior to discussing international carbon taxes, let us consider the case of a unilateral carbon tax introduced by a single national government.

Unilateral Carbon Taxes

First, take as one extreme the case of a carbon tax introduced unilaterally in a small country. For simplicity, we may assume here, and in what follows, that any pre-existing taxes on fossil fuels are second-best optimal with respect to *domestic* pollution as well as the distortions of all pre-existing taxes. Thus, the carbon tax under consideration would set out from that level. (For an example, see our earlier reference to the Swedish carbon tax on page 108.) Even if the tax would result in a drastic reduction in carbon emissions in this country, the effect on carbon concentrations in the atmosphere would be insignificant and hence fail to yield any noticeable direct environmental benefits. Thus, there would be no direct environmental benefits similar to those of a tax aimed at correcting for domestic pollution. However, the country is unlikely to introduce this tax (disregarding government tactics in a political environment where voters 'demand' a carbon tax), unless some indirect benefits could be expected to arise from doing so. For example, if by introducing the tax the country wants to demonstrate its willingness to make sacrifices, indirect benefits could eventually emerge should the carbon reductions be implemented by a larger set of countries cooperating for the common good. In fact, a self-interested, welfare-maximizing, national government would introduce a carbon tax for reasons of 'climate change policy' only at a rate that could be motivated on grounds of expected (indirect) environmental benefits from this tax (again reflecting correctly the prevailing second-best conditions, theoretically speaking). If so, the country would also benefit from the double dividend of this *non-distortionary* tax.

It is even more obvious that a large carbon-emitting country, which introduces a carbon tax reflecting the expected (significant) direct benefits of marginal-carbon reductions to this country alone (net of any carbon leakage), could regard its carbon tax as non-distortionary. Such a country would benefit from a potential double dividend, in exactly the same way as it would from an environmental tax, correcting for domestic externalities. In fact, the benefits would be even higher if the country had reason to expect that its carbon tax could influence other countries to take measures to reduce their emissions. If so, and in line with the preceding argument, the optimal tax rate would exceed the rate chosen on account of direct benefits only. If the tax elasticity of carbon emissions in the country remained below one in the relevant range – ie, so that the tax volume would continue to increase with the tax level – then the size of the double dividend would increase also.

International Carbon Tax Agreements

The opposite extreme to a unilateral carbon tax is a carbon tax agreement among all countries in the world. For simplicity, assume (1) that they are all capable of estimating and correctly revealing their expected marginal and total benefits from global carbon reductions, as well as predicting their marginal and total carbon-abatement costs; (2) that the agreement amounts to introducing a globally harmonized domestic carbon tax (in a first-best world) equal to the (vertically) aggregated marginal benefits where they coincide with the (horizontally) aggregated marginal abatement costs; and (3) to begin with, that carbon tax revenue is redistributed everywhere by domestic lump-sum transfers, hence initially disregarding any potential double dividend. For each individual party to the agreement, the harmonized carbon tax now defined, and hence the individual party's marginal-abatement costs, will be above, and probably far above, its marginal benefits from the global carbon reductions. Hence, the individual country would be exposed to a free-rider incentive. However, assuming that the agreement would gradually fall apart, if anyone were to defect, the (long-run) alternative for each party would be that of no carbon reductions at all. Hence, the individual country would be exposed to an incentive to agree to the treaty proposal as long as its benefits from the global emission reductions exceed its costs, and as long as other countries agree. This agreement on optimally harmonized domestic taxes can obviously be regarded as one where each party has committed itself to maintaining a certain tax level in its own country in exchange for (the benefits of) all other parties doing the same in their countries.

We disregard here all the enforcement problems connected with an agreement to harmonize domestic carbon taxes, where individual countries may use other instruments (if they so prefer) to mitigate indirectly the effect of the tax on domestic fossil-fuel use (see Hoel, 1993). The possibility of such obstructions of an international tax agreement tend to work in favour of using other policy instruments, where a potentially efficient alternative would be a system of internationally tradable carbon-emission quotas.

Given the assumptions made, the agreement means that aggregate total benefits exceed aggregate total costs, compared to the case of no agreement. If all countries were identical, and received the same marginal benefits from global carbon reductions, having the same marginal-abatement cost functions, benefits would exceed costs also for each individual country. In that case, the agreement as it is now designed – excluding any international financial transfers – would represent a welfare improvement for all countries and, in that respect, constitute a treaty acceptable to all. However, since countries do differ significantly in a number of ways, international (tax) transfers would most likely be required to attain an internationally acceptable agreement. Given an optimum where aggregate benefits – for an agreement to be worthwhile – significantly exceed aggregate costs, we may assume that there are transfer distributions that could make every country better off and also be accepted by all. More specifically, the individual net-transfer recipient country would require a financial transfer at least large enough to cover its abatement costs, net of its estimated benefits from the global-carbon reductions – and, we may now add, its benefits from using the transfer *plus* the domestic carbon-tax revenue for a reduction in pre-existing distortionary taxes. Similarly, the net-transfer payer country would accept to pay an amount at most equal to these benefits (which include second dividends from domestic carbon-tax revenue *minus* transfers to other countries), net of abatement costs. (It may be noted that agreed tax transfers from a (rich) country may very well exceed the domestic carbon-tax revenue of the country; see Bohm and Larsen, 1994, p 231, for an illustration of this point.)

In the two extreme carbon-tax contexts now discussed – a unilaterally imposed carbon tax and a globally harmonized one – the policy issue for an individual country on the verge of introducing such taxes turns out to be rather similar. Firstly, without an environmental policy reason, there would not be any carbon-tax issue at all. Secondly, given an environmental policy reason and a command-and-control alternative, there is a second dividend of the carbon tax. In both cases, the individual country's benefits from introducing the tax include, if relevant, the benefits obtained from recycling the net additional government revenue from the tax (agreement). Between the two extremes, there could be intermediate cases of (at least temporarily stable) agreements among a limited set of countries.

Assume as before, but now for any given incomplete set of countries, that if a country defects, the others would eventually do the same. Then, again, we end up in a situation similar to the fully global agreement, or to the unilateral case, where the agreement could be taken to have indirect benefits from exerting 'pressure' on free-riders to cooperate at a later stage in addition to direct (non-negative) environmental benefits. This argument could obviously be extended to any carbon-tax treaty proposal accepted by a self-interested and welfare-maximizing country. Just as in the case of an environmental tax introduced on account of a domestic externality, a carbon tax has a potential double dividend, which may be kept by the country itself or, in negotiations, be allowed to dissipate to other countries.

CONCLUSION

Recent contributions to the literature, questioning the capacity of environmental taxes, in particular carbon taxes, to make a reduction in pre-existing tax distortions feasible and hence to provide a 'second dividend', have been reviewed.

First, we have noted that there is always a positive (non-negative) 'second dividend' of an environmental tax, if the revenue of this tax is recycled in the most efficient (welfare-maximizing) way, and the outcome is compared: (a) to lump-sum redistribution of the environmental-tax revenue or (b) to an alternative command-and-control policy (the origin of the double dividend argument, it seems). This essentially restates 'conventional wisdom' that there exists a double dividend of environmental taxes.

Secondly, claims that the introduction of an efficient revenue-neutral environmental tax in some real-world cases could make the environmental tax costless, in the sense that the value of reduced tax distortions exceeds the costs of pollution abatement, were found to be incorrect except for the special case where, for some political reason, a tax reform could and would be carried out only in connection with the introduction of this tax. Otherwise, and more generally, such a costless outcome, when feasible, would be the result of two separate undertakings: a tax reform and the introduction of the *environmental* tax. By definition, the introduction of an environmental tax has a second dividend that falls short of abatement costs.

Thirdly, statements in the literature that an environmental tax is 'distortionary' were found to be incorrect or to imply a redefinition of this term as commonly understood. Such statements have been made in analyses that are limited to the general-equilibrium *costs* of the environmental improvements of a revenue-neutral environmental tax, on the grounds that the marginal-environmental effects – ie, the benefits – are uncertain. Uncertainty, which characterizes the cost estimates as well, in particular the estimate of the second dividend, means 'only' that the optimal (non-distortionary) environmental tax rate is uncertain. The environmental effect cannot be set to zero without eliminating the basis for analysing the tax as an environmental tax.

Fourthly, statements to the effect that 'environmental taxes typically exacerbate, rather than alleviate, pre-existing tax distortions' (Bovenberg and de Mooij, 1994) are found to be wanting in the absence of investigations of the extent to which different pre-existing tax bases and proposed environmental tax bases are independent, substitutes or complements. Moreover, from the perspective in which the double dividend argument originated – comparing environmental taxes and command-and-control – the latter option may well exacerbate (or diminish) pre-existing tax distortions. Specifically, as we have pointed out, the relevant consumer-price index, which is the vehicle for transferring the policy effect on to the labour-tax base, is likely to be influenced to a similar extent in both cases. If the extent is identical, the second dividend of the environmental tax replacing the alternative regulatory instrument is altogether unaffected by this argument.

These conclusions reconfirm earlier statements in the literature that the dividend from recycling environmental taxes are potentially important, in some cases possibly to the extent of making second-best optimal environmental taxes exceed marginal-environmental effects. While the revenue recycled may be small for many existing or proposed environmental taxes, it could be considerable for the case of a carbon tax – ie, a tax on the carbon content of fossil fuel.

Carbon taxes, which have been proposed only as an instrument for environmental policy, were found to be analytically identical to environmental taxes related to domestic environmental problems, even under the existing extreme uncertainty concerning the implications of carbon emissions. It was shown that, regardless of whether domestic carbon taxes today are imposed unilaterally or as a result of international agreements, such taxes cannot be regarded as distortionary in any conventional sense of the term. While second dividends arise here as well, it was noted that national carbon-tax revenues may be redistributed among countries in order to make international agreements possible, hence redistributing the capacity to reduce tax distortions among the participating countries.

Our discussion has explicitly concerned environmental taxes, but is equally valid for their substitute, next-of-kin, economic-incentive instrument, tradable emission permits. The reason is that such permits can be auctioned off so as to yield the same amount of government revenue, if the two options are designed to produce, in principle, the same effects on emissions and the same distributive implications for the tax-liable/permit-liable parties. Specifically this means that: (a) a domestic carbon tax without compensatory payments should be compared to government auctioning of all carbon permits – a likely design of the two options, at least in the very long run – and (b) a system of (temporarily) 'grandfathered' permits – eg, at the fossil-fuel wholesale level – should be compared to a carbon tax, the revenue of which is (temporarily) redistributed to those whom the policy-maker would want to shelter by grandfathering, and so on, for intermediate cases. Thus, the two comparable options provide, in principle, the same government revenue and hence, the same potential double dividend.

REFERENCES

Arrow, K (1970) 'Political and economic evaluation of social effects and Externalities', in Margolis, T (ed) *The Analysis of Public Output*, NBER, Columbia University Press, New York

Ballard, C, Shoven, J and Whalley, J (1985) 'General equilibrium computations of the marginal welfare costs of taxes in the United States', *American Economic Review*, 75, pp 128–38

Bohm, P (1994) 'Environment and taxation: the case of Sweden', in OECD *Environment and Taxation: The Cases of The Netherlands, Sweden and the United States*, OECD Documents, OECD, Paris

Bohm, P and Larsen, B (1994) 'Fairness in a Tradable-Permit Treaty for Carbon emissions reductions in Europe and the Former Soviet Union', *Environmental & Resource Economics*, 4, pp 219–39

Bohm, P and Russell, C (1985) 'Comparative analysis of alternative policy instruments', in Kneese, A V and Sweeney, J C (eds) *Handbook of Natural Resources and Energy Economics*, Vol I, North Holland, Amsterdam, pp 395–460

Bovenberg, L and Goulder, L (1994) *Costs of environmentally motivated taxes in the presence of other taxes: general equilibrium analyses*, Working Paper, Fondazione ENI Enrico Mattei, Milano

Bovenberg, L and de Mooij, R (1994) 'Environmental levies and distortionary taxation', *American Economic Review*, Vol 84, No 4, pp 1085–89

Goulder, L (1994a) 'Effects of carbon taxes in an economy with prior tax distortions: an intertemporal general equilibrium analysis', mimeo, Department of Economics, Stanford University, Palo Alto, California

Goulder, L (1994b) 'Environmental taxation and the "double dividend": a reader's guide'. Paper presented at the International Institute of Public Finance 50th Congress, Cambridge, Massachusetts, also NBER Working Paper, No 4896, Washington, DC

Hahn, R (1989) 'Economic prescriptions for environmental problems: how the patient followed the doctor's orders', *Journal of Economic Perspectives*, Vol 3, No 2, pp 95–104

Hoel, M (1993) 'Harmonization of carbon taxes in international climate agreements', *Environmental & Resource Economics*, 3, pp 221–31

Lee, D and Misiolek, W (1986) 'Substituting pollution taxation for general taxation: some implications for efficiency in pollution taxation', *Journal of Environmental Economics and Management*, 13, pp 338–47

Oates, W (1993) 'Pollution charges as a source of public revenue', in Giersch, H (ed) *Economic Progress and Environmental Concerns*, Berlin

Parry, I (1994) 'Pollution taxes and revenue recycling', *Journal of Environmental Economics and Management*, Vol 29, No 3, pp 64–77

Pearce, D (1991) 'The role of carbon taxes in adjusting to global warming', *Economic Journal*, 101, pp 938–48

Poterba, J (1991) 'Tax policy to combat global warming: on designing a carbon tax', in Dornbusch, R and Poterba, J (eds) *Global Warming: Economic Policy Responses*, MIT Press, Cambridge, Massachusetts, pp 71–97

Poterba, J (1993) 'Global warming policy: a public finance perspective', *Journal of Economic Perspectives*, Vol 7, No 4, pp 47–63

Proost, S and van Regemorter, D (1995) 'The double dividend and the role of inequality aversion and macroeconomic regimes', *International Tax and Public Finance*, 2, pp 205–17

Sandmo, A (1975) 'Optimal taxation in the presence of externalities', *Swedish Journal of Economics*, Vol 77, No 1, pp 86–98

Shackleton, R, Shelby, M, Christofaro, A, Brinner, R, Yanchar, J, Goulder, L, Jorgenson, D, Wilcoxen, P, Pauly, R and Kaufman, R (1992) 'The Efficiency Value of Carbon Tax Revenues', draft, US Environmental Protection Agency, Washington, DC

Whalley, J and Wigle, R (1991) 'The international incidence of carbon taxes', in Dornbusch, R and Poterba, J (eds) *Global Warming: Economic Policy Responses*, MIT Press, Cambridge, Massachusetts, pp 233–63

C h a p t e r   8

ON THE DIVIDENDS FROM ENVIRONMENTAL TAXATION

Paul Ekins

INSIGHTS FROM THEORY

The Environmental Dividend

It is generally agreed among economists that, in a situation where the production or consumption of some good results in a negative external effect – ie, one that is not reflected in the price of the good in question – then social welfare can be improved by imposing a tax on the good.

The theoretical case is most easily represented diagrammatically, as in Figure 8.1 (following Pearce and Turner 1990, p 86), in which the output of a good Q is associated with damaging pollution, P, which imposes a marginal external cost given by the MEC curve. The producer of the good derives a marginal net private benefit from production given by the MNPB curve. The figure is stylized in the sense that it assumes that the curves can be measured and remain stable as prices and outputs change, which may not be the case in practice, but they illustrate the basic theoretical position.

Without intervention the producer will produce at Q_1, P_1. However, this is clearly not socially optimal, because beyond Q^* all output incurs a net social cost. At Q_1 the total net cost of production beyond Q^* is given by the triangle *abc*. Conversely, the triangle *abc* becomes the benefit gained – the environmental dividend – of reducing output and pollution to Q^*, P^*. A tax, t^*, levied on the producer's output, such that t^* is equal to the MEC and MNPB at the point they intersect, will reduce the producer's net benefit to

Marginal costs/benefits

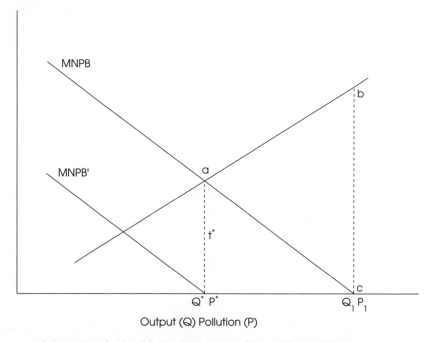

Output (Q) Pollution (P)

Figure 8.1 *Optimal best environmental tax with no abatement*

MNPB', giving the producer the incentive to reduce output to its optimal level, so that social welfare is maximized.

However, it is not the output *per se* that is responsible for the environmental damage, but the pollution associated with it, so that it is really the pollution which should be taxed. Of course, given the pollution/output relationship, a tax on output acts as a tax on pollution. But if the tax is levied directly on pollution – eg, through an emissions tax – then the producer has the opportunity of reducing pollution by abating it directly, rather than by reducing output. How much abatement will be undertaken depends on the marginal abatement cost (MAC) of reducing pollution below P_1.

In Figures 8.2a and b, three possible MAC curves are shown – MAC_1, MAC_2 and MAC_3. MAC_1 lies everywhere above MNPB. No abatement will take place. Given an optimal tax on pollution, t^*, pollution will be reduced only by reducing output, as in Figure 8.1, to reach the optimal pollution level P^*. MAC_2 lies partly above, and partly below, MNPB. Again, following Pearce & Turner (p 90), pollution reduction will take place along the arrowed line, through abatement up to P_2 (where MAC_2 lies below MNPB), and then through output reduction (where MAC_2 lies above MNPB). Where the environmental damage is given by MEC_1 optimal pollution will be P_2^*, achieved by a tax t_2^* through abatement only. Where the damage is higher, say MEC_2, optimal pollution will be $P_2^{*\prime}$, achieved by a tax $t_2^{\prime}$ through a combination of abatement and output reduction. With the tax t_2^*, the producer's MNPB will fall to $MNPB_2$; with the tax $t_2^{*\prime}$, it will fall to $MNPB_2^{\prime}$.

In Figure 8.2b, MAC_3 lies wholly below MNPB, so that pollution reduction will be only through abatement. Here the optimal polution is P_3^*, achieved by tax t_3^*, reducing the MNPB (per unit of pollution) to $MNPB_3$.

In Figure 8.1, the cost of the pollution reduction in terms of lost output is $Q_1 - Q^*$. In Figures 8.2a and b, with abatement curves MAC_2, MAC_3, the possibility of abatement at lower cost than output reduction means that the same pollution reduction as in Figure 8.1 can be achieved at lower cost. Thus it can be seen in Figures 8.2a and b that the lower the cost of abatement, the lower the level of pollution ($P_3^*<P_2^*<P^*$) that can be achieved with a lower tax ($t_3^*<t_2^*<t^*$).

Yet even this is only a partial equilibrium result. Several other effects can be identified which make the overall macroeconomic effect much more difficult to compute. First, the output of pollution abatement companies will have increased. Secondly, the price of the abating firm's output may have increased, with further knock-on effects through the economy. Thirdly, in response to any increase in the price of the abating firm's output, substitution towards other products will take place. Fourthly, it may be that the productivity of people or other firms will have increased owing to the reduction in pollution. Fifthly, it may be that the rise in the price of the use of the environmental resource will hasten the depreciation of the capital equipment affected; on the other hand, it may be that the shift in relative

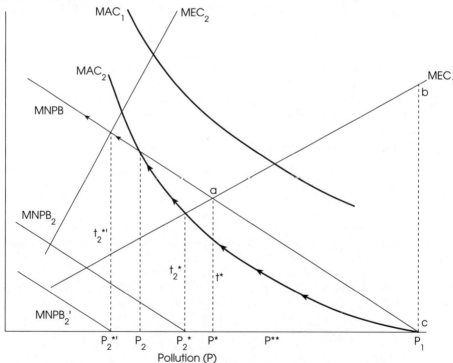

Figure 8.2a *Optimal environmental taxation with abatement*

Marginal costs/benefits

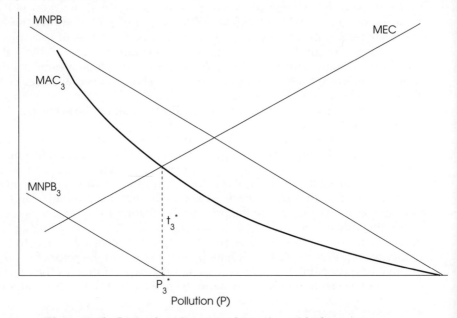

Figure 8.2b *Optimal environmental taxation with abatement*

prices will stimulate research, innovation and investment with a view to economizing on the resource, which may be economically beneficial. Sixthly, the tax will yield revenue, which will allow other taxes to be reduced, with yet more knock-on effects through the economy. Assessing the overall costs of pollution abatement even in this simple case is therefore no simple matter. The last point is revisited in some detail below.

Risk and Distribution

Making the theory of environmental taxation operational depends on being able to determine the MEC curve – ie, the damage inflicted by an additional unit of pollution, not just at current or experienced levels of pollution, but at all feasible levels. This is a daunting task, even for pollutants whose effects are relatively simple, local and can be clearly identified. For more complex, transboundary or global environmental effects, or where the pollutants have synergistic effects – the combined effect is larger than the sum of the individual effects – the task becomes so difficult that often only order-of-magnitude estimates, if any, are possible. Even these estimates, however, may need to be modified substantially for the purpose of arriving at the optimal tax in situations where there is substantial but uncertain risk, and to take account of distributional questions.

Both these issues are well illustrated in the case of the economics of global warming. It is universally acknowledged that the risk of climate change from the accumulation of greenhouse gases in the atmosphere

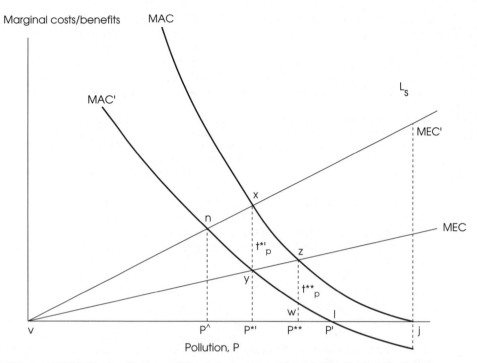

Figure 8.3 *Optimal pollution, taking into account risk and distributional effects*

carries with it a non-negligible risk of major, irreversible ecological and human disruption. It is clear that the position of the MEC line needs to take account of this risk. Where MEC is a 'best estimate' of external damage, the risk is equally distributed about this estimate, and where decision-makers on behalf of society are indifferent to risk, the position of the MEC curve does not need to be changed. However, where the risk of greater costs than the best estimate is greater than the risk of lesser costs, or where society is risk averse (a likely situation, perhaps, when confronted with potentially major disruptions), the effect will be to adjust the MEC curve upwards to, say, MEC' in Figure 8.3, thereby justifying more pollution abatement (to P'') and a higher tax ($t^{*''}_p$) to achieve this. The extra net abatement costs over the initial valuation of MEC (amounting to the triangle *xyz*) can be regarded as an insurance payment in case the expected damage given by MEC is under-estimated.

The incorporation of risk aversion into a benefit-cost analysis in this way can make a substantial difference to its outcome. In Cline's study of global warming, the application of risk-aversion weights of 0.125 to his low damage estimate, 0.5 to his central estimate and 0.375 to his high damage estimate converts the central estimate's benefit-cost ratio of 0.74, with no adjustment for risk, to a ratio of 1.26, thus economically justifying a programme of 'aggressive abatement action' (Cline, 1992, p 300).

Of course, risk aversion is only one consideration in the treatment of the huge uncertainties that characterize global warming, the attendant risks of which Chichilnisky and Heal (1993, p 67) describe as 'poorly understood, endogenous, collective and irreversible'. They stress the possible importance of the option value of controlling emissions given the irreversibilities attendant on climate change, pointing out that the analyses of both Cline (1992) and Manne and Richels (1992) fail to consider option values and consequently may underestimate the benefits of mitigating climate change:

> As the value of an option generally increases with increasing uncertainty about the future, and as uncertainty looms large in any projections regarding global warming, the extent of the underestimate could be important. It could, for example, be decisive in the endorsement of a global carbon tax.
> (*Chichilnisky and Heal, 1993, p 81*)

More generally, Nordhaus (1994, p 188) concurs as to the importance of uncertainty to the calculation in his model of an optimal carbon tax: 'Roughly speaking, the optimal carbon tax doubles when uncertainty is taken into account, and the optimal control rate increases by slightly less than half.'

The other important issue with regard to the position of the MEC curve is the weight attached to distributional questions. The *intergenerational* issues will be dealt with directly through the discount rate that is chosen. In general, the lower the discount rate that is applied, when costs are predominantly in the distant future, the higher will be the MEC curve. This, too, can make a substantial difference to the calculated optimum. Again, the effect of varying this parameter is shown in Cline's work, with regard to the different benefit-cost ratios obtained for his programme of 'aggressive abatement action'. With high damage assumptions, this ratio is 2.60 for a discount rate of 1.5 per cent, 1.09 for a discount rate of 3 per cent, and 0.56 for a discount rate of 5 per cent.

The *intragenerational* distributional issue can be illustrated by further reference to Figure 8.3. It will be seen that even at P^{**}, the position of optimum pollution given MEC, an external cost equivalent to the triangle *vzw* will be borne by the victims of the pollution. In the case of global warming, there is ample evidence (some of which is surveyed in Ekins, 1995) that the physical impacts from global warming will bear most heavily on people in the South, while the benefits from burning fossil fuels, the largest contributor to global warming, have largely gone to the North. In such a situation considerations of equity may suggest that a larger weight should be given to the costs than to the benefits.

In fact, this issue is normally ignored in damage cost calculations – that is to say, no extra weight is given to damage suffered by low greenhouse gas (GHG) emitters than to that suffered by high GHG emitters. Rather a negative weight is often implied, because high GHG emitters, being richer, have a higher willingness to pay to avoid damage, so the damage incident on them is valued more highly than the greater damage incident on poorer, low GHG emitters. If this was changed so that the damages facing low GHG emitters were given higher weight, this would also have the effect of shifting the MEC curve upwards, say to MEC' in Figure 8.3, again yielding a new optimum tax rate $t^{*'}_p$ ($>t^{**}_p$), and lower pollution, $P^{*'}$. In effect, the abatement benefit *kzm* would have been revalued at the higher level *k'xm*.

The conclusion of this analysis is that the position of the MEC curve in Figure 8.3, and hence the efficient position of economic activity, is powerfully dependent on considerations of uncertainty, risk, distribution and equity. This in turn affects both the level of the optimal pollution and the size of the environmental dividend from reducing pollution to this optimum. In general, the greater the pollution reduction, the greater the environmental dividend.

The cost of achieving the environmental dividend is the loss of real economic output incurred. Given that the environmental improvement can be envisaged as being brought about through the diversion of economic resources from producing marketed goods or services, to the production of unmarketed environmental goods or services, a loss of marketed output is to be expected. However, there exist several possibilities where this cost may be mitigated or even avoided.

One of these possibilities relates to the existence of technological potential or of technological capability that is underused, where 'underused' means that currently there exist unimplemented technological means to reduce CO_2 emissions through the conservation or more efficient use of energy, which are economically viable at current energy prices. This begs the question, of course, as to why these means are unimplemented. One possible response is that the institutional, or other, difficulties of implementation, left out of consideration in the purely technical analysis, are such that they impose costs that actually make these means uneconomic. On the other hand, some analysts have suggested that there are market failures preventing the implementation of some cost-efficient, energy-conservation measures (eg, Lovins and Lovins, 1991; Jackson and Jacobs, 1991; Jackson, 1995), with the implication that these failures could be remedied without removing the cost efficiency of the measures. Detailed review of this issue is outside the scope of this paper, but it may be noted that, after conducting such a review, Cline (1992, p 227) decided that a reasonable estimate was that the first 22 per cent of carbon emissions from his projected baseline could be cut back at zero cost. The possibility of such costless cuts could be illustrated in Figure 8.3 by an MAC curve such as MAC', which lies below MAC, and cuts the horizontal axis at the point corresponding to the costless reduction (P') and continues into the region of negative costs of abatement. This results, of course, in a lower optimal level of pollution ($P^{\wedge} < P^{**}$) and a higher environmental dividend ($k'nlm$) from abatement, where MEC' is the relevant external cost curve. (The triangle lmj represents an efficiency dividend arising from removing market failures and implementing negative-cost energy-efficiency measures.)

The environmental dividend arises solely from the benefits of reducing negative externalities, although its value depends, as has been seen, both on the valuation given to the externality and to the marginal cost of abating it. However, where abatement is effected through the imposition of a tax, the tax will raise revenues. These revenues can be rebated in some way, either directly or through the reduction of other taxes. If this can be done in such a way as to yield economic benefit, quite apart from the environmental benefit just discussed, then it may be said that there is a 'revenue-recycling' dividend from the tax, in addition to the environmental dividend. We now investigate the possibility of such a second dividend.

The Revenue-Recycling Dividends

A revenue-recycling dividend is here defined as an economic (and non-environmental) benefit resulting from the revenue-neutral imposition of a tax – ie, all the revenue from the tax is returned to taxpayers by cuts in other taxes or lump-sum rebates, rather than saved or spent by the government. Such a dividend can arise if the tax-plus-rebate (TPR) improves economic distribution (a distributional dividend), reduces involuntary unemployment (an employment dividend) or increases economic efficiency (thereby increasing output: an efficiency dividend).

It may be noted immediately that the possibilities for all these dividends depend on the economy being in a non-optimal state to start with. The existing tax structure must be non-optimal in some sense – for instance, because the tax base is related to employment – or there must be existing deficiencies in distribution and market failures in the labour and other markets. Any perception or assumption that the initial condition of the economy is characterized by perfectly competitive markets operating in equilibrium, with taxes imposed on a per-capita basis (a common enough assumption in, for example, general equilibrium modelling of such measures as a carbon tax), will *a priori* rule out the existence or possible achievement of such dividends (except for those related to improvements in distribution). However, with a less ideal, initial economic configuration, the existence of such dividends cannot be ruled out, and they will be investigated in turn.

The Distributional Dividend

There have been a number of proposals (reviewed in Atkins and Wilson, 1984) for TPR measures, in order to achieve distributional goals with less disruption than the alternatives entailed. They mainly concern the distribution of scarce goods that are also regarded as basic needs – food and housing – at times when the supply of the goods is particularly constrained. The TPR measure essentially involves a tax on the good in question, which increases its price and constrains the demand for it, accompanied by a distribution of the tax revenues that relatively favours a needy group; they can then afford to purchase more of the good than they could have done without the tax.

The advantage of such a measure is that it permits the market to operate in its normal way, while effectively rationing the good in question so that everyone can afford basic access to it, without being forced to consume it against their preferences (as happens with non-transferable ration coupons). Obviously, the perceived distributional benefit would have to be high enough to justify the administrative costs of the scheme.

The proposals for explicitly distributional TPR schemes came shortly after World War II, when the supply of specific goods to satisfy basic needs was constrained. As supplies have increased, the need to reduce demand for the goods has decreased or vanished, so that redistribution is now normally carried out through general taxation or the granting of entitlements to specific goods (for example, food stamps).

Perhaps more relevant in the context of the current discussion of environmental taxation is the possibility that environmental taxes, where they fall proportionately more heavily on the poor than on the rich, will cause a distributional disbenefit (effectively a negative-distributional dividend). Again, detailed discussion of this issue is outside the scope of this paper, but there is some evidence that a carbon tax, for example, could bear disproportionately on low-income households (Pearson and Smith, 1991). There is also evidence that it does not need to do so (Barker and Johnstone, 1993). The overall desirability of an environmental tax, as well as its likely political and ethical acceptability, depends on regressive effects being avoided. These points are developed more fully in the chapter that follows.

The Employment Dividend

Involuntary unemployment is a condition in which people who want to become employed cannot find a job at a wage which they are willing to accept. Because it is perceived that, if their asking wage were low enough, they would be able to find a job, unemployed people are thence assumed to have a 'reservation wage', set by the Social Security system or their perceptions of what is fair or worthwhile, below which they are not prepared to take a job.

Figure 8.4 shows (again in a stylized way, with assumptions about the stability, measurement and existence of the curves shown) how the existence of a reservation wage, R, leads to unemployment, where L_s and L_d are respectively the curves of labour supply and labour demand. At R L_1 people want to work, but firms only wish to employ L_2 people. Unemployment of $(L_1 - L_2)$ is the result. If wages were to fall to w^*, then the labour market would clear, with resulting employment at L^*.

Wages

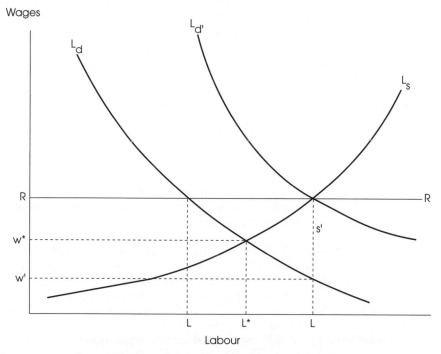

Labour

Figure 8.4 *The effect of wage subsidies on employment*

Now consider a situation in which there are no taxes on labour and firms are subject to an environmental tax, all the revenues from which are returned to them in the form of a labour subsidy (the more realistic equivalent case of a cut in non-wage labour taxes is discussed later). In aggregate, and ignoring adjustment and administration costs, firms would not experience net costs, by definition. Firms that are more than averagely environmentally intensive and less than averagely labour intensive would be net losers, while more labour intensive and less environmentally intensive firms would be net gainers. There should be no change in the overall price level. Because of the labour subsidy, all employers would experience an outward shift in their labour demand curve, as it becomes cheaper to employ people. If the subsidy was s', the L_d curve would shift to L_d'. If the reservation wage and labour-supply curve did not shift, employment would rise to L_1 and unemployment would disappear. This has occurred as a result of employers being prepared to pay the reservation wage R, because it is only actually costing them w', the difference s' being covered by the labour subsidy.

If it is not practical to focus the wage subsidy only on those parts of the labour market that are subject to the imperfection of a reservation wage, then the subsidy will still result in an outward shift in labour demand and employment will increase. The extra employment, however, will be at least partly the result of increased labour supply rather than reduced unemployment.

Returning to the situation with a reservation wage, the crucial question is whether – with a wage subsidy R and L_s would remain unchanged. Although the environmental tax would raise firms' costs, the lower labour costs would lower them. Overall there should be no increase in the price level; no increase in either the reservation wage or other wages would be justified, therefore, on inflationary grounds.

However, if nominal wages were to rise to absorb the subsidy, the result would be quite different. Firms' labour-demand curves would not shift outwards, because their labour costs would not change. There might be some initial movement up the L_s curve as workers initially perceive their returns from labour to have increased, but there would be general inflation as labour costs fail to fall to balance the rise in prices due to the environmental tax, and the labour supply would reduce if it became clear that inflation was eroding the value of the nominal wage increase. However, to the extent that the environmental tax may be passed on by firms in their prices to non-employed consumers, there would be a redistribution of income from the non-employed to wage-earners, and to this extent real wages and labour supply would rise, *increasing* unemployment (because L_d is unchanged).

If R remained nominally the same, then in real terms the increase in the price level would have caused it to fall, and some increase in employment might result. However, it is more likely that nominal R would rise with the price level, leaving real R the same. Moreover, the price increase would feed through into further wage rises and adverse competitiveness effects, leading to general macroeconomic deterioration.

Whether the wage subsidy increased nominal wages or not, there would be a further tendency to increase employment. Relative to labour, the price to firms of the taxed environmental input would increase, and this effect would be the greater where wages did not increase and firms' labour costs fell to w'. This would cause firms seeking to substitute other inputs, including labour, for the taxed environmental input. Moreover, the price of output which embodied the taxed environmental input would rise relative to that which did not (even if the aggregate price level remained unchanged). In so far as firms' labour costs fall because of the wage subsidy, the price of labour-intensive output would tend to fall relative to other output. All these shifts in relative prices would increase the demand for labour, tending to increase employment and reduce unemployment.

The shift in relative prices would also alter the productivity of the affected capital stock and, perhaps, hasten its depreciation. This adjustment effect could be minimized by introducing the taxation in a gradual, pre-announced way, so that the new relative prices are anticipated and allowed for in investment schedules. But in any case, where the environmental tax reflects an externality, it must be stressed that the adjustment to the new relative prices, and the resulting shift in resource allocation, should *not* be regarded as a 'distortion' due to the tax, but as a desirable adjustment to a higher level of allocative efficiency, where a distortion is removed through the externality's internalization. As Pearce (1991, p 940) has emphasized: 'While most taxes distort incentives, an environmental tax corrects a distortion, namely the externalities arising from the excessive use of environmental services.'

To summarize the employment dividend, the key question which determines the extent to which this dividend would arise is whether or not the wage subsidy results in higher wages. If it does, then the implications for employment are ambiguous: negative because of inflation and macroeconomic deterioration; and positive through the substitution effects in both production and consumption.

If the wage subsidy does not result in higher wages, then employment would unambiguously increase, through both the substitution effects and firms' falling labour costs. Although the higher employment would probably mean that overall labour productivity in the economy was lower, it is also likely that output would increase somewhat. Reaping an employment dividend would result in an efficiency dividend, as well. It is important to recognise that these dividends are not due to reducing distortions arising from the existing tax system (which will be discussed in the next section) but from removing the labour-market imperfection caused by the reservation wage, as illustrated in Figure 8.4, and increasing the employment of resources (in this case labour) in the economy. To achieve these dividends, and to reduce unemployment, perhaps substantially, it is only necessary that social dialogue and economic understanding should prevent wage demands from absorbing the labour subsidy from the tax-plus-rebate. Achieving such a dialogue and understanding must be the first political priority in the introduction of such a measure.

The Efficiency Dividend

Where the existence of a (negative) externality means that the marginal cost of the responsible activity exceeds the marginal benefit, then that activity is underpriced. This is the rationale for environmental taxation, as has been seen. But the underpricing of something in one market affects other markets, as well as its own. The income effect of the underpricing will cause all other goods to be overconsumed compared to the undistorted case. The sign of the substitution effect will differ depending on whether the other goods are substitutes (less will be consumed) or complements (more will be consumed). The environmental tax will not only remove the distortion in the market causing the externality (the environmental dividend); it will also cause the other markets to adjust. Whether these other adjustments are viewed as part of the move towards internalization and environmental optimality, or as distortions due to the environmental tax, makes a crucial difference on whether the environmental tax is perceived to be able to deliver an efficiency dividend or not.

An efficiency dividend from environmental taxation is here defined as an improvement in non-environmental economic welfare because of an increase in output, caused by a reallocation of resources, that is consequent on the imposition of an environmental tax. Such a dividend may be yielded by an increase in employment, here called an employment dividend, brought about by an environmental tax. But there are a number of other possible sources.

The possibility of an efficiency dividend associated with an employment dividend arose only because the labour market was distorted by the existence of a reservation wage. In general, the possibility of an efficiency dividend exists only where there is such a market distortion – ie, an allocation of resources that results in lower-than-potential economic output, prior to the imposition of the environmental tax.

That taxation (apart from impractical lump-sum or poll taxes or taxes internalizing externalities) leads to distortions in the economy, is generally and uncontroversially accepted. According to the static perfect-competition model, distortions arise from the taxes that change the prices facing both producers and consumers, so that factors no longer receive their marginal product and the cost of output does not reflect its true economic cost. Where the tax falls on labour, whether directly as a labour tax or indirectly as an expenditure tax which reduces the real value of the wage, it introduces a wedge between what the producer pays for labour and what the employee either gets or is able to purchase. Either labour demand, or labour supply, or both are lower as a result, and so are employment and output (it may be that unemployment is not higher, because this is the difference between labour supply and demand at a given wage).

Figures from the US suggest that distortions from taxation are substantial. Thus Ballard *et al*, (1985, p 128) calculate the marginal excess burden (MEB) of taxation in the US to be in the range of 17–56 cents per dollar of extra revenue. Jorgenson and Yun (1990, p 207) find that the MEB of the US tax system as a whole, even after the tax reform of 1986, which was widely held to have reduced the excess burden, is 38 cents per dollar of revenue raised. Some components of the tax system had far higher costs – for example, the MEB for individual capital taxes was 95 cents per dollar. Jorgenson and Yun (1990, p 6) acknowledge that their MEB estimates 'are considerably higher than previous estimates. This can be attributed primarily to the greater precision we employ in representing the US tax structure'. Nordhaus (1991a, p 316) notes that 'some have estimated (the marginal deadweight loss of taxes in the US) as high as $0.50 per $1.00 of revenue'.

While there are no comparable figures for Europe, EC 1994 (p 145) makes the point:

> Marginal costs of taxation increase more than proportionally with the level of taxation. In view of the much higher share of tax revenues in the Community than in the USA (the tax burden in the Community is nearly 50 per cent higher than in the USA and Japan) it would appear that the costs of fiscal systems in terms of foregone GDP and hence employment might be particularly high in the Community. Only if the structure of the Community's fiscal system were much more efficient than in the USA, would this not hold true.

In the absence of grounds for believing European tax systems to be more efficient than that of the US, it seems likely that the distortions from taxation in Europe are at least as great as those in the USA.

The key question, then, becomes whether the substitution of an environmental tax for a distortionary tax can reduce the distortions from the tax system as a whole and lead to an efficiency dividend. The focus here will be on substituting an environmental tax for a labour tax of two kinds: an income tax on employees and a Social Security tax levied on employers. Initially, the analysis will not consider so-called erosion and interdependency effects, but then will come on to do so.

Substituting for a personal income tax

Two immediate first-round effects of substituting an environmental tax for a personal income tax will arise:

S1. The environmental tax will raise the price of the affected items; the reduction in income tax will increase the disposable income of employees. In so far as the higher prices are paid by non-employees (unemployed, pensioners, other non-employed, foreigners) and income-tax rebates are received by employees, the substitution will raise the real wage. This will increase the labour supply.

S2. The price increases will be concentrated in the goods or activities subject to the tax. Where the tax falls on inputs, producers will tend to substitute away from the taxed input. Where it falls on final demand, consumers will shift demand away from the affected sectors to others that are relatively less environmentally intensive and so less affected by the tax. It is, of course, the intention of the tax to bring about this substitution by both producers and consumers, and it will occur irrespective of how the revenue from the tax is recycled.

In so far as there is an inverse correlation between labour-intensity and environment-intensity, the demand for labour-intensive goods and services will increase. Barker (1994, pp 20–1) has shown that such a correlation exists for the production and industrial use of energy (energy-intensive industries tend to use relatively little labour, labour-intensive industries tend to use relatively little energy). A revenue-neutral energy tax would therefore be expected to increase labour demand.

The increase in labour demand will either reduce unemployment (if it exists) or put to work the increased labour supply induced in S1. Either way, employment and output would increase, yielding both an employment and an efficiency dividend. The increased employment and output would result in second-round macroeconomic improvements (lower benefits, higher tax revenues, so lower tax rates, etc). The only way these positive benefits would fail to materialize would be if S2's increase in labour demand was far stronger that S1's increase in labour supply in the context of a tight labour market. The increased labour demand would then engender wage inflation with generally negative effects on employment and output.

The effect S1 comes about as a result of a reduced a distortion in the labour market (employees' disposable income moves closer to their marginal product as paid by their employers), through the simultaneous reduction or removal of a distortion in the market of the taxed good (an externality has been wholly or partially internalized). It is important to recognize that the labour-market distortion has *not* been reduced through the introduction of another distortion, but through the reduction or removal of one. However, even so, it is possible that, through interdependencies in the tax system, or the erosion of the environmental tax base, the reduction of the environmental distortion in the context of a labour market with pre-existing labour taxes could lead to *more* labour-market distortion rather than less. This possibility has been addressed in a number of recent papers (eg, Bovenberg and de Mooij, 1994; Goulder, 1994a, b; Parry, 1994) and is discussed below.

Substituting for an employers' Social Security tax (SST)
Consider an average firm using energy E_1 and employing labour L_1, which is subject to a SST of t_L. The firm pays tax of $L_1 t_L$.

Now let a tax t_E be imposed on energy, with full compensation by way of reduction in SST. Then, *initially*, the firm will pay energy tax of $E_1 t_E$, with a reduction in its SST to:

$$t_L - (t_E E_1)/L_1.$$

Now, with energy relatively more expensive and labour relatively cheaper, the firm changes its proportion of inputs, say to L_2 ($>L_1$) and E_2 ($<E_1$). The tax paid on energy use is now $t_E E_2$. Let the new tax rate on labour, t_L', be set so that the total tax paid by the firm is unchanged, so:

$$t_L L_1 = t_L' L_2 \qquad + t_E E_2$$

$$\rightarrow \quad t_L' = t_L(L_1/L_2) - t_E E_2/L_2 \quad (1)$$

$$\rightarrow \quad t_L' < t_L$$

The first term on the right hand side (RHS) of equation 1 can be thought of as the result of the substitution effect. The firm's tax rate on labour will be reduced in proportion to its increased employment. The second term is the revenue effect of the energy tax, further reducing the effective tax rate on labour.

The reduction in the effective tax rate on labour will reduce the overall marginal cost of labour to the firm, as long as the wage paid to labour is unchanged. If this is so, then the greater is the fall from t_L to t_L', and the greater is the fall in labour's marginal cost to the firm.

This situation is analogous to that analysed earlier using Figure 8.4. In this case, instead of s' being a wage subsidy, it is a reduction in the employers' SST, which has the same effect of reducing the marginal cost of labour and thereby increasing labour demand.

As in the earlier case, if all the SST decrease is passed through to employees as an increase in wages, then evidently the marginal cost of labour to employers will not fall, and so labour demand will not rise. Even so, because of the increased cost of energy, a substitution effect still takes place, but less strongly. The situation then parallels the case where recycling was achieved by reducing a personal income tax, as in S1 and S2 above.

Erosion and interdependency effects between environmental and labour taxes

The so-called erosion and interdependency effects will be discussed separately, although it will be seen that they actually arise from the same analytical position. The interdependency effect has been discussed in detail in Parry (1994).

Parry constructs a model that includes a good – the production or consumption of which entails a negative environmental externality – and labour taxes which distort the labour/leisure market, so that more than the optimal amount of leisure is taken.

Imposing an environmental tax raises the price of the polluting good and, where this good is a substitute for leisure, this causes still more leisure to be taken, thereby increasing the distortion in the leisure market. This not only imposes a welfare cost *per se*, but reduces revenue from the labour tax so that more labour taxes are required, thus increasing the welfare burden from that source. This combined effect Parry calls the 'interdependency effect' (IE) of environmental taxation.

Parry acknowledges that recycling the revenue from the environmental tax will reduce the welfare burden from the pre-existing labour taxes, which he calls the recycling effect (RE). However, his analysis finds that, where the polluting good is an average, or greater than average, substitute for leisure, RE/IE < 1. This means that the 'efficiency dividend', as defined above, cannot exist in such a situation. It means, moreover, that the optimal environmental tax will be less than the marginal environmental damage.

Parry's analysis can be questioned from several angles. First, his result only holds, generally, for polluting goods that are average or greater than average substitutes for leisure. For less than average substitutes, it depends on the values of other parameters. For *complements* to leisure, the results would be quite different: a rise in the price of the polluting good would reduce the amount of leisure taken, thereby reducing the pre-existing distortion in the leisure market, and also increasing the revenue from the labour taxes, thereby reducing the welfare loss from that source. For complements, both RE and IE would engender a welfare gain, yielding a substantial efficiency dividend and justifying an optimal environmental tax that was higher than the Pigouvian level. Parry dismisses complements to leisure in a footnote (1994, p 5), claiming that 'this is only applicable to a narrow range of goods (such as skis and video-cassette recorders), and will be ignored below'. But it is by no means clear that this issue can be dealt with so summarily.

Because leisure is the obverse of labour, which is the source of income, and all time that is not labour is counted as leisure, some leisure always has to be sacrificed to gain the income to buy goods. This is the income effect of any leisure/goods trade-off. Substitution or complementarity between leisure and goods needs to be assessed once such income effects have been compensated for, answering the question: given the increase in the price of the polluting good, will more or less leisure be taken, assuming that the budget constraint remains unchanged by the price change?

Leisure is measured in terms of time. Whether a good is a substitute or complement for leisure depends on whether its consumption is time-saving or time-using. Such a quality is implicit in the two examples given by Parry, but his assumption that they somehow comprise a 'narrow range' of goods is questionable. Few consumer goods actually save time. Many more are neutral with respect to time. A substantial number would seem to be time-using.

The point at issue is whether polluting goods are substitutes or complements to leisure. The EC Fifth Environmental Action Plan lists five sectors as particularly environmentally damaging: energy use, agriculture, transport, industry and tourism. Of course, tourism is time-using by definition. It is also the world's largest single industry. Private transport is also time-using, with motor-fuel being a prime example of a commodity that is both highly polluting and time-intensive in its consumption. Food is also time-using, whether it is bought for home consumption, requiring cooking, or bought in restaurants.

There are obvious complexities. For example, convenience foods are less of a complement to leisure than unprepared foods, but a strong substitute for such foods. A rise in the price of convenience foods could be expected to increase the consumption of unprepared foods and so the demand for leisure to prepare them. Convenience foods are therefore an effective substitute for leisure, through their impact on the demand for unprepared foods, which are a strong complement to it. However, it is not clear that an increase in the price of all foods, to internalize the externalities deriving from agriculture, would increase demand for leisure. In so far as unprepared food becomes proportionately more expensive than convenience foods, which might be expected because a greater proportion of its price is associated with agriculture rather than processing, the demand for leisure could be reduced.

Contrary to what Parry maintains, it is clear that the substitute/complement issue cannot be dismissed. In fact, his condition that, for there to be no efficiency dividend, the polluting goods must be average or greater than average substitutes for leisure begins to look rather restrictive. If most polluting goods, such as the examples above, are in fact complements to leisure, then an efficiency dividend begins to look more, rather than less, likely.

However, there is a second and more fundamental point to be made about Parry's analysis. The calculation of welfare losses from distortions due to environmental externalities, or the tax system, is obviously dependent on where the 'no-distortion' position is to be taken. For the market of the polluting good, this 'no distortion' position is rightly taken to be *after* the externality has been internalized. But for the leisure market, Parry's 'no distortion' position is *before* the externality is internalized, so that the effect on the leisure market of internalizing the externality of the polluting good is perceived to be distorting. This is inconsistent.

A more satisfactory treatment is as follows. Figure 8.5 uses Parry's notation and shows the supply-and-demand curves of the polluting good X_j and leisure N with no market distortions – ie, without a labour tax and after internalizing the externality associated with $X_j \bullet S_j + c$, S_N, D_j', D_N' are these undisturbed supply and demand curves respectively, where c is the external cost associated with X_j.

Before c is internalized, however, output of X_j is at X_j^o ($>X_j'$), with a welfare loss given by the triangle *abc*, because its price, S_j is below its true cost $S_j + c$. This distortedly low price for X_j has an effect (here also called a distortion) in the leisure market as well, comprising:

- an income effect which tends to increase the amount of leisure taken;
- a substitution effect which tends to decrease the amount of leisure taken, if X_j is a substitute for leisure, or increases it, if X_j is a complement.

If the income effect and possibility of complementarity are ignored for the moment (in order to make a direct comparison with Parry's analysis, which proceeds in this way), the demand for leisure will be decreased by the distortion in the X_j market, say to D_N^o in Figure 8.5, resulting in leisure taken of N_o ($<N'$) and a welfare loss given by the triangle *def*.

If a tax, t ($\leq$c), is applied to the polluting good, its consumption will be brought down towards Xj' as its effective price is raised. Let a tax t^1 bring consumption down to X_j^1, reducing the welfare loss in this market to *agh*. Simultaneously, the distortion in the leisure market will diminish, as the demand for leisure rises in response to the higher price of X_j. In Figure 8.5 it rises to D_N^1, leaving a reduced welfare loss of *iefr*. This is completely contrary to Parry's analysis; Parry had the tax *increasing* the distortion in

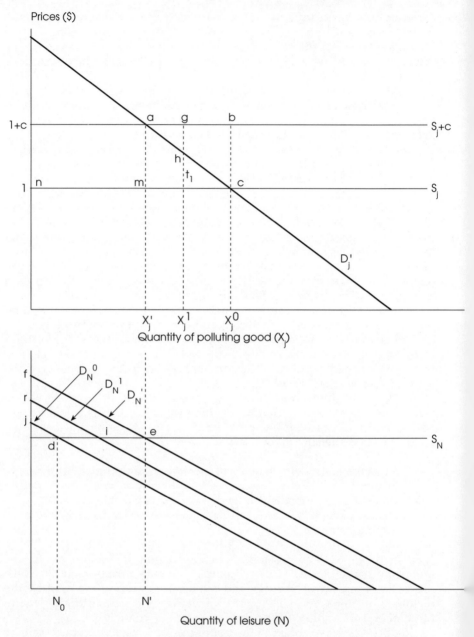

Figure 8.5 *Distortions in two markets and the effects of an environmental tax*

the leisure market because he took its undistorted position to be N_0 rather than N'.

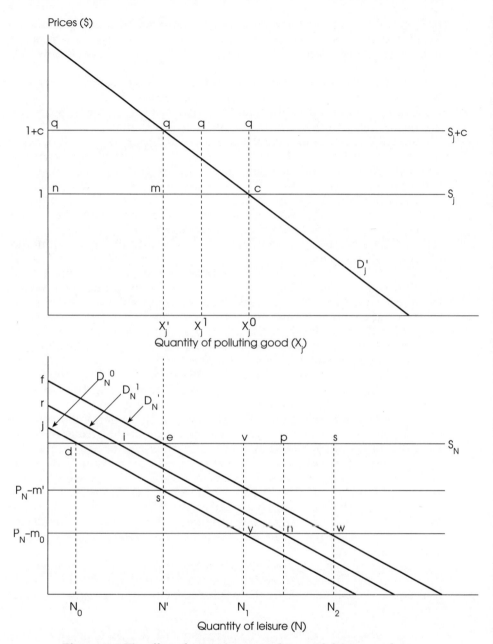

Figure 8.6 *The effect of an environmental tax with leisure market distortions from a labour tax*

Figure 8.6 adds the labour tax, shown here (as in Parry), as an effective subsidy to leisure, m. The first point to notice is that in the case before the tax t is imposed and leisure demand is D_N^0, subsidy to leisure reducing its price to m' will increase the amount of leisure taken from N_0 up to N'. Relative to D_N' this introduces a distortion *des*. The total distortion from the initial undistorted position (the intersection of S_N and D_N' at *e*) is now: *defj* + *des* = *sefj*.

Increasing labour taxation m beyond m' to m_0 (still before the imposition of any environmental tax) increases the leisure taken to N_1 and adds the further distortion *yves*. The total distortion is now *dvy*, due to the labour tax and, as before, *defj*, due to the uninternalized externality.

Imposing an environmental tax moves D_N^o back towards its undistorted position D_N'. At D_N^1 it can be seen that the distortion from the environmental externality is reduced to *iefr*, while that from the labour tax is unchanged at *ipn* (= *dvy*). Full internalization of the externality removes the distortion from that source entirely, leaving a labour-taxation distortion of *esw* (= *dvy*), unchanged by the imposition of the environmental tax.

Here it can be seen that, unlike in Parry's analysis, the correct identification of the no-distortion position of the leisure market separates out the distorting effects of the environmental externality and the labour tax, such that they do not interact. There is no direct 'interdependency effect' (IE).

However, there is still an indirect IE because the environmental tax does increase leisure, from N_1 to N_2, with a consequent loss of revenues from the labour taxation, given by the area *vswy*. If this revenue has to be raised by increasing the rate of labour taxation, then the distortion from this is V•*vswy*, where V is the marginal welfare distortion of labour taxation (ie, loss of welfare per unit of revenue raised).

The situation is then as follows. The IE, or increased distortion in the leisure market due to the environmental tax is V•*vswy* – *defj*. The recycling effect (RE), with full internalization of the externality, is V•*cX'*.

It is not clear *a priori* which of these effects is the larger. V depends on the wage elasticity of labour supply (leisure demand – the greater the elasticity, the larger is V). The RE depends on V, the level of the tax and the level of consumption of the polluting good. The IE depends on V, the level of the leisure subsidy (m), and the elasticity of substitution between leisure and the polluting good (the greater the elasticity, the greater will be both *vswy* and *defj*). All that can be concluded at this stage is that Parry's conclusion that there will be no efficiency dividend from an environmental tax when the goods are average or better than average substitutes, is no longer going to be generally true.

Before continuing, it should be noted that this analysis has ignored (as did Parry's) the effect of the leisure subsidy on the polluting good's market. If leisure and the polluting good are substitutes then the subsidy will have two effects:

- It will increase the leisure taken, and therefore reduce labour and income. This will reduce the demand for X_j.
- The substitution effect will reduce the demand for X_j. If leisure and the polluting goods were complements then demand for X_j would be increased.

Where X_j is reduced overall by these interactions, the leisure subsidy has the effect of compensating, to some extent, for the environmental externality. However, these effects complicate an already complicated situation, without shedding further light on the differences between Parry's analysis and that being advocated here. They will not be considered further, beyond noting that a full account of the taxes' interactions would need to take account of them.

We can now investigate what difference is made to the revised analysis by the income effect of the uninternalized environmental externality and the possibility of complementarity between leisure and the polluting good.

The income effect of non-internalization will tend to increase the amount of leisure that is taken, therefore reducing the distortion when leisure and the polluting good are substitutes, decreasing the size of *defj* and reducing the IE. If the income effect is greater than the substitution effect, then the non-internalization results in more leisure being taken than is optimal, and the following analysis of complementarity is relevant.

Where leisure and the polluting good are complements, the substitution effect of non-internalization will cause more leisure to be taken, say N_o, as illustrated in Figure 8.7. The effect of the externality in this case is to *increase* welfare in the leisure market, by defj. The introduction of a labour tax will increase leisure further, to N_1 say, giving rise to a distortion *ehg*. As the environmental tax is applied, the demand for leisure contracts towards D_N'. At D_N^1 the extra welfare from the externality has shrunk to *dmrj*, while the externality from the labour tax is now at *mlk* $(= ehg)$. When the externality is fully internalized, the extra welfare in the leisure market from the distortion has disappeared, while the distortion from the labour tax is still unchanged at *dry* $(= ehg)$.

However, in this case the indirect IE has increased welfare, because leisure has fallen from N_1 to N_1', so revenues from the labour tax will have risen, allowing it to be reduced. The associated welfare gain is V•*rygh*. The RE is again V•cX_j'.

The results of this analysis can be summarised thus. An efficiency dividend (defined as a situation in which RE + IE > 0), will arise in the following cases:

1. If the goods are substitutes, V•cX_j' – V•*vswy* + *defj* > 0 (Figure 8.6). This will be made the more positive (or less negative) the higher the revenue from the environmental tax (dependent on the tax rate and the quantity of the taxed good). It will be made the less positive (or more negative) the higher the labour tax. The higher the elasticity of substitution, the higher both *vswy* and *defj*, with an indeterminate effect. A large m (increasing *vswy*) or a small N' (reducing *defj*) will make an efficiency dividend less likely.

2. If the goods are complements, V•cX_j' + V•*rygh* – *defj* > 0 (Figure 8.7). Again this will be the more positive (or less negative) the higher the revenue from the environmental tax. The effect of the elasticity of substitution on the outcome is still indeterminate, but in this case a large m (increasing *rygh*) will make an efficiency dividend more likely.

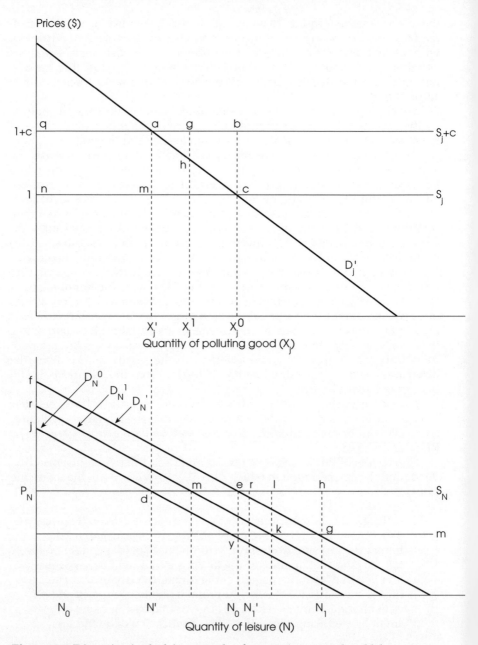

Figure 8.7 *Distortion in the leisure market from environmental and labour taxes when leisure and the polluting good are complements*

On balance, because the RE effect is always positive, while the terms in IE work against each other, it would not be unreasonable, on the basis of this analysis and the earlier discussion, to conclude tentatively that where there is a pre-existing labour tax, an efficency dividend is more likely than not.

Where Parry talks of an interdependency effect, Bovenberg and de Mooij (1994, pp 1087–88) find that the erosion effect of an environmental tax rules out an efficiency dividend. Their model shows that the imposition of an environmental tax has a negative effect on employment:

> The negative effect on employment is due to a decline in the real after-tax wage eroding the incentives to supply labour. The drop in the real after-tax wage comes about because the lower tax rate on labour income does not fully compensate workers for the adverse effect of the pollution levy on their real after-tax wage. This incomplete offset is due to the erosion of the tax base of the environmental tax. In particular, the higher environmental tax induces households to switch from dirty to clean consumption commodities. If the initial tax rate on the dirty commodities is positive, this behavioral effect erodes the base of the environmental tax and, therefore, produces a negative tax-base effect.

In other words, imposing the environmental tax (on final commodities) causes consumers to switch away from the affected goods. The price of the goods rises by the amount of the tax, but the erosion of the tax base means that not enough revenue is raised to compensate consumers fully by reducing their income taxes adequately. Consumers are worse off; their real wage has declined and so they will work less. This reduces employment and output (and, in Bovenberg and de Mooij's framework, would have further knock-on effects through raising reduced revenues from the labour tax, necessitating a further rise in tax rates and even greater losses in the after-tax wage, although Bovenberg and de Mooij do not push the analysis this far).

The problem with this analysis derives from a misperception of the nature of the distortion induced by an environmental externality, which can be illustrated in the following way. Imagine an economy with no market distortions except one that is due to an environmental externality in a single goods market, j. This is partially internalized by an environmental tax, t, levied on consumption of the commodity, which is less than the marginal social cost, c, imposed by the externality. All the tax revenues are returned by the government to consumers on a lump-sum basis.

Now suppose the government raises the environmental tax to c. The price of the commodity will rise by (c-t), but suppose that the erosion effect is such that no extra revenue is raised. The price of the good now equals its marginal social cost, so optimality has been reached in that market, and there have been no 'interdependency effects' with other taxes, because there are no other taxes. But consumers are worse off in market terms, because they have not been compensated for the price rise. Their real wage has therefore fallen and they will supply less labour.

This is precisely the effect derived by Bovenberg and de Mooij. They attribute it to the existence of pre-existing labour and/or environmental taxes, but, as the above discussion shows, these are incidental to the analysis. Bovenberg and de Mooij's analysis is correct in identifying an effect on the real wage but it is surely not correct to call this effect a 'distortion' from the environmental tax, when in fact it is an essential part of the process of internalizing the externality.

The basic point is analogous to the fundamental flaw in Parry's analysis. In the simple example above, the optimal allocation of resources is achieved by a tax rate c. Where the pre-tax price of the good is p, the *optimal* consumer price of the good is (p+c). This means that the optimal real wage is that which reflects a price level which incorporates the price of the good as (p+c). A real wage that is higher than this because the price level is lower, because the externality has reduced the price of the good below (p+c), is part of the distortion due to the externality. The process of raising the price to this level is a process of moving towards optimality, *not* of introducing a distortion, even though this process reduces the real wage of consumers. The externality means that, at any price below (p+c), consumers effectively receive a subsidy, making their real wage distortedly high.

It is possible to divide the welfare loss from imposing the environmental tax into two parts: (i) the reduction in consumption of the polluting good; and, where there is an erosion effect, (ii) the reduction in the real wage. However, it is implicit in the identification of the optimal level of pollution that this total welfare loss is less than the welfare gain arising from reducing pollution to this level.

It should also be noted that the reduction in the real wage will not necessarily reduce the supply of labour (as in Bovenberg and de Mooij's model), because it induces two effects working in different directions. In addition to reducing the incentive to supply labour, it also reduces the demand for all normal goods, including leisure, thereby reducing the disincentive to supply labour. The net outcome of these two effects cannot be determined *a priori*.

Now it is possible to see how an efficiency dividend can emerge, in fact, from the situation analysed by Bovenberg and de Mooij. First, it may be noted that the real wage effect is dependent on the price elasticity of the demand of the taxed good (ε). If $\varepsilon=0$, there will be no reduction in consumption of the taxed good, implying a vertical D_j' curve in Figure 8.7. The externality will be internalized, but there will be no change in the environmental damage. In this case, the revenue will rise in strict proportion to the tax increase, c/t, although this is unlikely in practice (although elasticities may be quite low). There will be no erosion.

At the other extreme, for $\varepsilon = \infty$ (the taxed good is infinitely elastic, D_j' in Figure 8.7 is horizontal) consumption of the taxed good, and therefore the revenue from taxing it, will fall to zero. The result of internalizing the externality will be its complete elimination. Between these two extremes, the revenue will stay unchanged ($r = 1$) if $c = -t/\varepsilon$, or $\varepsilon = -t/c$, where $-1 \le \varepsilon \le 0$. In this case the reduction in consumption of the taxed good will have eroded away all the potential revenue increase from the high tax (see the Appendix on p 159 for the derivation of this relation).

Where $r>1$ $\{(c/t)>(-1/\varepsilon)\}$ and $-1 \le \varepsilon \le 0$, there will be some erosion of the tax base and a real wage effect – ie, the tax will reduce the real wage. However, as has been stressed, this should not be regarded as a distortion due to the environmental tax, but as part of the movement towards optimality brought about by the increase of the tax to the Pigouvian level. By the definition of optimality, the welfare increase from internalizing the externality (the environmental dividend) will be greater than the welfare loss from the reduction of the real wage and the reduction in consumption of the taxed good. Nor is it certain that the real-wage effect will reduce employment and output, as in Bovenberg and de Mooij's model, for the reason given above.

However, if r>1, there is some extra revenue from the tax increase. If there are also distortionary taxes, then this extra revenue can be returned to consumers by reducing these, instead of through lump-sum rebates, which is the recycling effect discussed above. This always results in a welfare increase. Where the distortionary factor is V, an efficiency dividend of $(cX_j' - tX_j)V$ ($= cX_j'\{1 - 1/r\}V$) will be the result.

It is also possible that r<1 – ie, that the erosion effect is proportionately greater than the tax increase, so that the revenue from the environmental tax decreases. If this revenue loss has to be made up by increasing distortionary taxes, this will result in a 'negative' recycling effect and a negative efficiency dividend (ie, a welfare loss), because $(C \bullet X_j' - t \bullet X_j) < 0$.

The situation with regard to erosion and interdependency effects can now be summarized:

1. The erosion effect derives from raising the price of the taxed good consequent on internalizing an environmental externality. This price rise is part of a move towards optimality rather than the introduction of a distortion. Where erosion takes place – ie, $\varepsilon < 0$ – the price rise reduces the real wage, as well as the tax reducing the consumption of the polluting good. However, the consequent welfare losses are outweighed by the welfare gain from internalizing the externality. The environmental dividend is the environmental benefit due to internalization, less the welfare losses from reduced consumption of the polluting good and the real-wage effect. Where the environmental tax increases the revenues from the taxed good, this extra revenue can be used to reduce distortionary taxes. This recycling effect will produce an efficiency dividend, subject to the outcome of the interdependency effect discussed above. Where the environmental tax reduces the revenues from the taxed good, and extra revenue has to be found from distortionary taxes, this negative recycling effect will cause a welfare loss.
2. Parry's negative interdependency effect derives from ignoring the distortion in the leisure market due to the externality – ie, ignoring the interdependence between the markets – before the environmental tax is imposed, and then regarding the tax's effect on the leisure market as the imposition of a distortion instead of the removal of one. With a more consistent treatment of the interdependency between the two markets, an efficiency dividend emerges as the most likely outcome from the substitution of environmental taxes for distortionary labour taxes.

Conclusion on the Three Main Dividends

1. Where there is an environmental externality, the imposition of a

tax directed at the externality, at a level equal to or below the Pigouvian level, will yield an environmental dividend. If the tax falls on the commodity related to the externality, the environmental dividend will derive purely from a reduction in output, which is the cost of achieving this dividend. If the tax falls directly on the environmental externality – eg, on an emission – and if there are possibilities of abating the externality at a marginal cost lower than the tax levied, then some abatement will take place; the output/externality relation will be changed; the environmental dividend will be greater; and the loss of output will be less than if there is no abatement or a commodity tax is levied.

2. Where there is involuntary unemployment, it can be reduced by the imposition of an environmental tax, with the revenues used to subsidize wages in the part of the labour market where wages are inflexible, provided that the wage subsidy is not passed on to employees as a wage increase. Where the labour market imperfection is due to an employer's labour tax, then unemployment can be reduced by using the revenues from the environmental tax to reduce the labour tax, again provided that this reduction is not passed on to employees in the form of higher wages. In both cases the increase in employment – the employment dividend, will result in increased output – an efficiency dividend.

    An employment dividend also arises from the shift towards relatively labour-intensive production and consumption caused by the reduced price of labour relative to taxed environmental inputs. Where there is involuntary unemployment, this will also lead to an efficiency dividend in the form of increased output.

3. An efficiency dividend may be expected to arise whenever the revenues from an environmental tax can be used to reduce the distortions from other taxation, provided that the analysis properly identifies the undistorted position as one that fully internalizes the externality. For the efficiency dividend to arise, the recycling effect, which is positive whenever an increase in environmental taxation has resulted in increased revenues, will have to be greater than any negative outcome from the interdependency effect (caused by the interaction between the markets for the polluting good and for leisure/labour), which consists of two terms of opposite sign.

In short, in a situation with an environmental externality, involuntary unemployment and distortionary taxes, one would normally expect a triple dividend – environmental, employment and efficiency – to emerge from taxing the externality and using the revenues to reduce the distortionary taxation.

EVIDENCE FROM SIMULATION MODELS

The dis1cussion so far has been purely theoretical. Another way of gaining insights into the dividends of environmental taxation is from computer models that simulate the effects of such taxation on the economy. The link between theory and simulation is that the relationships in the simulation models are derived from theory. In a general-equilibrium model the simulations are normally exclusively driven by the specified theoretical relationships, in that the values of the model's parameters are calibrated from a single year, and all markets, including the labour market, are constrained to clear, which means, among other things, that these models show no unemployment. Macroeconometric models, on the other hand, which are also based on theory, derive their parameters from time-series estimation so that they are based on a whole range of past data which has been accepted by the model. While their markets may be constrained to clear in the long run, they can have non-clearing markets in the short and medium terms, so that they do yield insights into unemployment.

All models produce results that are determined by the relationships between specific variables, so that these results are entirely dependent on the assumptions and specifications of the modellers. This is particularly so in assessing the possibility of an efficiency dividend, which depends crucially on where the 'no distortion' position of the economy is taken to be.

The Environmental Dividend

All models agree that where there is a negative environmental externality, environmental taxation can yield an environmental dividend. The size of the dividend from a given environmental tax depends on the size of the elasticity of substitution of the affected input in production, and of the elasticities of demand and substitution of the affected products in consumption: the higher the elasticities, the higher the environmental dividend – ie, environmental damage can be reduced at less cost.

The variety of dividends that can be simulated by different models, with regard to the same issue, is well illustrated by an Energy Modelling Forum (EMF) exercise undertaken at Stanford University, which specified standardized scenarios for 14 widely differing economic models. In these models a carbon tax of $80 per tonne carbon brought about a change in CO_2 levels in 1990 of between –35 per cent and +20 per cent (Gaskins and Weyant, 1993, p 319). Obviously, had no carbon tax been levied, emissions in all cases would have been greater, but the range of these simulations is very large.

More general evidence of the environmental dividend from environmental taxation came from the DRI's wide-ranging report, commissioned by the European Commission (DRI, 1994). DRI modelled three scenarios for six of the larger European Union economies (EU-6): a Reference scenario (REF) containing 'all policy measures and actions agreed by the end of 1992' (DRI 1994, p 27); a Policy-in-the-Pipeline scenario (PIP), incorporating policies or proposals that had been the subject of a directive, mainly comprising 'command-and-control' measures, except for the European Commission's carbon-energy tax; and an Integrated scenario (INT), mainly using market instruments, including environmental taxation, to internalize environmental costs.

Table 8.1 shows the environmental results of the scenarios, in terms of changing environmental pressure in various areas. Much of the positive difference between PIP and INT may be attributed to environmental taxes and considered the taxes' environmental dividend.

Table 8.1 Changes in environmental pressures between 1990 and 2010 across themes

Theme	REF	PIP	INT
Climate change	−30	−10	0
Regional air quality			
acid deposition	+10	+40	+70
photochemical	−10	+20	+60
Urban environment			
air pollution	+10	+30	+80
other	−70	−40	−20
Toxic substances	+30	+20	+20
Nature and biodiversity	−20	−10	+10
Water quality	−20	+30	+50
Water resources	−20	−10	−10
Waste			
hazardous	−60	0	+50
non-hazardous	−30	−10	+40
Oil in the coastal zone	−20	+10	+30

Note: a + indicates an environmental improvement, and a − an environmental deterioration – ie, a decrease or increase in environmental pressure – of the percentage indicated.

Source: DRI, 1994, p 62

The Employment Dividend

DRI also modelled a variant of the INT scenario, called INT+, in which all the revenues from INT's environmental taxes were used to reduce employers' non-wage labour costs, such as Social Security payments, or, in the UK, employers' National Insurance Contributions. This was analysed theoretically earlier. The scenario results showed that the employment dividend was not insubstantial. INT revealed an increase over REF by 2010 of 1.1 million jobs (an employment increase of 1 per cent), while INT+ showed an increase of 2.2 million jobs (DRI, 1994, p 53). The increase in INT will have come about from the substitution of now relatively cheaper labour for environmental resources in production, and a shift away from environmentally intensive goods and services in consumption, as discussed earlier. The further effect in INT+ is due to an intensification of these effects through the reduction in firms' labour costs from the recycling of the environmental taxes' revenues.

A number of other studies, reviewed by Majocchi (1994), have produced similar results. The QUEST model indicated that a 10 per cent reduction in employers' Social Security Contributions (SSCs), financed by a carbon-energy tax, would increase employment after seven years by 1 per cent, reducing unemployment by 0.9 per cent (Majocchi, 1994, p 14). Financing the cut by increasing personal income taxes only increased employment by 0.7 per cent (because of the lack of any shift away from energy-intensive commodities), while increasing VAT brought no employment increase at all. Another study, using the HERMES model, found that a similar cut in SSCs, also financed by a carbon-energy tax, produced a 0.64 per cent rise in employment in the EU-6 (Majocchi, 1994, p 16).

The employment dividend can be made even greater by targeting the SSC reductions on the lower paid. Several studies suggest that such targeting could increase employment by 2 to 3 percent (Majocchi, 1994, pp 23–5). For example, the QUEST model shows that, with full recycling of revenues to achieve budget neutrality, employment could increase by 3 per cent and unemployment decrease by 2.7 per cent across the EU from such a measure (Majocchi, 1994, p 25; see also EC, 1994, p 160).

All these studies tend to confirm the theoretical conclusions discussed earlier that an employment dividend from environmental taxation is both probable and significant.

The Efficiency Dividend

It is to be expected that the increase in employment shown by the models, as discussed in the previous section, would lead to an increase in output, and the models do indeed show this too. Thus the INT and the INT+ scenarios in the DRI report indicate that GDP increases over REF by 2010 of 0.9 per cent and 1.06 per cent respectively. For the untargeted case using the QUEST model, the GDP increase after seven years was 1 per cent, rising to 1.8 per cent in the targeted case.

QUEST's albeit small increases in GDP from an imposition of a carbon tax are in contrast to the GDP decreases, or costs, from such a tax that many other models have found and which tend to predominate in discussions of this issue. For example, the Stanford Energy Modelling Forum exercise mentioned earlier found: 'The costs of achieving a 20 per cent reduction in CO_2 emissions (in the US) relative to today's level range from 0.9 per cent to 1.7 per cent of US GDP in 2010' (Gaskins and Weyant, 1993, p 320).

However, these cost results were generated by returning the carbon-tax revenues to households on a lump-sum basis, rather than by reducing distortionary taxes. It is clear that such a procedure is suboptimal. For example, Jorgenson and Wilcoxen (1993, p 20) argue: '(Lump-sum recycling) is probably not the most likely use of the revenue. ... Using the revenue to reduce a distortionary tax would lower the net cost of a carbon tax by removing inefficiency elsewhere in the economy.' This is precisely the effect that is obtained in all models that do, in fact, reduce distortionary taxes to offset a carbon tax. Jorgenson and Wilcoxen themselves (1993, Table 5, p 22) find that a 1.7 per cent GDP loss under lump-sum redistribution is converted to a 0.69 per cent loss and a 1.1 per cent gain by reducing labour and capital taxes respectively.

This effect has also been shown in the work of Nordhaus. Nordhaus (1991a), on the basis of an abatement-cost curve derived from his survey of extant models (in Nordhaus, 1991b), and his own calculation of a global-warming damage function, arrived at an efficient level of a carbon tax of $7.33 per ton CO_2 equivalent (Nordhaus, 1991a, p 934). By 1993, using his own DICE model, the optimum carbon tax had fallen to $5.24 per ton CO_2 equivalent. Using a carbon tax of $56 per ton to cut emissions in 1995 by 20 per cent from 1990 levels caused an annualised global GDP loss of $762 billion (Nordhaus, 1993, p 315). However, these DICE results came from recycling the carbon-tax revenues through lump-sum rebates. When instead carbon taxes are used to reduce other, burdensome taxes, assumed to have a dead-weight loss of 30 cents per dollar of revenue raised, then the opti-mal tax rate becomes $59 per ton, emissions go below the 20 per cent cut, and annualised GDP rises by $206 billion. Nordhaus (1993, p 317) notes: 'The importance of revenue recycling is surprising and striking. These find-ings emphasize the critical nature of designing the instruments and use of revenues in a careful manner. The tail of revenue recycling would seem to wag the dog of climate-change policy.'

Barker (1992, p 9) has consistently argued against lump-sum rebates to offset revenues: 'An alternative treatment would be to find which existing tax creates the largest distortions in the economy and the highest loss of welfare and then to use the carbon tax revenues ... to reduce the marginal rates of this tax.' Boero et al (1991, p 93) agree: 'Economically we should seek to reduce the most distortionary (tax)'. On Jorgenson and Yun's figures this would mean initially offsetting taxes with an MEB of 95 cents per dollar. Because of interaction effects between the taxes, it is not possible to argue that, for this tranche of offset, each dollar of carbon tax revenue raised would generate a 95 cent increase in welfare because of distortionary reduc-tions elsewhere; but it may be noted that this rate of offset is more than three times that used by Nordhaus in his 'tail-wagging' calculation discussed earlier, and could thus be expected to yield a substantially higher optimal tax rate than his $59 per ton CO_2 equivalent.

While they do not report the MEB figure they used, Gaskins and Weyant (1993, p 320) confirm the importance of this approach to revenue recycling: 'Simulation with four models of the US economy indicate that from 35 per cent to more than 100 per cent of the GDP losses could ulti-mately be offset by recycling revenues through cuts in existing taxes.' Models that do not take account of the possibly beneficial effects of revenue recycling may be expected to overstate the costs of carbon reduction under rational policy-making.

It must be emphasized that these model results do not 'prove' the exis-tence of multiple dividends from environmental taxation. They arise from the specification of the model that is being used. If these specifications had included the 'interdependency' and 'erosion' effects discussed earlier, then the multiple dividends would not have emerged. Goulder (1994b) believes that the models should include these effects. For example, Goulder (1994b, p 27) dismisses the Nordhaus results presented above on the grounds that 'they do not capture the tax interaction effect because the model did not include pre-existing taxes. Including pre-existing taxes in the benchmark data would likely reverse the Nordhaus results.'

However, even this is far from certain. In a simulation using the Jorgenson-Wilcoxen model, which does contain pre-existing taxes, multiple dividends arise when either labour or capital taxes are replaced by a carbon tax, a result which Goulder (1994b, p 24) finds 'difficult to account for'. Simulations from other models reported in Goulder's paper, replacing a personal income tax, do not show multiple dividends. However, in so far as replacing a personal income tax (as opposed to SSCs) does not bring about substitutions in production as well as consumption, one would have expected smaller multiple dividends in this case anyway.

Moreover, if the interdependency and erosion effects, which Goulder claims prevent an efficiency dividend from occurring, in fact arise from a mis-specification or misperception of the 'no-distortion' economic position, then the models that illustrate such effects are only expressing their mis-specification. On balance, the conclusion drawn here is that a triple dividend from environmental taxation – with appropriate revenue-recycling – yielding increases in environmental quality, employment and output, is both predicted theoretically and emerges from simulations often enough to be regarded as a likely outcome.

EVIDENCE FROM IMPLEMENTATION

Tax systems, and environmental taxes within them, are complex and subject to restructuring, so that it is no easy matter to compare how the imposition of environmental taxes has changed over time. However, three OECD reports (1989, 1994, 1995) do enable some comparisons of recent experience to be made.

Table 8.2 shows how the percentage of tax in the price of petrol has changed between 1990 and 1994 in the G7 and some non-G7 European countries. The percentage has increased in all countries, in some quite markedly.

Between 1990 and 1994 five countries – Denmark, Finland, The Netherlands, Norway and Sweden – introduced carbon or carbon-energy

Table 8.2 *Total taxes as per cent of end-user price of petrol (households)*

Country	1990	1994
Belgium	65.5	74.2
Canada	42.4	50.0
France	74.3	80.8
Germany	63.1	76.9
Italy	74.9	76.1
Japan	45.6	48.2[1]
Netherlands	64.5	75.9
UK	61.9	73.5
US	26.7	34.4

[1] 1993

Source: OECD, 1995, Table 2, p 48

taxes as part of a reconfiguration of their systems of energy taxation according to environmental criteria. Norway also introduced taxes on SO_2 emissions, and Sweden imposed taxes on SO_2 and NO_x. While the changes involved in these reconfigurations are limited (see OECD, 1994, and the assessment by Barde in Chapter 11), they remain important examples of environmental tax reform. Table 8.3 gives the revenues yielded by the carbon/carbon-energy taxes, in absolute terms and as a percentage of GDP. Table 8.4 gives details of some other environmental taxes with comparisons, where possible, between OECD 1989 and OECD 1995. It can be seen

Table 8.3 *Revenues from carbon taxation in five European countries*

Country		CO_2 Revenues	
	Domestic Currency millions (year)	ECU[1] millions	As % of GDP[1]
Denmark	DKr 3,174 (93)	420	0.36
Finland	Mk 1,450 (94)	208	0.3
Netherlands	Gld 1,400 (95)[3]	645	0.25
Norway	NKr 6,000 (94)	715	0.81
Sweden	approximately SKr 6,000 (94)	750	1.1

[1] Exchange rates to ECUs and GDP figures from *International Financial Statistics Yearbook 1994* (IMF, Washington, DC)

Source: OECD, 1995, pp 27–36

that a fairly wide range of taxes have been imposed, but by a relatively small group of countries, principally the Nordic countries. Tax rates have tended to be increased and some new taxes have been introduced, especially by Denmark. It is hard to know how environmentally effective the taxes have been. Where the tax rates have been increased, but the revenues have not by the same amount, it is possible that the taxes' incentive effects are working – for instance, lubrication oil in Norway. Similarly, where revenues have increased more than taxes, then the incentive effect would appear to be weak – for instance, air pollution in France. Some taxes have been abolished – such as Finland's tax on fertilizers (in 1994) and Sweden's tax on beverage containers (in 1993). Some new taxes are also in prospect. Belgium, having recently introduced taxes on disposable razors, cameras and beverage containers, is planning taxes on a range of other products, including paper, pesticides, batteries, glue, oil and solvents. The UK is planning to introduce a landfill tax in 1996.

If multiple dividends from environmental taxation do not exist, then policy-makers should evaluate such taxation purely on the basis of whether its environmental benefits are worth its economic costs. But there is substantial evidence that this is not, in fact, the way that policy-makers are currently assessing environmental taxes; nor are the environmental benefits the only reason for their slowly but steadily increasing introduction.

Table 8.4 *Some environmental taxes in some OECD countries*

Type of Tax	Country	Tax Rate		Tax	
		OECD 1989 ECU	*OECD 1995 ECU[1]*	*OECD 1989 mil.ECU (1987)*	*OECD 1995 mil. ECU[1] (year)*
CFC/halons	Australia	–	0.15/kg	–	0.1 (89)
	Denmark	–	3.97/kg	–	0.68 (93)
	USA	–	variable	–	479 (92)
Sand, gravel, etc	Denmark	–	0.66/m³	–	15.9 (93)
Packaging	Denmark	–	variable	–	40.4 (93)
Disposable tableware	Denmark	–	33%[2]	–	7.7 (93)
Rechargeable batteries	Denmark	–	variable	–	1.03 (93)
Batteries	Sweden	variable	variable	2.1	1.55* (91/92)
Beverage containers	Finland	substantial increase between two periods		1.6	3.85* (93)
Lubrication oil	Finland	29/tonne	27.6*/tonne	3	2.3* (93)
	France	6/tonne	19.2*/tonne	4	14.9* (94)
	Norway	0.06/litre	0.09*/litre	6.5	2.8* (94)
Pesticides and fertilizers	Norway	*na*	13% (pesticides) approx. 20% (fertilizers)	1.5	17.4* (94)
Pesticides	Sweden	0.64/kg	1.82*/kg	approx. 1	*na*
Pesticides	Denmark	–	variable	–	1.46 (93)
Air pollution (SO₂)	France	19/tonne	19.2*/tonne	13	25.7* (94)
Aircraft noise	Netherlands	*na*	*na*	4.4	15.7* (93)

[1] Exchange rates to ECUs and consumer-price indices (for deflation to 1987 values, but only where marked *, when data from both periods are available for comparison) from *International Financial Statistics Yearbook 1994* (IMF, Washington, DC)

[2] Percentages relate to the wholesale price of a product.

[3] The abbreviation *na* denotes data not available.

Sources: OECD, 1989; OECD, 1995

As an example of the shift in perception on this point, it is striking that, in 1989, the OECD survey of 'economic instruments for environmental protection', which include environmental taxes, made no mention at all of possible multiple dividends. Although the study noted increasing interest in economic instruments, it attributed this to a desire for more cost-effective environmental protection; for greater policy integration, both within environmental policy and between it and other policy areas; and for a more preventive rather than curative approach. Yet by 1993 the European Commission's white paper *Growth, Competitiveness, Employment* (EC, 1993, p 150) was making the employment dividend a core *raison d'être* for environmental taxes: 'If the double challenge of unemployment/environmental pollution is to be addressed, a swap can be envisaged between reducing labour costs through increased pollution charges.' This idea was explicitly endorsed by the UK Chancellor of the Exchequer in his 1994 Budget (Clarke, 1994, p 35), when he stated: 'Taxes can play an important role in protecting the environment. ... But I am determined not to impose additional costs on business overall. ... In brief, I want to raise tax on polluters to make further cuts in the tax on jobs.' More strikingly still, an OECD study (1994, p 57) of the Swedish introduction of environmental taxes concluded: 'It seems fair to say that, without the opportunity offered by the need felt to reduce income taxes, while keeping the total volume intact, environmental taxes would not have been introduced to the extent that now is the case.' In other words, the environmental dividend from environmental taxation was perceived as of less importance than the benefits of reducing distortionary taxes elsewhere.

CONCLUSION

Of course, the fact that policy-makers seem to have been converted to the idea of the possibility of multiple dividends from environmental taxation does not necessarily mean that such dividends either exist or will be achieved in practice. This paper has sought to show that there are sound theoretical reasons for believing that the systematic shift of the tax burden, from labour and capital to the use of environmental resources, can improve environmental quality and increase employment, thereby reducing unemployment and raising output. The theoretical arguments against this belief rest on an inconsistent view of the 'no-distortion' position of the economy. This inconsistency derives from a perception that the environmental externality only causes a distortion in the market containing the process or product which, in turn, contain the externality, so that when the environmental tax is introduced, it causes distortions in the other markets; this inevitably causes a loss in welfare. A more logical view is that the environmental externality, through market-interaction effects, actually distorts all markets to some extent. The economy is in a position of no-distortion when the externality has been internalized. When the environmental tax is introduced, therefore, it does not distort other markets; the internalization of the costs in the market that is most affected actually returns the other markets to a no-distortion position. In short, it seems that both theory and logic suggest that the internalization of environmental externalities should be regarded as distortion-reducing in all markets rather than distortion-increasing.

Modelling of environmental taxes with appropriate revenue-recycling suggests, though with exceptions, that multiple dividends exist. However, the output dividend is likely to be small. The chief significance that it exists lies in the fact that it suggests that environmental tax reform may be a way of improving environmental quality without negatively affecting the economy – fear of which has tended to militate against environmental improvement. The employment dividend may be more substantial than the output dividend. While it certainly will not 'solve' unemployment on its own, it seems likely that it could make a useful contribution towards reducing it. There are not many macropolicies for reducing unemployment. Environmental tax reform is not a policy that can be ignored by those committed to such reduction.

But the principal dividend of environmental taxation remains the environmental dividend. Those who have questioned the existence of multiple dividends have performed an important service in re-emphasizing 'the critical importance of attending to the environmental benefits' (Goulder, 1994b, p 31). It is not likely to result in an optimal policy to allow the introduction of environmental taxation to be driven by the perception that income, or other distortionary or unpopular taxes are too high. The principal purpose of environmental taxation is, and should remain, the improvement of environmental quality through the internalization of environmental costs. But what this analysis of other possible dividends does suggest is that this process is not likely to involve the economic costs that have often been attributed to environmental improvement in the past. Rather, it may yield net non-environmental economic benefits. This should make environmental tax reform attractive even to policy-makers who are more sensitive to economic performance than to environmental damage. The evidence suggests that, despite the political difficulties of introducing environmental taxes (discussed in Hanley *et al*, 1990, and, more briefly, OECD, 1994, pp 43– 45, but outside the scope of this paper), this is proving to be the case.

APPENDIX

Let t, c be the initial and Pigouvian tax rates respectively, where c>t. Let X_j, X_j' be the quantity of the taxed good demanded under tax rates t and c respectively. Then, when R_1, R_2 are the initial and Pigouvian revenues respectively, and r is the ratio between them:

$$R_1 = tX_j \text{ and}$$
$$R_2 = cX_j' \text{ and}$$
$$r = (R_2/R_1) = cX_j'/tX_j$$

Now, if ε is X_j's average price elasticity of demand over the relevant range:

$$\varepsilon \quad = (dX_j/dt)(t/X_j), \text{ where } dX_j/dt = (X_j' - X_j)/(c\text{-}t)$$

$$\rightarrow \varepsilon(X_j/t) = (X_j' - X_j)/(c\text{-}t)$$

$$\rightarrow X_j' \quad = X_j\{1 + \varepsilon(c\text{-}t)/t\}$$

$$\rightarrow r \quad = (c/t)\{1 + \varepsilon(c\text{-}t)/t\}$$

When $\varepsilon=0$, $r=c/t \rightarrow X_j'=X_j$ so there is no erosion effect.

The condition for revenue to be unchanged ($r=1$), is as follows:

$$r \quad = (c/t)\{1 + \varepsilon(c-t)/t\} = 1$$

$$\rightarrow t/c \quad = 1 + \varepsilon(c-t)/t$$

$$\rightarrow \varepsilon c^2 + tc(1-\varepsilon) - t^2 = 0$$

Using the quadratic formula

$$c \quad = t \text{ or } -t/\varepsilon \text{ (where } -1 \leq \varepsilon \leq 0)$$

$$\text{or } \varepsilon \quad = -t/c$$

REFERENCES

Atkins, L V and Wilson, D G (1984) 'Origins and Implications of Tax-Plus-Rebate Policies', *Journal of Resource Management and Technology*, Vol 13, No 3, November, pp 163–69

Ballard, C L, Shoven, J B and Whalley, J (1985) 'General Equilibrium Computations of the Marginal Welfare Costs of Taxes in the United States', *American Economic Review* Vol 75, No 1, March, pp 128–38

Barker, T (1992) 'The Carbon Tax: Economic and Policy Issues', Energy-Environment-Economy Modelling Discussion Paper No 3, Department of Applied Economics, University of Cambridge, Cambridge; also published in Carraro, C and Siniscalco, D (eds) (1993) *The European Carbon Tax: an Economic Assessment*, Kluwer, Dordrecht, pp 239–54

Barker, T (1994) 'Taxing Pollution instead of Employment: Greenhouse Gas Abatement through Fiscal Policy in the UK', Energy-Environment-Economy Discussion Paper No 9, June, Department of Applied Economics, University of Cambridge

Barker, T and Johnstone, N (1993) 'Equity and Efficiency in Policies to Reduce Carbon Emissions in the Domestic Sector', *Energy and Environment*, Vol 4, No 4, pp 335–61

Boero, G, Clarke, R and Winters, L (1991) *The Macroeconomic Consequences of Controlling Greenhouse Gases: a Survey*, Department of the Environment, HMSO, London

Bovenberg, A L and de Mooij, R A (1994) 'Environmental Levies and Distortionary Taxation', *American Economic Review*, Vol 94, No 4, September, pp 1085–89

Chichilnisky, G and Heal, G (1993) 'Global Environmental Risks', *Journal of Economic Perspectives*, Vol 7, No 4, pp 65–86

Clarke, K (1994) 'The Chancellor's Speech', Budget 1994, *Financial Times*, 30 November, pp 33–5

Cline, W (1992) *The Economics of Global Warming*, Institute for International Economics, Washington, DC

DRI (1994) *Potential Benefits of Integration of Environmental and Economic Policies: an Incentive-Based Approach to Policy Integration*, report prepared for the European Commission, Graham and Trotman, London, Kluwer, New York

EC (European Commission) (1993) *Growth, Competitiveness, Employment: the Challenges and Ways Forward into the 21st Century*, white paper, Bulletin of the European Communities Supplement 6/93, European Commission, Brussels

EC (European Commission) (1994) 'Taxation, employment and environment: fiscal reform for reducing unemployment', Study No 3, *European Economy*, No 56, Directorate-General for Economic and Financial Affairs, European Commission, Brussels, pp 137–77

Ekins, P (1995) 'Rethinking the Costs Related to Global Warming', *Environmental and Resource Economics*, 6, pp 231–77

Gaskins, D W and Weyant, J P (1993) 'Model Comparisons of the Costs of Reducing CO_2 Emissions', *American Economic Review* (AEA Papers and Proceedings), Vol 83, No 2, May, pp 318–23

Goulder, L H (1994a) 'Effects of Carbon Taxes in an Economy with Prior Tax Distortions: an Intertemporal General Equilibrium Analysis', July, mimeo, Department of Economics, Stanford University

Goulder, L H (1994b) 'Environmental Taxation and the "Double Dividend": a Reader's Guide', paper prepared for the International Institute of Public Finance 50th Congress, 'Public Finance, Environment, and Natural Resources', August, mimeo, Stanford University, California

Hanley, N, Hallett, S and Moffatt, I (1990) 'Why is more notice not taken of economists' prescriptions for the control of pollution?', *Environment and Planning*, Vol 22, pp 1421–39

Jackson, T (1995) 'Price Elasticity and Market Structure – overcoming obstacles to ensure energy efficiency' in Barker, T, Ekins, P and Johnstone, N (eds) *Global Warming and Energy Elasticities*, Routledge, London, pp 254–66

Jackson, T and Jacobs, M (1991) 'Carbon Taxes and the Assumptions of Environmental Economics' in Barker, T (ed) *Green Futures for Economic Growth*, Cambridge Econometrics, Cambridge, pp 49–67

Jorgenson, D and Wilcoxen, P (1993) 'Reducing US Carbon Emissions: an Econometric General Equilibrium Assessment', *Resource and Energy Economics* Vol 15, No 1, March, pp 7–25

Jorgenson, D and Yun, K Y (1990) 'The Excess Burden of Taxation in the US', Harvard Institute of Economic Research, Discussion Paper No 1528, November, Harvard University, Cambridge, Massachusetts

Lovins, A B and Lovins, H L (1991) 'Least Cost Climatic Stabilization', *Annual Review of Energy and Environment*, Vol 16, pp 433–531

Majocchi, A (1994) 'The Employment Effects of Eco-Taxes: a Review of Empirical Models and Results', paper presented at the OECD Workshop on Implementation of Environmental Taxes, Paris, 14–15 February, mimeo, Department of Economics, University of Pavia

Manne, A S and Richels, R G (1992) *Buying Greenhouse Insurance*, MIT Press, Cambridge

Nordhaus, W (1991a) 'To slow or not to slow: the economics of the greenhouse effect', *Economic Journal*, 101, July 1991, pp 920–37

Nordhaus, W (1991b) 'The Cost of Slowing Climate Change: a Survey', *The Energy Journal*, Vol 12, No 1, pp 37–65

Nordhaus, W (1993) 'Optimal Greenhouse Gas Reductions and Tax Policy in the 'DICE' Model', *American Economic Review* (AEA Papers and Proceedings), Vol 83, No 2, May, pp 313–17

Nordhaus, W (1994) *Managing the Global Commons: the Economic of Climate Change*, MIT Press, Cambridge, Massachusetts

OECD (Opschoor, J and Vos, H) (1989) *Economic Instruments for Environmental Protection*, OECD, Paris

OECD (1994) *Environment and Taxation: the Cases of The Netherlands, Sweden and the United States*, OECD, Paris

OECD (1995) *Environmental Taxes in OECD Countries*, OECD, Paris

Parry, I (1994) 'Pollution Taxes and Revenue Recycling', paper given to the International Workshop on Environmental Taxation, Revenue Recycling and Unemployment, 16–17 December, Fondazione Eni Enrico Mattei, Milano

Pearce, D (1991) 'The Role of Carbon Taxes in Adjusting to Global Warming', *Economic Journal*, 101, July, pp 938–48

Pearce, D W and Turner, R K (1990) *Resource and Environmental Economics*, Harvester Wheatsheaf, Hemel Hempstead, Herts

Pearson, M and Smith, S (1991) *The European carbon tax: an assessment of the EC's proposals*, Institute of Fiscal Studies, London

TAXING POLLUTION INSTEAD OF JOBS: TOWARDS MORE EMPLOYMENT WITHOUT MORE INFLATION THROUGH FISCAL REFORM IN THE UK

Terry Barker

SUMMARY

Fiscal changes designed to achieve the objectives of a substantial increase in employment, and at the same time a large reduction in CO_2 emissions, are explored using an energy-environment-economy model of the UK: the Cambridge Multisectoral Dynamic Model (MDM). Two options to achieve these objectives are considered in detail: the road-fuel duty escalator, intro-

Acknowledgement
When this paper was written, the author was a Principal Investigator with Paul Ekins on a project *Greenhouse gas abatement through fiscal policy*, funded under the Global Environmental Change Initiative (project L320253107) of the UK Economic and Social Research Council (ESRC). The ESRC is gratefully acknowledged for providing support for the project. This paper is a companion to that published in *Energy and Environment* in 1995, entitled 'Taxing pollution instead of employment: greenhouse gas abatement through fiscal policy in the UK', but includes new scenarios and places more emphasis on achieving higher employment without higher inflation. It reports on an application of a large model of the economy which involves the work of many people; acknowledgements are due to other members of the team in Cambridge who have worked on aspects of the model relevant to the research: Rachel Beaven, Clare Bryden, Nick Johnstone and Peter Madsen. Acknowledgements are also due to Susan Baylis and Richard Lewney of Cambridge Econometrics for comments on the paper, to Rob Wilson of the Institute for Employment Research, University of Warwick, UK, who worked on the specification of the employment equations, and to Robert Lindley, Director of the Institute, for comments. Any views expressed in the paper are strictly those of the author.

duced in the March 1993 Budget at 3 per cent in real terms and increased to 10.1 per cent from 1996, and the EC's proposed carbon/energy tax rising to $10 per barrel by 2000 and then to $20.4 by 2005. Revenues for each tax are recycled via reductions in employers' National Insurance Contributions (NIC) calculated to keep the ratio of the public-sector borrowing requirement (PSBR) to GDP at base scenario rates. The changes are introduced in 1996 and standardized so that each option increases employment by some half a million by 2005. A detailed analysis is made of the effects on industrial employment of the options; both appear to generate a pattern of extra employment which is different from that seen in the 1987–89 boom and also different from that which might be expected under conditions of more rapid economic growth in the 1990s. Most of the extra jobs created are full-time, especially male full-time when compared with historical experience. Both options appear to provide substantial environmental net benefits as well as economic gains. In addition, the road-fuel duty option is expected to have no impact on the rate of inflation, since the effect of the increases in the duties on consumer prices is offset by that of reductions in NIC on industrial costs. Each option has its strengths and weaknesses and a combination may allow the UK to increase the number of jobs by one million by 2005 and at the same time reach the Toronto target of a 20 per cent cut in CO_2 emissions below 1988 levels by 2005.

INTRODUCTION

The objective of reducing long-term structural unemployment has moved to the top of the international political agenda following the apparent establishment of a regime of low inflation in OECD countries (EC, 1993, OECD, 1994a and b). At the same time, governments are considering and implementing fiscal measures to reduce greenhouse gas emissions to levels which are sustainable in terms of climate change. Bringing the two objectives together suggests an intriguing set of options: that the fiscal system be reformed by switching the burden of taxation from employment to pollution (fiscal reform or 'ecological tax reform' – see von Weizsacker and Jesinghaus, 1992; Majocchi, 1994). The switch in taxation appears to offer a route towards full employment, at the same time benefiting the environment (see OECD, 1993 a and b for case studies, and EC, 1994, for a thorough exploration of the issues in the context of the European Union).

This paper explores two such options to achieve an extra one million jobs by 2005 in the context of the UK fiscal system and the UK Government's measures to meet the Rio target (UK DoE, 1994). One option is the continued escalation in road-fuel duties; although the purpose of the measure is partly to raise revenues, once the PSBR is brought down to acceptable levels these new revenues could be used to reduce employers' National Insurance Contributions, which are effectively a tax on employment.[1] A second option is the introduction of the proposed EC carbon/energy tax, again the revenues being recycled through the reduc-

---

[1] At present (1993 estimates from UK CSO's *Financial Statistics*, March 1994) the revenues from duties on hydrocarbon oils are approximately £12bn and those from employers' NIC are £23bn, approximately 10 per cent of total central government current receipts from all sources, so the switch in taxation involved in the removal of the NIC is fairly marginal, although the effect on petrol prices will be more substantial.

tion in employers' NIC.[2] These options have been explored in detail using an E3 (energy-environment- economy) model of the UK economy which was developed to analyse greenhouse gas abatement, and some of the results are reported below.[3]

The paper concentrates on the spending of the revenues raised by escalating road-fuel duties or a carbon/energy tax in the form of reductions in employers' NIC. The analysis is not intended as a comprehensive programme to reduce unemployment in the UK (which would at the very least require more discussion and modelling of many employment-creating measures), but as a preliminary quantitative exploration of the industrial and economic effects of some important potential components of such a programme. The purpose is to answer the questions: what is the scale of the extra employment generated by such fiscal reform? In what sectors will employment increase and what type of employment is generated? How can the risks of escalation of wage inflation be reduced? What additional economic and environmental benefits might be expected?

One reason for the introduction of the higher road-fuel duties was the government's stated requirement to reduce the PSBR; it is assumed, therefore, that the reduction in NIC takes place after 1996, when the PSBR ratio to GDP has been reduced to below 3 per cent, the Maastricht upper limit for participation in full Economic and Monetary Union. However, considered as a greenhouse gas abatement policy, the effects of the higher duties on CO_2 emissions are fairly modest and much higher levels of duty may be required to bring down emissions to long-term sustainable levels. One option for fiscal reform explored in the paper is the use of the large revenues generated by higher duties to reduce NIC sufficiently to generate some half million jobs by 2005; this option is compared to a second one of introducing a carbon/energy tax, on the lines suggested by the EC, but continuing to escalate after the year 2000[4] and at a rate also sufficient, via the reduction of employers' NIC, to generate half a million jobs by 2005. However, the comparison of the two options is an expository device in the analysis of the measures and presentation of the results and does not mean that they may not both be implemented together. Since they have rather different effects on the environment and the economy, it could well be sensible to combine

---

[2] The paper is confined to consideration of the taxation of pollution associated with the burning of fossil fuels. Although there is a case under the polluter-pays principle that pollution of water and land should also bear more taxation, the tax instruments are not in place, and the tax base does not appear to be large or robust enough to generate the large revenues required to replace employers' NIC.

[3] The results in the tables below often show values to the nearest one million or thousand and percentages to one decimal place. This is necessary for an analysis which considers industries of very different sizes and should not be taken as an indication of the accuracy of the projections. The uncertainties and projection errors mean that the numbers should be taken only as indicating general trends as discussed in the text.

[4] The effects of the EC carbon/energy tax rising to $10 per barrel oil-equivalent in 2000 and remaining at that level are considered by Barker (1995b); with recycling of revenues via reductions in NIC, employment is some 250,000 higher than base (1 per cent) by the year 2000, results which are exactly in line with those for the EU quoted in EC, 1994, p 150, using the QUEST and HERMES models.

them in a comprehensive programme of employment generation providing an extra one million jobs by 2005.[5]

The next section briefly describes the Cambridge model of the UK economy. This includes an overview of the economics of the model and of the treatment of energy demands and the emission of air pollutants. The following section describes the policy instruments which are the focus of the analysis, namely:

- The escalator: this is the main measure introduced by the government to reduce the growth of greenhouse gas emissions, through the escalating excise duty on road fuels.
- The carbon/energy tax: the EC proposal adapted to start in 1996.
- Employers' NIC: the measure chosen to reduce employment costs in the study.

The section sets out the detailed econometrics of the model which lie behind the effects of changing real fuel prices and real labour costs in the scenarios. The next section explains the scenarios which have been constructed and how they relate to one another; this section then presents the main results for employment, CO_2 emissions, government revenues and expenditures, the main macroeconomic variables and a summary of the environmental effects. The following section presents the results for the labour market in detail. Finally some conclusions are given in the last section.

AN E3 MODEL FOR THE UK

The Cambridge Multisectoral Dynamic Model (Barker and Peterson, 1987), a large-scale model of the UK economy, has been extended to include energy-environment-economy interactions to become an E3 model. The model already contained an energy sub-model (Peterson, 1987); this has been replaced by a new version based closely on UK Department of Energy work (UK DEn, 1989). The energy sub-model allows a detailed analysis of the demand for energy and the substitution between fuels following the imposition of a carbon/energy tax. The projection of fuel use, distinguished by user and type of fuel, is then available to calculate emissions of CO_2, allowing for different qualities of fuels. Details of the sub-model and applications to assess the effects of the carbon/energy tax are given in Barker and Lewney, 1991; Barker, Baylis and Madsen, 1993; and Barker, Ekins and Johnstone, 1995.

---

[5] This treatment differs from that adopted in the optimal tax literature, where each tax is assessed independently, usually in the context of a general-equilibrium model with strong assumptions regarding competition etc, against a 'neutral' base, usually taken to be a *per capita* tax or subsidy on private consumers (rather like the discredited UK poll tax). The scenarios in this paper could have been designed to include recycling of revenues via a *per capita* subsidy and then reductions in NIC compensated by a corresponding *per capita* tax, but this was regarded as rather artificial and more likely to confuse than to assist in the analysis. The EC study (1994) draws on the optimal tax literature to justify fiscal reform. The basic argument is that the substantial tax revenues from new taxes proposed to correct externalities must go somewhere, and they can be used to correct distortions in the existing tax system, such as taxes on employment when European economies are experiencing substantial unemployment.

In the course of 1993, the model was re-estimated on new data based on a new Standard Industrial Classification (SIC92), a new price base, 1990, the CSO's input-output tables for 1990 and the 1993 edition of the *National Accounts*. The number of industrial sectors was extended to 49, with an emphasis on service-sector disaggregation. The model is used by Cambridge Econometrics to provide forecasts for UK industrial and regional prospects. This paper relies on the February 1994 forecast (Cambridge Econometrics, 1994) to provide a base scenario to compare with the higher employment scenarios. The following discussion of the model summarizes and extends the earlier published descriptions.

General Models and Double Dividends

The model used in this paper is one which is in some ways more general than the General Equilibrium Models (GEM) which have dominated the approach in the early literature on US and global CO_2 abatement (Boero, Clarke and Winters, 1991). It does not assume that the economy is at full employment all the time (the usual GEM assumption), although in the long term, given assumptions about the growth of world markets and the UK working population, the model's projections normally reach full employment. Furthermore, it does not assume constant returns to scale or perfect competition in production (two usual GEM assumptions) on the grounds that these assumptions do not hold for many sectors of the economy. Finally, it is an econometric model, utilizing annual time series of some 30 years' data; GEM models are often calibrated on one year's data, although one important US GEM (Jorgenson and Wilcoxen, 1993) is also estimated on time-series data.

These features mean that the model can be used to analyse the year-to-year dynamics of new policies over a long projection period, such as to the year 2020, simulating the changes introduced in successive budgets and the lagged effects of the policies.

It also means that the term 'double dividend' must be interpreted with care. In a GEM framework, the environmental dividend comes from the introduction of social environmental costs into the prices of the model and the economic dividend comes from the removal of a distortionary tax. The two dividends are measured against a theoretical optimum assumed in the model's construction and projections. In the framework adopted in most time-series econometric models there may be no optimum in this sense. The environmental dividend in these models comes from the reduction of CO_2 and associated reduction in other emissions; and the economic dividend comes from the extra employment from the tax shift. The extra employment can mean lower short-term unemployment with the long-term level unaffected, or it can also mean a higher non-inflationary level of full employment.[6]

---

[6] Bovenberg and van der Ploeg (1993) use a theoretical model to investigate fiscal reform in a small open economy under conditions of involuntary unemployment. They find that if substitution between labour and resources is easy, if the production share of labour is large and if initial tax rates on resources and profits are small, fiscal reform can yield a triple dividend: increases in employment, improvements in environmental quality and higher profits.

The new version of the model (MDM9)

MDM9 follows closely the economics and methodology of version 8 used in the previous forecasts. A comprehensive account of an earlier version of the model is given by Barker and Peterson (1987) and this remains the main reference for the research results. Since then, the model has become an energy-environment-economy model of the UK and many of the equations have been cast into pairs of a co-integrating long-term form and a dynamic-adjustment equation, but the basic structure of the model has remained unchanged.

Two features of the changes to the database, comparing MDM9 with MDM8, as used in earlier analyses of the carbon tax, are worth noting in the context of this paper.

1. Revised Commodity, Industry, Investment and Stockbuilding Classifications. The new SIC92 is a fundamental change to the classification system for industries and their principal products (and therefore for commodities), bringing the UK system into line with common European standards used by the EU statistical office Eurostat. The industry and commodity classification remain identical to each other in MDM, with the new industries defined on the SIC92. In summary, the order of industries has changed compared to that in MDM8, with electricity and other utilities appearing after manufacturing rather than before; several more service industries are distinguished; and general government output is included in several of these new industries, rather than appearing as a separate activity.

Although the time-series data are weak (with the exception of the employment data) for several of the new service industries, it was thought worthwhile to include them because they are important for economic fore-casting, and the new input-output table gives the necessary cross-section data to disaggregate them in the model.

2. Input-Output Tables for 1990. The input-output tables published for 1990 in *Economic Trends* (October 1993) are in purchasers' prices and they have to be converted to basic prices for MDM9. This mainly involves the realloca-tion of the duties on alcohol, tobacco and petrol to final consumers, and the reallocation of distribution and other margins from the valuation of each commodity's demand to wholesale and retail-distribution commodity output.

The estimates of final demand in the input-output tables are classified by commodity rather than function as shown in the national accounts. The conversion is done by calculating classification converters from the input-output tables in as much detail as possible – for instance, at a 123 commodity and 68 functional category level for consumers' expenditure. The converters are then aggregated to the 49-commodity level of MDM. In the model these are applied to the time-series functional data given at a detailed level in the national accounts – for example, the 68 categories of consumers' expenditure in 1990 prices. Estimates for components of demand for 1993 published at the time of the November 1993 Budget are included in the database. Estimating intermediate demand is less straight-forward. First, input-output coefficients are calculated for commodities absorbed in production by industries from the input-output tables and aggregated to the MDM groups. These coefficients are then projected one year at a time to allow for known and expected technical and other changes. The coefficients for any year are applied to estimates of gross output for that year to give intermediate demand.

MDM91 as an energy-environment-economy model

The economic model is designed to analyse and forecast changes in economic structure. To do this, it disaggregates industries, commodities and consumer and government expenditures, as well as foreign trade and investment. In fact, it disaggregates all of the main variables that are treated as aggregates in most macroeconomic models. The detailed variables are linked together in an accounting framework based on the United Nations System of National Accounts. This framework ensures consistency and correct accounting balances in the model's projections and forecasts.

The model is a combination of orthodox time-series econometric relationships and cross-section input-output relationships. Although it forms aggregate demand in a Keynesian manner, with a consumption function and investment equations, it also includes an average-earnings equation (based on the notion of a target real-wage increase). The supply side comes in through the export and import equations, in which innovation and capacity utilization affects trade performance, as well as a set of employment equations which allow relative wages rates and interest rates to affect employment, and therefore industry-level productivity growth.

The model's main exogenous variables are as follows:

1. World growth in industrial production.
2. World inflation in wholesale prices and in prices of traded goods, such as crude oil.
3. UK population, labour force and natural resources (the main natural resources being coal, oil and natural gas).
4. Current and capital spending of the UK Government.
5. UK tax rates and allowances.
6. The sterling-dollar and other exchange rates.
7. UK and US interest rates.

Energy and environment modelling

The energy modelling is done in energy units (therms) and prices (pence per therm). The methodology is close to that adopted by the UK Department of Energy (now a branch of the Department of Trade and Industry) (UK DEn, 1989). The modelling is done in two stages. There are equations for aggregate energy demand by fuel users allowing for the substitution between energy and other goods and services as a result of relative price changes. The equations also include terms for output and other measures of activity and a temperature variable. At the second stage, the substitution between different fuels for each user is done by share equations, also allowing for relative price effects. The projection of fuel use by user and type of fuel is then available to calculate emissions of carbon dioxide and other gases and particulates to the atmosphere, allowing for different qualities of fuel and different processes of combustion.

MODELLING TAX EFFECTS ON POLLUTION AND EMPLOYMENT

Modelling Road-Fuel Demand

There are many studies of the demand elasticities for gasoline (see Dahl and Sterner, 1991, and Goodwin, 1992, for reviews, and Franzén and Sterner, 1995, for a discussion of some long-run estimates from time-series/cross-section data) which give a wide range of estimates for the long-term price elasticity of demand – which is of most interest in an analysis of the effects of a potentially substantial price rise. The first version of the Cambridge E3 model (reported in Barker, 1995) imposed a long-term price elasticity of –0.3 for fuel consumption by road transportation in the UK (this includes both gasoline and diesel fuels and covers both private and commercial road transport); but it was clear that the data would support the imposition of much higher – ie, more negative – elasticities.

The recent literature on estimates for the UK (Virley, 1993 and Dargay, 1993) covers the same ground but comes to different conclusions. Virley estimates an unrestricted error-correction equation for first differences in road-transport fuel consumption, annual data 1950–90, and finds a long-run price elasticity of –0.46 and income elasticity of 1.22 (calculated for 1990). Dargay, reporting preliminary results, adopts a more disaggregated approach, dividing the demand for transport fuels into fuel consumption per kilometer driven, vehicle use and vehicle ownership. She finds a long-run price elasticity for petrol consumption by passenger cars of about –0.7 to –1.4 and an income elasticity of about 1.5. The high price elasticity comes from a large response of vehicle (car) ownership to petrol price.

In the face of these differences and given the danger of serious biases in time-series estimates on non-stationary data, it is worth exploring the cross-section evidence. Franzén and Sterner (1995), taking note of Pesaran and Smith's (1995) warning of the difficulties of using pooled time-series and cross-section data, have found high long-run prices elasticities (–1.2 to –1.4) for OECD gasoline demand and low income elasticities (0.6 to 0.75) from such data. Since it is clear from the engineering data that substantial savings in fuel use have taken place over the sample period and that more improvements are possible by further increasing engine efficiency, a high long-run price elasticity seems plausible for the UK and accordingly it has been imposed on the single equation for road-fuel consumption (gasoline and diesel). Demand is related to economic activity and relative prices with a non-linear specification as follows (DEn, 1989, p 78):

$$\ln E = 0.621 \quad + 0.695 \text{*}(\ln Y \quad - 0.900 \text{*} \ln Y(-1))$$
$$ (4.0) \quad\quad (6.1) \quad\quad (\text{***})$$

$$- 0.120 \text{*} \ln RPE \quad + 0.001 \text{*} time$$
$$(\text{***}) \quad\quad\quad\quad (2.1)$$
$$+ 0.900 \text{*} \ln E(-1) \quad + e$$
$$(\text{***})$$

equation 1

Annual data 1970–92; Rbar sq=0.99; Durbin-Watson Statistic=1.84
where ln denotes natural logarithm
(–1) denotes a lag of one year
numbers in brackets are t-statistics and (***) denotes an imposed parameter
E is total delivered energy in million therms
Y is a measure of economic activity
RPE is the price of energy relative to that of all goods and services
time is a time trend
and e is an error term.

Note that parameter 0.900 appears twice, with the parameter -0.12 representing the price elasticity and 0.900 the lag on the price effect, both being imposed to give the long-run elasticity of –1.2. The long-run income elasticity is estimated as 0.8, in line with the cross-section estimates. A full discussion of the logic behind the equations and their properties is given by UK DEn (1989, pp 77–91); the specification allows for lagged effects of relative prices but not of any other variable. The reasoning behind this lagged response is that the history of energy prices up to the previous year is embodied in the stock of energy-using equipment (road vehicles) used in the current year; it is this stock, combined with the level of activity in the current year, which determines road-fuel demand. One important difference in this approach compared with that of Virley (1993) is that lagged responses are only imposed on the price effects, not on both income *and* price effects. An improvement on this specification might be the use of the co-integration procedure in estimating responses; but a satisfactory set of results could not be obtained in time to be included in the model.

The March 1993 Budget included a commitment to raise road-fuel duties by 3 per cent per annum in real terms indefinitely, and in the December 1993 Budget this was increased to 5 per cent. The energy sub-model distinguishes the use of gasoline (motor spirit) and diesel (derv) by road transportation –ie, freight and passenger transport, and private cars – with, as discussed above, an own-price elasticity estimated to be –0.12 in the short term (current year) and –1.20 (imposed) in the long term. Within total energy use, the model then distinguishes the shares supplied by gasoline and diesel (and other fuels). The cross-price elasticities between gasoline and diesel is potentially large, but due to problems with the data no estimates have been made and the shares are projected on the basis of past trends. The road-fuel duties are imposed on both fuels, but since diesel engines are more efficient, there is likely to be a further switch to diesel. This effect is not taken into account in the scenarios. For the reasons discussed by Virley (1993, p 44), it is not likely to make much difference to the CO_2 results, but it may make a difference to the other environmental effects, since diesel consumption generates much more pollution in the form of air-borne particulates. A further switch to diesel fuel may offset some of the potential environmental benefits of the road-fuel duty escalator.

Since spending on road fuels is likely to increase by 1–2 per cent per annum as real incomes increase, with a long-term price elasticity of -1.2, real prices must rise by slightly less than 1–2 per cent per annum in order to hold consumption constant in the long term. However, in the short term, with a low short-term price elasticity (–0.12), real prices must rise by some 8 per cent to 17 per cent per annum to achieve the same effect. Since the tax only affects fuels used in road transport and since CO_2 emissions from road transport are only about 20 per cent of total emissions, real prices have to rise very sharply in order to reduce total emissions substantially.

Modelling the EC's Carbon/Energy Tax[7]

The EC proposals are modelled by assuming that imports and domestic supplies of fuels will bear the tax according to their carbon and energy content, with exports exempted from the tax coverage and the tax being introduced unilaterally in the UK. The treatment is assumed to be very close to that adopted for excise duties on hydrocarbons (see Barker, Baylis and Madsen, 1993, for a fuller analysis of an EU-wide or OECD-wide tax). If it is also assumed that all the tax is passed on to the user of the fuels, and that the industrial user then passes on the extra costs in the form of higher prices, then the new prices for all goods and services in the economy can be calculated. The increase in price will be a result of the direct and indirect carbon and energy content of each of the 49 commodities and 68 consumers' expenditure categories (to take two important sets of prices in the model).

It is worth explaining how the model predicts the impact of the carbon/energy tax on prices and tax revenues. The effects on total energy consumption and the use of fuels are derived entirely from the effects of the tax on prices. The carbon and energy components of the EC tax are treated separately. The *carbon* tax is converted from a $1 per barrel oil-equivalent ($3 in 1996, rising to $5 by 2000) in 1996–2000 (in real 1993 prices) to a rate in £ sterling (using the fixed exchange rate of $1.75=£1) per tonne of carbon emitted for each year 1996–2000. The carbon-tax liability of all fuels is calculated on the basis of their carbon content, and converted into pence per therm on the basis of their heat content. The *energy* component of the tax is expressed in pence per therm, and again indexed on the consumer price index. A matrix of total carbon/energy tax rates for each fuel and user can be constructed for each year and average rates calculated. Tax revenues can then be calculated from energy consumption for conversion, own use by energy industries and for secondary uses. The potential revenues will be reduced if consumption falls when the tax is imposed.

The original EC proposal has been accompanied in the scenario with indexation of benefits for any rise in prices from the tax and special additional payments to pensioners to compensate for higher fuel bills. In addition, given imperfections in the market for insulation and energy-saving appliances in the domestic sector, an energy-saving programme of £1.1 billion in total over the period 1996–2000 has been included in the scenario, with the costs met from the tax revenues.

---

[7] Details of the tax as originally proposed are given in (EC, 1991, 1992a). There have been many studies, besides those referenced in the text, of the possible effects of the tax on member states of the EU, notably (EC, 1992b; DRI, 1991, 1992; Karadeloglou, 1992).

Modelling the Employment Demand

This section explains how employment is determined in the Cambridge model, defined in terms of numbers of people in jobs, both full-time and part-time and both employees and self-employed. The approach is highly disaggregated, with employment being divided into 49 industrial sectors, each in 12 regional labour markets; however, for this paper, only the aggregate 49 UK industrial sectors are considered. For each industry, employment is determined by a set of co-integrating equations in which the long-term labour demand function includes both output and factor price terms (see Briscoe and Wilson, 1991, and Nickell, 1984). Expected direction of effects on employment (E) are as follows:

output (Q)	positive effect
real wages (RW)	negative effect
average weekly hours (H)	negative effect
real oil prices (ROP)	negative effect
cost of capital (BR)	positive effect

Note that the substitution effects of the cost of capital dominate the effects from the implicit change in economic activity.

This theoretical approach is contrasted with that previously adopted in the Cambridge model (Peterson, 1987) and that adopted, for example, by Jorgenson and Wilcoxen in their general equilibrium model of the US (1993) in which the employment functions were derived from the neoclassical factor-demand model. The assumption of constant returns to scale imposed in the general equilibrium model is not justified in many UK employment equations and has been rejected in favour of a more flexible approach which allows employment typically to grow less than output. The approach requires the further estimation of a set of hours-worked equations, which are required to solve simultaneously with the employment equations. Briefly, hours worked are determined by 'normal' hours and the rate of unemployment with allowance for lagged adjustment. (These equations are very stable because the exogenous normal hours have a large, dominating effect.)

The econometric estimation combines the technique of co-integration (Engle and Granger, 1987) and a methodology for developing parsimonious and robust time-series models in a comprehensive and efficient manner developed by David Hendry (1985) and summarized by Gilbert (1986). Most of the variables discussed above were tested and found to be integrated of order one – ie, I (1). The next step was to test whether groups of variables which economic theory suggests should be related in the long run, such as employment, the real wage and output, are co-integrated. This was done by running a regression, in terms of current levels only, for each industry, and testing whether the residuals from this regression are stationary. Once the existence of a stable long-run relationship had been established, a more dynamic form of the model could be estimated with a very general specification, which was then progressively simplified to achieve a final efficient model form.

In the vast majority of cases the results suggest that an error-correction formulation can be applied, so this model was imposed in all industries. In this form, the residuals from the first-stage co-integrating regression (which represents the long-run relationship between employment and its determinants) are used in a second-stage dynamic specification, which incorporates various lagged terms to reflect adjustment lags. The inclusion of the residuals from the first stage ensures that the long-run solution, given by the co-integrating regression, is imposed.

In the search for a satisfactory specification, various additional regressors were introduced or, alternatively, other variables were tried in place of output and real wages. It is perhaps worth mentioning some variables which were considered as regressors in the original specification search, but which were finally discarded from the specification. From a wide set of factor price variables under analysis, time series measuring material input prices, investment good prices and user cost of capital, were discarded. Equally, series measuring the capital stock and the level of capacity utilization in each industry were left out of the final specification. A number of proxy variables, such as time trends, for approximating technological change, were also examined and discarded. Other variables, such as exchange rates and generalized measures of aggregate demand, were considered but were not found to improve the specification consistently.

The preferred general specification for employment (E) contains, in addition to the output (Q) and real wage (RW) variables, an average hours-worked term (H), a variable measuring the real price of oil (ROP) and an interest rate variable (BR) (bank base rate). These last two variables constitute the preferred general-factor price terms. The coefficient on both hours worked and the real price of oil is expected to be negative, while that on bank rate is expected to be positive, given that firms substitute labour for capital as the price of capital rises. Almost all of the coefficients in the co-integrating regressions for this general specification take their expected sign. Most are also significant at the 5 per cent level (although it is important to bear in mind that they are probably biased (see Stock, 1987). The general explanatory power is good.

The tests on the residuals generally confirm that the residuals are stationary. All of the co-integrated regression Durbin Watson test statistics are acceptable. Using Engle and Granger's approximate guidelines, most industries pass the basic and augmented Dickey-Fuller tests to establish stationarity in the residuals. Given the qualifications on the power of these tests, these results are taken to indicate a co-integrated specification, such that a stable long-run equilibrium relationship exists between employment and this set of variables.

The effects of output, relative wages and hours worked, together with those for the oil price and banks' base rate, as estimated in MDM91, are presented in Table 9.1. Estimated elasticities of the wrong sign have been restricted to zero to maintain sensible long-term properties of the model. For the most part, the output elasticities are below one, showing that as output increases, employment rises proportionately less. Increases in relative wage rates and in hours worked tend to reduce the numbers employed. The elasticities vary markedly across industries and are often less than –1, especially for hours worked. Increases in real oil prices have small effects in

Table 9.1 *UK Co-integrating Employment Equations: Estimates of Long–term Elasticities*

Industry	Output elasticity	Real wage elasticity	Hours effect	Oil price effect	Interest rate effect
1 Agriculture, etc	0.314	−0.451	0.000	−0.128	0.052
2 Coal, etc	1.155	−0.545	−3.633	0.000	0.137
3 Oil and gas	0.037	−0.002	0.000	0.000	1.756
4 Other mining	0.756	−0.684	0.000	0.000	0.000
5 Food	0.200	−0.494	−1.459	−0.087	0.066
6 Drink	1.268	−1.392	0.000	0.000	0.172
7 Tobacco	1.906	−1.191	−1.646	0.000	0.120
8 Textiles	0.613	−0.717	−3.480	−0.055	0.000
9 Clothing and leather	0.638	−0.608	−1.410	−0.055	0.052
10 Wood and wood products	0.483	−0.528	−1.318	−0.144	0.130
11 Paper, printing and publishing	0.238	−0.437	−0.208	−0.057	0.043
12 Manufactured fuels	0.753	−1.152	−1.043	−0.248	0.000
13 Pharmaceuticals	0.296	−0.463	−1.634	−0.003	0.051
14 Chemicals	0.370	−0.686	−2.176	−0.036	0.069
15 Rubber and plastics	0.426	−0.601	−0.301	−0.003	0.031
16 Non–metallurgical mineral products	0.846	−1.189	−1.716	−0.172	0.021
17 Basic metals	1.018	−1.268	−4.589	−0.106	0.000
18 Metal goods	0.680	−0.756	−1.651	−0.044	0.000
19 Mechanical engineering	0.664	−1.006	−2.154	0.000	0.032
20 Electronics	0.200	−0.307	−3.864	−0.093	0.056
21 Electronic engineering	0.637	−0.609	−1.378	−0.022	0.054
22 Instruments	0.179	−0.561	−2.153	−0.032	0.043
23 Motor vehicles	0.692	−1.215	−1.929	0.000	0.059
24 Aerospace	0.200	−0.727	0.000	−0.032	0.000
25 Other transport equipment	0.976	−0.535	−2.724	−0.019	0.000
26 Manufacturing necessities	0.425	−0.142	0.000	0.000	0.007
27 Electricity	0.408	−0.684	−0.579	0.000	0.072
28 Gas supply	0.200	−0.401	0.000	0.000	−0.075
29 Water supply	0.665	−0.389	0.000	0.000	0.093
30 Construction	0.523	−0.241	0.000	0.000	0.049
31 Retailing	0.610	−0.299	0.000	0.000	0.066
32 Distribution necessities	0.267	−0.177	−0.115	−0.042	0.112

33	Hotels and catering	0.323	−0.022	−1.603	0.000	0.021
34	Rail transport	0.200	−0.736	−2.968	−0.107	0.020
35	Other land transport	0.200	0.000	0.000	−0.121	0.000
36	Water transport	0.275	−0.563	0.000	0.000	0.113
37	Air transport	0.421	0.000	−0.762	−0.080	0.139
38	Other transport services	0.200	−0.227	0.000	−0.026	0.060
39	Communications	0.288	−0.251	−0.541	−0.024	0.041
40	Banking and finance	0.521	−0.018	−0.987	−0.043	0.026
41	Insurance	0.234	0.000	−0.278	−0.081	0.091
42	Professional services	0.753	−0.318	0.000	−0.027	0.084
43	Computing services	0.835	−0.189	0.000	−0.219	0.121
44	Other business services	0.882	−0.617	0.000	0.000	0.000
45	Public administration	0.200	−0.429	−0.364	0.000	0.000
46	Education	0.328	−0.034	−2.994	0.000	0.111
47	Health and social services	1.018	0.000	0.000	−0.190	0.228
48	Waste treatment	0.200	0.000	−0.472	−0.045	0.023
49	Miscellaneous	0.902	−0.663	0.000	0.000	0.071
	Total	0.533	−0.336	−0.754	−0.042	0.072

Note: The total is calculated using shares in total employment in 1990 as weights.

Source: Cambridge Econometrics, 1994

reducing employment. Finally, increases in interest rates slightly increase employment in the long term as labour is substituted for capital.

Having identified stable long-run relationships, it remains to derive a general dynamic specification which can be simplified into a final efficient form. Following the modelling methodology of Hendry (1985) an initially over-parameterized model containing the five key regressors with lags on all variables is proposed.

The general equation form may be written:

$$
\begin{aligned}
\Delta E_t = a &+ b_0 * \Delta Q_t + b_1 * \Delta Q_{t-1} \\
&+ c_0 * \Delta RW_t + c_1 * \Delta RW_{t-1} \\
&+ d_0 * \Delta Ht + d_1 * \Delta H_{t-1} \\
&+ e_0 * \Delta ROP_t + e1 * \Delta ROP_{t-1} \\
&+ f_0 * \Delta BRt + f_1 * \Delta BR_{t-1} \\
&+ g_1 * \Delta E_{t-1} + g_2 * \Delta E_{t-2} \\
&+ b_2 * Q_{t-1} + c_2 * RW_{t-1} + d_2 * H_{t-1}
\end{aligned}
$$

$$+ e_2 * ROP_{t-1} + f_2 * BR_{t-1} + g_3 * E_{t-1}$$

Equation 2

It is specified in terms of first differences. It can be seen how equation 2 in its unrestricted form has some 19 independent terms, including the constant. Given that the present set of data only has some 37 observations, or 34 after taking into account the proposed lag structure, the number of degrees of freedom is comparatively small.

A restricted version of the general VAR model can be obtained by replacing the last six terms in equation 2 by a single variable which is the residual, lagged one period, from the long-term co-integrating equation. This error-correction model may be written:

$$\Delta E_t = a + b_0 * \Delta Q_t + b_1 * \Delta Q_{t-1}$$
$$+ c_0 * \Delta RW_t + c_1 * \Delta RW_{t-1}$$
$$+ d_0 * \Delta H_t + d_1 * \Delta h_{t-1}$$
$$+ e_0 * \Delta ROP_t + e_1 * \Delta ROP_{t-1}$$
$$+ f_0 * \Delta BR_t + b_1 * \Delta BR_{t-1}$$
$$+ g_1 * \Delta E_{t-1} + g_2 * \Delta E_{t-2} \div EC_{t-1}$$

Equation 3

where EC is the error-correction term. Again, the model is formulated in first differences. Since the data are annual, no lags beyond the second period are considered, because it was felt that the number of observations would not support a fuller lag structure. Note that since the model is specified in terms of first differences, this implies a lag of up to two years in terms of levels of each variable. Equation 3 is a restricted version of equation 2 and as such it needs to be tested to ascertain whether or not the restrictions placed on the lagged levels of the independent variables are significant. In the vast majority of industries, this restriction was acceptable.

When the general version of equation 3 is estimated, inevitably many of the 14 coefficients turn out to be insignificant and it is clear that the equation remains over parameterized. The model was therefore further simplified and reparameterized to achieve a more parsimonious representation of the data-generating process. This task was achieved by sequentially eliminating the least significant variables and testing the resulting residual sum of squares to ensure that it does not differ significantly from the original sum of squares found in the most general unrestricted specification.

In the preferred form of the restricted error-correction equations, there are a preponderance of significant and correctly signed coefficients. The dominant variables in these regressions are output, real wages and the lagged dependent variable. For individual industries, the other variables (hours worked, real oil price and bank rate) each contribute significantly to the explanation of employment change. The unadjusted coefficients of determination are sometimes quite low for this set of equations, but this is only to be expected when modelling first differences. All the generalized F-statistics are significant and the standard errors are acceptably low. The results indicate quite complex adjustment processes extending over two years in some industries. The final equations are generally free from problems of serial correlation, heteroscedasticity, and show little indication of parameter instability.

To complement the employment equations, a set of hours-worked equations have also been estimated, which relate average weekly hours worked by industry to normal hours, and capacity utilization. The specification adopted broadly follows the rationale set out in Neale and Wilson (1987). The final specification also includes lagged terms in average weekly hours and normal hours to allow for adjustment processes. In a few cases a Cochrane-Orcutt adjustment process has also been incorporated.

The above estimated employment equations give an indication of the effects of NIC on employers. NIC accounted for some 7.5 per cent of total wages and salaries in 1993, increasing the cost of labour to employers by this amount. If it were removed, then the direct effect on employment may be expected to be an increase of some 2.5 per cent of the total (7.5 per cent times the average elasticity of 0.34), or some 600,000 jobs. This will reduce unemployment, although by a smaller amount due to the discouraged worker effect, and the lower unemployment will increase hours worked slightly. Since hours worked also enters the employment equation, this reduces the original increase in employment as a count of heads.

Why Switching the Tax Burden Will Increase Employment

A shift in taxation from employers' NIC, personal income tax, corporation tax, or indeed the standard rate of VAT towards higher excise duties on road fuels, VAT on domestic fuels, or a carbon/energy tax, will generally tend to increase employment in the economy. This section considers the structural reasons for the increase; there will also be macroeconomic effects which will tend to strengthen the increase because the higher employment leads to higher incomes and expenditures. The macroeconomic effects are discussed below.

The basic cause of the structural effect is related to the main distinguishing characteristic of the UK energy industries – and indeed these industries worldwide – namely, that oil, coal, gas and electricity are all highly capital-intensive. They require large investments in the location and exploitation of reserves, as well as in distribution systems, and require much more investment in physical capital in relation to output than other industries. Figure 9.1 illustrates this characteristic by showing the capital and employment intensities for 35[8] UK industrial sectors. Here 'capital' is measured by cumulated gross domestic fixed-capital formation in 1990 prices over 1960–92 (INV); employment is measured by numbers employed (both part-time and full-time) in 1990 (EMP); and output is measured as value-added in 1990 (YVA). Thus a tax burden on the energy industries tends to affect the use of capital and natural resources rather than labour;

---

[8] There are only 35 sectors shown in the chart because this is the greatest level of detail available for investment in the UK CSO's *National Accounts*. Industrial employment and value added defined over the 49 sectors distinguished in MDM have been aggregated to a comparable grouping in order to prepare the chart.

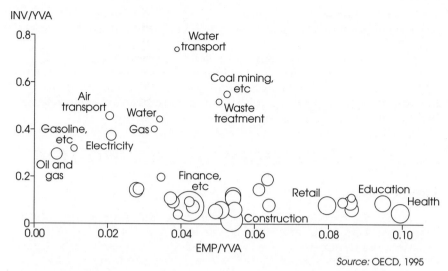

Figure 9.1 *Labour and employment intensities for industries in the UK*

and relieving the burden of NIC, income tax or VAT leads to more use of labour. The size of the bubbles in the chart is proportional to output.

The extra employment does not come through large-scale incentive effects to increase the willingness of workers to accept employment at a given take-home wage, except effects related to the availability of jobs. It comes from incentive effects for employers to take on more labour and substitution effects in the market for goods and services. In the market for labour and the market for goods and services (commodities), there are both demand-side and supply-side effects.

More demand for labour-intensive commodities

As relative prices change in favour of labour-intensive commodities, consumers will tend to substitute towards such items; this is not an obvious process because the shift in relative prices will affect all commodities to a greater or lesser extent, depending on the production process – ie, all goods and services require labour.

More demand for labour

As described above, the lower real cost of labour will induce employers to increase employment. Although the reduction in NIC cuts real labour costs, the effect is offset by the increase in wage rates brought about by the effect of the road-fuel escalator or the carbon/energy tax on the general price level, and hence on wage rates and labour costs through pay negotiations.

More supply of labour

As the labour market tightens and unemployment falls, more people will be encouraged to enter the market and apply for jobs. To the extent that this occurs, unemployment will fall more slowly (in absolute numbers) than employment will rise. This effect helps to reduce what would otherwise be a marked response of wage rates to the higher demand for labour, a response which would increase real labour costs and reduce the impact of lower NIC on these costs.

As the level of employment – and therefore employment income rises, so real incomes rise in general – and thus real consumption rises further, adding to the original increase in employment. As employment rises and unemployment falls, so expenditure by government on unemployment benefits and Social Security benefits falls more generally.

FISCAL POLICY REFORM TO RAISE EMPLOYMENT

The Scenarios

The design of the scenarios is illustrated in Figure 9.2. The starting point is a base derived from a Cambridge Econometrics forecast for the UK to 2010 (Cambridge Econometrics, 1994) incorporating the November 1993 Budget changes. In the base scenario, as shown at the left-hand centre of the chart, the road-fuel duty escalator is reduced from 5 per cent in real terms in 1994–95 to zero in 1996 and thereafter on the grounds that the PSBR is

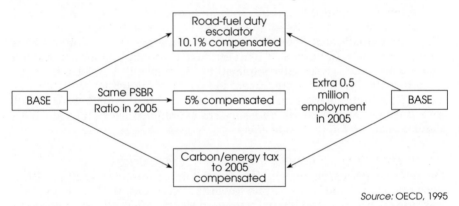

Source: OECD, 1995

Figure 9.2 *The scenarios used in the model*

projected to fall below 3 per cent of GDP in 1996, so achieving the Maastricht target.[9] In the base, the rate of employers' NIC is held at 7.5 per cent of wages and salaries. The three main scenarios are shown in the centre of the figure: in the top one, the escalator is continued at 10.1 per cent above the rate of inflation from 1996, this rate being calculated at that required (via reductions in NIC) to raise employment (defined as a count of jobs) by half a million above base in 2005.[10] Over the projection period, the PSBR/GDP ratio is held constant at base levels by allowing the rate of employers' NIC

---

[9] In the Cambridge Econometrics forecast the escalator is allowed to continue at 5 per cent; after 1998, employers' NIC are progressively reduced to prevent the PSBR turning into a large public debt repayment.

[10] The exercise was done by trial and error in repeated solutions of the model: in fact each option increased employment by about 492,000 by 2005. Given the uncertainties in the exercise, this was regarded as sufficiently close to the 'half a million' extra jobs chosen as the target.

to fall, if necessary allowing it to go negative so that it becomes an employment subsidy. The middle scenario is a variant in which the escalator is held at 5 per cent, the rate proposed in the November 1993 Budget. With the high price elasticity for road fuels, the rate may be sufficient to bring to an end the long-term increase in CO_2 emissions from the road-transport sector. In the other scenario, a carbon/energy tax is introduced in 1996, with the rate rising to \$10 per barrel by the year 2000 and then continuing to rise at a faster rate so as to reach \$20.4 by 2005, a rate which also achieves an increase of half a million in employment above base by reductions in employers' NIC, keeping the PSBR/GDP ratio at base levels.

Comparison of 10.1 per cent escalator and carbon/energy tax scenarios shows the differences between two options, both achieving the same increase in employment above base and both with the same PSBR ratios as the base.

The codes identifying the scenarios in the tables and charts which follow are:

1. BASE: VAT on domestic fuels, no road-fuel duty escalator after 1995, no carbon/energy tax.
2. A 5 per cent escalator: as BASE but with the road-fuel escalator continued at 5 per cent in real terms from 1995, compensated by lower rates of employers' NIC so as to keep the ratio of the PSBR to GDP (current market prices) at the levels expected in the base scenario.
3. 10.1 per cent escalator: as 5 per cent escalator but at the rate of 10.1 per cent from 1996.
4. Carbon/energy tax: as BASE but with a carbon/energy tax rising to \$10 per barrel oil-equivalent (pb) by the year 2000 and accompanied by a £1.1 billion energy-saving programme for the domestic sector and then rising steadily to \$20.4 pb by 2005 with compensation via reductions in employers' NIC to keep the PSBR ratio at base levels.

Employment

Employment is expected to rise and unemployment to fall over the medium term for the UK economy. However, unemployment is expected to remain high at over 2 million into the next century, and there is considerable room for policies to reduce unemployment. Table 9.2 shows employment in the scenarios. Both options achieve an increase in employment of around 492,000 in 2005 by design; unemployment is some 300,000 down at 1.9 million in 2005. The effects of the escalator are more gradual as they build up over time, so the increase is only about 150,000 by 2000, compared with an increase of about 250,000 with the carbon/energy tax. The continuation of the 5 per cent escalator after 1996, with revenues recycled via reductions in employers' NIC, is expected to lead to an increase of 191,000 in employment above base by 2005.

Table 9.2 *UK employment in three scenarios*

	1995 (thousands)	2000 (thousands)	2005 (thousands)
Base	24,698	25,534	26,446
Differences from base:			
10.1% escalator		152	492
5% escalator		65	191
carbon/energy tax		253	491

Source: Cambridge Econometrics
Ref: C32F8K&F, April 1993

CO$_2$ Abatement

The UK Government's target on CO$_2$ emissions to comply with the Rio Convention is a reduction of 10 mtc (million tonnes carbon equivalent) by the year 2000 (UK DoE, 1993, 1994). This is to be achieved by a number of measures, the most important from the point of view of fiscal policy being the extension of VAT to domestic fuels and the road-fuel escalator. Table 9.3 shows CO$_2$ emissions for the base scenario, which includes the escalator to 1995 and the extra VAT. The Rio commitment is met with a substantial margin for error, with a reduction of some 8 mtc below 1990 levels by the year 2000. This is partly a result of the Government's measures, but also arises from the switch to gas as a fuel in electricity generation and by the depth of the 1990–92 recession.

Table 9.3 *UK CO$_2$ emissions in three scenarios (mt carbon)*

	1970	1980	1990	2000	2005
Base	182.3	163.8	158.6	149.8	165.5
Differences from base:					
10.1% escalator				–3.7	–13.4
5% escalator				–1.9	–6.9
carbon/energy tax				–12.7	–27.5

Source: Cambridge Econometrics
Ref: C32F8K&F, April 1994

Both Table 9.3 and Figure 9.3 show that the other scenarios have emission levels below those of the base in the years 2000 and 2005. The options (10.1 per cent escalator and carbon/energy tax) combine to reduce emissions substantially, with the carbon/energy tax achieving much larger reductions for the same employment impact. The Toronto target is a level of emissions in 2005 of some 127 mtc, calculated as a reduction of 20 per cent below 1988 levels of 159 mtc. The results imply that this target could be reached by a combination of the carbon/energy tax and the escalator at 10 per cent.

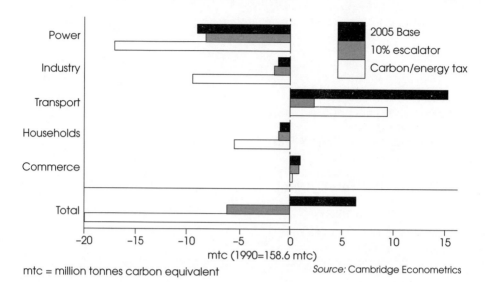

mtc = million tonnes carbon equivalent   *Source:* Cambridge Econometrics

Figure 9.3 *UK CO_2 abatement on three scenarios, 1990–2005*

Even the 5 per cent escalator, as proposed by the government, achieves a
significant reduction in CO_2 of 1.9 mtc by 2000 and 6.9 mtc by 2005; indeed,
if stabilization of emissions, and not reduction, continues to be the objective, then the 5 per cent escalator may well be sufficient at least to 2005. If
the taxes are not compensated, the economy would be more depressed, and
the emission saving would be achieved through reduced output and activity rather than through a change in structure.

Macroeconomic Effects and Petrol Prices

A number of important macroeconomic indicators are shown in Table 9.4
for the three scenarios over the period 1995–2005 or for the year 2005.

Overall, GDP and consumption growth are significantly higher for the
road-fuel option, approaching some 0.2 per cent for consumers' expenditure over a ten-year period. In fact, for all macroeconomic indicators, the
outcome is expected to be favourable: higher real growth at lower inflation,
lower unemployment and a higher balance of payments surplus. The retail
price index is marginally lower, but inflation in home unit costs (the price
deflator for GDP at factor cost) is 0.3 per cent lower than base as the burden
of taxation is shifted from industry to consumers. The increase in the trade
surplus is partly due to the reductions in oil use when road-fuel duties are
raised; this reduces imports directly since the output of North Sea oil and
gas is held constant by assumption. Of course, there are private costs which
are borne by those paying the higher duties, most notably those leading to
a reduction of 31 per cent in consumers' expenditure on petrol and oil by
2005, although these costs are ameliorated by the long adjustment time
allowed in the scenario. For example, the vehicle owner can switch to a
more fuel-efficient model when the vehicle becomes due for replacement.

The macroeconomic differences from base for the carbon/energy tax

Table 9.4 *Main macroeconomic indicators according to two UK scenarios*

	Base	*10.1% escalator*	*Carbon/ energy tax*
GDP (% pa, 1995–2005)	2.8	3.0	2.9
Consumers' expenditure (% pa, 1995–2005)	2.2	2.4	2.2
Home unit costs (% pa, 1995–2005)	5.0	4.7	5.3
RPI (% pa, 1995–2005)	4.8	4.8	5.1
Unemployment (million in 2005)	2.4	2.1	2.1
Balance of payments (% GDP in 2005)	3.9	4.0	2.8
PSBR (% GDP in 2005)	–0.4	–0.4	–0.4
Employers' NIC (% wages and salaries in 2005)	7.8	–1.0	1.0

Source: Cambridge Econometrics
Ref: C32F8K&F, April 1994

are so small as to be almost negligible: slightly higher growth and inflation and a small fall in the balance of payments.

An increase in the rate of duty of 10.1 per cent per annum in real terms from 1996 has the effect of increasing the price of road fuels to the private consumer by 33 per cent by 2000 and nearly doubling them (up 84 per cent) by 2005, compared to the base. Petrol prices would be an extra 16–42 pence per litre, compared with about 50 pence per litre at present. However, the rise is progressive, being only 5 per cent in 1996, 6 per cent in 1997, then accelerating as the tax becomes a larger and larger component of the prices. For comparison, implementation of the carbon/energy tax, rising to $10 per barrel oil-equivalent in real terms in 2000 and $20.4 pb in 2005, is estimated to increase real road-fuel prices by 38 per cent by 2005. This increase is lower because the carbon/energy tax is applied as a specific tax on the carbon and energy content of the fuel inputs. Other taxes on road fuels and a high value-added by refining mean that the fuel input costs are a small percentage of the final product price and therefore any tax on the fuel inputs represents only a small percentage of the total final price to consumers.

Public Sector Revenues and Expenditures

Table 9.5 shows the structure of UK public finances in the scenarios for 1990 and 2005. The table shows some large aggregates, highlighting the main taxes and those changing the most. The results are all for complete simultaneous solutions of the model – ie, they take into account all indirect effects on all revenues and expenditures of the public sector, including price effects, such as prices of goods and services bought by the government, and real effects, such as the loss in revenues caused by a drop in petrol consumption and the reduction in unemployment benefits paid out by the government when unemployment falls. The PSBR is shown for comparison: the PSBR ratio to GDP is the same in the three scenarios, but since GDP is different, the absolute level of the PSBR is also slightly different.

Table 9.5 *UK public finances according to two scenarios*

	1990 £ billion	2005 Base £ billion	10.1% escalator £ billion	Carbon/ energy tax £ billion
				Differences from base
Public sector revenues:				
Duties on road fuels	9	32	36	–2
Carbon/energy tax	0	0	0	33
VAT	33	109	3	6
Other indirect	20	33	1	1
Income taxes and employees' NIC	102	227	6	11
Employers' NIC	20	49	–51	–44
Public sector expenditures:				
Goods and services	113	335	–8	10
Unemployment benefits, etc, to persons	59	118	–3	–2
PSBR	–2	–5	–1	–1

Source: Cambridge Econometrics
Ref: C32F8K&F, April 1994

On the revenue side, although the scenarios show a marked change in structure, income tax and VAT remain the largest taxes in terms of revenues raised, with income tax on persons and companies estimated to raise over £200 billion by 2005 after the changes announced in the 1993 Budget. The road-fuel escalator is estimated to raise £36 billion in additional road-fuel duty revenues, about one-third of the revenues from VAT, allowing for reductions in fuel use, compared to £32 billion in the base. (The small fall in road-fuel duties shown for the carbon/energy tax is due to a reduction in road-fuel consumption in this scenario.) The carbon/energy tax is expected to raise a similar £32 billion. The effects on other tax revenues are significant. With the escalator, these revenues (VAT, other indirect taxes and income tax) are up by £10 billion; with the carbon/energy tax they are up £18 billion. Both scenarios show a radical shift for employers' NIC: with the escalator, a £49 billion revenue in the base becomes a £2 billion subsidy; with the carbon/energy tax, the NIC rate is cut to 1 per cent of the wage and salary bill.

On the expenditure side, the higher employment and lower unemployment means that there are substantial reductions in the cost to the government of unemployment and other Social Security benefits. The reduction is £3 billion by 2005 in the scenario with the road-fuel duty escalator and £2 billion in the case of the carbon/energy tax. However, there is a much more dramatic change in government spending on goods and services: spending is down by £8 billion (2.5 per cent of the total) on goods and services with the escalator as labour costs come down sharply and prices in general are lower than in the base; but spending is up by £10 billion with the carbon/energy tax as prices in general are higher. Thus, although the NIC reduction is £51 billion for the escalator, compared with only £46 billion direct extra revenues, £8 billion of the reduction is due to lower costs for government itself in its wage bill and other costs of goods and services.

The Effects on Equity

In order to reduce the adverse equity effects of the carbon/energy tax on domestic consumers of fuel and power, the tax is assumed to be accompanied by a £1.1 billion (1992 prices) programme for insulation and improvement in domestic energy-using equipment targeted at households in the lowest quintile of the income distribution (see Brechling, Helm and Smith, 1991 and Barker and Johnstone, 1993, for a discussion). This produces net welfare gains for the sector through improvements in the energy efficiency of their homes and heating and lighting equipment, with the benefit being not only through the saving of carbon/energy tax but also through the consequent saving of VAT. In addition, in the scenario, pensions are further increased to offset the extra fuel cost to pensioners.

The energy-saving programme creates some of the further jobs in the 491,000 total, alongside those following the reduced NIC. The modelling of the effects of an energy-saving programme is still at a provisional stage and is intended only to give the order of magnitude. A detailed simulation of the domestic energy sector is well advanced and in due course will provide more accurate estimates of the effects on equity and consumption.

In contrast, the road-fuel duty escalator is expected to be a progressive tax. The proportion of household spending on petrol rises from 1.5 per cent for the lowest quintile group to 2.6 per cent for the highest quintile group (Pearson and Smith, 1991, p 42). The relative responses across income groups suggest that the reduction in real spending will be more or less the same for the different groups. However, some groups will face much higher costs – for example, those living and motoring extensively in rural areas where there are no public transport alternatives to the private car.

The Effects on Industrial Competitiveness

This issue has been of great concern in the carbon/energy tax literature and is treated at length by Barker (1995). In the application in this paper, the carbon/energy tax is assumed to be introduced in the UK unilaterally, in order to give an indication of the potential extent of loss of competitiveness. The results are summarized here.

The road-fuel duty escalator affects industrial costs indirectly through raising consumer prices in general (although the effect in the scenario as shown in Table 9.4 is masked by the effect of the reduction in NIC); this leads to higher wage rates through wage bargaining and so higher labour costs and higher industrial prices. However, since there are very small direct effects on industrial costs, through the increased costs of road transportation of goods, and since there are substantial reductions in labour costs via the reduction in NIC, net industrial costs fall in nearly all sectors. In effect, the tax burden is being transferred from industrial activity to private motoring, with a consequent increase in international competitiveness.

With the carbon/energy tax, since employers' NIC are reduced to keep the PSBR ratios at base levels, all industries' labour costs fall depending on their use of labour – and the most labour-intensive industries will have the largest reduction in costs. On the other hand, energy-intensive industries will have sharp increases in costs, so that in aggregate there is a slight increase in industrial costs and a slight loss in international competitiveness.

The Effects on the Environment

Barker (1995a) gives a detailed analysis of how the options for fiscal reform are also likely to provide substantial extra benefits in the form of environmental improvements, in addition to reductions in greenhouse gas emissions. The reason is that there are emissions of other air pollutants and other social costs closely associated with the emission of CO_2. Table 9.6 gives estimates of reductions in these other pollutants which are attributed to the policy options under the assumption of constant 1991 emission rates. When the implications of these reductions for improvements to health, reductions in damages to buildings and crops, reductions in accidents, noise, road damage and congestion from reduced traffic flow are calculated in monetary terms, there is an additional benefit in both fiscal reform options of some 0.5 per cent of GDP, although there are many qualifications surrounding the basis of the calculations.

Table 9.6 *Reduction in air emissions and road traffic assuming constant emission rates[1]*

	1990	2005 base	10.1% escalator	Carbon/ energy tax
Emissions[2]	thousand tonnes		% reduction from Base	
CO_2	158,630	165,527	–8.1	–16.6
SO_2	3780	2405	–0.6	–23.9
NO_x	2779	3326	–19.2	–15.0
CO	6701	9289	–28.4	–14.0
CH_4	3388	3619	–0.1	–5.1
PM	473	502	–20.7	–15.0
VOC	1760	2163	–17.5	–8.6
	million litres			
Petrol consumption	46,330	68,866	–31.0	–16.8
Road traffic flow[3]			–15.5	–8.4

[1] The reduction in emissions is calculated assuming that the ratio of emissions to activity remains constant at 1991 rates (1992 rates in the case of CO_2).
[2] NO_x includes all oxides of nitrogen; PM is particulate matter; VOC is volatile organic compounds.
[3] Road traffic flow is assumed to decline at half the rate of that of petrol consumption – ie, it is assumed that half of the reduction in consumption is a result of improved engine efficiency and half is a result of reduced traffic.

Source: Cambridge Econometrics
Ref: C32F8K&F, April 1994

THE EFFECTS OF THE POLICY OPTIONS ON THE LABOUR MARKET

The effects on the labour market in the policy options are dominated by the effects of reducing the rate of employers' NIC from about 7.5 per cent of the wage and salary bill at present to nearly zero in both options (–1 per cent for the escalator and 1 per cent for the carbon/energy tax). In fact, the NIC option for recycling the revenues has been chosen deliberately to give the greatest employment effects: several studies – such as EC, 1994 – provide evidence that recycling via income tax or VAT reductions has smaller effects on employment and output.

Table 9.7 shows the increases in gross output (in per cent) and employment (in thousands), compared with the base, for the 49 industries distinguished in the model. There are several interesting features in the results. First, overall output is 0.9 per cent above base for the escalator but only 0.1 per cent above for the carbon/energy tax. The loss of competitiveness with a carbon/energy tax shows in the fall in output of several energy-intensive sectors and some very price-competitive sectors, such as motor vehicles. In the escalator option, there is a gain in competitiveness and in output. Secondly, most of the extra employment is in just 6 of the 49 industries: construction, (wholesale) distribution, hotels and catering, other business services (real estate, rental of equipment, recruitment agencies, security services, industrial cleaning), health and social services and miscellaneous services (NGOs, sporting activities, entertainment, personal services, domestic services). These industries all have considerable employment to begin with; and analysis of past performance shows (Table 9.1) that they have either a large response to the lower real wage costs or, in the case of health/social services, a high response of employment-to-output changes. Thirdly, the energy-saving programme in the carbon/energy tax option shows up in an increase in output of public administration above base, although the extra employment associated with the programme is in construction and non-metallic minerals (insulation materials), not in public administration.

Figure 9.4 illustrates these industrial results in a summary form. The chart shows changes in employment from 1995 to 2005; note that most of the increases are in the service sectors.

Table 9.8 shows the type of employment in the 492,000 extra jobs in both options in 2005. Just over half the extra jobs are full-time, with most of these being for men; there is a considerable increase – over 100,000 – in part-time jobs for females. Figure 9.5 illustrates these results; note that male full-time employees are expected to fall during 1995–2005; the effect of fiscal reform is to slow the reduction.

Table 9.9 shows the regional distribution of the extra jobs: they are spread across the regions more or less in proportion to employment in the base projection. Figure 9.6 summarizes the regional employment results, showing how the north of England and Scotland benefit relatively more from fiscal reform, but that no region loses employment.

Tables 9.10, 9.11 and 9.12 present the same basic information, but scaled to a total of 250,000 extra jobs from 1995 to 2000, and compared to the

Table 9.7 *Increases in output and employment in the scenarios in 2005[1]*

Industry	Output % above base		Employment thousands above base	
	10.1% escalator	Carbon/energy tax	10.1% escalator	Carbon/ energy tax
1 Agriculture, etc	1.5	0.2	9	14
2 Coal, etc	0.5	0.4	0	0
3 Oil and gas	0.1	0.2	0	0
4 Other mining	0.4	–0.6	1	1
5 Food	1.3	0.2	7	7
6 Drink	1.4	0.9	2	2
7 Tobacco	0.3	–0.0	0	0
8 Textiles	0.4	–0.3	7	5
9 Clothing and leather	0.4	–0.2	6	4
10 Wood and wood products	1.4	0.3	4	3
11 Paper, printing and publishing	0.8	0.1	8	
12 Manufacturing fuels	–10.1	–7.7	1	12
13 Pharmaceuticals	0.3	–0.2	1	1
14 Chemicals	–0.2	–0.3	9	9
15 Rubber and plastics	0.3	–0.2	5	4
16 Non–metallurgical mineral products	0.6	–0.4	4	5
17 Basic metals	0.3	–1.5	6	13
18 Metal goods	0.6	–0.2	7	7
19 Mechanical engineering	0.2	–0.4	16	20
20 Electronics	0.9	–1.4	3	1
21 Electronic engineering	0.9	–0.6	5	5
22 Instruments	0.3	–0.1	3	2
23 Motor vehicles	–0.3	–1.3	5	4
24 Aerospace	0.1	0.3	3	2
25 Other transport equipment	–0.4	–0.1	1	2
26 Manufacturing necessities	1.7	0.8	3	1
27 Electricity	0.7	–8.6	2	12
28 Gas supply	–0.6	–10.3	1	10
29 Water supply	0.2	–0.6	1	1
30 Construction	1.8	0.6	53	42
31 Retailing	2.5	1.2	18	9
32 Distribution necessities	1.0	0.2	24	18
33 Hotels and catering	7.8	5.2	61	58
34 Rail transport	0.7	–0.1	4	6

35	Other land transport	0.9	0.6	1	1
36	Water transport	0.4	0.5	0	0
37	Air transport	0.1	−0.5	0	0
38	Other transport services	1.0	0.5	3	2
39	Communications	0.7	−0.5	6	7
40	Banking and finance	0.5	0.4	2	3
41	Insurance	1.2	0.3	1	1
42	Professional services	1.0	0.4	9	9
43	Computing services	1.2	0.5	2	2
44	Other business services	1.4	1.2	64	52
45	Public administration	0.0	2.6	13	7
46	Education	0.3	0.2	1	1
47	Health and social services	0.7	0.5	60	69
48	Waste treatment	1.4	1.6	1	1
49	Miscellaneous services	3.3	4.9	50	48
50	Unallocated	0.0	0.0	0	0
	Total	0.9	0.1	492	491

[1] This table shows scenario results, less base results, for 2005 gross output (% difference) and employment (in thousands).

Source: Cambridge Econometrics
Ref: C32F8AN&CN, June 1994

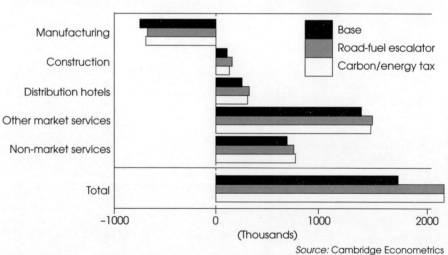

Source: Cambridge Econometrics

Figure 9.4 *UK employment by industry, 1995–2005, according to three scenarios*

Table 9.8 *Increases in employment by type in the scenarios in 2005[1]*

	10.1% Escalator	Carbon/energy tax
Male employees full-time	166	178
Female employees full-time	98	100
Male employees part-time	38	35
Female employees part-time	107	103
Male self-employed	66	59
Female self-employed	17	16
Total	492	491

[1] This table shows the increases in employment scenario less base for 2005 in thousands

Source: Cambridge Econometrics
Ref: C32F8K&F, June 1994

composition of the historical increase in employment in 1987–89, and the increase which might be expected in a scenario in which the UK economy grows by about 0.5 per cent, per year faster each year in the context of faster world growth in general. Comparison between the results shows some of the special features of the extra employment coming from fiscal reform. These can be summarized as follows:

- Although the extra employment is largely in those industries which normally gain employment in the upturn of the cycle and in conditions of long-term higher growth – ie, mainly in the services industries – there is more employment in health/social

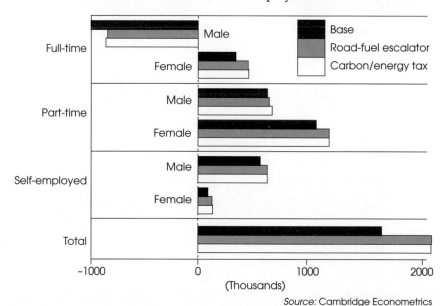

Source: Cambridge Econometrics

Figure 9.5 *UK employment by type, 1995–2005, according to three scenarios*

Table 9.9 *Increase in regional employment in the scenarios in 2005[1]*

		10.1% Escalator	Carbon/energy tax
1	Greater London	55	50
2	Rest of South East	115	112
3	East Anglia	20	17
4	South West	33	31
5	West Midlands	43	42
6	East Midlands	39	35
7	Yorkshire and Humberside	45	48
8	North West	56	64
9	North of England	22	24
10	Wales	22	22
11	Scotland	35	38
12	Northern Ireland	7	7
	Total	492	491

[1] This table shows the increases in employment scenario less base for 2005 in thousands

Source: Cambridge Econometrics
Ref: C32F8K&F, June 1994

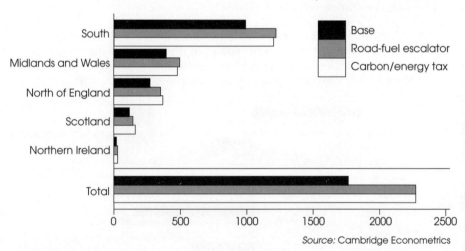

Source: Cambridge Econometrics

Figure 9.6 *UK employment by region, 1995–2005, according to three scenarios*

services, much more employment in miscellaneous services (personal services, etc), more employment in construction than if the economy had grown faster, and much less expansion in retailing than might be expected from the 1987–89 boom.

• Most of the extra jobs created are full-time, especially male full-time when compared with historical experience, and this offsets to some extent the expected decline in male full-time employment over the next decade.

Table 9.10 *The industrial composition of 250,000 extra jobs in the UK*[1]

Industry	1987–89 average	1995–2000 projection		
		Higher growth	10.1% escalator	Carbon/ energy tax
1 Agriculture, etc	–5	–1	4	6
2 Coal, etc	–10	0	0	0
3 Oil and gas	2	0	0	0
4 Other mining	0	0	0	1
5 Food	0	3	4	4
6 Drink	–2	3	1	1
7 Tobacco	–1	1	0	0
8 Textiles	–4	3	5	4
9 Clothing and leather	–1	9	4	3
10 Wood and wood products	2	1	2	2
11 Paper, printing and publishing	4	5	4	4
12 Manufacturing fuels	0	1	0	4
13 Pharmaceuticals	1	1	1	1
14 Chemicals	–1	3	4	4
15 Rubber and plastics	3	7	3	2
16 Non–metallurgical mineral products	0	2	2	3
17 Basic metals	–1	7	3	7
18 Metal goods	5	7	3	4
19 Mechanical engineering	2	14	9	11
20 Electronics	–1	11	1	1
21 Electronic engineering	0	5	3	3
22 Instruments	–1	2	2	2
23 Motor vehicles	0	8	2	2
24 Aerospace	–1	1	1	1
25 Other transport equipment	–4	–2	1	1
26 Manufacturing necessities	4	4	1	1
27 Electricity	0	0	1	4
28 Gas supply	–1	0	0	5
29 Water supply	0	0	1	1
30 Construction	44	20	31	27
31 Retailing	35	18	6	3
32 Distribution necessities	7	9	15	14
33 Hotels and catering	21	13	18	18
34 Rail transport	–2	0	1	2
35 Other land transport	8	4	0	0
36 Water transport	0	2	0	0
37 Air transport	2	1	0	0
38 Other transport services	3	2	2	1

39 Communications	4	5	3	3
40 Banking and finance	16	7	0	1
41 Insurance	5	2	0	0
42 Professional services	21	16	4	4
43 Computing services	7	7	1	1
44 Other business services	33	24	28	24
45 Public administration	−7	0	12	9
46 Education	17	6	0	0
47 Health and social services	35	7	38	40
48 Waste treatment	0	1	0	0
49 Miscellaneous services	12	10	28	25
Total	250	250	250	250

[1] This table shows total increases in employment over the periods shown, each scaled to a total of 250.000 (0.94% of total employment in 1990) to give a standard comparison. The 1987–89 extra jobs are increases over time; the projected changes are differences from base.

Source: Cambridge Econometrics
Ref: C32F8AN&CN, June 1994

- Slightly more of the extra employment is in part-time jobs and for the self-employed than might be expected from faster growth or recent historical experience.
- No region experiences a fall in employment; the extra employment is particularly concentrated in the North West, Yorkshire and Humberside, and Scotland, with fewer jobs than

Table 9.11 *Types of employment in 250,000 extra jobs in the UK (thousands)[1]*

	1987–89 average	Higher growth	1995–2000 Difference from Base 10.1% escalator	Carbon/ Energy tax
Male employees full-time	21	114	88	97
Female employees full-time	80	52	51	52
Male employees part-time	10	12	17	14
Female employees part-time	56	38	52	49
Male self-employed	66	27	33	30
Female self-employed	17	7	8	8
Total	250	250	250	250

[1] This table shows the increases in employment over the period 1987–89 scaled down to a total of 250,000 for comparison, and differences from base 1995–2000 for the scenarios shown, also scaled to 250,000.

Source: Cambridge Econometrics
Ref: C32F8K&F, June 1994

Table 9.12 *Regional composition of 250,000 extra jobs in the UK (thousands)[1]*

		1987–89 average	Higher growth	1995–2000 Difference from Base 10.1% escalator	Carbon/ Energy tax
1	Greater London	23	28	28	27
2	Rest of South East	62	56	55	54
3	East Anglia	15	13	11	9
4	South West	28	18	16	15
5	West Midlands	23	23	22	22
6	East Midlands	15	22	20	20
7	Yorkshire and Humberside	20	21	24	25
8	North West	24	22	30	32
9	North of England	6	13	11	12
10	Wales	17	15	10	10
11	Scotland	15	16	19	21
12	Northern Ireland	4	4	3	4
Total		250	250	250	250

[1] This table shows the increases in employment over the period 1987–89 scaled down to a total of 250,000 for comparison, and differences from base 1995–2000 for the scenarios shown, also scaled to 250,000.

Source: Cambridge Econometrics
Ref: C32F8K&F, June 1994

might be expected in Wales and the South in general, outside Greater London; this is partly accounted for by the historical success of Wales in obtaining extra employment for inward investment in industries with good long-term prospects.

The conclusion which emerges is that fiscal reform will generate most jobs for those in full-time employment, especially for men, and more jobs (than might be expected from a general expansion of the economy) for part-timers and the self-employed. The more employment is created for part-timers, the less likely it is that unemployment will be reduced, so some of the general benefits of reform are lost. The conclusion that there will be appreciably more jobs in segments of the labour market already close to full employment suggests that there may be more upward pressure on wage inflation. However, it is implicit in the projections that extra training will supply the extra skills in demand.

It is also worth noting that the reductions in employers' NIC are assumed to be across-the-board and not targeted at any particular groups – for instance, those previously unemployed, those on low incomes, or young workers. There are a number of proposals for reducing employment costs (Layard and Philpott, 1991; EC, 1993; Drèze and Malinvaud, 1993; Michie and Grieve Smith, 1994) which will have different effects on the labour market, and which may increase employment overall, as well as in the particular groups (more than if the reduction were a general one). Some detailed research has been done on the impact of such schemes for The Netherlands, reported in EC, 1994, and it is clear that they are capable of producing much larger increases in employment than the simple reduction in NIC for all employees. It appears that plausible schemes are worth modelling in more detail than has been attempted in this paper.

CONCLUSION

Balanced changes in the fiscal system can lead to increases in employment by reducing the real cost of labour, and at the same time they can make a substantial contribution to reducing UK emissions of CO_2. The effects on GDP – the balance of payments – and inflation are likely to be small, but more favourable in the road-fuel option than in the carbon/energy tax option. The overall effects on industrial competitiveness are small, since the loss of competitiveness from the increase in fuel costs is offset by the gain in competitiveness from the decrease in labour costs.

Two options to raise employment by just half a million jobs by 2005 have been compared: an escalation of just over 10 per cent per annum in real duties on road fuels starting in 1996 and a carbon/energy tax rising to $20 per barrel oil-equivalent by the year 2005. Both options are balanced in the sense that the ratio of the PSBR to GDP is exactly the same as in the base scenario. The conclusions for the comparison are as follows:

- Each option achieves the increases in employment similarly through the reductions in employers' NIC, but the effect on reductions in CO_2 is quite different: the escalator focuses all the reductions on road transport while the carbon/energy tax spreads the reductions across all sectors that burn fossil fuels.
- The increases in employment appear to favour full-time workers, especially men; however since there is expected to be a decline in this type of employment, this may not lead to more wage inflation; the extra employment is spread across all the regions and countries of the UK; and fiscal reform is likely to be a more favourable employment-creating option for governments than general fiscal expansion.
- The effect on the rate of inflation in the escalator option is negligible, while the carbon/energy tax might raise the rate by 0.3 percentage points from 4.8 per cent to 5.1 per cent per annum 1995 to 2005; these results assume that wage bargainers are able to pass on any increase in consumer prices and that the NIC reduction is not targeted at those with little market power. If the fiscal reform were to be accompanied by some form of social contract between the government and the trade unions and/or the extra employment incentives were targeted at the young, or those on low pay, the effects on inflation might be much less.

This paper has considered two rather stylized options for raising employment over the next ten years. The main conclusion is that perhaps a million jobs could be created without adding to inflation by recycling the revenues from a carbon/energy tax and a road-fuel duty escalator into targeted reductions in employment costs and employment subsidies. In addition to the extra employment, the measures will lead to a substantial reduction in CO_2 emissions, probably sufficient to meet the Toronto target of a 20 per cent cut below 1988 levels by 2005, more general environmental benefits and an improvement in overall macroeconomic performance.

REFERENCES

Alfsen, K, Brendemoen, A and Glomsrod, S (1992) *Benefits of Climate Policies: some tentative calculations*, Discussion Paper 69, Central Bureau of Statistics, Oslo, Norway

Barker, T (1993) 'Secondary Benefits of Greenhouse Gas Abatement: The Effects of a UK Carbon/Energy Tax on Air Pollution, Energy-Environment-Economy Modelling', Discussion Paper No 4, Department of Applied Economics, University of Cambridge, Cambridge

Barker, T (1995a) 'UK energy price elasticities and their implications for long-term CO_2 abatement', in Barker, T, Ekins, P and Johnstone, N (eds) *Global Warming and Energy Demand*, Routledge, London, pp 227–53

Barker, T (1995b) 'Taxing pollution instead of employment: greenhouse gas abatement through fiscal reform in the UK', in *Energy and Environment*, Vol 6, No 1, pp 1–28

Barker, T, Baylis, S and Bryden, C (1993) 'Achieving the Rio target: CO_2 abatement through fiscal policy in the UK', *Fiscal Studies*, 15 (3), pp 1–18

Barker, T, Baylis, S and Madsen, P (1993) 'The UK carbon/energy tax: macroeconomic effects', *Energy Policy*, 21, (3), pp 296–308

Barker, T, Ekins, P and Johnstone, N (1995) (eds) *Global Warming and Energy Demand*, Routledge, London

Barker, T and Johnstone, N (1993) 'Equity and efficiency in policies to reduce carbon emissions in the domestic sector', *Energy and Environment*, Vol 4, No 4, pp 335–61

Barker, T, Johnstone, N and O'Shea, T (1993) *The EC Carbon/Energy Tax and Secondary Transport-Related Benefits, Energy-Environment-Economy Modelling*, Discussion Paper No 5, Department of Applied Economics, University of Cambridge, Cambridge

Barker, T and Lewney, R (1991) 'A green scenario for the UK economy', in Barker, T (ed) *Green Futures for Economic Growth*, Cambridge Econometrics, Cambridge, pp 11–28

Barker, T and Peterson, A W A P (eds) (1987) *The Cambridge Multisectoral Model of the British Economy*, Cambridge University Press, Cambridge

Boero, G, Clarke, R and Winters, L A (1991) *The Macroeconomic Consequences of Controlling Greenhouse Gases: A Survey*, UK Department of the Environment, Environmental Economics Research Series, HMSO, London

Bovenberg, Lans A and van der Ploeg, F (1993) 'Consequences of environmental tax reform for involuntary unemployment and welfare', available from Department of Applied Econometrics, University of Cambridge, Cambridge

Brechling, V, Helm, D and Smith, S (1991) 'Domestic energy conservation: environmental objectives and market failures', in Helm, D (ed) *Economic Policy Towards the Environment*, Blackwell Publishers, Oxford, pp 263–88

Briscoe, G and Roberts, C J (1977) 'Structural breaks in employment functions', *The Manchester School*, 1, pp 1–15

Briscoe, G and Wilson, R A (1991) 'Explanations of the demand for labour in the United Kingdom engineering sector', *Applied Economics*, 23, pp 913–26

Cambridge Econometrics (1994) *Regional Economic Prospects Analysis and Forecasts to 2005*, Cambridge Econometrics, Cambridge

Dahl, C and Sterner, T (1991) 'Analysing gasoline demand elasticities: a survey', *Energy Economics*, 13 (3), pp 203–210

Dargay, J M (1993) 'The demand for fuels for private transport in the UK', in Hawdon, D (ed) *Recent Studies of the Demand for Energy in the UK*, Surrey Energy Economics Discussion Papers Series No 72, University of Guildford, Surrey, pp 25–40

Drèze, J H and Malinvaud, E (1993) *Growth and Employment: The Scope of a European Initiative*, Department of Economics, University of Louvain, Louvain, Belgium

DRI (1991), *The Economic Impact of a Package of EC Measures to Control CO_2 Emissions*, Final Report prepared for the European Commission, European Commission, Brussels

DRI (1992), *Impact of a Package of EC Measures to Control CO_2 Emissions on European Industry*, Final Report prepared for the European Commission, European Commission, Brussels

EC (1991) *A Community Strategy to Limit Carbon Dioxide Emissions and to Improve Energy Efficiency*, SEC(91) 1744, European Commission, Brussels

EC (1993) *White Paper on Growth, Competitiveness, Employment*, Supplement 6/93 Bulletin EC, Brussels, European Commission, Brussels

EC Directorate-General for Economic and Financial Affairs (1992a), *The Climate Challenge: Economic aspects of the Community's strategy for limiting CO_2 emissions*, European Economy No 51, European Commission, Brussels

EC Directorate-General for Economic and Financial Affairs (1992b), *The Economics of Limiting CO_2 Emissions*, European Economy, Special Edition No 1, European Commission, Brussels

EC Directorate-General for Economic and Financial Affairs (1994) 'Taxation, employment and environment: fiscal reform for reducing unemployment', *European Economy*, Annual Economic Report for 1994, No 56, pp 137–178

Ekins, P (1995) 'Revisiting the costs of CO_2 abatement', in Barker, T, Ekins, P, and Johnstone, N (eds) *Global Warming and Energy Demand*, Routledge, London, pp 283–304

Engle R F and Granger, C (1987), 'Cointegration and error correction: representation, estimation and testing', *Econometrica*, 55, pp 251–76

Franzén, M and Sterner, T (1995) 'Long-run demand elasticities for gasoline', in T Barker, Ekins, P and Johnstone, N *Global Warming and Energy Demand*, Routledge, London, pp 106–20

Gee, D and von Weizsacker, E U (1993) *Ecological Tax Reform*, WBMG Environmental Communications, London

Gilbert, C L (1986) 'Professor Hendry's econometric methodology', *Oxford Bulletin of Economics and Statistics*, 48, pp 283–307

Glomsrod, S, Vennemo, H and Johnsen, T (1990) *Stabilization of emissions of CO_2: a computable general equilibrium assessment*, Discussion Paper 48, Central Bureau of Statistics, PB 8131, Dep 0033, Oslo, Norway

Goodwin, P B (1992) 'A review of new demand elasticities with special reference to short and long run effects of price changes', *Journal of Transport Economics and Policy*, 26, pp 155–170

Hawdon, D (1992) (ed) *Energy Demand: Evidence and Expectations*, Surrey University Press, Guildford, Surrey

Hendry, D F (1985) *Empirical Modelling in Dynamic Econometrics*, Nuffield College, Oxford

Hendry, D F (ed) (1986) 'Economic Modelling with cointegrated variables', special issue of the *Oxford Bulletin of Economics and Statistics*, Vol 48, No 3

Jorgenson, D W and Wilcoxen, P J (1993), Reducing US carbon emissions: an econometric general equilibrium assessment, *Resource and Energy Economics*, Vol 15, No 1, pp 7–25

Karadeloglou, P (1992) 'Energy tax versus carbon tax: a quantitative macroeconomic analysis with the HERMES/MIDAS Models', in Laroui, F and Velthuijsen, J W (eds) *An Energy Tax in Europe*, SEO-rapport nr 281, Amsterdam, pp 127–152

Layard, R and Philpott, J (1991) *Stopping Unemployment*, The Employment Institute, London

Majocchi, A (1994) 'The employment effects of eco-taxes: a review of empirical models and results', paper presented to the OECD Workshop on the Implementation of Environmental Taxes, Organization for Economic Cooperation and Development, London

Michie, J and Grieve Smith, J (eds) (1994) *Unemployment in Europe*, Academic Press, London

Neale, A J and Wilson, R A (1987) 'Average weekly hours of work in the United Kingdom, 1948–80: a disaggregated analysis', in Bosworth, D L and Heathfield, D F, *Working Below Capacity*, Macmillan, London, Chapter 9

Nickell, S (1984) 'An investigation of the determinants of manufacturing employment in the United Kingdom', *Review of Economic Studies*, 51, pp 529–57

OECD (1989) *Economic Instruments for Environmental Protection*, Organization for Economic Cooperation and Development, Paris

OECD (1993a) *Eco-Taxes in OECD Countries: a Survey*, OECD Environmental Monographs, No 71, Organization for Economic Cooperation and Development, Paris

OECD (1993b) *Environment and Taxation: The Cases of The Netherlands, Sweden and the USA*, Organization for Economic Cooperation and Development, Paris

OECD (1994a) *The OECD Jobs Study: Facts Analysis Strategies*, Organization for Economic Cooperation and Development, Paris

OECD (1994b) *The OECD Jobs Study: Evidence and Explanations*, Organization for Economic Cooperation and Development, Paris

OECD (1995) *Environmental Taxes in OECD Countries*, Organization for Economic Cooperation and Development, Paris

Pearce, D (1991) 'The role of carbon taxes in adjusting to global warming', *The Economic Journal*, 101, pp 938–48

Pearce, D (1992) 'The secondary benefits of greenhouse gas control', CSERGE Working Paper 92–12, University of East Anglia, Norwich

Pearce, D, Bann, C and Georgiou, S (1992) *The Social Costs of Fuel Cycles*, CSERGE, University College London, London

Pearson, M and Smith, S (1991) *The European Carbon Tax: An Assessment of the European Commission's Proposals*, The Institute for Fiscal Studies, London

Pesaran, M H and Smith, R (1995) 'Alternative approaches to estimating long-run energy demand elasticities: an application to Asian developing countries', in Barker, T, Ekins, P and Johnstone, N (eds) *Global Warming and Energy Demand*, Routledge, London, pp 19–46

Peterson, A W A P (1987) 'Employment', in Barker, T and Peterson, W (eds) *The Cambridge Multi Sectoral Model of the British Economy*, Cambridge University Press, Cambridge

Pezzey, J (1991) *Impacts of greenhouse gas control strategies on UK competitiveness: a survey and exploration of the issues*, A report for the Department of Trade and Industry, HMSO, London

Read, C (1991) *Air Pollution and Child Health*, Greenpeace, London

Stock, J H (1987) 'Asymptotic properties of least squares estimators of cointegrating vectors', *Econometrica*, Vol 55, No 5, pp 1035–56

UK Central Statistical Office (1993), 'Input-output tables for the United Kingdom in 1990', *Economic Trends*, HMSO, London

UK Department of Energy (1989) 'The demand for energy', in Helm, D, Kay, J and Thompson, D (eds), *The Market for Energy*, Clarendon Press, Oxford, pp 77–91

UK Department of the Environment (1992) *Digest of Environmental Protection and Water Statistics 14*, HMSO, London

UK Department of the Environment (1992) *Climate Change: Our National Programme for CO_2 Emissions, A Discussion Document*, Department of the Environment, London

UK Department of the Environment (1993) *Climate Change: Update on the UK's CO_2 Programme*, Department of the Environment, London

UK Department of the Environment (and other Government Departments) (1994) *Climate Change: The UK Programme*, Cm 2427, HMSO, London

UK Department of the Environment and Department of Transport (1990) *Oxides of Nitrogen in the United Kingdom*, The Second Report of the United Kingdom Photochemical Oxidants Review Group, HMSO, London

UK Warren Spring Laboratory, Department of Trade and Industry (1983) *Acid Deposition in the United Kingdom*, The United Kingdom Review Group on Acid Rain, HMSO, London

Virley, S (1993) 'The effect of fuel price increase on road transport CO_2 emissions', *Transport Policy*, Vol 1, No 1, pp 43–8

Watkins, L H (1991) *Air Pollution from Road Vehicles*, State of the Art Review, Transport and Road Research Laboratory, HMSO, London

Weizsacker, E U von and Jesinghaus, J (1992) *Ecological Tax Reform: A Policy Proposal for Sustainable Development*, Zed Press, London

C h a p t e r   1 0

REFLECTIONS ON THE DOUBLE DIVIDEND DEBATE

Daniel McCoy

INTRODUCTION

Environmental taxation to enhance economic policy performance has attracted increased interest in the 1990s both among policy-makers and academics. While there has been a long tradition in advocating the use of taxation for environmental purposes, recent attention has placed emphasis on the opportunities of using environmental taxes to achieve a range of other policy objectives. This interest in the additional benefits from using environmental taxes has become categorized as the 'double dividend' debate. Intuitively, the double dividend hypothesis seems easy to grasp; the recycling of revenue raised from a corrective environmental tax can lead to two dividends. The first dividend is the improvement in environmental quality, while the second or additional dividend is any extra benefits derived from using the revenues to reduce pre-existing distortions in the economy. However, this would seem to be the extent of the consensus in this particular debate. Beyond this basic notion there seems to be no clear definition of what exactly these double dividends are. Different forms of the second dividend abound, with some groups rejecting the prospect of double dividends while others go further, claiming multiple dividends. There are, it seems, a number of double dividend debates occurring at once and these criss-cross in a manner that leads to a confusing path from theory to empiricism to policy recommendations. This is the path that I will try to explore in this chapter.

This debate is not merely an academic squabble, even though it has all the hallmarks of one. It assumes its significance in the fact that most industrialized countries are looking for new ways to tackle, simultaneously, problems of environmental deterioration, rising government budget deficits, high unemployment and losses in trade competitiveness. Policy-makers, eager to show their green credentials, are particularly keen on the notion of being able to do so while reaping increased economic benefits, so obtaining the proverbial, but ultimately unattainable, 'free lunch'. It is within this context that society needs to reflect on what the double dividend debates imply for the use of environmental taxes in practice.

There is an inherent logic in the taxing of 'bads', such as pollution, rather than taxing 'goods', such as employment, a logic which has a ready appeal. Policy-makers in industrialized countries are increasingly making use of environment-related taxation to achieve this sort of tax shift, as indicated clearly by David Gee in Chapter 6 of this book. These policies are presented to the taxpayer as obtaining environmental improvements at little or no cost. In fact, taking the strongest form of the double dividend hypothesis to its full consequences, the implication is that the improvements can be gained at a *negative* cost, so it is seen as an attractive win-win package. For instance, the European Commission (1991) proposal for a carbon-energy tax was put forward as part of a 'no regrets' policy measure: if global warming turned out not to be as significant as was feared, then the additional benefits from the tax, such as energy savings, would be worth pursuing regardless. The proposal also had the condition that it was to be a revenue-neutral measure, in that the revenues had to be recycled to reduce other taxes. The favoured scenario was to reduce labour taxes as one way to tackle the European Union's unemployment problems. The most recent environment-related tax was introduced in early 1996 in The Netherlands, as summarized by Hans Vos in Chapter 12. This is a tax on electricity and on natural gas for both households and low-energy using firms. There is a compensatory mechanism arising from the new revenue in the form of reduced income taxes. The policy claim is that if people do not change their behaviour, their incomes will remain approximately the same. If they cut down their energy consumption, the objective is that their net income will increase. The double dividend claim inherent in these policies is based both on the incentive to reduce pollution and the revenue-raising potential of these environmental taxes.

Naturally, having got the scent of some form of economic nirvana, policy-makers have sought the advice of economists to provide both the evidence and the means to achieve these double dividends. The economics profession was not found wanting in its willingness to provide answers. There was already a substantial body of theory with which to tackle the issues, as summarized by Peter Bohm and Paul Ekins in Chapters 7 and 8. In addition, there were plenty of models to these theories empirically, as outlined by Paul Ekins and Terry Barker in Chapters 8 and 9. Economists are often lampooned for having the attitude of 'That is all right in practice, but how does it work in theory?' which may be seen as the opposite perspective of politicians. However, the benefit of economic theory is to distinguish between coherent and incoherent arguments in order to provide sound policy advice rather than to have a policy based on unreliable intuition. As Stern (1990) points out: 'taxation is a subject in which intuition has to be carefully tutored by theoretical inquiry and empirical investigation'. The next section will look more closely at the theoretical developments, while the section that follows it will examine how the double dividend hypothesis has been assessed using different economic modelling techniques, and will report on some of the mixed evidence in its support. The subsequent section considers the extent to which the theoretical and empirical findings are incorporated in the adoption of environmental taxes internationally. The final section contains some concluding impressions about the state of the debate thus far.

THEORETICAL UNDERPINNING

Much of the theoretical work on the double dividend claim is based on the theory of externalities and the theory of optimal taxation. The main body of work drawing on these theories is found in the subfields of environmental and public economics. Environmental economists have long recognized the role of taxation in delivering the first dividend of environmental improvement, by the use of what are called Pigovian taxes for correcting externalities caused by pollution (Pigou, 1920). Taxation, though, is just one of a number of policy instruments that policy-makers could use to achieve an environmental improvement. Measures like standards, subsidies and marketable permits are frequently used in practice for environmental policy purposes, but the double dividend story implies that environmental taxation may be a superior instrument because of its potential to raise revenues. The literature on this angle of comparing different environmental policy instruments has been rather limited, with some notable exceptions like Pezzey (1992).

The theoretical approaches take the overall welfare of society as the objective of policy-makers in deciding how efficiently to allocate scarce resources. The question then becomes, 'Can the use of environmental taxes improve this efficiency?' In order to answer this, it is necessary to set a benchmark against which any environmental tax reform can be assessed in terms of whether it improved overall societal welfare or not. If welfare has increased, how much of that can be attributed to the improvement in the environment – the first dividend – and how much is due to the recycling of the tax revenues – the second dividend? Differences in the benchmark position and in the manner in which the revenues are recycled make the opposing theoretical interpretations arising from the literature difficult to compare. Indeed, it is even difficult to derive a consistent decomposition of the two dividends to ensure that they are both welfare improving. To clarify this dilemma, these two theoretical approaches may be somewhat simplistically divided into an 'environmental' view and a 'public finance' view.

The 'environmental' view could be described as treating environmental taxation as a corrective instrument which aims to reduce the welfare distortion caused by an externality, such as pollution. Pigovian taxes force agents to take account of the full social costs of their actions. The optimal Pigovian tax in a competitive market would be set equal to the marginal external damages at the optimum level of pollution. Because of the huge unknowns associated with this optimal point, it is possible to set the tax either too high or too low. Both have welfare losses attached because society would not be using scarce resources in their most productive activity. Once recognition of the potential welfare impacts of using the revenues collected are accounted for, then the efficient pollution tax rate will differ from the Pigouvian rate, depending upon the tax elasticity of pollution demand. When Lee and Misiolek (1986) investigated the efficiency implications of substituting pollution taxation for general taxation, they found that the pollution tax should be set higher than the conventional Pigouvian rate where the more inelastic is the tax elasticity of pollution demand.

Once the externality is recognized as a welfare distortion, the theoretical models in the 'environmental' view assume that the environmental tax is normally set at its optimal rate, taking account of the revenue requirements of the policy-makers. Thus, it forms part of an overall optimal tax system. As Ulph (1992) points out, if the taxes initially chosen were just an arbitrary set of taxes, then it would be fairly trivial to show that a switch to an optimally designed set would confer a double dividend. An optimal tax system in this context is one which would minimize the excess burden in terms of welfare losses associated with using a set of distortionary taxes to finance a government's revenue requirement. All taxes cause distortions except those which are merely lump-sum transfers – ie, payments which are unaltered by the actions of the agents involved.

The problem of designing a tax system to ensure efficiency in raising government revenue is an age-old problem. The Ramsey (1927) rule for optimal taxes in the absence of externalities is that the rates are chosen so that the weighted sum of the compensated cross-price elasticities is the same for all goods. In the case of independent goods, this rule reduces to what is referred to as the inverse elasticity rule – ie, those goods that are relatively demand-inelastic should be taxed heavily. From the government's point of view, this means that those goods whose consumption will not decline by much in response to higher prices should be taxed more heavily so that the tax base remains intact. This tends to be a property more associated with necessity goods, such as petrol, which should be a luxury good, but in the near term is fairly price resistant in demand because of structural requirements on mobility. But higher petrol prices affect travellers and income groups very differently, so there has to be a trade-off between a system which is efficient and one which is equitable. This is where the allocation of the tax-derived revenue comes in.

In the presence of an externality which is the motivation for environmental taxes, Sandmo (1975) shows that the optimal tax structure is weighted between a Ramsey-type efficiency term and a Pigouvian externality term, where the latter only applies to the externality-generating commodity. This result assumes that all taxes are alterable so that policy-makers can ignore complementarity and substitutability between the externality-producing good and all other goods. Often in practice policy-makers cannot tax the externality-generating commodity directly, so welfare can be improved by taxing complementary or subsidizing substitute goods to reflect the distortion. This raises a crucial point of difference in the theoretical models used, depending on whether the aim is tax redesign or tax reform. The environmental view tends to deal with tax redesign, where the policy-maker seeks to alter the whole tax system by starting afresh. Tax reform means working with the existing tax system, with all its pre-existing distortions, by trying to make changes to reallocate these distortions so as to improve welfare.

Given the possibility of tax redesign, Ulph (1992) suggested a decomposition that contrasts two distortionary tax systems. One ignores the externality but raises the required revenue optimally, and is called the Ramsey system. The other optimally raises the revenue accounting for the externality, and is termed the Pigouvian system. The Pigouvian system will obviously have a higher welfare than the Ramsey system because it optimizes the correct welfare function by recognizing the externality. The way that Ulph interprets the double dividend claim is whether this overall welfare improvement comes both by a lower externality distortion and a lower revenue distortion. The disentanglement of these separate effects is difficult even in theory. In practice, it is probably impossible to distinguish how much of an energy price rise is externality correcting and how much of it is revenue raising.

However, the usefulness of the Ulph decomposition is that it shows that the double dividend claim can fail. It is sensible that both the externality and revenue distortions could be higher, although not simultaneously, under the welfare-improving Pigouvian system. Put more starkly, while the second dividend may be positive, the first dividend can be negative. As Baumol (1991) points out: 'theory can be helpful to policy-makers by pointing out surprising relationships unlikely to be recognized by unaided common sense; by noting significant exceptions to principles widely accepted; and by offering generalizations of its own'. Environmental improvement can be expensive, so it is quite conceivable that we could get too much of a good thing in terms of too much pollution reduction at too high a social cost.

The widespread agreement that environmental taxes normally deliver the first dividend of environmental improvement has, therefore, to be seriously questioned. This agreement is based on the premise that detrimental externalities are excessive and so should be reduced using an instrument like an environmental tax in order to increase welfare. However, as Baumol and Oates (1988, Chapter 7) demonstrate, this policy rule will break down if any one of the following conditions are met:

1. The initial situation is one of imperfectly competitive markets.
2. There are multiple interacting externalities involved.
3. Abatement of the externality is possible.

Most of the theoretical work assumes that these conditions do not hold. This is at variance with the reality in which these tax reforms are being proposed.

Another version of the double dividend referred to by environmental economists applies to the additional benefits from using environmental taxes over traditional command-and-control instruments, such as regulatory standards. The revenue-raising property of environmental taxes, in addition to their incentive for polluters to find innovative ways to limit pollution to reduce their tax liability, are seen as the advantages of tax measures over standards. An alternative instrument containing similar efficiency properties as taxes, in terms of cost minimization of pollution abatement and incentive for pollution-reduction innovation, are tradable permits. Some economists, such as Peter Bohm in Chapter 7 of this book, argue that tradable permits are also capable of delivering a double dividend in that they can be utilized to provide government revenue by auctioning off the rights to pollution. The experience of using tradable permits has been confined mainly to the US and the revenues raised have been relatively too small to be taken seriously for general tax reform. But, appropriately designed, tradable permits could be a feasible alternative to environmental taxes in delivering double dividends.

The 'public finance' view of the double dividend issue concentrates on the second dividend from environmental taxes. As Goulder (1994) says: 'the preoccupation with the possibility of a second dividend, in my view, reflects the uncertainties about the magnitudes of the first'. Given the uncertainty about the extent of the costs and benefits of environmental reform, policy-makers are looking for the prospect of no-cost options. In order to analyse the environmental reform in cost-benefit terms, the policy-maker needs to determine the value of uncertain environmental benefits with the 'gross costs', which are the costs of abatement, and any efficiency costs involved in recycling the revenues. When the policy-maker can be assured that the environmental gross benefits are positive (another version of the first dividend), it is not necessary to engage in the difficult task of putting a value on these benefits if the gross cost can be shown to be negative. The value and sign of these gross costs are used to determine whether there is a second dividend. But these gross costs are as uncertain as are the benefits.

Goulder has distinguished several versions of the double dividend claim where the environment dividend is taken as given, so the distinguishing variable is the recycling of the revenues collected to ensure a revenue-neutral budget change. The first version is described as the *weak form* where the revenues are recycled to reduce distortionary taxes, usually on clean goods or on labour, rather than on recycling the revenue to taxpayers in a non-distortionary lump-sum transfer. Typically, the gross costs are lower (although not necessarily zero) by recycling revenue to cut distortionary taxes compared to the gross costs of lump-sum returns. This finding is used as evidence of a double dividend in its weak form. This is equivalent to Pezzey's (1992) decomposition based on a comparison between a revenue-ignoring policy, where policy-makers ignore the potential efficiency gains by using lump-sum transfers, with a revenue-recognizing policy that tries to exploit this additional dividend. This is best described as the *revenue recycling effect*. The weak-form claim is fairly uncontentious and receives broad support from numerical simulations using these theoretical models. However, the more realistic benchmark against which any tax reform should be measured is not a lump-sum tax system but one where government revenue is raised using distortionary taxes or, as economists describe them, second-best taxes.

The *strong form* of the double dividend claim put forward by Goulder is that of a revenue-neutral swap of an environmental tax for a 'representative' distortionary tax, involving a saving in gross costs. The strong claim is that the second dividend comes about from improving the efficiency of raising taxes. It is not like an intermediate form where the policy-maker can identify a particularly distorting tax which could be reduced if an alternative source of revenue could be found. The strong form claims that environmental taxes are themselves intrinsically more efficient than other average types of taxation. The benefit of finding that the strong form holds would be, of course, that the policy-maker need only ensure that the sign of the net benefits is positive to claim the double dividend, so side-stepping the difficult issue of valuing the benefits. The support for the strong form, both theoretical and numerical, is rather mixed. One would expect this to be the case, given the powerful conditions required for what amounts to be a free lunch.

Economists, like the general public, believe that there is no such thing as a free lunch, so the theoretical work of the public finance tradition used in the double dividend debate has set out to show why this must be the case. Parry (1994) has made use of partial equilibrium or the 'triangles and rectangles' approach, also drawn upon by Paul Ekins in his contribution to this book, to show that in addition to the revenue-recycling effect of the tax swap, there is another effect which depends on the interaction of the taxes. This is the *tax interaction effect* where policies, which in isolation may increase efficiency, can decrease it when interaction with pre-existing taxes are accounted for. Because pre-existing taxes in other markets affect the welfare costs of any new tax, the impacts of a new tax depend on the degree of substitutability and complementarity between commodities. For instance, a tax which creates an excess burden in one market may lead to a substitution toward another commodity whose pre-existing excess burdens decline such that the overall welfare increases. In principle, a carbon tax would penalize coal at the expense of lower CO_2-generating and CO_2-emitting gas – one of the objectives of a climate-change avoidance tax policy. In effect, this is what the second dividend is about. The public finance argument is that pre-existing distortions are likely to be exacerbated such that the tax interaction effect is negative and stronger than the positive revenue-recycling effect. Therefore, gross costs are positive and the strong form of the double dividend hypothesis fails.

Partial equilibrium approaches are normally inadequate to account for the welfare impacts of a tax reform because every market needs to be assessed in order to account for the interactions involved. However, at the theoretical level, many practitioners using general equilibrium models often make assumptions about the separability between commodities to overcome the complexity of dealing with the cross-effects between markets. One important theoretical piece on the second dividend by Bovenberg and de Mooij (1994) uses a simple general equilibrium model to cast doubt on the strong form of the double dividend claim, where an environmental tax is increased to reduce an existing tax on labour. The result is pivotal on the uncompensated wage elasticity of labour supply: if it is positive, as most empirical work suggests, then the strong form fails. A positive wage elasticity means that workers respond in aggregate to higher wages by supplying more hours of work. The elements of the two arguments behind this result are that the higher price for the environment-harming good increases the price level, so reducing real after-tax wages. The fall in the labour tax of equal revenue yield is not sufficient to compensate the worker fully for the higher price of the commodity bundle. This leads to, at least, as great a distortion as that which pre-existed in the labour market. However, in addition, the higher price of the dirty good leads the consumer to substitute towards alternative commodities such that the tax base will decline, making it more costly to raise the finance for government revenue. The *tax interaction* effect is thus greater than the *revenue-recycling* effect. Accordingly, the second dividend, in terms of a more efficient tax system, fails to materialize. This theoretical result is consistent with that of Parry (1994) who argues, using US data, that the environmental tax should be set at a lower rate than the externality-correcting Pigouvian tax.

These analytical results are derived using simplified models and numerical simulations. More complex theoretical models have been constructed, extending these models to analyse additional factors of production, such as capital (Bovenberg and van der Ploeg, 1994a), taxation of intermediate inputs, not just final consumption, and different models of the functioning of the labour market. The results of this work suggest that the prospect of a double dividend depends ultimately on the initial conditions regarding the environment for the first dividend and the initial tax system for the second dividend. Goulder (1994) suggests that the prospects for the second dividend are greater when:

1. The initial differences in the marginal-efficiency costs of the different tax rates are large.
2. The tax burden from the environmental tax falls primarily on those factors with low marginal-efficiency costs.
3. The environmental tax base is sufficiently broad.
4. The recycled revenues are targeted to reduce tax rates on factors with high marginal-efficiency costs.

The mixed conclusions from the theoretical work seem to imply that the validity of the double dividend hypothesis as an empirical issue is dependent on the underlying conditions of the economy and the environment.

EMPIRICAL SUPPORT

For the empiricist, the main lesson from the theoretical work on the double dividend hypothesis has to be the importance of capturing the interactions in the economy which will result from any environmental tax reform. Consequently, partial equilibrium approaches typically will be of limited value for providing answers for policy-makers, although they are used, for example, by Shah and Larsen (1992). The more widely used approaches to testing the hypothesis involve the use of macroeconometric models and computable general equilibrium models (Fankhauser and McCoy, 1995). The empirical support from these models for the double dividend claim also has been mixed, which makes it difficult for policy-makers to draw robust conclusions to support environmental tax reform.

Empirical modelling typically consists of a series of simulations carried out by making changes to values such as the tax rates, and comparing the resulting outcomes against a baseline forecast. General equilibrium models treat welfare explicitly by modelling consumer-utility (satisfaction) maximization, given their available preferences, income and technology. This accords well with microeconomic foundations which makes computable general equilibrium (CGE) models attractive to the academic economic community. However, CGE models are generally not estimated empirically using historical time series, but are calibrated to replicate the data of the base period. The impact is that they are quite suitable for looking at the likely long-run outcome of an environmental tax reform, but can bear very little resemblance to reality. Indeed, they have been referred to as 'numerical implementation of theoretical models' (Boero *et al*, 1991). In contrast, macroeconometric models, like that used by Terry Barker in Chapter 9 of this book, do not treat welfare explicitly, but focus more on the transitional impacts of reforms on activity measures such as GNP, inflation, unemployment and balance of payments etc. Very often these are the high-profile macroeconomic numbers that interest policy-makers in the short to medium term – namely, the time profile for which macroeconometric models are most suitable.

As a consequence of the variations in the interests of the policy-makers and the different models being used, the notion of empirically testing double dividend has changed. Alternative versions of the second dividend have arisen including reduced unemployment, higher growth, greater profits and more competitiveness. The European perspective has focused particularly on the prospect of more jobs and less pollution as the version of the double dividend for policy prescription, as noted by David Gee in Chapter 6. The North American interest seems to be one of tax reform to improve the efficiency of revenue collection, primarily to reduce the fiscal drag from crippling budget deficits. This point is touched on by Paul Ekins in Chapter 8.

The main spur for the recent spate of empirical work on environmental tax reform has come from the European Commission proposals on a carbon tax and in the US from the Clinton Administration's proposed BTU (British thermal unit) energy tax. Both of these proposals have failed to be adopted, despite positive empirical support. While the support for the strong form, in terms of negative gross cost, is rather feeble, there is much more optimism that an *intermediate form* of the second dividend would hold. This form suggests that it is possible to find a particularly distortionary tax to be substituted by the environmental tax. Given the extent of distortions in the present tax system, this would seem a likely prospect. However, this is probably more of an argument for tax reform in general than merely an issue with environmental tax reform *per se*.

The prospect of welfare improvement with negative gross cost for a revenue-neutral environmental tax reform in the US is reported by Goulder (1994) using the results from two CGE models, two macroeconometric models and a partial equilibrium model. In general, these reject the strong form of the double dividend claim. However, the general equilibrium approach of Jorgenson and Wilcoxen (1994) support the strong double dividend claim, particularly when the revenues are used to reduce taxes on capital. The European focus rests on using the revenues to reduce labour taxes as a way to cure the unemployment crisis in the European Union. The question of whether environmental taxes can increase employment while simultaneously improving the environment depends fundamentally on the operation of the labour market. Issues of whether it is better to reduce personal income taxes or National Insurance payments for employers also depend on whether the labour market is flexible or contains rigidities from union behaviour and job-search frictions.

The extent of factor substitution and the passing of the tax incidence on to other sectors domestically or to competitors are crucial assumptions in determining whether there is an employment dividend. Unsurprisingly, the econometric estimates based on the recycling of the proposed European carbon-tax revenues are mixed in support of the employment dividend across the EU (Capros *et al*, 1994). There is evidence that some member states may find it beneficial to proceed unilaterally with such tax reforms in order to tackle unemployment (Fitz Gerald and McCoy, 1992) though this ironically may be at the expense of the environment (Brunello, 1994). Some studies have suggested that there may be triple or even multiple dividends to be gained from the recycling of revenues (Bovenberg and van der Ploeg, 1994b). In addition to the improved environmental quality (green dividend), there might be more employment (pink dividend), higher profits (blue dividend) and more public goods (red dividend).

The extent of the differences between the models in terms of their structure, assumptions made, the size of the tax changes and the mechanism used for recycling contrive to make it hazardous for a policy-maker to try to make comparisons between them. The complexity of the real world and the context in which policy decisions are made are obviously inappropriately captured in these models, and so their results are of limited value for policy advice.

POLICY USE

On the basis of the quite cryptic theoretical and empirical debate, it is useful to consider the extent to which double dividend ideas have influenced environmental policy in practice. Morgenstern (1995) reports that Pigouvian-type taxes were used in one or more cases in 10 out of 19 OECD countries. The majority of these taxes were used more for their revenue-raising potential than for their incentive effects, both in their original purpose and in practice (OECD, 1989). In the majority of cases the revenues collected are quite small and often earmarked for environmental improvements, and are not part of a package of wider tax reform. The main category of environmental price measures occur in the form of indirect taxes. This point is taken up by Jean-Philippe Barde Chapter 11. In most OECD countries, the share of environment-related taxes in total tax revenues began to increase in the 1990s with the introduction of measures like carbon taxes (Scandinavia), road-fuel levies and landfill taxes (UK), and energy taxes (The Netherlands). On average, the revenues from environment-related measures in OECD countries is about 6.5 per cent of total taxes, while employment would constitute close to 30 per cent (OECD, 1995). On the face of it, there would seem to be plenty of scope to initiate further tax shifts away from employment towards the environment.

The problem faced by policy-makers, of course, is one of uncertainty, the fundamental risk being that the switch to environmental taxation may improve the environment but could do so at the expense of growth, jobs and the country's competitiveness. This might then lead to the flight of factors of production to countries with more lax pollution-control policies. This fear is played upon by those industries and sectors which feel that they would be hardest hit by the environmental reform. This strategy has been successful in blocking the EU proposed carbon tax, for instance. Policy-makers have responded to this worry about the impact on the vulnerable sectors and industries in the economy by introducing measures of compensation and exemptions. For example, the recent energy tax introduced in The Netherlands mirrors the EU carbon-energy tax proposal by exempting those firms which use energy most intensively. This may seem a rather odd exemption if the sole objective was for environmental or energy-efficiency concerns. However, any benefits from environmental improvement and extra revenue sources could be outweighed by competitiveness losses among the economy's more energy-intensive industries. It seems that policy-makers have yet to be convinced that it is something other than a 'jobs versus the environment' choice that they have to make.

CONCLUSION

The concept of a double dividend from environmental taxes is still a relatively recent phenomenon, so it is not surprising that it is an issue that is far from resolved. Initially, policy-makers were seen to be running faster than the economic theorists and empiricists when they reacted to the emergence of environmental problems, particularly the threat of global warming, by proposing the use of environmental taxes to help tackle the problem. Given the uncertainty about the benefits of abatement and the prospect of large transitional costs for the economy, policy-makers were quite willing to accept the idea of extra benefits other than an improved environment. The empirical models used by analysts such as Terry Barker in Chapter 9 provided much scope for optimism. This is because, in general, the empirical support for the additional benefits was positive, with some suggestions of multiple dividends as if environmental tax reform were a panacea for all economic ills. But the theoretical work has been used to cast doubt on the strength of the hypothesis. Theorists are seeking to alert policy-makers to the complexity of economic interactions, which could result from any pattern of revenue recycling, by giving rise to greater distortions than the initial environmental externality. Indeed, the prospect of government failure to use the additional revenues responsibly is something that would also need careful consideration, the condition of revenue neutrality notwithstanding. However, it would be wrong to conclude that the theoretical disputes on the claim have dealt it a fatal blow, even though they have cast doubt on the ease of achieving the double dividend.

The main deficiency in this debate is the lack of connection between the environmental and the economic impacts in the models used. The environmental gains which underline the first dividend receive cursory treatment. Usually the impact of the taxes on the environment are considered positive in economic terms, but this is just an assumption which, in general, may be valid but is not necessarily so. Just as the interactions in the economy from the revenue recycling are important, so too are the environmental interactions as a result of the reduction in the taxed pollutant. Much of the analysis carried out has taken the two dividends to be somehow separate from each other, such that the recycling of the revenues will have no further environmental impact. This obviously is not the case, but it highlights an important aspect of much of the current interest in environmental taxes. It would seem that any environmental benefits are only secondary considerations to the main virtue for policy-makers who are interested in more fundamental tax reforms. From an environmental viewpoint, this is not in itself a bad thing because, from both the empirical and the theoretical evidence discussed above, it seems that the strong form of the double dividend claim is likely to fail – ie, the gross costs of any tax reform are likely to be positive. Thus, it will be necessary to determine more precisely the nature, timing and social incidence of any resulting environmental benefits associated with any proposed tax change. It is not sufficient to assume that such benefits will *ipso facto* be positive.

To conclude this reflection on a hopeful note, it would seem that despite the confused debate there is still plenty of optimism that environmental taxes have an important role to play, both in helping to improve the environment and the efficient functioning of the economy. Whether these taxes are capable of delivering a double dividend depends as much on the perspective of the policy-maker and the general public as on the crucial economic and social circumstances into which they are introduced. One thing seems certain, over the coming decade: the double dividend debate is as unlikely to disappear as it is to be resolved.

REFERENCES

Baumol, W J (1991) 'Toward enhancement of the contribution of theory to environmental policy', *Environmental and Resource Economics*, 1, pp 333–52

Baumol, W J and Oates, W E (1988) *The Theory of Environmental Policy*, Cambridge University Press, Cambridge

Boero, G, Clarke, R and Winters, L A (1991) *The Macroeconomic Consequences of Controlling Greenhouse Gases: A Survey*, UK Department of the Environment, Environmental Economics Research Series, HMSO, London

Bovenberg, A L and de Mooij, R A (1994) 'Environmental levies and distortionary taxation', *American Economic Review*, 94, pp 1085–89

Bovenberg, A L and Goulder, L H (1994) 'Optimal Environmental Taxation in the Presence of Other Taxes: An Applied General Equilibrium Analysis', Working Paper, Department of Economics, Stanford University, Palo Alto, California

Bovenberg, A L and van der Ploeg, I F (1994a) 'Green policies and public finance in a small open economy', *Scandinavian Journal of Economics*, 96, pp 343–63

Bovenberg, A L and van der Ploeg, I F (1994b) 'Environmental policy, public finance and the labour market in a second best world', *Journal of Public Economics*, 3, pp 349–90

Brunello, G (1994) 'Labour Market Institutions and the Double Dividend Hypothesis: An Application of the WARM Model', paper presented at the International Workshop on Environmental Taxation, Revenue Recycling and Unemployment, Fondazione Eni Enrico Mattei, Milan

Capros, P *et al* (1994) *Double Dividend Analysis: First Results of a General Equilibrium Model (GEM-E3) Linking the EU-12 Countries*, Fondazione Eni Enrico Mattei, Milan

European Commission (1991) *A Community Strategy to Limit Carbon Dioxide Emissions and to Improve Energy Efficiency*, SEC(91) 1744, European Commission, Brussels

Fankhauser, S and McCoy, D (1995) 'Modelling the economic consequences of environmental policies, in Folmer, H, Gabel, H L and Opschoor, H (eds), *Principles of Environmental and Resource Economics: A Guide for Students and Decision-Makers*, Edward Elgar Publications, London, pp 221–37

Fitz Gerald, J and McCoy, D (1992) 'The Macroeconomic Implications for Ireland' in Fitz Gerald, J and McCoy, D (eds) *Economic Effects of Carbon Taxes*, Research Paper Series, No 14, The Economic and Social Research Institute, Dublin

Goulder, L H (1994) 'Environmental Taxation and the Double Dividend: A Reader's Guide', Working Paper, Department of Economics, Stanford University Palo Alto, California

Jorgenson, D W and Wilcoxen, P J (1994) *The Economic Effects of Carbon Taxes*, Department of Economics, Harvard University, Cambridge, Massachusetts

Lee, D R and Misiolek, W S (1986) 'Substituting pollution taxation for general taxation: some implications for efficiency in pollution taxation', *Journal of Environmental Economics and Management*, 13, pp 338–47

Morgenstern, R D (1995) 'Environmental Taxes: Dead or Alive?', Discussion Paper 96:03, Resources for the Future, Washington, DC

OECD (1989) *Economic Instruments for Environmental Protection*, Organization for Economic Cooperation and Development, Paris

OECD (1995) *Environmental Taxes in OECD Countries*, Organization for Economic Cooperation and Development, Paris

Parry, I W H (1994) 'Pollution Taxes and Revenue Recycling', paper presented at the International Workshop on Environmental Taxation, Revenue Recycling and Unemployment, FEEM, Milan

Pearce, D W (1991) 'The role of carbon taxes in adjusting to global warming', *Economic Journal*, 101, pp 938–48

Pezzey, J (1992) 'Some Interactions Between Environmental Policy and Public Finance', University of Bristol Discussion Paper No 92/317, Department of Economics, University of Bristol, Bristol

Pigou, A C (1920) *Economics of Welfare*, Macmillan, London

Ramsey, F (1927) 'A contribution to the theory of taxation', *Economic Journal*, 37, pp 47–61

Repetto, R, Dower, R C, Jenkins, R and Geoghegan, J (1992) *Green Fees: How a Tax Shift Can Work for the Environment and the Economy*, World Resources Institute, Washington, DC

Sandmo, A (1975) 'Optimal taxation in the presence of externalities', *Swedish Journal of Economics*, 77, pp 86–98

Sandmo, A (1994) 'Public Finance and the Environment', Institute of Economics Discussion Paper 9/94, Department of Economics, University of Stockholm, Stockholm

Shah, A and Larsen, B (1992) *Carbon Taxes, the Greenhouse Effect and Developing Countries*, World Bank Policy Research Working Paper Series No 957, The World Bank, Washington, DC

Stern, N H (1990) 'Uniformity Versus Selectivity in Indirect Taxation', *Economics and Politics*, 2, pp 83–108

Ulph, D (1992)' A note on the "double benefit" of pollution taxes', Department of Economics, University College London, London

Part III

ECOTAXATION IN PRACTICE

EDITORIAL INTRODUCTION TO THE PRACTICALITIES OF ECOTAXATION

In its review of the Fifth Environmental Action Plan, the European Commission (1995, p 47) admitted that the implementation of the wide range of economic instruments envisaged for the plan at its inception in 1992 has proved much more difficult than expected. Nevertheless, the Commission remains undeterred. Its aim is to increase the acceptance of such approaches because their role in promoting greater efficiency of implementation and in generating revenue to cover administrative costs, if nothing else, is appealing.

The group of chapters that follow suggest that there is still a long way to go before such taxes become both tolerated and effective. Jean-Phillippe Barde expresses the institutional spirit of the times – namely, that OECD countries recognize the economic significance of devices that correct market distortions yet reduce, in theory at least, the cost of regulation. The willingness to experiment with environmental levies is now much more dynamic than was the case a decade ago. This is especially the case in relatively high income and egalitarian nations such as Sweden, Denmark and Norway, where the attractiveness of a lower public-sector burden on regulation is indeed very alluring.

More significantly, however, is a change of economic thinking. The original theoretical principles rested on the analysis of Pigou who regarded waste discharges as discrete, identifiable and correctable with redirected market signals. Conceptually these discharges were supposed to be exceptional and occasional, but as Repetto (1994, p 1) pointed out in a powerful re-analysis of Pigouvian taxes, this has never been the case: 'Environmental externalities are ubiquitous – yet economists have not yet incorporated this fundamental fact into their models in analysis.'

Repetto and various analysts at the Wuppertal Institute in Germany, as well as increasing numbers of other researchers, are therefore looking at models of industrial materials and energy flows which are designed to reduce the link between such flows and wealth creation. This focus of attention is called dematerialization and is likely to become the late 20th-century version of Pigouvian taxation. Thus, the main zone of interest lies not so much with the traditional wastes emission tax, as with a restructuring of the price signals of a whole economy towards penalizing the use of energy, materials and resource depreciation and away from labour and underemployment. Slowly but surely, the basis of an environmentally influenced social policy based on fairness and opportunity, coupled to cleaner technology, and closing formerly open production and consumption loops, is taking hold.

Repetto (1994, p 15) points out that over 93 per cent of 1993 tax receipts in the US came from payroll, personal and corporate income taxes, estate and gift taxes, and capital gains taxes. By contrast, only around $5 billion of the $1.1 trillion tax revenue came from taxes or natural resources losses. At least $20 billion of direct federal aid goes to encouraging resource depletion in grazing, forestry and soil erosion.

Repetto appeals for a removal of the Pigouvian approach and favours a much more comprehensive, if still very simplistic, set of studies of ecological tax reform. He illustrates his point with an imagined tax of $20 per tonne on all unprocessed materials drawn from the natural world each year into the US economy. This would yield $100 billion in revenues if it was simply levied *pro rata*. Any differentiation as to toxicity or degree of dissipation would yield more revenue and be better targeted. The days are past, notes Repetto (1994, p 19), when it was in the national interest to encourage resource exploitation as an end in itself.

We could be at a momentous age in ecological tax reform. Up to a century of misdirected taxation is now in the dock and is found wanting in an age where sustainable development means far more than maintaining low tax rates, low inflation and strict monetary controls. A recent study of the German tax system (Jarass and Obermair, 1994) concluded that jobs and income taxes rose from 45 to 51 per cent of total tax revenue, while the proportion of revenue coming from natural resource depletion declined from 12 to 9 per cent. When two of the most powerful economies come to realize just how much of their resources are being misdirected in this way, there is scope for change.

So much for a head of steam. At the point of implementation, the picture is far different. This is the prime purpose of the chapters that follow. Any new tax is going to hurt powerful and politically potent interests, mostly industrial but generally in the usually elitist wealth-creating sector. This suggests that any moves to ecological tax reform will have to be presaged by clever little experiments, careful analysis of pilot schemes, and a great deal of patient explanation to otherwise suspicious parties. Even variants of Pigouvian taxes, simply picking up some of the obvious 'polluter-pays principles' are looked upon with intense suspicion by industry and the financial community.

The Clinton proposal for an energy tax – the BTU tax – was a notable early casualty. Dawn Erlandson (1994, pp 173–76) suggests that the cause of failure was very unsurprising: Clinton himself was not terribly committed to the idea, and the lobbying of influential opinion was very poor. Concessions to the coal lobby, in particular, were made too early, so congressional committees scented blood. The two main features – a physical energy basis for taxation, not carbon or source price, and no exceptions – were removed quickly. This opened up the disjointed remains of the proposal to the baying of a host of hunting dogs who could spot a carcass long before the proposal was finally killed.

The EU carbon/energy tax proposal also fell foul of big energy-intensive industry and the legal structures of the union which require unanimous agreement over any proposal to change either energy or fiscal policy. So sensitive are both these arenas to national economic autonomy that it is unlikely in the foreseeable future to expect any agreement over this issue. In any case, World Trade Organization rules can require such taxes to be stripped at the border, adding to the bureaucratic burden of implementation. Britain opposed the idea on doctrinaire fiscal grounds – namely, it wanted to run its own fiscal matters, although it claimed that it was already imposing carbon/energy taxes of a sort in its fuel-price escalator and in the operations of its Energy Saving Trust. The former is more a fiscal move than an environmental one because real petrol prices are falling, so the mopping up of consumers' surplus is very attractive. The latter is seriously impaired by the battle of wills between consumer protection and environmental protection of the utilities industries, and indeed, may become a rump organization (Owen, 1955). Despite these inherent weaknesses in the semblance of carbon taxation in the UK, Britain successfully fought the introduction of the carbon/energy tax, as did France (which sought derogation on the energy part because of its low carbon-emissions per capita) and the cohesion countries who looked for a better deal on regional redistribution.

A promising idea, well within the 'sin' area of a modified Pigouvian tax, was kicked into touch because the political alliances and advocacy coalitions, that are vital to promote and push radical economic reforms of this scale, were simply not in place.

As Terry Barker introduced in Chapter 9, a study by Ikwue and Skea (1995) concluded that the very purpose of the carbon/energy tax – namely, that it would reduce the demand for goods which are created intensively from carbon sources and energy provision – is undermined by industrial lobbies who cannot separate ecotaxation from any threat to their competitive position or deregulatory ideologies. In addition, they added this list of warning about ecotaxation implementation:

1. Do not push tax policies as a matter of political urgency thereby short-circuiting consultation with key groups: the subsequent antagonism will live to haunt you.
2. Avoid creating a situation where the beneficiaries are not obvious and the losers are .
3. Ensure that the objectives of the tax are clear, even when these objectives fail in the spaces between policy arenas.
4. Where international agreements are necessary, make sure that the political will across nations is in place before the blocking coalitions have to be faced.

Hans Vos in Chapter 12 also accepts that new tax regimes require more political preparation than refined economic theory. The experience with ecotaxation is a story of partial implementation, but growing acceptance of an imperfect arrangement. The key to the change lies in the emergence of industrial eco-audits which provide information on avoidable waste flows and potentially bad publicity over toxic and other releases, and in the scope for industry-wide regulatory compacts. These allow groups of like-minded individual groupings to come up with agreed targets for emissions and waste reduction, as long as the regulatory interference is minimal. The idea is that responsible industry agrees to work in some sort of cooperative environmental framework, then finds its own ways to reduce emissions by internal pricing and managerial controls. The external pressure groups are deeply suspicious of these voluntaristic and seemingly non-scrutinized aspects, and want the whole initiative enshrined in law. So far, there is no serious change in regulatory policy, while all sides study the possible implications. But as the new breed of integrated regulatory agencies take on more cost-recovery charging approaches to their work, there will be a greater call for self-regulation and internalized pricing regimes.

In the UK, an obvious target for environmental pricing is water. Paul Herrington explains why in Chapter 13. It is a resource that is likely to be in shorter supply and greater demand as climates change and society becomes more dispersed and affluent. There is a greater public interest and economic valuation in water as an environmental asset in the ground, or in rivers and lakes, simply keeping ecosystems alive. Policy changes in the guidelines to the Environment Agency indicate that ecological economic methods of pricing and valuation should be incorporated into the allocation measures for determining how much water remains *in situ*, and in what quality.

So the policy setting favours greater use of environmental taxation for water, but the political setting does not. Judith Rees explains that the Office of Water Supply (Ofwat) is ambivalent over the introduction of demand-reducing measures involving pricing, although it favours the use of metering and other innovative techniques. The basic problem here is that water privatization is deeply unpopular because it has led to rises in prices, mostly due to the needs to meet European Community water-quality objectives that were ignored in the 1980s, and because of the high payouts to directors, takeover bids that further raised the value of shares, and general adverse publicity over mismanagement.

This sorry saga, mostly structural in a commercial regime that is supposed to provide a public service, but made worse by serious miscalculations in management, suggests that environmentally and socially supportive pricing cannot be guaranteed to be popular, no matter how cleverly or accurately it is presented. If an organization is regarded unfavourably, untrustworthy and generally unsympathetic to public opinion, it will not be able to take more revenue from the customer, whatever the policy setting. This is a salutary lesson for the ecotaxation evolution. The popular image of both government and industry has to be reasonably favourable before even well-intentioned tax reforms are put in place.

The other main problem with any environmental tax, as already indicated in the BTU tax and carbon/energy tax stories, is the political matter of how to gain acceptance among lobbies whose obstructiveness can scupper the strategy. In the case of the UK landfill tax, the government was originally committed to a single rate based on the volume of waste disposed in a landfill. Nine months later, as Jane Powell and Amelia Craighill disclose in Chapter 15, the Treasury and the Customs and Excise backed down to favour the more environmentally and economically sensible two-tier tax based on toxicity and inertness. Even then, the waste-disposal contractors and the navigation interests were very unhappy that dredging would be charged even when it was not destined for a designated landfill site. The bill currently before Parliament defines landfill as deposits on or under the land and does not confine the practice either to controlled wastes (ie, spoil) or to statutory sites (ENDS, 1996, No 252, p 21). In classic British tradition, the final definition will be subject to a wide range of interpretation. The quarry, coal and chemical industries are all lobbying the MPs on the scrutiny committee to try to get exemptions. The sugar-beet and electricity industries are equally agitated to get the 'temporary storage' of sugar-beet soil waste and fly-ash waste exempted before it is reused on agricultural or construction land respectively.

All of this is to be expected, but it shows how any ecotax, no matter how bold in principle, is not readily accepted either for its principle or for its unfairness. And inevitably there will be unfairness when such a regime is imposed on a plethora of activities and waste streams in a relatively unsophisticated manner. Yet if no concessions are made, mostly for politically doctrinaire reasons, then inevitably some big players will cry 'foul' and seek to subvert the process.

Underlying this story is a serious problem for enthusiasts of ecological tax reforms. As concessions such as dredging wastes are granted, so the clamour for more special pleading will grow. If more concessions are made, as Bill Clinton found to his cost with his BTU tax proposals, the door will be widened into a hostile dispute over injustice. Yet concessions mean lowering the income base and also increasing the problem of handling wastes. According to the British Government's non estimates, the landfill tax revenue will be £450 million in its first full year, while the offset of National Insurance Contributions (from 10.2 per cent at present to 10 per cent) will be £500 million. By 1997–98, the gap could more than double to £120 million. Inevitably, the tax rate will have to rise in the future, hence the frantic lobbying and deep suspicion at present. Who could possibly say that environmental taxation was an economic measure?

Take another case. Local authorities will pay £150 or so million in landfill tax in 1997–98, but only about £30 million of this will be offset by lower labour charges, leaving the local councils to find new revenue from rate-capped budgets. Labour is advocating a system of tax credits where methane is extracted from landfill sites and used for energy production. But this does not get round the point that a well-meaning tax set in a policy environment that is inherently unforgiving and unfriendly may make matters worse in the name of the sustainability transition. This is why debates on how to present and implement ecotaxation have to be very open, participatory and educational. There is no substitute for carrying the argument to the classroom, to the media studio or newspaper office, to the rotaries and to local round tables. Without informed consent and much attention to the distributional implications, ecological tax reform will remain a marginal and contested policy arena. It deserves better.

The command-control regulations may have to be tightened to ensure willingness to accept a charge in order to avoid excessively costly regulatory burdens. This also increases resentment, as industry becomes suspicious that the regulatory squeeze is to encourage compliance with ecotaxes. It may be so, but it may not. There are plenty of good reasons why touch-regulatory controls should surround any strategy of ecological tax reform.

As the tax policy becomes successful and the revenue stream falls, as could be likely in the UK, for example, over diminished solid-waste streams, so the political temptation to raise the levy or to widen the basis of the tax take will grow. If, at that point, the tax regime is seen as a traditional macroeconomic policy measure by another guise, rather than a sustainable development initiative, then the public acceptance of the new regime may fall away and become very antagonistic.

All this suggests that governments have to be very careful about how they approach ecotaxation. Pilot schemes, progressive pricing, plenty of evidence of revenue targeting and a wide array of round tables and other consultative devices ideally need to be set in motion in attendance to the actual measures on the ground. After all, in any democracy it is what is possible to achieve that gets done, not that what, in principle, is desirable.

REFERENCES

Data Research Institute (1994) *Potential Benefits of Integration of Environmental and Economic Policies*, Graham and Trotman, London

Environmental Data Services (1996) 'Arguments over the landfill tax get down to the nitty-gritty', *The ENDS Report*, No 252, pp 20–3; No 253, pp 28–9

Erlandson, D (1994) 'The BTU tax experience: what happened and why it happened', *Pace Environmental Law Review*, Autumn, pp 173–84

European Commission (1995) 'Second Progress Report on the Fifth Environmental Action Programme: Points to Integrating Environmental Policy', COM (95) 634, European Commission, Brussels

Ikwue, T and Skea, J (1995) 'Business and the genesis of the European Community carbon tax proposal', *Business Strategy and the Environment*, February, pp 1–10

Jarass, L and Obermair, G (1994) *More jobs, less pollution: a tax policy for improved use of production sectors*, Department of Economics, Weisbaden Polytechnic, Weisbaden

Owen, G (1955) *Energy Policy: The Government and the Energy Regulations. A Case Study of Energy Saving Trust*, GEC 95-35, CSERGE, University of East Anglia, Norwich

Repetto, R (1994) *Shifting taxes from value added to material inputs*, mimeo, World Resources Institute, Washington, DC

C h a p t e r   1 1

ENVIRONMENTAL TAXATION: EXPERIENCE IN OECD COUNTRIES

Jean-Philippe Barde

Over the last few years, the idea of using economic, in particular fiscal, instruments for environmental protection has gained increasing support; indeed, a number of practical experiments have taken place in OECD countries. The tax-environment interface is becoming all the more important now that the need for structural adjustment in both industrialized and developing economies is high on the economic and political agendas. Furthermore, the potential contribution of tax instruments to tackle transfrontier and global environmental problems is subject to intense analysis and debate. This evolution is the result of significant changes in environmental policies, in particular a stronger reliance on the use of so-called 'economic instruments' in environmental policy. The use of environmental taxes must be put in this context.

THE CONTEXT: A GROWING RELIANCE ON ECONOMIC INSTRUMENTS

When environmental policies were initiated in industrialized countries in the early 1970s, they relied almost exclusively on direct regulations or so-called 'command and control' measures, such as licences and standards. At the same time, economists were arguing that this approach was not economically efficient and that better use of market forces ought to be

Acknowledgement
The opinions expressed in this paper are the author's own and do not necessarily reflect the views of the OECD. The author is grateful to Béatrice Fournier for comments on an earlier draft; the author, of course, bears full responsibility for this text.

made. The issue of using 'economic instruments' for environmental protection progressively, but slowly, gained support and a limited number of such approaches were implemented – for instance, waste-water pollution charges in France and The Netherlands in the early 1970s.

The OECD has long been advocating for a more intensive and consistent use of economic instruments, such as charges and taxes on polluting emissions and products, tradable emission permits and deposit-refund systems (see Box 11.1). As a matter of fact, the last decade witnessed a significant increase in the use of such instruments in OECD countries. There are at least six main reasons for this evolution:

1. The often limited performance of direct regulations, which are costly and difficult to enforce.
2. The move toward 'deregulation' or regulatory reform in various areas of intervention.
3. The search for economically more efficient policy instruments.
4. The search for revenue either for the general government budget or for financing specific environmental programmes.
5. The need for an effective 'integration' between economic and environmental policies reflected by the declaration of OECD environment ministers in 1991 (OECD, 1991).
6. The new policy context created by the Brundtland Report and the Rio Conference, to the extent that economic instruments are an essential condition for a sustainable development.

A Significant Evolution

A first OECD survey (OECD, 1989), which reflected the situation in 1987 in 14 OECD countries, identified 150 cases of economic instruments (EIs) (including subsidies), out of which 80 were environmental charges/taxes. Since then, the situation has continued to evolve and a number of countries have implemented or are intending to introduce new EIs (OECD, 1994). In some countries, the number of EIs has increased by 50 per cent between 1987 and 1993 (see Table 11.1). This is particularly true for Nordic countries (Denmark, Finland, Norway, Sweden), The Netherlands and the United States. The great number of new product taxes, in particular 'green' energy taxes, is a key feature of this evolution. Carbon taxes have been introduced in Denmark, Finland, Norway, Sweden and The Netherlands; Switzerland is presently considering the introduction of a carbon tax. Sulphur taxes are applied in Denmark, France, Norway and Sweden, and tax differentiation between leaded and unleaded gasoline has contributed significantly to the increased use of unleaded gasoline in several countries. A variety of polluting products are also subject to ecotaxes – for example, pesticides, fertilizers, lubricants and packaging (Table 11.2).

The application of emission taxes and charges has not evolved to a great extent, and in fact constituted the first 'wave' of economic instruments introduced during the 1970s and 1980s. These relate mainly to water effluent and solid-waste charges. There is also a marked increase in the use of deposit-refund systems (35–100 per cent increase according to countries), due in particular to the steep increase in packaging waste (140

BOX 11.1 TYPES OF ECONOMIC INSTRUMENTS

1. *Charges and taxes.* Charges are usually construed as payments made for a specific service or benefit, such as collective water-treatment plants or waste collection and disposal. Generally speaking, charge revenue is earmarked to cover the cost of these services. Environmental taxes are based on the environmental characteristic of the taxed item, but the revenue is not affected to specific environmental purpose and goes to the general budget.

Emission charges or taxes are direct payments on the quantity and quality of the pollutant discharged. They are applied in many environmental fields and in most countries, although with varying intensity. For instance, water effluent charges form the backbone of water-management systems in France, Germany and The Netherlands, but are also used to varying degree in many other countries. Waste charges are also quite common, but with different levels of sophistication and coverage (applying to industrial waste only in a few instances). In OECD countries, air pollution charges and taxes are increasingly implemented in a number of countries; this takes the form of special energy (fuels) taxes or emission charges – eg, a charge on SOx emissions in France, charges on NOx emissions in Sweden, and, increasingly, carbon taxes in Nordic countries and in The Netherlands. Noise charges, ranging from crude to more elaborate systems, are applied to aircraft in a few countries.

User charges are payments for the cost of collective collection and treatment services. They are commonly used by local authorities for the collection and treatment of solid waste and sewage water. They are primarily a financing device.

Product charges or taxes are applied to products which create pollution either as they are manufactured, consumed or disposed of – eg, fertilizers, pesticides, batteries. Product charges or taxes are intended to modify the relative prices of the products and/or to finance collection and treatment systems. For example, see Chapter 16 on the role of product charges in British Columbia.

2. *Marketable (tradable) permits* (also referred to as emissions trading) are based on the principle that any increase in emission must be offset by a decrease of emission of an equivalent, and sometimes greater, quantity. For example, when a statutory ceiling on pollution levels is fixed for a given area, a polluting firm can set up or expand its activity only if it does not increase the total pollution load. The firm must therefore buy 'rights' or permits to pollute from other firms located in the same control area, which are then required to abate their emission by an amount equal to the additional pollution emitted by the new activity. The objective of this approach is twofold: first, to achieve cost-minimizing solutions (by inducing firms with high marginal-abatement cost to purchase abatement from firms with low marginal-abatement cost). Secondly, to reconcile economic development activity with environ-

mental protection by allowing new activities to set up in a control area without increasing the total amount of emission within it.

3. *Deposit-refund systems* are widely applied in OECD countries, in particular for beverage containers. A payment is made when purchasing a product contained in a designated type of packaging. The payment (deposit) is reimbursed when the packaging is returned to the dealer or a specialized treatment facility.

4. *Subsidies* also constitute an important EI. They are used in many OECD countries, although to a limited extent. The main forms of financial assistance are grants, soft loans and accelerated depreciation.

million tons in OECD countries). These schemes usually prove quite effective, with an 80–100 per cent return of waste packaging and used containers (OECD, 1994).

Tradable permit systems are implemented only in a few countries. There are provisions for pollution trading in Australia, Canada and Germany, but with limited scope and application. Tradable permits are applied on a large scale only in the United States, in particular in the context of the acid rain programme.

Finally, the use of EIs to tackle global environmental problems – for example, global warming, oceans, biodiversity and transfrontier pollution – is high on political agendas, in particular the issue of carbon taxes, in the context of the Framework Convention on Climate Change. However, no significant progress has occurred so far on the international scene, despite the strong plea made by the European Commission.

The Existence of Mixed Systems

Past controversy about EIs was principally focused on the issue of EIs versus regulation. In fact, the present situation is characterized by the prevalence of 'mixed systems' where EIs are used as an adjunct to direct regulations. In such systems EIs complement regulation by providing *additional incentive* for pollution abatement and a *source of revenue* for financing environmental measures, such as the treatment of effluents, waste collection and processing.

The actual combination of EIs and regulations varies considerably between countries and according to the type of pollution. In some cases, EIs constitute the cornerstone of the policy – in particular, waste-water charges in France, Germany and The Netherlands, and air pollution in Sweden. In other instances, EIs only provide an additional financial incentive device – for instance, some types of product taxes. Yet in others, EIs constitute an optional tool and opportunity for cost savings – such as tradable permits in the United States. However, this situation may evolve in the future, as in several countries it is intended to give a more pre-eminent role to EIs, not only by introducing new ones but also by making them more

Table 11.1 *Economic instruments per country, 1 January 1992*

	Charges on emissions (of which user charges)	Charges on products (of which tax differentiations)	Deposit refunds	Tradable permits	Enforcement incentives
Australia	5 (2)	1 (0)	3	1	2
Austria	3 (1)	4 (2)	3		
Belgium	7 (2)	2 (2)	1		
Canada	3 (2)	7 (3	1	2	2
Denmark	3 (2)	10 (2)	2		
Finland	3 (2)	10 (2)	2		
France	5 (2)	2 (1)			
Germany	5 (2)	3 (3)	2	1	
Greece		2 (1)	1		
Iceland	1 (1)	1 (1)	2		
Ireland	2 (2)	1 (1)			
Italy	3 (2)	2 (0)			
Japan	3 (1)	1 (1)			
Netherlands	5 (2)	4 (2)	2		
New Zealand	1 (1)				
Norway	4 (2)	8 (2)	3		
Portugal	2 (0)	1 (1)	1		
Spain	3 (2)				
Sweden	3 (2)	11 (2)	4		2
Switzerland	3 (2)	2 (2)	1		
Turkey			1		
UK	1 (1)	1 (1)			
USA	5 (2)	6 (1)	4	8	2

Source: OECD, 1994

Table 11.2 Overview of environmentally related taxes and charges in OECD countries (1 January 1995)

Environmental tax measures

	Australia	Austria	Belgium	Canada	Denmark	Finland	France	Germany	Greece	Iceland	Ireland	Italy	Japan	Luxembourg	Mexico	Netherlands	New Zealand	Norway	Portugal	Spain	Sweden	Switzerland	Turkey	United Kingdom	United States
Motor fuels																									
Leaded / unleaded (differential)	●		●		●	●	●	●		●	●	●		●	●	●	●	●	●	●	●	●	●	●	
Diesel (quality differential)					●	●										●	●	●			●				
Carbon / energy taxation					●	●												●			●				
Sulphur tax																		●							
Other excise taxes (other than VAT)	●	●		●	●	●	●	●	●		●	●	●	●	●	●	●	●	●	●	●	●	●	●	●
Other energy products																									
Other excise taxes	●	●	●		●	●	●	●	●		●	●	●	●		●		●		●	●	●		●	●
Carbon / energy taxation					●	●									●	●		●			●				
Sulphur tax					●		●									●		●			●				
NOₓ charge							●														●				
Vehicle-related taxation																									
Sales / excise / registration tax difference (cars)			●	●	●	●		●	●	●	●	●	●		●	●		●	●	●	●	●	●		●
Road / registration tax difference (cars)			●	●	●					●	●	●			●	●		●			●	●	●		
Agricultural inputs																									
Fertilizers																		●			●				
Pesticides					●	●												●			●				

Source: OECD, 1995

Other goods
Batteries
Plastic carrier bags
Disposable containers
Tyres
CFCs and/or halons
Disposable razors
Disposable cameras
Lubricant oil charge
Oil pollution charge

Direct-tax provisions
Environmental investments/accelerated depreciation
Employer-paid commuting expenses part of taxable income
Free parking part of taxable income
Commuting expenses deductible from taxable income only if public transport used

Air transport
Noise charges
Other taxes

Water charges and taxes
Water charges
Sewerage charges
Water-effluent charges

Waste disposal and management charges
Municipal waste
Waste-disposal charge
Hazardous waste charge

effective through higher rates of taxes and charges which will be capable of inducing real changes in polluters' behaviour – for instance, carbon and sulphur taxes and NO_x charges in Sweden.

ENVIRONMENTAL TAXES

The greatest number of environmental instruments in use in OECD countries relate to various types of charges and taxes. What basically differentiates charges from taxes is that a charge is usually a payment for a service rendered – such as collective waste or water-treatment facilities, while tax revenues are not earmarked to specific environment or other purposes. However, this distinction is not always clear cut and both terms are often used interchangeably. Nevertheless, both have a fiscal or quasi-fiscal character and so called ecotaxes have proliferated over the last five to ten years in OECD countries (OECD, 1995a).

The 'greening' of taxes can be done in two complementary ways.

1. One way consists in restructuring existing taxes in an environmentally friendly manner. Such an approach aims at modifying relative prices by taxing those products and activities that pollute relatively more than others. This approach is developing in several countries and is attracting growing interest in others. For instance, twenty countries introduced tax differentiation on leaded vs unleaded gasoline. In sixteen countries, car sales and/or annual vehicle taxes have been modified in order to stimulate the use of less polluting vehicles.

2. Another way is to introduce new ecotaxes. For instance, product taxes are applied to products which create pollution as they are manufactured, consumed or disposed of. Examples are lubricants, fertilizers, pesticides non-returnable containers, mercury and cadmium batteries, 'feedstock' chemicals and packaging (see Table 11.2). In most cases, ecotaxes are implemented to tackle specific environmental issues on an *ad hoc* basis. For instance, in France, a sulphur tax was introduced in 1985 and taxes on H_2S, NO_x and HCl emission by industry in 1990. In Belgium, a more systematic approach is followed whereby a series of ecotaxes are introduced with the 'Ecotax Law' of 1993; these taxes apply to a variety of products – eg, drink containers, disposable razors and cameras, selected packaging for industrial use, pesticides, paper and batteries. The UK will apply a 'Landfill Tax' in 1996, as discusssed in some detail in Chapter 15. Switzerland intends to implement taxes on VOC (volatile organic compounds) and a CO_2 tax in the near future.

One more comprehensive approach implies the greening of taxes in the broader context of tax reforms.

Environmental Tax Reforms

The proliferation of new environmental taxes and the restructuring of existing (mainly energy) taxes raises the issue of the compatibility and coordination of these taxes with existing fiscal structures and policy. On the one hand, the compatibility of current non-environmental taxes with environmental goals needs to be reviewed; on the other hand, new ecotaxes must be properly integrated in fiscal structures. The issue is thus whether new ecotaxes should be part of a tax 'package' – ie, a comprehensive tax reform.

The first issue (adapting existing taxes) is an urgent, albeit complex one. While a number of current taxes, such as energy, vehicle or other transport related taxes, can be identified easily as 'environmentally relevant', some other taxes may have perverse environmental implications; indeed, there exist many distortionary taxes which are the origin of market failures. For instance, land taxes can induce the degradation of wetlands or the over exploitation of forests – for instance, through tax breaks for agricultural or industrial usage of land, and preferential tax treatment for felling trees (OECD, 1992). In the field of transport, many tax provisions result in adverse environmental effects: the preferential taxation of company cars and the tax deductability of commuting expenses induce the overuse of private cars, hence congestion, pollution, noise and accidents (Figure 11.1). The lower taxation of diesel fuel for motor vehicles (in many countries diesel-fuel taxes are half the level of gasoline taxes) induce an over development of road transport (in particular freight) and the multiplication of diesel automobiles which are a significant source of pollution (particulates) and noise. Agricultural support measures, such as price support and lower input prices, have potentially adverse environmental effects. Some countries have already started to identify such environmentally distortive taxes;

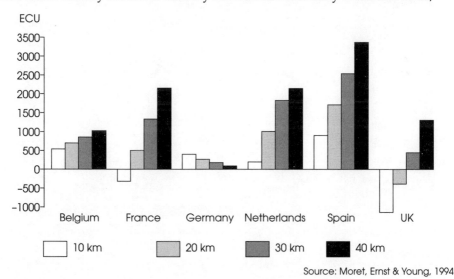

Source: Moret, Ernst & Young, 1994

Figure 11.1 *The tax advantage of a company car, compared with a privately owned car (home–work distance: 10, 20, 30 and 40 km)*

this exercise is technically difficult, but is also likely to be politically perilous as invariably it affects conflicting interests and pressure groups such as farmers and road transport lobbies. It is, nevertheless, an essential prerequisite for an efficient 'green' tax reform.

The issue that economic subsidies have detrimental effects on the environment – for example, in the fields of energy, transport, agriculture and manufacturing – should also be seen in this context of broader tax reforms (subsidies are negative taxes). The G7 (the group of seven leading industrial nations) in 1995 expressed concern about this issue and instructed the OECD to undertake work in this area.

As energy is a major source of pollution and tax revenue, restructuring of energy taxation is the most pressing and obvious path to tax reforms. Existing energy taxes may be restructured and/or additional ecotaxes levied. For instance, as gasoline taxes are high in most OECD countries, there is ample room for restructuring (Figures 11.2 and 11.3). Instead of a flat rate – eg, per litre – the fuel tax should be, at least in part, based on the carbon and sulphur content. Several countries, in particular Nordic countries, have done so. For instance, in Sweden, in 1991, general energy taxes were cut by 50 per cent, while a new CO_2 tax was introduced (SEK 0.25 per kilo of CO_2 for all fuels) (see Table 11.3). This resulted in a significant increase of energy taxation. In 1993, however, for reasons of international competitiveness, manufacturing industry and commercial horticulture

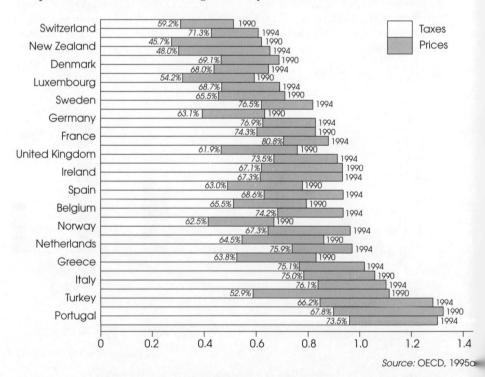

Source: OECD, 1995a

Figure 11.2 *Prices and taxes on leaded gasoline: sold to households (including VAT) in US purchasing-power parities per litre*

were granted a total exemption of energy tax and a 75 per cent rebate on the carbon dioxide tax. The basic tax rate for industry is SEK 0.08 per kilogram of CO_2 and SEK 0.32 for other sectors (household, services and transport). A similar approach, involving a reduction in energy tax and the introduction of a CO_2 tax, has been followed in Norway (1991) and in Denmark (1992). Obviously, tax exemptions may run against the environmental objective of the ecotax. This underlines the need for international harmonization and cooperation.

Comprehensive environmental tax reforms are usually applied in a revenue-neutral context implying that additional ecotaxes are compensated by the reduction of other taxes, in order not to increase the total fiscal burden. This is a fundamental aspect of tax reforms and, to a large extent, a key condition to ease implementation. Hence, the 1991 Swedish tax reform was mainly based on a significant decrease in income taxes, compensated by the introduction of a variety of new ecotaxes, in particular on CO_2, sulphur and NO_x. This resulted in a redistribution of 6 per cent of the GDP. A similar path has been followed in Norway since 1992. Denmark is also implementing a comprehensive tax reform over the period 1994–98. The European Commission (1993a) has made a strong plea for comprehensive green tax reforms, as discussed in detail by David Gee in Chapter 6.

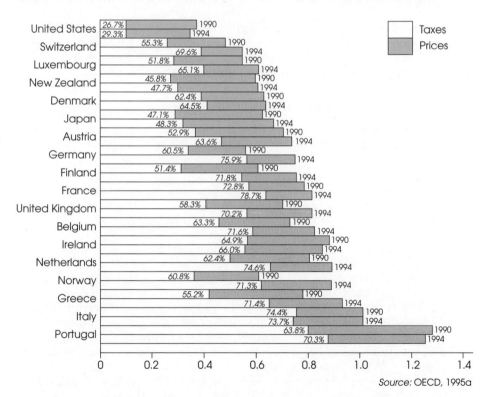

Source: OECD, 1995a

Figure 11.3 *Prices and taxes on unleaded gasoline (95 RON) sold to households (including VAT) in US purchasing-power parities per litre*

Table 11.3 *Swedish general energy tax (GET) and CO_2 tax*

Fuel	SEK	GET	GET	CO_2	Total	GET	CO_2	Total	GET	CO_2	Total
			1990			1991–92			Industry 1993		Others 1993
Coal	ton	460	230	620	850	0	200	200	230	800	1030
Oil	m³	1078	540	720	1260	0	230	230	540	920	1460
Natural gas	km³	350	175	535	710	0	170	170	175	680	855
LPG[1]	tonne	210	105	750	855	0	240	240	105	960	1065
Electricity	ore/ kWh	5	5			0			0		
									0 district heating		

1 LPG: liquid petroleum gas

Source: Swedish Ministry of the Environment, 1994

THE POLITICAL ECONOMY OF ENVIRONMENTAL TAXES

Although the experience in environmental taxes is fairly recent, their increasing and potential role in environmental policy has raised a number of economic, fiscal and political issues which are still the subject of debate and scrutiny. These will be reviewed briefly in this section.

Implementation Issues

Any attempt to introduce new taxes is always confronted with a variety of technical and political problems (see OECD, 1996).

The need for clear goals

First, the objectives that environmental taxes are supposed to achieve must be defined clearly: what specific environmental problem is the tax aiming at? This is not always a trivial question. For instance, the purpose of a tax on packaging may not be explicit: is it designed to promote recycling, volume reduction or specific ways for disposal? Similarly, whether 'green' energy taxes are primarily designed for reducing polluting emissions (in this case which pollutant?) or energy conservation is often far from explicit, even though both are interrelated. In fact, ecotaxes have sometimes multiple policy goals, based on the right or wrong assumption of 'double dividend' or 'no regret' arguments. Some of these were spelt out by Daniel McCoy in Chapter 10. Energy taxes are a case in point, where the energy-conservation argument is compounded with the emission-reduction objective. What makes implementation delicate is when these multiple goals are not well founded in technical and economic terms, and worse, they are not made explicit to stakeholders and the public. The issue becomes more blurred when the environmental and fiscal objectives are not clearly separated and defined. The 'greening' of taxes may be a political argument to justify or to hide the real purpose of revenue raising.

Confusion may also arise with 'double dividend' arguments – for instance, employment and the environment. Combining policy aims can be a double-edged sword: on the one hand, a good selling argument, and on the other hand, a source of confusion and opposition when the multiple purpose is not made explicit. Moreover, each responsible party fears that it will lose. Environmental policy-makers are nervous that the environmental purpose of the tax becomes secondary or lost. People in charge of the other related policy area – eg, employment – may also fear reduced effectiveness (see below).

Designing environmental taxes

Ideally, the amount of tax paid should reflect the environmental-damage cost caused by the taxed product or activity. This will not be possible in practice, but nevertheless, the closer the link between the tax paid and the environmental impact, the greater its effectiveness. This means that the effectiveness of an environmental tax is the function of two main parameters: the basis and the rate of the tax.

Linkage. The determination of the basis of the tax raises the so called 'linkage' issue. In case of an emission tax, the payment should be linked with the externality – ie, the quantity of polluting emissions. Measuring emissions is not always easy and can be costly, and emission taxes may prove difficult to implement. It becomes all the more complex when the discharge of a given activity is a complex mix of different substances – for instance, discharges into water from chemical or pulp-and-paper industries comprise a mix of organic matters, particulates and chemicals such as chlorine and heavy metals. Taxing all these discharges may prove complex. In a number of cases, a compromise must be found between complex and sophisticated linkage formulas, and over-simplified ones. On the other hand, a loose linkage will produce little incentive to the taxpayer for taking emission-reduction measures. Generally speaking, the linkage should be as clear and as explicit as possible.

When emissions are a function of inputs in the production process, taxing these inputs can be a convenient solution – eg, taxing the sulphur or carbon content of fuels, certain 'feedstock' chemicals, fertilizers. This proves to be a workable approach, provided the linkage is made sufficiently explicit to induce environmental protection measures – for instance, changing input mix. In some cases, the linkage is made closer when input taxes are refunded to polluters in proportion to the quantity of emission abated. For instance, the Swedish sulphur tax is reimbursed to industry in proportion to the quantity of sulphur removed by end-of-pipe technologies. Care must be taken that the linkage remains direct and stable.

The existence of substitutes. So-called 'product taxes' – ie, taxes on damaging products such as pesticides, packagings, lubricants and different types of fuels – are a convenient solution. The user of the product is faced with two alternatives: to reduce the consumption or use of the taxed product, or to switch to substitute products. This raises the delicate issue of demand-price and substitution elasticities. The existence of appropriate substitutes may not be straightforward: if given categories of fuels are taxed in proportion to their carbon or sulphur content, the user must be able to choose between alternative fuels. For instance, a tax differentiation between three categories of diesel fuels was introduced in Sweden in 1991; the tax was extremely effective as it induced oil companies to supply 'clean' diesel fuels whose share of the market rose in two years from 1 per cent to 60 per cent (Swedish Ministry of the Environment, 1994). The case of the Belgian taxes on disposable razors and cameras is also one where close substitutes are available and are clearly identifiable. But when no substitutes or only poor ones are available, the environmental effectiveness of the tax will be reduced (notwithstanding the fact that the tax continues to internalize the environmental cost and acts as a permanent incentive to reduce consumption and/or to develop substitutes). In this case, the tax may be judged as a pure revenue-raising device and may be contested on both environmental and fiscal grounds. When only imperfect or not easily identifiable substitutes exist – for example, pesticides, fertilizers and certain chemicals – an information campaign should be deployed to inform users about possible substitutes or alternative courses of action.

Tax rate. The rate of the tax is the other key parameter. Leaving aside the ideal Pigouvian tax where the unit rate would equal the marginal damage cost, the rate should be sufficiently high to ensure the achievement of environmental goals. In reality, taxes will often turn as compromises between conflicting aims and interest groups. While taxpayers will exert pressure to minimize the tax level, conflicts may also arise on the government side: the more effective a tax, the faster its revenue will decrease over time as the taxable base diminishes. Thus, while environmental authorities will try to apply a rate which is sufficiently high to achieve the environmental purpose of the tax, the Treasury would rather opt for a lower tax, which may be less environmentally effective but with a more sustainable revenue yield. This raises again the issue of the insertion of the ecotaxes within the global fiscal system. Ideally, ecotaxes should be designed so that revenue will decrease over time, although there should always be a tax on residual pollution – ie, that degree of pollution that is cheaper to discharge than to abate. The residual level of pollution is where the marginal cost of abatement is equal to the unit rate of the tax. Assuming that a government wants to keep constant its total tax revenue (and this is a strong assumption), this implies the introduction of new taxes over time or the increase in existing ones. Hence, where environmental taxes play a growing role, it implies regular adjustments in the tax system. For instance, the Swedish sulphur tax has triggered a 40 per cent decrease in the sulphur content of fuel oil between 1990 and 1992, which resulted in a much lower tax revenue than expected (Swedish Ministry of the Environment, 1994).

Phasing in the implementation of the tax

The political acceptability and the effectiveness of the tax can be improved considerably through proper timing. First, a pre-announcement allows stakeholders to take at an early stage appropriate measures, such as emission-abatement technology, changes in production methods and input mix.

Secondly, a progressive and carefully planned and announced increase in the tax level avoids brutal disruptions and enables industry to plan its investment strategy. In Germany, long before water-effluent charges came in force (in 1981), abatement measures were put in place by industry to minimize charge payments. In Sweden, while the government's Commission on Environmental Charges was envisaging the introduction of a tax on chlorine, industry opposed strongly but took drastic measures to cut emissions; finally, the tax was not implemented but the announcement effectively induced industry to take control measures. The Danish ecological tax reform is being implemented over a four-year period (1994–98). In France, water-effluent charges were doubled over a five-year period (1992–96) and another 25 per cent increase is proposed for the seventh programme of French Water Agencies (1997–2007).

Political barriers

Taxes are never popular and environmental taxes do not escape that rule. The main opposition comes from industry as emission taxes add an additional burden to the cost of abatement measures (tax paid on 'residual' emissions). Also, environmental taxes can be suspected to be a purely fiscal instrument dressed in green. It is important to involve stakeholders in the policy process. The Swedish Commission on Environmental Charges was a forum for discussion with industry. In Belgium, an Ecotax Commission was instrumental in the passing of the 1993 Ecotax Law. A 'follow-up commission', where industry can argue its case, is charged with the evaluation of the new system.

Clearly, imposing a series of new environmental taxes is made much easier if it is done in the context of a 'package' of measures, such as the reduction of other existing taxes (the revenue-neutrality argument), the correction of regressive distributional impacts, and the mitigation of possible adverse trade effects. These issues are briefly reviewed below.

The Use of Tax Revenue

What should be done with the revenue of ecotaxes? This is a key issue as it impinges on the political acceptability of taxes, their environmental effectiveness and 'double dividend' arguments, whereby ecotaxes could be designed to provide benefits in two or more fields. If tax revenue is allocated to the general budget of the government, it can have any impact, including the reduction of public deficits. What matters politically is that the use of the ecotax revenue be clearly identified.

Generally, three main options are considered: earmarking to specific environmental purposes; compensation for possible regressive distributional implications of the tax; reducing other existing distortionary taxes.

Earmarking.

It is strongly debated whether ecotax revenue should be earmarked, in particular for environmental purposes; there are environmental, fiscal and political arguments at stake. The various arguments appear in Chapters 12, 13 and 14 of this book.

First, it must be recognized that earmarking environmental taxes and charges is widely used in OECD countries. Indeed, this was historically the driving argument for the implementation of such taxes and charges. In the late 1960s, water-effluent charges were introduced in France and The Netherlands; their basic purpose was to raise funds for financing collective water-treatment facilities, and to provide financial assistance to the private sector for pollution-control investment. A comparable system was introduced in Germany in the early 1980s. In such systems, funds are entirely 'recycled' in pollution-control activities. Other similar systems, albeit much more limited in scope, are applied in other fields such as waste recovery and recycling – used lubricants, packaging, batteries – and air pollution (the SO_x tax in France and the NO_x charge in Sweden). Note that where earmarking is the intended objective, the word 'charge' should be used rather than 'tax' as the revenue is to be used for a specific purpose.

The main advantage, from an environmental point of view, is that such earmarked charges (in fact, 'user charges' in most cases) provide a guarantee for a continuous flow of financial resources. Earmarking also strongly reinforces the political acceptability of charges, first because the charge paid is in a sense 'returned' to taxpayers in the form of services, collective facilities, grants and other assistance; secondly, because the distribution of the tax revenue is made explicit and transparent to the public (in particular environmental groups) and polluters. Earmarked charges are also seen as a powerful means to finance a transition period for 'catching up' accumulated investment lags and pollution backlogs. This approach of 'environmental funds' is widely used and promoted in economies in transition (Eastern and Central Europe) (OECD, 1995c).

There are, however, many issues and pitfalls with earmarking. First, when revenue is allocated to specific environmental purposes, earmarked taxes are remote from any type of environmental tax that economists would favour. Even if Pigouvian taxes, whereby the tax rate is based on the marginal pollution-damage cost, are hardly feasible, at least taxes should be designed to influence behaviour – for example, to induce polluters to reduce their discharge. This objective will not, or will only partially, be achieved with earmarked taxes. Furthermore, if earmarked taxes happen to reach this incentive level, this would induce over-investment and over-capacity in pollution-control facilities – hence, economic inefficiency. This is the case in The Netherlands where, in certain river basins, high levels of water effluent charges led to a 20 per cent over-capacity in treatment facilities.

Secondly, earmarking runs against conventional wisdom in tax policy. Earmarked funds may lead to inefficient uses of public money and prevent the introduction of new ecotaxes in a revenue-neutral context. The Treasury will hate to lose access to and control of the revenue because such funds are usually managed by environmental agencies (*a contrario*, this is a reason why environmentalists prefer earmarking). Earmarking systems, introduced for transitory periods, will tend to perpetuate, and lobby groups will endeavour to 'capture' the system in order to keep control of and benefit from the money.

As ecotaxes are gaining in importance, especially as new 'green' energy taxes are introduced, the allocation of the revenue, and in particular the issue of earmarking, acquires significant fiscal, economic, environmental and political dimensions. This issue must be seen in a long-term and global perspective, in particular in the context of tax reforms. As was pointed out in Part II of this volume, this is why ecotaxation rarely relates to economic theory, and why it is more of a social and political measure than an economic one.

Distributive Implications

Ecotaxes have potential distributive implications at several levels: within a country, some regions may be more affected than others, depending on industrial structure and environmental endowment; various sectors of industry may also be hit unequally; finally, within the household sector, income categories will be affected unequally. Although there is still little evidence of the nature of the distributive implications of environmental taxes, this is now a matter of growing potential concern, and hence a key aspect of the implementation of such taxes.

As a number of ecotaxes may apply on mass consumption products such as packaging, batteries, motor vehicles and energy, these are likely to affect people on lower incomes. Ecotaxes paid by the production sector – eg, input taxes on industry and agriculture, and emission taxes – will also be reflected in consumer prices. Yet a distinction must be made between rather low and limited ecotaxes on packaging, batteries, fertilizers and detergents, and higher and more general taxes such as energy taxes. The first category, in fact, reflects the situation prevailing in most OECD countries where ecotaxes are still limited in scope and probably hardly have any discernible distributive impacts, although there are no empirical studies to imply or contradict this rule-of-thumb.

The case is quite different when major taxes – in fact, energy taxes – are concerned. Several studies have estimated the potential distributive incidence in the case of carbon taxes. Pearson and Smith (1991) made an analysis of the distributional incidence of the proposed EC carbon/energy tax in the UK. They showed that the tax would have a significantly larger impact on the energy consumption of poorer households than on other households: while a carbon tax of $10 per barrel would reduce overall domestic consumption by 6.5 per cent, it would reduce by 10 per cent the consumption of the 20 per cent poorest households (Pearson and Smith, 1991). However, there seem to be large differences in the regressivity of carbon taxes in European countries (Pearson, 1992); in most cases the regressive incidence seems small except for Ireland (Scott, 1992).

Nevertheless, despite the lack of convincing evidence, the likely increase in the number and level of ecotaxes will require sustained vigilance over their potential distributive implications. Financing corrective measures for the regressive impact of taxes will depend on the significance of these impacts and the type of policy chosen: one might opt for *ex ante* mitigation measures, such as tax rebates or exemptions, or *ex post* lump-sum transfers to the affected sectors or income categories. Generally speaking, mitigation measures such as tax rebates will jeopardize the environmental purpose of the tax.

Ecotaxes and Employment: Is There a 'Double Dividend'?

Between 1990 and 1994, the number of unemployed people in OECD countries rose from 25 million to 35 million (8.5 per cent of the labour force). By the end of 1995, the unemployment rate in OECD countries was 7.5 per cent, and 11 per cent in the European Union. This is why a considerable number of studies have attempted to evaluate whether green fiscal reforms could be devised to provide benefits both in terms of the environment and employment. This so-called 'double dividend' argument is attracting a great deal of attention and controversy in academic and political circles, as summarized by Daniel McCoy in Chapter 10. In particular, the European Commission is making a strong plea for a reduction of labour taxes (in particular, Social Security Contributions paid by employers) which would be financed by the proposed EU carbon/energy tax: the double dividend would be a reduction in carbon emissions and an increase in employment. Various simulation models seem to indicate a positive employment impact, especially if the reduction in employers' Social Security Contributions (SSC) is targeted to low-skilled, low-income workers (European Commission, 1993b).

It is not the purpose of this chapter to discuss this complex issue, which is still the subject of a great deal of analysis and controversy. The hypothesis of the double dividend is a function of a number of factors and uncertainties, in particular regarding the structure and functioning of labour markets, labour and capital mobility. It is important, however, to underline the strong policy dimension of this argument. The key policy issues are:

- Distortionary taxes, which are targeted to be reduced or withdrawn, must be significant and clearly identified. In particular, it must be ascertained that the reduction of these taxes would in all probability provide the expected benefit (the first 'dividend'). Hence, the employment benefit of reducing SSC must be established clearly. Available evidence seems to indicate some potential for employment creation by reducing the tax wedge on labour (employers' SSC and income taxes on low-income categories) in countries where this tax burden is high.
- A significant employment effect will require a substantial reduction of labour charges – hence the imposition of ecotaxes which are sufficiently high to finance this reduction. Such taxes do not seem to exist yet, and may prove politically difficult to pitch at a sustainably high level.
- As mentioned earlier, an effective ecotax implies shrinking revenue over time, as emissions decrease. Thus, keeping a constant revenue yield to finance the reduction in other labour taxes would require regular adjustments in the fiscal system – eg, by introducing new ecotaxes or increasing existing ones.
- As high taxes would be required, so international coordination would be needed. No country will be ready to embark in, say, high carbon taxes, if a similar approach is not implemented by trading partners. However, ecotaxes can also provide trade advantage, as

noted in the section that follows.
- Environmentalists tend to fear that the employment argument would jeopardize the environmental purpose of the tax; ecotaxes must first and foremost be used for environmental protection.

Nevertheless, the double dividend issue remains high on political agendas in several countries. Interestingly, the new UK 'landfill tax' to be introduced in October 1996 will be accompanied by a reduction in employers' SSC. The difficulties of implementing this policy are examined in more detail in Chapter 15.

The Trade Implications of Ecotaxes

Last, but not least, ecotaxes are often contested by industry which claims that such taxes will hurt its competitiveness. Another concern is that industries will be induced to locate in other countries where ecotaxes do not exist or are lower: this is the so-called 'leakage effect'. Without entering into details, four remarks are in order.

1. Environmental policy as such has a potential impact on trade and competitiveness; ecotaxes are but one of the instruments applied and it is the compounded effect of the mix of policy instruments applied that matters (regulations, tradable permits, etc).
2. There is no firm evidence that environmental policy has so far had significant effects on trade. Models indicate ambivalent results: either a slightly positive or a slightly negative impact on the balance of trade. Similarly, there is no convincing evidence of industrial flight to so-called 'pollution havens' (Dean, 1992).
3. The alleged minimal effect of environmental policy on trade is probably a reflection of the limited magnitude of these policies (environmental expenditures in OECD countries vary between 1 and 2.5 per cent of GDP). However, as these policies may gain in importance, the trade effect may become more significant.
4. A distinction must be drawn between short-term and long-term adjustments. In the short term, some industry sectors or plants may be more affected than others as the economy is adjusting to the tax in the longer term. In fact, industry's opposition is stronger against taxes than against command-and-control regulations because taxes impose an additional burden (polluters must pay the abatement cost plus the tax on residual pollution). However, at the global level, the tax is a transfer payment within the nation and should not affect the competitiveness of the domestic economy. Moreover, in the longer term, taxes should lead to a minimization of the over-all abatement cost within a country or an economic sector, compared to command-and-control regulations (the so-called 'static efficiency' argument): indeed this should be the primary purpose of ecotaxes. Hence, the competitive position of the economy should be improved. In the current debate, there is often a confusion between short-term competitiveness issues and longer-term adjustments in trade patterns.

Note that the competitiveness effect will depend on how the tax revenue is used. For instance, reducing labour charges may improve the competitiveness of labour-intensive industries. Increased energy taxes may affect energy- and capital-intensive industries.

This does not mean, however, that the trade implications of environmental taxes should be disregarded. In fact, rightly or wrongly, this issue has become the main stumbling block for the introduction of new ecotaxes. The EC carbon energy tax proposal has failed so far largely on trade grounds. Member countries do not want to apply such a tax as long as other main EU competitors will not apply similar measures (hence, the so-called 'conditionality clause'). When ecotaxes are introduced unilaterally, exemptions are often granted to sectors that are subject to international competition. As mentioned earlier, in Sweden industry was granted a total exemption of the general energy tax and a 75 per cent rebate on the carbon dioxide tax; in Denmark, a 50 per cent rebate on the CO_2 tax is granted to industry; in Norway, certain industries are exempted from the CO_2 tax. In fact, the much criticized EC carbon/energy tax proposal provides for the exemption of certain industrial sectors. Exemptions are certainly not a good solution and in fact will create trade distortions while eroding the environmental effectiveness of the tax.

In the case of product taxes, there is room for the application of 'border tax adjustments': exported products are exempted from the tax while imported ones are subject to the domestic tax; hence, domestic and imported goods are treated equally. This approach conforms with the country of destination principle and is consistent with rules under the General Agreement on Tariffs and Trade (GATT). The issue is far less clear in case of emission or input taxes; under the current interpretation of GATT rules, emission taxes do not qualify for border tax adjustments. The issue is unclear for input taxes such as energy taxes; while the Uruguay Round allows energy taxes to be remitted on exported goods, it is not clear whether a border tax adjustment could be applied to imports. There is a strong need for clarifying these rules. Note that, in practice, border-tax adjustments may prove difficult and costly to enforce. This example illustrates the problem of the implementation burdens raised by Daniel McCoy in Chapter 10.

CONCLUSION

The use of environmental taxes increased significantly over the last decade, with an acceleration in the last four years. However, future developments are not very clear. It seems that industrialized countries are in a transition period characterized by six main features and uncertainties.

1. There are uncertainties as to the real effectiveness of environmental taxes (and indeed of economic instruments in general). No feed-back evaluation systems of the taxes have been installed so that, except in a few cases, little is known about the economic and social consequences beyond the vagaries of economic models. This is, of course, partly attributable to the small time span since these

taxes were introduced. But there is also a lack of analytical capability to carry out such evaluations, which are all the more difficult in that taxes are usually implemented in conjunction with other policy instruments. Disentangling their effect is likely to be arduous. To overcome these difficulties, countries should devise 'in-built' evaluation systems, even though these will add to the implementation costs.

2. We are in a 'grey' area where most existing environmental taxes, including carbon taxes, are still fairly small. If we want environmental taxes to be really effective and efficient, their level must increase significantly. Carbon taxes are a case in point: in OECD countries, even a moderate carbon tax rate of $50 per ton of carbon would raise approximately $150 billion (based on 1990 carbon emissions) – ie, about 2.5 per cent of the total OECD tax revenue (OECD, 1995b). Stabilizing CO_2 emissions at 1990 levels by the year 2050 would necessitate much higher taxes. Clearly, such tax levels would imply significant economic effects and restructuring, even in a revenue-neutral perspective. The prospects for significant increases in ecotaxes are far from clear for the time being.

This 'grey area' is also characterized by uncertain political moves towards taxation reforms and the effective streamlining of tax systems to correct government failures and various externalities. The EU has undertaken a systematic review of tax systems to identify such distortionary taxes. This approach is surely to be recommended, but will obviously be subject to many political flaws.

3. If a real move towards incentive taxes takes place, the issue of revenue stability will arise: effective ecotaxes mean decreasing revenue. Hence, the government will have to adjust by introducing new (perhaps precautionary environmental) taxes. Taxation reform will thus become a permanent process, with all the pitfalls of a political democracy.

4. There are great uncertainties as to the international scene: unless environmental taxes are internationally coordinated, their implementation at the domestic level will be limited or subject to exemptions which erode their environmental effectiveness. This is all the more true for policies that are designed to cope with global environmental issues such as global warming. The prospects for the application of carbon taxes at the international scale are quite uncertain. Even though the international coordination of environmental taxes seems a prerequisite for any further significant progress, countries are still caught in the 'prisoner's dilemma'.

5. Environmental taxes are a typical and outstanding case where key actors in the economy must cooperate. In particular, environmentalists and tax experts must be in dialogue to make sure that both environmental and tax policies are compatible and, indeed, mutually reinforcing. The OECD (1993) has taken a clear standpoint on environmental taxes, stating that:

...environmental and fiscal policies can and should be made mutually reinforcing. While there exists a great potential role for environmental taxes in environmental policy through the introduction of new taxes and/or the modification of existing taxes, the removal of existing distortionary taxes will also improve the tax structure and increase the efficiency of the economy. Furthermore, the main fiscal issues related to environmental taxes, such as tax and revenue neutrality and earmarking, can be solved through a proper design and implementation process of taxes.

This means that ecotaxes will be implemented successfully if, and only if, both parties cooperate – in particular, ministries of the environment and of finance. Cooperation and dialogue must also prevail with other stakeholders, such as industry, farmers, consumers and environmental NGOs.

6. It seems that environmental taxes are at some kind of cross-road: both fiscalists and environmentalists have come to an agreement as to their usefulness and potential and a number of such taxes have been applied in most OECD countries. Yet only a small number of countries have put in place comprehensive 'green' tax reforms. It seems that further progress is largely conditional upon stronger political will to improve the efficiency and effectiveness of environmental policy and more intense international cooperation to mitigate the real or alleged trade implications. David Gee, in Chapter 6, notes that public opinion may be more supportive of ecotaxation than politicians currently imagine. But public opinion is notoriously fickle, and the success of ecotaxation is generally not recognised unless the policy justification is carefully and repeatedly presented. In any democracy, that is a tough path to follow, unless there awaits a long period of possible economic pain before the benefits become real commitment and concerted action.

REFERENCES

Dean, J M (1992) 'Trade and the Environment: A survey of the literature', in Low, P (ed) *International Trade and the Environment*, World Bank Discussion Paper 159, World Bank, Washington, DC

European Commission (1993a) *Growth, Competitiveness and Employment*, The European Commission, Brussels

European Commission (1993b) *Taxation, Employment and Environment: Fiscal Reform for Reducing Unemployment*, The European Commision, Brussels

Moret, Ernst & Young (1994) *Tax provisions which have an impact on the environment*, Report for the European Commission, Brussels

OECD (1989) *Economic Instruments for Environmental Protection*, Organization for Economic Cooperation and Development, Paris

OECD (1991) *An Environmental Strategy in the 1990s*, Communiqué, Organization for Economic Cooperation and Development, Paris

OECD (1992) *Market and Government Failures in Environmental Management: Wetlands and Forests*, Organization for Economic Cooperation and Development, Paris

OECD (1993) *Taxation and Environment: Complementary Policies*, Organization for Economic Cooperation and Development, Paris

OECD (1994) *Managing the Environment: The Role of Economic Instruments*, Organization for Economic Cooperation and Development, Paris

OECD (1995a) *Environmental Taxes in OECD Countries*, Organization for Economic Cooperation and Development, Paris

OECD (1995b) *Global Warming: Economic Dimensions and Policy Responses*, Organization for Economic Cooperation and Development, Paris

OECD (1995c) *The St Petersburg Guidelines on Environmental Funds in the Transition to a Market Economy*, Organization for Economic Cooperation and Development, Paris

OECD (1996) *Implementation Strategies for Environmental Taxes*, Organization for Economic Cooperation and Development, Paris

Pearson, M (1992) 'Equity issues and carbon taxes', in OECD (ed) *Climate Change: Designing a Practical Tax System*, Organization for Economic Cooperation and Development, Paris, pp 92–106

Pearson, M and Smith, S (1991) *The European Carbon Tax: An Assessment of the European Commissions*, The Institute of Fiscal Studies, London

Scott, S (1992) 'Theoretical considerations and estimates of the effect on households', in Fitzgerald, J and McCoy, D (eds), *The Economic Effects of Carbon Taxes*, Policy Research Series, The Economic and Social Research Institute, Dublin

Swedish Ministry of the Environment (1994) *The Swedish Experience: Taxes and Changes in Environmental Policy*, Ministry of the Environment, Stockholm

C h a p t e r   1   2

ENVIRONMENTAL TAXATION IN THE NETHERLANDS

Hans Vos

INTRODUCTION

Environmental taxation is a frequently studied and occasionally hotly debated subject in The Netherlands. Environmental pressure groups are in favour of the subject, as much as industry is against it. The government, next to searching constantly for appropriate instruments of environmental policy (Ministry of the Environment), although attracted by the financial function of taxes (the Treasury), is cautious for political reasons (Ministry of Economic Affairs).

Application of environmental taxes in The Netherlands is of a diverse nature. Pigouvian taxes are scarce, but a number of charges exist of which the revenues are earmarked for environmental allocation, some of them substantial in financial impact. A small but increasing part of fiscal taxes is environmentally based. Recently, a further extension of such taxation has been introduced after ample political discussion. A new regulatory tax on energy use was introduced in 1996. Greening the fiscal system is studied by a dedicated commission. This chapter aims to provide an outline of the history of environmental taxation in The Netherlands, its application, and the current debate on and perspectives of this issue.

The first section briefly explains the basic argument of environmental taxation and lists a number of practical problems, encountered in the preparation and implementation of environmental taxation. There follows a short history of the debate on and the implementation of environmental taxes. Some key policy documents are discussed and the fate of the major general fuel tax and its recent extensions is discussed. Then an overview of the present application of environmental taxes in The Netherlands is presented. The final section outlines the current debate on 'ecotaxes' and discusses the current role of environmental taxation in environmental policy. Crucial to this role and its developments are the basic principles of financing environmental policy, the eco-paradox, the 'double dividend' argument, and initiatives for discussing the greening of the fiscal system. The recent introduction of the waste-disposal and groundwater taxes, of the new regulatory tax on energy and the installation of the Commission for Greening the Fiscal System are discussed.

ENVIRONMENTAL TAXATION: THE BASIC ARGUMENT AND PRACTICAL PROBLEMS

The basic argument of environmental taxation has been described more than once. Comprehensive descriptions are given in Opschoor *et al*, (1994) and O'Riordan (1994), just to mention two recent sources. It is repeated very briefly below.

Environmental pollution and the depletion of natural resources means using too much of the 'services' provided by our natural environment – for instance, as a 'dustbin' for polluted gases, waste water and solid waste. This over-exploitation is possible because these services are not bought on the market, but received for free. Over-exploitation causes damage to the environment, which in its turn negatively affects human welfare and economic positions. If we should be able to connect prices to environmental services, an equilibrium would be created in which the environment is only exploited up to sustainable levels ('in short, getting the prices right'). Such prices will be artificial because no proper markets exist. This is where environmental taxation becomes effective: the government or other institution should calculate prices that could be applied as surtaxes on to the market prices of raw materials, commodities, consumer goods or various types of pollution, such as air pollution, waste water and solid waste. Thus, taxation should be an incentive to change people's behaviour towards the environment.

As was stated in the editorial introduction to this section, environmental (Pigouvian) taxes, compared with policy instruments of the command-and-control type, are a cost-effective instrument and promote both static and dynamic efficiency. Why is it, then, that such taxes are so scarcely found in practice in almost all countries, including The Netherlands, which strive after least-cost solutions for their severe environmental problems? Many financial, political, economic and policy problems lie ahead (see de Savornin Lohman, 1994, for a good discussion). A few points include:

1. *Calculation of the right prices.* Since environmental services, in general, cannot be marketed, only artificial prices can exist. A number of methods for directly or indirectly assessing environmental values have been suggested, but they hardly escape from the theoretical level. Any tax rates set in practice are at best remote proxies.

2. *Practical definition problems.* There is considerable confusion about the real character of so-called environmental taxes/charges when they are put into practice. Systems such as the Dutch and French water-pollution charges and the household-waste collection charges, in operation in many countries, are not environmental taxation in a strict sense, but, as noted by Michael Spackman in Chapter 3, are essentially recovery charges for services rendered in the field of waste-water treatment and household-waste removal. Of course, such charges increase production costs or commodity prices and may act like environmental taxation in the Pigouvian sense, but the objectives differ fundamentally because they raise revenues instead of creating price incentives. The charge rates are not dictated by the value of the environmental commodities they reflect, but by the targeted revenues. Environmentally based and defended taxes with revenues flowing into the public purse have a hard time in parliament, and very few survive.

3. *Implementation issues.* Environmental policy is very much command-and-control oriented. Environmental taxation as an instrument is not mainstream government policy. Many government bodies are dominated by legally skilled people, who may overrule economists pleading for a more market-based approach.

4. *Direct and indirect economic impact.* Next to the targeted impact, environmental taxation may also affect other, mainly economic, parameters such as employment, income distribution, trade and international competitiveness. Industry generally opposes environmental taxation. Their spokespeople point at the competitive disadvantages in the international economic arena, if taxes are implemented unilaterally. They complain about the disadvantages in relation with other OECD or non-OECD trade partners if, for example, the EU were to introduce taxes. Besides, industry has a better negotiating position in case of individually arranged environmental licences than under a generic tax system.

5. *Allocation of the revenues.* Revenues are not the main objective of environmental taxation. Central to this whole book is the question of how these revenues should be allocated. Simply pocketing them by the Treasury leads to an increasing overall tax burden, which is deeply unpopular. Returning the revenues to the taxpayers would help to focus on the real purpose of environmental taxation: right prices. This can be done in two ways: either by returning the revenues to those who have paid this specific tax, or by returning the revenues to all taxpayers by implementing a balanced tax reduction elsewhere in the fiscal system. Returning the revenues of taxes might be considered to be in violation with state aid regulations, which are in force in the European Union.

The way that tax revenues should be spent is one of the key issues in the debate about the value of environmental taxation. Another aspect of this issue concerns the double dividend, as reviewed in the previous section. The matter of allocating tax revenues is discussed below.

6. *International issues*. European Union rules also forbid discriminating taxation and taxation on imports; this restricts options for environmental taxation. Multilateral introduction of environmental taxation may remove some of these objections, but the carbon/energy tax dossier that finally failed during the Essen Summit in October 1994 showed, as indicated in the editorial introduction to this section, how difficult this is in practice. Also, GATT-rules restrict free taxation in international trade. International competitiveness will further discourage unilateral implementation of environmental tax systems.

To date, these and other factors have also impeded an extensive introduction of environmental taxation in The Netherlands. However, a long history of discussing economic instruments, particularly charges and taxes, resulted in several new taxes and in a more positive attitude in bringing about ecological elements in the fiscal system, as will be shown in the following sections.

ENVIRONMENTAL TAXATION: THE DUTCH HISTORY

At the beginning of November 1993 a bill on Environmental Taxes passed the Second Chamber of the Dutch Parliament. This bill contained new fiscal taxes on waste disposal (Dfl 30 per tonne; expected revenue Dfl 150 million), on groundwater (Dfl 0.34 per m3; expected revenue Dfl 435 million) and on uranium (expected revenue Dfl 10 million, to be paid mainly by Holland's single nuclear power plant for electricity generation). These new taxes were planned to be introduced on 1 January 1994, but the bill was turned down in the First Chamber whose function is the control of new legislation, passed by the Second Chamber. Members of the First Chamber, wary of the possible negative effects of these new taxes, wished to have more information at their disposal before it approved the bill.

The new taxes, which were introduced finally on 1 January 1995 by the Second Chamber, are the culmination of a long history of environmental charges and taxes in The Netherlands. More fiscal taxes with an environmental basis are under discussion. In this section, a concise overview of the history of the role and use of economic instruments in general and environmental charges/taxes in Dutch environmental policy is presented on the basis of a few highlights (see also Vos, 1993).

Academic Discussion of Economic Instruments: 1970–88

Paradoxically, perhaps, the start of the period described as academic discussion is also marked by the start of the application of economic instruments in environmental policy, notably the introduction of the major water-pollution charge system. This system, however, remained the single significant charge for almost two decades, whereas its structure, at least by intention, had nothing to do with environmental taxes in the Pigouvian sense.

One of the reasons why the regulatory function drew little political attention during the early years of environmental policy was the negative attitude of the Dutch green movement. At that time, environmentalists dogmatically rejected the idea that the right to pollute could be bought from the government. In later years, the green movement changed their position and eventually became fierce advocates of environmental taxation.

1970: The Surface Water Pollution Act (1969) + Water Pollution Charge system.
The revenues of this charge have played a key role in reducing the severe water pollution of the 1960s by collective treatment of waste water to acceptable levels at the present time (more thant 80 per cent as far as oxidizable matter-type is concerned). This charge has the character of a user charge, comparable with fees for collecting household waste. Skou Andersen (1993), however, cites a Dutch parliamentary document on the (future) water pollution charges that stated 'for those affected (the levies) will be an incentive to reduce water pollution as far as possible'. Notwithstanding its purely financing character, the incentive impact was reported (see, for example, Bressers, 1983; Schuurman, 1988).

1972: Adoption of the Polluter-Pays Principle (OECD/EC).
The formal adoption of the polluter-pays principle in international frameworks served as a basis for the introduction of new financing charges, to begin in 1972.

1972: Air-pollution Charge.
The air-pollution charge was imposed as a surcharge on the price of fuels. Its purpose was to raise revenues for financing some of the activities of the recently established Ministry of the Environment. Its significance was modest. Full earmarking was accepted at that time.

In the following years, a number of documents played an important role in formulating government positions on environmental taxation (see Wash, 1992).

1974: Memorandum on Instruments for Environmental Policy, Charges and Physical Regulation.
The polluter-pays principle was taken as one of the cornerstones of Dutch environmental policy. The memorandum described the role of environmental charges as financial and regulatory instruments of environmental policy. Physical regulation was preferred over market-based instruments. Charges were considered to be potential sources of money for financing environmental policy. Charges could also have a regulatory function, although this function was not put in the forefront. No new charge/taxes were proposed in this document.

1978: Memorandum on Environmental Charges.
Statements regarding the role of charges as incentive instruments were still

of an academic nature. A less strict interpretation of the polluter-pays principle was accepted for reasons of efficiency. Government measures with regard to environmental quality included direct measures, such as building collective waste-water treatment plants, and indirect measures, such as establishing legislation, rules for enforcement, and so on. The memorandum states that only direct measures should be financed from the revenues of charges.

1978–85: The Introduction of Five (Sectoral) Financial Charges.
These charges were imposed on air pollution from cars (on fuels), on noise from cars (on fuels), on lubricants, on chemical waste, and on industrial noise. Their proceeds were modest, but the execution of the schemes absorbed a fair amount of money for administration and control.

1985: Discussion Paper on Alternative Schemes for Financing
Environmental Policy.
Owing to its considerable inefficiency, the government decided to restructure the system of sectoral charges. Prior to a definitive decision, a discussion paper was produced in which economic instruments, notably environmental charges, were generally reviewed. The then sectoral system of minor charges was criticized for its administrative inefficiency. Consistent continuation of this policy would result in a large number of rather insignificant charges. The paper discussed four alternative systems. First, a categorical system of charges aimed at groups of polluters such as transport and agriculture. Secondly, a system of charges to be imposed on basic products such as raw materials, intermediary products and fuels. Thirdly, a system of fuel charges. A final system would exclude all charges; all environmental policies would have been paid for from the general budget. The latter system was not in accordance with the polluter-pays principle and immediately was rejected for that reason. The paper showed a more positive attitude towards the potential incentive function of the charges, but their principal function remained a revenue-raising one.

1988: General Environmental Provisions Act; Chapter on Financial
Provisions + the General Fuel Charge.
The third system described above, a general fuel charge, was chosen as a basic financial instrument of environmental policy. This system was found to be in accordance with the polluter-pays principle, because fuel consumption was considered to be a major source of pollution. This charge – with revenues increasing from Dfl 200 million in 1988 up to Dfl 1,500 in 1993 – replaced the sectoral charges discussed earlier. This policy reflected the generally held belief that streamlining and simplifying the financial system of environmental policy was necessary.

Environmental charges were still relished for their money-raising potential. Earmarking of the revenues for financing policy institutions and policy measures was still accepted by the Treasury. The Ministry of the Environment itself collected the charge and allocated the revenues.

Increasing Policy Interest of Economic Instruments: 1989-91

The year 1988 may be considered a turning-point in Dutch environmental policy. The Chernobyl incident and an impressive Christmas speech by Queen Beatrix brought the environmental issue to the very top of the societal and political agenda. In 1989, the new centre-left Cabinet, built on the ruins of the old centre-right coalition that tripped over environmental issues, published the National Environmental Policy Plan-plus (NEPP-plus). Although physical regulation still maintained its prevalent position, economic instruments impressively gained attention.

With the preparation of the NEPP-plus, a process of environmental policy integration was started. Four ministers signed the plan – namely, the Ministers for Environment; for Economic Affairs; for Transport and Public Works; and for Agriculture, Nature Conservation and Fishery. This integration also implied a heavy involvement of the Minister of Finance with respect to the general fuel charge, which has had consequences for the direction of thinking about environmental charges and their role in environmental policy (see the following section).

In the NEPP-plus, a programme for actions, research and discussion was launched. It contained several elements, including:

- active promotion of and a contribution to discussions of economic instruments in international frameworks;
- research into a number of concrete economic instruments as to their practical feasibility;
- stimulation of new clean technology by introducing a scheme of accelerated depreciation for such investments;
- experiments with incentive charges and deposit-refund systems if these instruments are proved feasible in principle;
- investigation of several aspects of incentive energy charges.

The General Fuel Charge rates were increased substantially. A CO_2 tax was introduced, and discussion started on extending the General Fuel Charge to a broad-based general environmental tax. The fuel charge was brought under the competence of the Minister of Finance and became a real fiscal tax, without any earmarking. Henceforth, the budget of the Ministry of the Environment was fully dependent on the public budget, since generating own sources was no longer allowed.

Political Struggle for the Implementation of Economic Instruments: 1992 to present

1992: Environmental tax (fuels).
The start of the third period is marked by the introduction of the Environmental Tax and discussions on extending its base, first to the dumping of solid waste, the extraction of groundwater and the use of uranium, and secondly to other environmental subjects. The Ministry of Finance decided that the environmental tax would have to rise considerably, from

Dfl 400 million in 1989 up to a projected Dfl 2,1 billion in 1994, of which amount some Dfl 600 million would have to be covered by new taxes.

1995: Environmental tax (fuels, waste, groundwater, uranium).
It was considered to be unjust only to tax energy consumption in such circumstances. The government decided to broaden the tax base to other objects with an environmental or natural resource bearing: solid waste, groundwater, nutrients and pesticides. Farmers' organizations strongly protested against the taxation of nutrients and pesticides; there is already a strong policy in this field, and the Ministry of Finance dropped these two elements in the regulatory tax base.

Originally, plans were made to put a charge of about Dfl 10 per ton on all solid waste, and a tax of about Dfl 0.25 per m^3 on groundwater. Later, politicians argued that waste for incineration should be exempted. In Holland, tariffs for incinerating waste are substantially higher than tariffs for landfills. The Dutch policy is to try to reduce the cost differences between the incineration and the dumping of waste, because dumping must be reduced substantially. The Ministries of Environment and Finance agreed, but the Ministry of Finance had already counted the revenues, so a deficit arose. This could only be repaired by increasing the tax rate for dumping.

Another problem occurred. Oil refineries, which are a very important industry in Holland, produce residual gases that formerly were burned at the plant. The government persuaded the refineries to make a better use of these gases by recycling them into their processes. However, that implied that taxes must be paid for the use of these gases as a fuel. The oil refineries protested that they would have to bear the additional costs of residual gas recycling and whould be punished on top of that by additional taxation. This happened to be a reasonable argument and the Ministry of Finance withdrew this proposal in the bill, by which another deficit occurred. After all, the tariff on solid waste for dumping increased to about Dfl 30 per ton. Finally, a new tax on uranium as a fuel in nuclear power plants was proposed.

As already mentioned, the First Chamber requested a more sound justification and solid motivation of the newly proposed taxes. The Ministry of Finance was asked to produce a so-called Note of Refinement (Second Chamber, 1993–94, 22 849, no. 27) in which the potential negative environmental and economic impact of the taxes was analysed. This analysis resulted in several modifications of the Bill on Environmental Taxes, including:

- a differentiated tariff for the tax on groundwater: Dfl 0.34 per m^3 of groundwater removed by drinking-water companies, and Dfl 0.17 for industrial and agricultural groundwater removal;
- exemption of the tax on groundwater for the removal of groundwater during soil or groundwater remediation operations;
- exemption of the tax on groundwater if it is used in a closed circuit for cold and heat storage;
- refunding of the tax if drinking-water produced from groundwater is used for the rinsing of returnable drink packaging;
- zero-rate tax for the incineration of waste;

- exemption of the tax on solid waste for separately collected organic waste;
- refund of the tax for dumping ink residues from paper and cardboard recycling, and for plastic waste generated in plastic recycling.

The tariff for waste dumping is fixed on Dfl 29.20 per ton of waste. The tax on uranium was also introduced, although the tax rate is nil for the present. The Act on Environmental Taxes came into force in January 1995.

1996: Regulatory tax on energy (small-scale use of electricity and gas).
As a political compromise between the coalition partners who constituted the so-called Purple Cabinet in 1994, and as a reaction to the failure to introduce a CO_2/energy tax on the European level, a new tax on energy use came under discussion and was introduced in January 1996 by the Ministry of Housing, Spatial Planning and Environment. The tax is levied on gas and electricity and affects small-scale use only. Its purpose is regulatory as the tax should contribute to achieving the national goals set for CO_2 levels in the year 2000.

For gas, the bracket taxed is 800 up to 170,000 m^3 per year; for electricity, amounts of 800 up to 50,000 kWh per year are taxed. Also, mineral oil products which are not used for transport (such as home-heating oil) are taxed up to certain levels. Tax rates for gas and electricity are increasing up to 9.53 cents per m^3 and 2.95 cents per kWh respectively. These rates reflect the original proposed EU tax rate on CO_2/energy of up to $10 per barrel.

The tax affects all households and approximately 95 per cent of all commercial activities. About 40 per cent of all non-transport, non-feedstock use of energy is covered. Only the consumption of natural gas in greenhouses is exempted from the tax.

The tax is expected to raise about Dfl 2.1 billion in 1998: about Dfl 1.2 billion will be paid by households and about Dfl 900 million by business. These revenues are recycled back to the households through three changes in personal income tax (affecting the first income tax brackets, the tax-free allowance, and the standard tax deduction for senior citizens), and to business through a reduction of social premiums paid by employers.

The history of the Act on Environmental Taxes and the introduction of the new tax on energy use is typical of the current discussion on ecotaxes in The Netherlands.

THE DUTCH PRACTICE OF ENVIRONMENTAL TAXATION

Table 12.1 presents charges and taxes which are currently applied in The Netherlands. Out of the eight systems described, five charges happen to have a purely financing purpose. The tax differentiation regarding leaded and unleaded petrol, principally, is a good example of Pigouvian taxation: a price difference was created to support the phasing-out of leaded petrol, whereas no revenues were aimed for. The environmental taxes (on fuels, waste, groundwater, uranium) had the advantage of two options: the creation of price incentives, and the raising of revenues. This dual purpose

Table 12.1 *The current application of environmental charges and taxes in The Netherlands (1996)*

Charges/Taxes	Description
Water-pollution charge	Levied on effluent emitted into surface waters; based on the pollution load actually measured or flat rates; revenues used for pollution treatment ⇨ Dfl 1,300 million
Aircraft noise charge	Levied on incoming aircraft; based on weight and type of aircraft; revenues spent for noise abatement ⇨ Dfl 25 million
Soil protection charge	Levied on volumes of phosphates in manure that exceed certain levels; revenues spent to support nutrients policy ⇨ Dfl 40 million
Municipal waste-user charge	Levied on all those who are served by the municipal waste-collection service; normally a flat rate per household ⇨ Dfl 900 million
Sewerage user charge	Levied on all those who are connected to the municipal sewerage system; a flat rate charge ⇨ Dfl 500 million
Tax differentiation: leaded/ unleaded petrol	Calculated as a differentiation of the excise levied on car fuels; differentiation amounts to approximately 8 per cent of the sales price ⇨ no revenues
Environmental taxes	Taxes are levied on all fuels except on those used as a raw material, and on waste and groundwater (for exemptions, see text); tax rates partly based on the carbon content of the fuel and partly on its thermic value (Dfl 4.70 per tonne of CO_2, and Dfl 0.39 per gigajoule (GJ)); tax on waste dumping: Dfl 29.20 per tonne; tax on groundwater: Dfl 0.34 per m^3 (drinking-water companies) or Dfl 0.17 per m^3 (industry and agriculture) ⇨ Dfl 2,100 million
Regulatory tax on energy use	Taxes are levied on the small-scale use of gas and electricity, and certain oil products; tax brackets for gas and electricity are 800–170,000 m^3 and 800–50,000 kWh; tax rates are 9.53 cents per m^3 and 2.95 cents per kWh respectively ⇨ no net revenues (through recycling)

concerns one of the aspects of the current discussion on environmental taxation. This discussion resulted in the introduction of the regulatory tax on energy use with no net revenues, and in the installation of the Commission for Greening the Fiscal System.

THE DUTCH DEBATE ON ENVIRONMENTAL TAXATION

Four issues are important for understanding the Dutch debate and the developments of environmental taxation:

- The basic principles of financing environmental measures.
- The above-mentioned, two-options character of the new environmental taxes, also known as the ecotax paradox (Menninga, 1993).
- The double dividend (or 'double-edged sword') argument, and the introduction of the regulatory energy tax.
- The creation of the Commission on Greening the Fiscal System.

Principles of Financing Environmental Measures

In 1989, the National Environmental Policy Plan reformulated the basic principles of the financing of environmental measures and the role of taxes therein:

1. Following the polluter–pays principle, polluters should pay themselves for the environmental measures they have to take as a consequence of direct regulation; this is the general rule.
2. Specific revenue-raising taxes could be applied if the costs of pollution or of collective measures can be allotted to identifiable groups of polluters. Examples include the municipal waste-user and sewerage-user charges, and also the water-pollution charge.
3. General revenue-raising taxes could be applied for covering environmental costs if no identifiable group of polluters exist or if it is undesirable to charge specific groups. An example was the former environmental charge (including the CO_2 tax) for financing general environmental policy costs. This principle was abandoned in 1992, when the environmental charge system was terminated and replaced by the fiscally administered environmental tax system, which was imposed initially on fuels, but later on waste, groundwater and uranium.
4. Public budget: in extreme cases when it is impossible or undesirable to charge any groups in society – for example, the costs of the remediation of abandoned hazardous waste sites – the public purse will finance the cost.

There is strong preference for applying financing rules according to the first principle: the polluter-pays principle. If this is impossible, or when it is more desirable to abate pollution in a collective way (for instance, water pollution), the second principle is applicable. General revenue-raising charges are no longer applicable, whereas financing from the public budget is unacceptable, except in extreme cases. The termination of the general revenue-raising charges facilitated the introduction of ecotaxes, and the possibility of using environmental taxation as a general source of income for the government, as well as being a vehicle for shifting the tax burden from direct taxation (labour) to indirect taxation (environmental pollution or the exhaustion of natural resources). However, the ecotax paradox remains to be talked over, if not solved.

The Ecotax Paradox

Ecological taxation has two different effects, but, in accordance with the well-known Tinbergen rule that one instrument cannot optimally serve two goals, it creates at least one non-optimal solution if it is used both for raising general government income and for regulatory purposes in environmental protection policy. In terms of the metaphor of the double-edged sword, one of the edges will inevitably be blunt. Wolfson (1994) argues that since ecological taxation primarily is a fiscal instrument aimed at the optimization of the fiscal structure, the environmental tax base should be inelastic. Otherwise, the tax would damage its own basis and cannot be used for the desired direct-to-indirect shift of the tax burden. This implies that the environmental edge is the blunt one, and that ecotaxes are poor instruments in the Pigouvian sense.

In February 1995, the Government Working Group on Greening Taxation, established by the State Secretary of Finance, started discussing the desirability, feasibility and practical aspects of ecological taxation. This Working Group may put the ecotax paradox on its agenda.

Double Dividend

Raising indirect taxation – for example, by introducing environmental taxes – and reducing income tax while levelling the total tax burden might reduce the overall distortionary costs of taxation, as was discussed in the previous section. This double dividend argument has dominated the discussion of ecotaxes in The Netherlands. The Fiscal Plan for the Budget Year 1992 proposed to reduce the tax burden on labour by introducing fiscal taxes on groundwater and waste. Such a shift was expected to contribute to an improved functioning of the labour market and hence to increased employment.

Bovenberg and Cnossen (1991) commented on this proposal and rejected the train of thought. They argued that a budget-neutral shift of direct to indirect taxation would result in an increased demand for labour under strict and rather unlikely conditions only. In the case of taxes in the consumption stage (product taxes on polluting consumer goods), some increase in labour demand might be expected, only if such taxes had a weak regulatory impact, if dodging such taxes by foreign purchasing could be prevented, and if the negative effects on purchasing power (primarily for the non-active) will not be compensated. In the case of taxes in the production stage (emissions, raw materials and intermediary products), environmental taxes would work positively on the labour market, only if the labour market were sufficiently flexible, if the higher environmental costs of consumption would not be rolled off to the producers, and if border effects could be prevented. The authors state that the real impediment for the higher demand for labour is the level of the tax burden itself, not the composition of the tax burden. The total tax burden should be decreased, either by reducing direct taxes (or social premia) or by reducing indirect taxes. They conclude that the double-edged sword would prove to be a fiscal mirage if budget neutrality and income neutrality (constant income distribution) were maintained.

Bovenberg and Cnossen started a debate on the topic of the double dividend. Bos and Mulder (1992) stated that it is the marginal tax burden that matters, and that it is possible to reduce the marginal burden without reducing the average burden, as budget neutrality requires. Then the demand for non-taxed, labour-intensive products would increase at the expense of the demand for environment-intensive products. The demand for labour would therefore increase.

In their reaction, Bovenberg and Cnossen (1992) point out that it is exactly the income neutrality condition that is crucial in this respect. Also referring to a study by Pearson and Smith (1991), they state that a better functioning of the labour market and an improved environmental quality through ecotaxes can be reached, if, and only if, the negative effects on the lower-income class are not repaired.

In a more recent article, Bovenberg and Keuzenkamp (1993) argue that, contrary to the situation in 1991 and under the circumstances of that time, the double dividend of ecotaxes could be realized. Early 1993 inflation forecasts were reduced dramatically, whereas most wage contracts were concluded already. This implied an unintended increase of net wages for a large part of the labour force for the time period of the wage contracts (one to two years). The rolling off of higher indirect environmental taxes would not be expected. Moreover, there was more political room for increasing the income differences by omitting compensation for higher burdens for the lower-income class (the inactive population). Consequently, dropping the income neutrality condition was no longer impossible: ecotaxes could work both for the environment and for the labour market.

Obviously, the question of whether shifting the tax burden from income to indirect taxation has positive effects on employment yields no general answer. It depends on specific economic conditions which may vary over time. Besides, the magnitude of the impact on employment also depends on the exact way that the revenues of the indirect taxation are spent, since decreasing income tax can be done in different ways, while other restitution options might be applied.

In a review of recent studies of the double dividend argument, de Wit (1994) points out that most of the empirical studies show a small though positive impact on employment, whereas the majority of theoretical studies seem to conclude to a negative impact. De Wit stated that most of the empirical studies concentrate solely on positive substitution effects (the substitution of environmental inputs by labour) and ignore possible negative output effects. Negative output effects may arise when higher prices for inputs result in a lower return on capital, inducing entrepreneurs to reduce the output under the domestic tax system – for example, by moving their business to foreign countries with a more favourable tax regime. If negative output effects exceed positive substitution effects, the overall impact on employment is negative. De Wit concludes that positive effects on employment may arise if factor mobility is limited. He also points to other factors that may have a positive employment impact and that are often ignored in the discussions. They include:

1. the impact of burden shifting on technological innovation;
2. the 'first-mover advantage';
3. the fact that less environmental damage could increase productivity; and
4. the removal of market imperfections which render such measures more effective.

Applying a general equilibrium model for The Netherlands (developed at the Central Planning Bureau), Gelauff (1992) examined five different options for refunding the revenues of environmental taxes. They include:

1. decreasing of the tariff in the first bracket of the income tax;
2. decreasing of the tariffs in all three brackets (35, 50 and 60 per cent respectively);
3. increasing the personal tax allowance;
4. increasing the labour-cost tax allowance; and
5. decreasing the VAT tariff.

He concludes that the first option, decreasing the tax tariff in the first bracket, has the strongest impact on employment.

The Commission on Greening the Fiscal System.

By the regulation of 24 March 1995 (WV 144, Strcrt 1995, p 62), the Dutch Finance Secretary of State constituted the Commission on Greening the Fiscal System. The Commission's task is to review options within the fiscal system for serving the interest of environmental protection and promoting sustainable economic development. Members of Parliament, officers of the Ministries of Finance, Environment and Economic Affairs, academicians, and representatives of societal groups (employers and environmentalists) are members.

The commission set out to investigate the greening options, by type of tax; all taxes will be reviewed. Taxes include:

- wage and income taxation; profit tax;
- environmental taxes according to the Act on Taxes on an environmental basis; existing taxes and options for new bases;
- aspects of mobility, including fuel excise duties, car-sales taxes, annual car taxes, and property transfer taxes;

- turnover tax and other state taxes;
- non-state taxes;
- other options.

On the basis of numerous ideas that recently emerged, the commission is aiming to come up with options as practicable and as feasible as possible for greening the fiscal system. In its first report of October 1995, the focus is on mobility-cum-income tax issues, including fixed travel-cost deduction, car-cost fiction, tax-free allowance for commercial travelling with private cars, income deduction of the costs of moving house, car pooling, and income tax. It also contains a recommendation that the purchase of very low-energy cars should be encouraged through the adaptation of the annual car taxes. Finally, an advice on groundwater taxation was included.

The commission is expected to publish its final report in late 1996.

CONCLUSION

The introduction of the regulatory tax on small-scale energy use in 1996 and the installation of the Commission on Greening the Fiscal System are important steps in the Dutch environmental taxation dossier. The government kept its promise to introduce, unilaterally, a substantial CO_2 tax, although the system has been adapted in order to avoid important negative effects on the Dutch exporting sector. Also referring to the three points discussed above, the following considerations may have played, and continue to play, a role in deciding on the introducion of the regulatory tax.

First, additional measures are required in order to achieve targets of the Dutch CO_2 policy in the year 2000 and beyond. Besides, The Netherlands has always advocated in international forums the introduction of such CO_2/energy taxes. After the Essen Summit, the Dutch expressed their willingness to continue preparing such a tax unilaterally or together with a smaller number of EU-member states.

Secondly, abandonment of raising direct taxes would cut off a (potential) source of government income. New options would be welcomed. Besides, shifting the competence for administering environmental taxation from the Ministry of Environment to the Ministry of Finance has stimulated the interest of the fiscal authorities for environmental taxation. Since the Ministry of Finance governs such taxes, they are less reluctant to consider new (environmental) tax bases which they can control fully.

Thirdly, in spite of good economic forecasts, the Dutch economy continues to suffer from persistent unemployment. Measures that might help to solve this problem are treated kindly. Since economists disagree on the overall impact on employment of shifting the tax burden, environmental (and fiscal) policy-makers are inclined to embrace the positive studies.

Finally, there is an institutional element. The constitution of the so-called Purple Cabinet in 1994 marked a breakthrough in the political history. Major political movements in The Netherlands are the Socialists, the Christian Democrats, the Liberals, and since the early 1990s, the Liberal Democrats. For over 50 years a coalition between Socialists and Liberals in The Netherlands was as unthinkable as a coalition between Labour and the

Conservatives in the UK. As a result of the declining popularity of the Christian Democrats and the political mistakes by their leaders after the 1994 elections, open-minded leaders of the Socialists, Liberals, and also the Liberal Democrats, found each other in a new coalition. The Socialists managed to bring the regulatory tax on energy use into the government agreements, and succeeded in materializing this system with the help of the Liberal Democrats.

The installation of the Commission on Greening Taxation also shows a positive attitude towards investigating the possibilities for adapting or creating fiscal provisions that can work for the environment. Comparable initiatives in a number of European countries, particularly in Scandinavia (Vos and Nooteboom, 1996), and the work of the Dutch Commission, especially as far as new taxes are concerned, are likely to reinforce each other. New elements covered in the Dutch approach include green fiscal measures in the direct income system; among other things, these measures regard mobility.

However, despite the installation of the Commission on Greening the Fiscal System, the dossiers of the tax on waste disposal and groundwater, and the regulatory tax on energy, show that new environmental tax bases or green fiscal provisions will only be adopted after very careful and thorough consideration.

REFERENCES

Bos, M and Mulder, R (1992) 'Fiscale luchtspiegelingen?', and Bovenberg, L and Cnossen S, 'Fiscale luchtspiegelingen!', *Economisch-Statistische Berichten* pp 37–8

Bovenberg, L and Cnossen, S (1991) 'Fiscaal Fata Morgana', *Economisch-Statistische Berichten* pp 1200–3

Bovenberg, L and Keuzenkamp, H (1993) Het aangescherpte tweenÿdend zwaard. *Economisch-Statistische Berichten*, 10 February

Bressers, H (1983) 'The role of effluent charges in Dutch water quality policy', in Downing, P B and Hanf, K (eds), *International Comparisons in Implementing Pollution Laws*, Kluwer-Nijhoff, Boston, pp 79–91

De Savornin Lohman, A (1994) 'Economic incentives in environmental policy: why are they white ravens?', in Opschoor, H and Turner, K (eds), *Economic Incentives and Environmental Policies*, Kluwer Academic Publishers, Dordrecht, pp 111–23

De Wit, G (1994) *Werkgelegenheidseffecten van een belastingverschuiving van arbeid naar milieu*, CE Delft

Gelauff, G M M (1992) 'Belastingen en werkgelegenheid', in *Economisch-Statistische Berichten*, 30-9, pp 950–3

Menninga, J (1993) 'Eco-tax paradox', *Milieu en Recht*, 11, p 593

Ministry of Housing Spatial Planning and Environment, (1996) *The Netherlands' Regulatory Tax on Energy – Questions and Answers*, The Hague

Opschoor, J B, de Savornin Lohman, A and Vos, H B (1994) *Managing the Environment: The Role of Economic Instruments*, Organization for Economic Cooperation and Development, Paris

O'Riordan, T (1994) 'Environmental taxation', CSERGE Working Paper PA 94-04, CSERGE, University of East Anglia, Norwich

Pearson, M and Smith S (1991) *The European carbon/energy tax: an assessment of the European Commission's proposals*, Institute for Fiscal Studies, London

Schuurman, J (1988) *De Prijs van Water*, Quint, Gouda

Skol Andersen, M (1994) *Government by Green Taxes: Making Pollution Prevention Pay*, Manchester University Press, Manchester

Skou Andersen, M (1993) *Governance by Green Taxes: Implementing Clean Water Policies in Denmark, France, Germany and the Netherlands 1970–1990*, PhD thesis, Aarhus, Denmark, p 158

Vos, H B (1993) 'The Dutch experience of economic instruments', in *Environmental Economics in Practice*, IBC Communications, Seminar Documentation, London

Vos, H B and Nooteboom, S (1996) *Groene belastingen in het buitenland*, DHV Milieu, Amersfoort

Wash, E P J (1992) *Principles of Environmental Charges*, FED, Deventer

Wolfson, D (1994) 'Regulerende heffingen is discussie', in *Economisch-Statistische Berichten* 21-1, pp 72–6

C h a p t e r 1 3

PRICING WATER PROPERLY

Paul Herrington

INTRODUCTION

Whether economic growth is defined and measured using traditional national income accounts or alternative environmental sustainability frameworks, higher living standards and rising levels of economic activity will normally lead to increasing demands for the core water services (piped-water supplies and sewage disposal, direct abstractions and direct discharges). In many countries population growth and more urbanization continue to add to these flow demands. Simultaneously, water consumers in other guises – such as swimmers, anglers, boaters and species-protectors – are increasing their *in situ* demands upon the resource. The result on every continent is a rapidly growing and increasingly complex array of competing claims on surface and groundwater resources, at a time when the usable supply is often deteriorating because of the lack of attention paid to pollution management in the past. Add in only a small dose of likely climate change over the next 25 years, inducing permanent effects upon both yields and demands, and it is found that serious supply-demand imbalances are threatening in even some of the wetter countries of northern Europe.

RECONCILING SUPPLIES AND DEMANDS

The traditional response to such problems has usually been supply-augmentation: the 'requirements' or engineering approach to policy in which demand increases are accepted without question and supply-expansion passively follows. In this context, large subsidies – from taxpayers in the richer countries and aid donors in developing countries – have helped to shield water users from the true resource costs of their activities, and enormous public investment programmes have resulted, increasing the world's freshwater storage 25 times in the 20 years after 1950. Since the 1970s, however, attitudes and policies have begun to change. A radically different macroeconomic climate has induced a more searching appraisal of public expenditure (less capital for new supply projects, operating subsidies for old and new ones scaled down); major droughts in the developed world (California, Australia and Western Europe) have brought home the costs of demand neglect; and, probably of greater importance, increasing recognition of both the adverse social and environmental effect of large-scale supply solutions (especially dams) and the long-term effects of increased water-borne pollution have prompted fundamental policy rethinks – for instance, by the World Bank.

The result is that freshwater today is more generally regarded as an economic good: scarce and often precious. Expansion of its supply is now often associated with increasing marginal costs in every sense: financial, economic and environmental. To be sure, the environmental costs of supply-side expansion – eg, permanently or more frequent lower river flows and groundwater mining – can *in principle* nearly always be ameliorated, since the technology is available. The consequence, however, would be to increase the marginal *economic* costs of supply-expansion even more through, respectively, extra support works for rivers and additional artificial aquifer replenishment (plus the necessary treatment) when rivers are otherwise running to waste to the sea.

As a result of these considerations, interest among policy-makers is now focusing on demand-management, which may be defined as: the organization and practice of structural, operational, economic or voluntary measures which seek to bring demands for water services into line with supplies, rather than the other way round. In an important sense, of course, demand-management is nothing new for water resources, since the increasing costs incurred because of inadequately managed abstractions from, or discharges to, rivers, lakes and groundwater have frequently prompted new or amended legislation to manage demands in recent history. In this way regulations, licences, permits and, in a few countries, pricing systems have a fairly long track record in the developed world, with varying degrees of success.

Furthermore, within a growing role for demand-management, the prospect of *increasing* demands in the future is sufficient to suggest that regulations alone cannot shoulder all or even most of the burden of the demand-supply reconciliation. This is because, first, more regulations and laws require additional information-gathering and policing; secondly, homogeneous regulations bear upon increasingly heterogeneous water uses inequitably in that they allow little or no scope for the preferences of the individual water-using economic agent to be expressed; and, thirdly, while sufficiently strong regulations may, in principle, always be able to achieve optimal aggregate demand-management in the short run, their weak incentive signals and inability to achieve the optimum at least cost counsel strongly against exclusive reliance in the long run.

The flip side of this particular coin is that, in the long run, the sensible use of water requires the proper pricing of the resource and the services it provides. Only in that context may the issues of allocative and productive efficiency, of environmental protection and resource sustainability, and of equity all be satisfactorily addressed.

Demand-Management Literature

Evidence concerning the escalating costs of supply-led approaches has been documented, and the principles and practice of demand-management expounded, in major documents published since the mid 1980s by international organizations (eg, OECD, 1987; OECD, 1989a; OECD, 1989b; United Nations, 1991; United Nations (1992)), national governments (eg, Tate, 1990; Department of the Environment, 1992; Department of the Environment, 1995) and the conservation movement (eg, CPRE, 1991; CPRE, 1993; RSPB, 1995). Reference should also be made to the recent works of Postel (1992) and Winpenny (1994) which argue persuasively for the treatment of water as an economic resource.

Plan of the Chapter

What, then, is the scope for demand-management today? How strong are the current arguments for metering and the use of tariffs and other economic instruments to influence demands for clean and dirty water services? In the sections which follow, I first consider past and likely future demand growth for core services in Europe, and then turn to examine the role of pricing for, in turn, the piped-water services and direct abstractions, before conclusions are reached.

Demand Trends and Forecasts

Demand trends and forecasts in England and Wales
First, let us consider in some detail demand trends for piped public-water supplies in England and Wales, making use of work recently undertaken at the University of Leicester (for the Department of the Environment) about the effect of climate change on water demands (Herrington, 1996).

Table 13.1 suggests that domestic demands in England and Wales had been increasing at an annual rate of about 1.5 lhd (litres per head per day) over 1971–91, to reach an estimated 140 lhd in a climate-normalized 1991. In the five National Rivers Authority (NRA) regions then comprising the South and East of the country, the 1991 figure is estimated to be 5 per cent larger (147 lhd), and, for the same area, micro-component analysis of the present and future ownership, use and technology of individual water-using habits and appliances suggests a most likely domestic demand figure for 2021 of just over 178 lhd.

This gives a rather lower annual increase of about 1 lhd over 1991–2021, largely because of increased shower usage (especially by power showers) and higher garden use, but constrained by expected 25–30 per cent reductions in water use per cycle in washing-machines and dish-

Table 13.1 *Public water-supply trends and forecasts in England and Wales, 1971–2021*

| | England and Wales | | South and East only | | |
	1971[e]	1991[e]	1991[e]	2021[f] No climate change	2021[f] With climate change
Domestic only					
Population (m)	48.854	50.878	25.440	28.411	28.411
Persons/household	–	–	2.60	2.35	2.35
No of households (m)	–	–	9.785	12.090	12.090
Average water consumption (l/h/d)	108	140	147	178.4	185.6
Typical peak* consumption (l/h/d)	–	–	206	293	338
Public water supplies (Ml/d)					
Domestic	5276	7123	3740	5069	5273
Industrial and commercial	5189	4614	1939	2106	2131
Miscellaneous unmeasured[†]	272	333	164	194	199
System losses	2888	4587	2340	2340	2340
Total	13625	16657	8183	9709	9943

Notes:
e   estimate
f   forecast
†   assumed to be 2 per cent of total public water supplies
m   millions
l/h/d litres per head per day
Ml/d megalitres per day
*   average daily demand in peak seven days for a typical water-supply zone

Sources: Waterfacts, various issues (Water Services Association, London), and author's own estimates

washers. Domestic water use outside the house (garden use and car-washing) is forecast to increase, even in the absence of climate change, from 5 per cent in 1991 to about 10 per cent in 2021, although in the peak May-August period average ex-house demands are forecast to rise from 12 per cent to 24 per cent of all domestic use. Their greater importance in peaks suggests that the domestic element of peak seven-day demands, which often determines the sizing of much of the local public-water supply infrastructure, may rise by more than 60 per cent over 1991–2021, once typical forecast population increases are taken into account, even without any allowance for climate change.

Our 'most likely' forecasts, including estimates of the effects of climate change (largely driven by an assumed 1.1°C warming in summer months), generate a figure of 186 lhd for 2021, with the ex-house proportion up to 12 per cent for the year as a whole and to 28 per cent for the May-August period. Typical forecast peak seven-day demands for the domestic sector in 2021 are about 80 per cent higher than 1991 figures, again including the effect of forecast population increases. Average year-round demands in the South and East are most likely to increase by about 35 per cent if forecast population growth is included.

Adding in climate change suggests that average domestic demands may increase by about 40 per cent by 2021. Industrial and commercial use, for which no particular forecasting methodology has gained acceptance among water planners, is likely to increase only very slowly (if at all), and Table 13.1 then shows that even a complete halt to increases in system losses (which is *not* a forecast) would still generate an overall public water-supply increase of nearly 19 per cent (22 per cent with climate change built in). Note that these increases, largely emanating from the domestic sector, are based on the assumptions of no spread in domestic metering (which therefore stays at the 3 per cent of homes estimated for 1991) and no other significant new demand-management initiatives over the whole 30-year horizon.

Of course, these figures are spuriously precise. The accuracy which may seem to be implied by growth forecasts such as 'nearly 19 per cent' in reality is not present and therefore not claimed. The data do give, however, an idea of the possible orders of magnitude of public water-supply growth over the next 25 years and thus draw attention to the widening demand-supply gaps referred to above and already highlighted in early NRA planning documents (NRA, 1992 and NRA, 1994). The addition of other direct abstraction forecasts gives a much less homogeneous picture across the South and East; a cursory examination of possible agricultural and industrial abstractions suggests total direct abstractions increasing by between 15 per cent and 35 per cent over the next 30 years.

Demand satiation in Europe

Trend analysis and forecasting exercises in continental European countries give a varied picture for the public water supply (see Table 13.2), but surveys suggest increasing withdrawal demands into the long-term future in most regions (OECD, 1987). The typical picture has been of steadily increasing, but lower, forecast increases for public water-supply and irrigation purposes but a more uncertain prospect for industrial abstractions. Claims of the satiation of domestic demands have long come from Sweden (at 190–200 lhd), Switzerland (260–270 lhd) and various United States cities (in-house 275–285 lhd, but ex-house use apparently still increasing); but the more recent experiences of Denmark and Germany are of greater interest.

Demand trends in Denmark

The data in Table 13.2 for Denmark shows domestic use no higher in 1991 than in 1975, but more detailed information for 1983–92 for councils covering about 40 per cent of the population shows domestic consumption steady at 170–175 lhd over 1983–89 and then declining steadily to 158 lhd

Table 13.2 *Recent public-water supply, domestic-consumption trends in European countries (all data in litres per head per day)*

	1970	1975	1980	1985	1988–89	1991
Austria	121	130	130	131	145	
Belgium	72	93	103	108	108	116
Denmark		174	175	191	190	175
England and Wales[a]	106	114	121	130	136	140
Germany[b]	118	133	140	145	145	144
Finland			148	155	151	150
France		106	109	141	159	161
Italy		202	215	220[c]		214
Luxembourg			177		176	177
Netherlands[a, d]	119	133	141	157	167	173
Norway		200[e]		175		
Spain		145			126	
Sweden	229	207	196	195	194	195
Switzerland[b]	270	258	229	259	270	260

Notes:
a   Adjusted for 'average' climate
b   Includes households and 'small business' use
c   1984 figure
d   Series significantly higher than central government estimates reported for OECD (1987) and data reported in Achttienribbe (1993)
e   1976 figure

Sources: ISWA data, including most recent revisions; England and Wales figures include author's own estimates for 1970–80

in 1992 (Dansk Vandteknisk Forening, 1993). If, as is likely, the post-1989 data are at least partly climate-driven (supply restrictions?), a near-constant data series emerges. Why should this be the case when living standards have been rising? One possible answer is not hard to find, for the same Danish publication records that average water-supply and sewerage-volumetric charges in nearly half the councils rose by 134 per cent over 1983–92 (20 per cent for water supply and 220 per cent for sewerage), which is equivalent to a 65 per cent increase in real terms.

Demand trends in Germany

In Germany, the constancy of water use by 'households and small businesses' is even more remarkable; for further information, BGW, 1993 shows no net increase over 1981–92 and therefore confirms the data in Table 13.2. Here two 'explanations' are offered by German water professionals: first, a possible price effect on demand (German water prices are now by far the highest in Europe, but large increases have only taken place since reunification and therefore cannot account for the pre-1990 data); and, secondly, the growth of a very pronounced 'green consciousness' which informs domestic and industrial water use both in general terms and specifically in the design of water-using appliances. The German data are, in fact, even more striking than at first appears, for allowance for the small business element in the figures quoted in Table 13.2 (estimated as 10–15 per cent of the total by R Stadtfeld, BGW, in a personal communication) suggests a satiation of domestic use at 120–130 lhd. German water planners seem quite certain that these trends are here to stay:

> ...water consumption in the Federal Republic of Germany will not rise any further in the short or long run – there is a general decoupling of water consumption from economic growth.
>
> (BGW,1990)

Demand trends in The Netherlands

Much at variance with the German experience and prognosis is some recent evidence on Dutch water use assembled by VEWIN, The Netherlands Waterworks Association (Achttienribbe, 1993). Using the results of a diary study undertaken by 1000 households in April 1992, domestic use was broken down into its appliance ownership, frequency and unit-water use micro-components. When reassembled, these suggested a very large increase in domestic use from 107 to 135 lhd over 1980–92 (mostly due to increased ownership, frequency of use and unit-water use of showers) and a further increase of 16 per cent (over 20 lhd) over the 1992–2010 period, giving a rate of increase very similar to that forecast for England and Wales above.

Experience in other developed economies is consistent with the two deductions to which we are driven: in the absence of demand-management, domestic demands will continue to rise at a substantial rate; however, in those countries recently showing a levelling off, it seems that economic factors may have been at work.

PIPED PUBLIC-WATER SERVICES

Domestic Metering

Despite several official enquiries into household water metering in Britain in the last 20 years (the last two of which are reported in the Department of the Environment 1985 and 1993), this issue continues to generate controversy and passions to a degree that interested parties abroad find incomprehensible.

Economics and economists have traditionally concentrated on the efficiency aspects of the domestic-metering decision and pushed equity to one side. Recently, environmental considerations have also begun to figure prominently in debate. Regarding one important input into the efficiency and environmental questions, the position is now very clear. All the evidence, from Britain and abroad, shows a significant and enduring impact effect from a switch to domestic metering. The OECD listed 22 studies (1987) with reported consumption reductions usually in the 10 per cent to 30 per cent range. Since then, some additional work has been reported. In

Moss, Norway, the whole population of 25,000 was switched to domestic metering over the period 1979–83. Average daily demand fell about 9 per cent, while peak week demands fell from 21.6 Ml/d (megalitres per day; average over 1974–78) to 14.2 Ml/d (1984–89 average), a reduction of 34 per cent (Christian Raestad, personal communication).

Recent UK Metering Trials

The results of the recently completed UK trials are set out in Table 13.3. In the 11 small-scale trials about 8,600 domestic properties in total (areas ranged from 320 to 1174 properties) had their consumption estimated for a year before charging began (1988–89) and then, mostly, for three further years while they were charged under a wide variety of different volumetric tariff structures (1989–92). By comparing the consumptions in trial areas with those in unmeasured but (supposedly) otherwise similar control areas in each of the 11 districts, a demand effect due to metering, usually averaged over three years, could be estimated. In the Isle of Wight, however, a universal metering policy was adopted, with the result that the proportion of the population living in metered homes rose from 1 per cent in 1988-89 to 97 per cent in 1991–92 (involving 50,000 properties). Careful comparisons of estimates of unmetered and metered per capita consumption on the island and the mainland led to the estimate that the consumption of those transferred to volumetric charging was 21.3 per cent lower than it would have been had they not been transferred.

Table 13.3 *Estimated effect of domestic metering in UK trials, 1988–92*

	'Official' estimate	*Revised estimate*	*Tariff*
Bristol	+1.6%	Omit	Flat rate
East Worcester	–17.2%	⎤	Seasonal
Three Valleys (Bookmans Park)	–8.4%		Peak rate/flat rate
Mid-southern	–7.3%		Flat rate
Northumbrian	–16.1%	as	Declining block
Three Valleys (Chorleywood)	–11.7%	'official'	Flat rate
Southern	–12.3%	estimate	Seasonal
Thames	–10.9%		Increasing block
Wessex (Turlin Moor)	–10.5%		Flat rate
Wessex (Broadstone)	–12.4%	⎦	Peak rate
Yorkshire	–13.7%	Omit	Increasing block
Small-scale sites (average)	–10.8%	–11.9%	
Isle of Wight	–21.3%	–21.3%	Increasing block

Source: 'Official' estimates and tariff details taken from the Department of the Environment (1993); revised estimates derived as described in the text.

The Water Metering Trials Final Report (Department of the Environment, 1993) estimated that the simple unweighted average effect of metering in the 11 small-scale trial areas over the three years was -10.8 per cent – ie, an average of 10.8 per cent less water was used each year as a result of the introduction of charging. An alternative, and arguably superior, average effect can be obtained by omitting the two trial areas (Bristol and Yorkshire), where the mean trial area and the mean control area consumptions per property in the pre-charging year were particularly (and inexplicably) out of line, with trial area figures 38 per cent and 26 per cent lower respectively. Table 13.3 shows this revised average effect to be –11.9 per cent.

Metering Evidence Summarized

These recent results, together with earlier UK domestic-metering evidence, are set out in Table 13.4. It is seen that three out of four studies suggest metering effects in the often-quoted 10–15 per cent range, with only the Isle of Wight significantly greater. Domestic metering will also affect peak

Table 13.4 *Impact effect of domestic metering on average domestic water use: UK evidence*

Area	Years	Type of evidence	Effect	Notes
Fylde Water Board	1971–72	Time-series (291 households)	11.0–14.5%	Individuals' meter readings
Malvern/Mansfield	1976	Cross-sectional (c700 households)	8–17% (mean = 12.5%)	Individuals' meter readings
11 'small-scale' trial sites	1989–92	Comparisons of about 12,000 (in total) trial-and-control households	Average: 10.8%	District meters read
9 'small-scale' trial sites	1989–92	Comparisons of about 10,000 (in total) trial-and-control households	Average: 11.9%	District meters read
Isle of Wight	1989–92	Time-series of water put into public water supply	21.3%	Absolute reduction and estimate for 'normal' and climate-induced growth

Sources: Coopers & Lybrand Associates, Water Metering, mimeo (Department of the Environment, 1985); Department of the Environment, 1993.

demands, with theory indicating a greater effect because of the concentration of largely luxury ex-house use at particular times in the summer. The importance of this for the planning of the local water-supply infrastructure has already been recognised.

Table 13.5 collects together relevant evidence from the UK metering trials and foreign studies. UK figures show that in relatively hot summers (which occurred in 1989–90 and 1990–91) metering seems to reduce monthly, weekly and daily peaks by about 25–35 per cent, whereas in a wetter summer (as in 1991–92) reductions were of the order of 15 per cent, not far above the estimated impact for the year as a whole. Because of the forecast growth in peaks already documented, this evidence is powerful and may add significantly to the case for domestic metering in locations where environmental criteria and the rising costs of traditional supply-enhancement are already arguing for demand-management policies.

Table 13.5 *Impact effect of domestic metering on peak demand: foreign and UK evidence*

	Foreign studies 1974–83 (1)	UK small-scale trial areas 1989–91	1991–92 (3)
Peak quarter-hour	–	52% (2)	–
Peak hour	52%	39% (2)	4%
Peak day	21–58%	27% (3)	15%
Peak week	34%	35% (3)	19%
Peak month	41–72%	27% (3)	15%
Summer (6 months) peak	–	24% (2)	–

Sources: Effect on public water-supply peaks from OECD, 1987. Effects on domestic water-supply peaks from Binnie, 1992 and Water Research Centre, 1994.

Efficiency and Equity

To quantify the net economic value of these effects on demands, domestic metering should be subject, like any other demand-management initiative, to cost-benefit analysis. To pass this test, a positive net benefit (or net present value) should emerge. But cost-benefit analysis, and indeed the whole concept of economic efficiency, ignores the issue of equity. Equity (or 'fairness'), however, is of the utmost importance; the likely incidence of a major tariff change, in terms of who gains and who loses and by how much, will help to determine whether it is acceptable or not. Certainly it is naïve to pretend, as some do, that the social security and tax systems can be left to deal with any consequent undesirable redistribution of income; it is therefore incumbent upon those who enter into this debate to examine seriously the question of incidence.

Distributional Implications of Water Metering

The Institute of Fiscal Studies (1993) reported to OFWAT on the distributional effects of four possible alternative methods of charging households in Britain for water and sewerage services. These were:

1. A fixed annual licence fee.
2. A charge based on the number of people in each household.
3. A charge based on the type of property occupied (detached, semi-detached, bungalow/terraced, or flat/other).
4. Water metering, with the fixed part of the bill reflecting only the costs of meter reading, billing and collection, and all other costs lumped together into a single volumetric charge per cubic metre.

Table 13.6 summarizes some of the main results. As would be expected, the severest impact on poorer households would be the equalized licence fee, the 'poor' being defined as either the lowest quintile or decile in the household income distribution. The proportion of annual household income devoted to water charges would increase, for the lowest decile, from 3.2 per cent to 3.7 per cent. What is much more surprising, however, is that metering turns out to be the alternative that bears on poorer households least harshly in average terms. Indeed, the lowest quintile households would on average gain a very small amount (about £2 per annum in 1991–92 prices), although that cloaks a very small average loss (of a similar amount) for the lowest-income 10 per cent of households. Similarly, the groups of the best-paid 10 and 20 per cent of households on average gain least from switches to water metering and property banding (as compared to the other

Table 13.6 *Estimated effects on average household incomes of high-income and low-income households, following changes to the different methods of charging for water services*

New basis of charge	Average loss (–) or gain (+) in £/year		Average loss or gain as % of household income	
	Lowest 10% of households	Highest 10% of households	Lowest 20% of households	Highest 20% of households
Licence fee	–£22	+£43	–0.5%	+0.1%
Number of people in household	–£5	+£57	+0.02%	+0.1%
House-type banding	–£8	+£30	–0.3%	+0.05%
Water metering	–£2	+£34	+0.04%	+0.05%

Source: Data collected from various tables to be found in the Institute of Fiscal Studies, 1993

options). Judged by the quintile and decile data estimated, therefore, of the four possible changes, water metering leads to the least overall disturbance from the present incidence of charges.

The reasons for this superficially surprising result are not hard to find; pensioner households (typically 1–2 persons) have most to lose from an equalized licence fee but gain significantly from a change to a number-of-people basis (by £41 per annum, on average) and to a metered basis (by £27 per annum). It follows that somewhere within the poorer groups there must be pronounced losers (since there are also gainers). Clearly, they must be larger, poor families: typically, one or two adults with two or more children.

Policies to Deal with Equity Problems

Are there, then, any ways of coping with that incidence problem, within a framework of charging by volume? Two methods can be considered. The first one recognizes that, for a typical household, domestic water supplies serve both basic needs and luxury purposes, and seeks to design a volumetric tariff accordingly. A free or low-price *tranche* of water for basic needs would thus be established (often known as a lifeline allowance). It would be no help to allow this on a household basis, however, since it would then benefit most below-average-sized households (especially pensioners) and the necessarily higher volumetric charge for 'excess' use would tend to make the relative position of large poor households even worse.

Ideally, the allowance needs to be geared to the number of people in each household, but it is doubtful if any feasible arrangements could be made to establish and monitor this figure accurately in the United Kingdom. As a second-best alternative, the low-price allowance might be geared to an assumption of one adult, plus the number of children, in the household, with the existing Social Security child benefit entitlement effectively being used as a passport to the concession (with, for example, 60 litres per person per day being allowed at a special low price). In this way, any risks to public health arising from the phenomenon of 'water poverty' should be minimized. There would result some cross-subsidization of households with children and single-person households by others, but efficiency and environmental criteria would be maintained.

The other interesting feature of such a tariff is that it can be made broadly consistent with what is known about the structure of present, and likely future, water demands in the home. Calculations using the data generated in the climate-change study referred to above suggest that, on a relatively broad definition of 'basic' water use in the South and East (responsible for about two-thirds of estimated 1995 domestic demands), *all* the forecast increases for domestic purposes up to the year 2021 would be for luxury purposes.

This sort of three-part tariff (a separate standing charge would continue to be included) can help to resolve the dispute between those who, in debates about paying for water, implicitly argue for a *social service* model of the water industry (stressing the consumer's right to potable water and the importance of consumption externalities arising in the form of public health benefits, and those who commend a *business or public corporation* approach to the water services, emphasizing the commercial nature of the industry's outputs, which are produced in response to consumer demands. If, as is maintained here, *both* models capture important elements of the nature of domestic water use, it would seem to be appropriate – and, indeed, given the often conflicting positions adopted, imperative – to devise a tariff which combines *both* approaches. In this way, efficiency, environmental and broad equity objectives could all be pursued.

A second way of dealing with the problems thrown up by water metering for larger poorer households is to accept other concessions – for example, family credit and income-support beneficiaries – as providing eligibility for certain percentage rebates on water and sewerage charges. This is the situation in, for example, Melbourne, Australia, where a wide variety of concession cards are accepted by the water utility as providing eligibility for up to a 50 per cent rebate on water and sewerage charges (with a maximum of A\$135 rebate per household per year).

That may leave one group inadequately covered: those whose medical situation requires them to use significantly more than an average amount of water. Recently, arrangements have been finalized for assistance from the UK Department of Health for those on home kidney-dialysis machines; and Severn Trent Water has announced the capping of a family's metered bill in a much-publicized case involving a mother suffering from multiple sclerosis (*Water Bulletin*, 1 September 1995). Precedents have thus been established in the health area.

The remaining problem that needs to be addressed is the general one of *transition*. As OFWAT proposed in its 1990 consultation document on charging policy (OFWAT, 1990, p 9), changes in charging methods should be introduced in a manner that 'avoids undue discrimination, hardship and cost'.

Pricing Principles and Public-Water Supplies

Once consumers are metered, there are strong efficiency arguments that prices should be geared to the marginal social costs of system expansion so long as demand elasticities are significantly different from zero (which seems to be true; see OECD, 1987). Changes in bills will then reflect potential changes in costs and a sensible use of resources should result. Furthermore, it is long-run marginal cost (LRMC) that matters, since investment choices by water consumers – eg, concerning complex domestic sprinkler systems or recirculation equipment for industry – need to be influenced by price signals which embody information about the cost of water over several years ahead.

What evidence is there of marginal costs actually being used in tariff determination for piped-water supplies? The best-known example abroad is that of Japan where the spread of progressive tariffs in the last 25 years has been driven by the desire 'to reflect the increased cost of the development of new water resources, etc' (OECD 1987, p 44). In England there is indirect evidence of LRMC estimation causing the volumetric element of the metered tariff to be reduced in a northern water service company with large excess capacity (and therefore low LRMC) and to be increased in a large water company in the south where LRMC was found to be high relative to average costs (ESRI, 1994). Otherwise, examples are hard to find. This, of course, does not prevent price changes being used to manage demand, even in the absence of LRMC estimation. For example, although reported domestic-consumption elasticities are small in Europe (–0.1 to –0.3; OECD, 1987), government policy in The Netherlands apparently includes a proposal to shift all household water charges (including fixed elements) on to a volumetric basis, in the hope of reducing the expected increase in water demands.

Further pricing initiatives come from other dimensions of tariff design; highlighted briefly here are seasonal, time-of-day and 'conservation' tariffs. Seasonal tariffs are rare, and almost completely confined to the United States. A recent US water-rate survey (Ernst and Young, 1992) listed tariff details for 121 US water utilities and identified only five with seasonal water-supply tariffs and seven with seasonal waste-water charges. Studies in the US in the 1980s showed that system peak-day ratios fell by 10 per cent to 15 per cent following the introduction of seasonal tariffs in four utilities in the late 1970s. Two of the small-scale areas in the recent UK trials used seasonal tariffs over a three-year period; in Chandlers Ford (Southern Water) and East Worcester, summer volumetric charges were pitched at 62 and 65 per cent above those in winter, and metering effects which averaged out at nearly 15 per cent over the whole year were reported (Department of the Environment, 1993). The breakdown of this effect between summer and winter has not been reported.

Time-of-day tariffs are almost unknown in the domestic sector. One UK trial, in Wessex (Broadstone), fixed a daily (6 pm to 9 pm) peak volumetric charge 77 per cent above that for the rest of the day, but it is impossible to tell to what extent the estimated effect of metering (–12.4 per cent over the three years) was influenced by the tariff. The celebrated example is in the industrial sector in Antwerp, where consumers can take advantage of a sophisticated night/day tariff. From 1955 to 1985 this appears to have been responsible for reducing the peak-hour to average-hour ratio from 1.6 to 1.1 (IWSA, 1990). One suspects, however, that only in rare cases would efficiency gains be large enough to outweigh the costs of the complex meter technology required.

Increasing-block (or progressive) tariffs are becoming more common in developed as well as developing economies. Two rationales have been offered: the pursuit of social objectives (the 'lifeline allowance' argument referred to above) and an underlining of the conservation message via escalating prices for more and more consumption. Strictly speaking, there is no efficiency argument for an increasing-block tariff, but if there is evidence of a 'psychological' effect on demand, the benefits may outweigh the intellectually subtle allocative-efficiency costs. The OECD survey (1987) found some evidence of effects deriving from progressive tariffs in Japan, Italy, Denmark and Switzerland (Zurich), but the two examples in the UK metering trials (Thames and Yorkshire) proved inconclusive.

Charging for Piped Waste-Water Services

For households the costs of sewerage and sewage disposal are generally recovered either through local taxation (the theory of public goods may be used to support such collective provision), or as an addition to the public water-supply tariff, whether that is volumetrically based or not. It is usually sufficient with domestic consumers for the input of water to be used as a proxy for the volume of sewage generated, although significant ex-house water use will upset the balance.

Industrial use of public sewers poses a much more serious problem, and from the 1970s onwards relatively sophisticated charging systems reflecting different charges for the treatment of different waste characteristics have become much more common in Western countries. Because their introduction was driven by fairness (as between dischargers) and cost-recovery, the schemes have invariably been designed on an average cost basis (originally historic, now usually replacement costs). The Mogden formula as used in the United Kingdom is of this type, charging for trade effluent according to an additive function which reflects the costs of reception and conveyance, volumetric and primary treatment, biological treatment, and sludge treatment and disposal. In at least one application of the formula (by Severn–Trent Water), when new or additional treatment capacity is required for business customers the future capital costs are reflected in the charges. Severn-Trent thus claim that its pricing approach is based on long-term average incremental costs, a surrogate for LRMC (ESRI, 1994; OECD 1987, Annex 2).

As tighter discharge standards have become reflected in higher tariffs in a number of countries, firms' interest in undertaking their own effluent treatment has grown. For industry to engage in its own treatment only when it would be 'cheaper' to do so (in overall economic and environmental terms), it is important to get the structure and level of waste-water utility tariffs right. Invoking the usual arguments for the smoothing of future years' marginal capital costs (because of the need to provoke sensible decisions by dischargers about investments which are complementary to, or substitutes for, the use of water services), the cheapness objective is best achieved by the utility basing tariffs on its own forward-looking marginal costs. These should relate to administration, capacity availability and actual discharges (see the discussion of these three elements below in the context of direct abstractions).

Probably one of the most thoroughly researched practical proposals for such a tariff has been published recently in Ireland (ESRI, 1994) where waste-water disposal is at present undertaken by 88 legally separate authorities, which mostly receive large subsidies on both capital and operating accounts (although no grants are likely in future for new treatment plant catering for industrial demands). The core of the suggested tariff is based upon the amount of peak-time capacity that a firm wishes to reserve and the incremental cost of such new plant, which is broken down into flow, chemical-oxygen demand and suspended-solids dimensions. Annual charges are then derived from assumptions concerning the discount rate and asset lives.

The ESRI report has now been distributed by the Irish Department of the Environment to interested parties as a consultative document, part of an on-going process of policy development. Following an ESRI workshop, at least one local authority is believed to be actively examining the proposals for possible application (Scott, 1995).

DIRECT ABSTRACTIONS

Introduction

Behind public-water supplies lie the direct abstractions of water undertakings from rivers, lakes and groundwater. In England and Wales, if the water companies are the retailers, then the NRA is best perceived either as a monopoly wholesaler or, where support works are required, a monopoly producer of raw water, charged with allocating the limited resource between a whole range of sometimes competing abstractors: water undertakings, industrialists, power generators, farmers, etc. It must also make or share in decisions about the development of new sources, and new control and regulatory works. And the familiar criteria apply: its allocation mechanisms should be equitable (should further environmental goals, in particular, be consistent with sustainable use) and should be economically efficient.

Of these objectives, broad equity should be easier to handle in the case of direct abstractions, since no precise equivalent of the water poverty issue associated with the introduction and operation of volumetric pricing in the domestic sector arises (see above). The closest analogy is the difficult position some farming communities would experience following the introduction of 'efficient' pricing of irrigation water. In that situation, however, the options are clearer. On the one hand, the issue may be treated as an exercise in the management of change, with perhaps a staged increase in tariffs and parallel assistance (technical and financial) for farmers concerning:

1. radical changes in irrigation practices;
2. fundamental changes in farming activities; or
3. the decline of the agricultural sector.

Alternatively, a political decision may be taken somehow to compensate irrigators so that they can afford the higher charges.

Allocative efficiency and environmental objectives for direct abstractions may then be pursued through the employment of a tariff which combines administrative, availability and actual abstraction charges. Administrative (or access) charges are either one-off or regular payments to cover the monitoring, billing, payment and other administrative costs borne by the responsible water agency. Availability charges ideally should reflect the long-run marginal costs incurred or imposed as a result of extra supplies being reserved by an abstractor. They would be charged on the size of the abstraction authorized in the licence and would reflect the capital costs of either support works or resource depletion (the latter being, for example in the case where lower river flows result, what it would have cost to add any necessary support works or other extra capacity). Actual abstraction charges should then be based on the short-run marginal opportunity costs of actually supplying more raw water. These would include system operating costs – eg, extra pumping – as well as any environmental damage costs (estimated directly or, as above, via necessary amelioration activities).

However, aquatic economic life is, of course, in reality much more complicated than this. Return flows at or very close to the point of abstraction without significant quality reduction should reduce charges since it is arguably *consumption* rather than *abstraction* that causes costs to be incurred. Put another way, returns separated spatially from the 'originating' abstraction may cause problems and therefore costs for other watercourse users or habitat – as (often) will polluted returns. If there is no charging system for direct discharges in existence, the financial 'credit' for a return flow could be linked positively to its quality, thus providing a surrogate incentive scheme encouraging pre-discharge treatment.

Further complications may arise. Integrated water-resource systems argue for common charges, but administrative complications may restrain the extent to which 'individual' resource locations should give rise to unique, locally based payments. Extra winter abstractions from rivers may normally have no implications for support works or other users, which suggests zero availability and actual abstractions charges; but the *possibility* of winter opportunity costs – eg, more abstractions meaning less aquifer replenishment in a dry winter – suggests either occasional winter surcharges or more regular payments based on the probability of the distribution of winter flows. Finally, in a dry-year resource-shortage situation, it can be argued that the notion of marginal-user opportunity cost should dominate. Rationing by price then occurs. This may cause political difficulties, but it has clear efficiency advantages over the alternative: to balance the effects of the shortage years with the surplus years by generating probability-driven 'average' LRMC-based charges, and therefore having to accept the need for bans or restrictions on abstractions in occasional years.

Abstraction Charges in Practice

As domestic and agricultural demands grow, enhanced perhaps by climate change, failure to set economically and environmentally appropriate charges for abstractions will impose increasing costs on the water-resource system and its users. Subsidized water for irrigators means that too much or the 'wrong' crops are produced and water is wasted; pricing at less than the marginal cost of supply means in the long run the over-utilization of resources and increasingly frequent (and economically inefficient) restrictions in dry summers. Yet the Environment Agency, constrained by the 1995 Environment Act to cost-recovery charges and concentrating its tariffs almost exlusively on *authorized* abstractions (the exception is for spray irrigation), is obliged to send out what are clearly misleading price signals in areas of resource shortage. For example, because of the probability of many rivers being able to support up to a considerable volume of abstractions without any significant costs being incurred, the marginal costs of further abstractions may be way above average costs. It has been estimated recently that the current implicit price of abstractions in the Thames region is only one-tenth of the marginal-capacity expansion costs (with no allowance for environmental costs). Thus cost-recovery through average-cost pricing may seriously underprice water (Dubourg, 1994).

At the last count, volume-related abstraction charges were being levied in all or part of only eight countries (France, Germany, The Netherlands, England and Wales, the United States, Japan, Canada and Australia), although relevant legislation has recently been passed in three more (Spain, Portugal and Italy – see Rees *et al*, 1993). In France, the Agences de Bassin administer very comprehensive charging schemes geared exclusively to *actual* abstractions, with complex weighting factors determined by location, source type, abstraction purpose (as a surrogate for the proportion not returned to the watercourse) and season. Although the weights used appear to be broadly correlated with opportunity costs in a weak ordinal sense, charges are set merely to recover costs and therefore suffer from the same criticisms as those in England and Wales. Germany passed the relevant abstraction-charges legislation in 1989 and directs the proceeds to a variety of purposes, including compensation to farmers for reduced land use which results from the need to protect groundwater sources. The first state to introduce charges, Baden-Wurttemberg, had an income from charges of DM 160 million in 1990: 80 per cent of the NRA's income but with only 20 per cent of its population. Abstractions for the public-water supply were charged at DM 0.10/cubic metre in 1992, about four times a typical figure in Southern England. In Hessen, the groundwater charge was DM 0.20/cubic metre (Muller and Scheele, 1993).

What of the evidence for effects on demands? Largely because of very low abstraction charges, the few known studies have concluded that industrial demands are relatively price-inelastic, whereas the opposite is often true for irrigation (OECD, 1987). Rees *et al*, (1993), in an extensive study undertaken for the NRA, therefore undertook questionnaire studies of 72 farm irrigators and 82 industrial abstractors in Eastern England. By examining preparedness-to-pay, they concluded that unit pricing based on economic principles has an important role to play in influencing irrigation abstractors in the short-to-medium term (particularly in changing the timing of abstraction from summer to winter) and in the longer term (in reducing demands overall). Industrial demands, however, would take much longer to show any response, since margins are far less tight and sunk costs in water-consumption specific processes very large. In the longer term, however, even industrialists would be likely to rethink recycling factors and process equipment if faced with substantially higher abstraction charges.

In its recent document on water conservation (Department of the Environment, 1995) the UK Government reiterated its intention to publish a consultation paper on incentive charging, emphasizing the additional benefits this might generate in encouraging water companies to reduce leakage in public water-supply distribution systems.

Tradable Licences?

It is sometimes suggested that tradable abstraction licences are the best answer to scarcity problems, since they leave it to the self-interest of actual and potential abstractors to sort out through voluntary transactions who gets how much water. Distribution decisions are thus automatically taken care of by 'the market', self-interest being seen as a much more assured way of generating allocative efficiency than 'command-and-control' policies. At the same time an efficiently functioning market will be able to provide valuable information to guide investment, since market prices reflect marginal private values in use and these in turn feed into water-agency capacity augmentation/diminution decisions.

Most recent interest in voluntary transfers has centred on market activity in the United States and Australia. The former is unsurprising, given the tradition of appropriative rights for water in parts of the western United States. Permanent or temporary transfers of rights between abstractors have been commonplace in half a dozen states for many years, being reflected in isolated transactions, water banks (also occurring in riparian traditions) and mature water markets. Most of the permanent transfer markets have facilitated a significant shift from irrigation to industrial and (more markedly) municipal use in recent decades, but in some areas – such as North Colorado – a strong rental market has also been established with potential surplus units (typically municipalities) renting back to irrigators in individual years when, for climatic reasons, potential supplies are high. In the North Colorado Water Conservancy District, about 30 per cent of total water deliveries is rented out each year, suggesting a flexibility in allocation that must produce sizeable efficiency benefits (Howe, Schurmeier and Shaw, 1986).

The Australian experience is more interesting because of the innovation of imposing water-rights transferability on a riparian framework (in this tradition, where the right to use water is derived from ownership of the adjoining, underlying or overlying land, the strict land-water complementarity in sales and purchases has usually prevented resources being attracted to their most highly valued uses). In the 1980s, transferable water entitlements were introduced into three states – South Australia (1983), New South Wales (1983–84) and Victoria (1987–88) – generally applying only to the irrigated sector (Australian Water Resources Council, 1986). Since then, temporary schemes have become permanent, market practices have spread (new abstraction licences have been allocated by tender or auction in a number of states), and in at least one state (South Australia) intersectoral water trades are free of restrictions (Pigram, 1993). Early analysis of water sales in that state, comparing prices to those imputed from land sales before 1983, suggested that marginal units of water had doubled in value following the introduction of transferability. More recent calculations in Victoria led to forecasts that between 3 and 10 per cent of water deliveries would be traded after 1987–88; in fact, only 1.2 per cent of deliveries was traded up to 1992, and no reliable estimates of efficiency gains have been made for that scheme (James, 1993).

Market Failure with Abstractions Licences

An inefficient water-rights market arises because of imprecision concerning what is being traded as well as market failure. Imprecision can arise in terms of quantity, quality, reliability, security of tenure and conditions of use; while market failure may occur for four reasons:

1. The existence of a dominant seller or buyer.
2. Third-party effects which are ignored.
3. The existence of 'public interest' and environmental values which are ignored or undervalued.
4. Market distortions resulting from taxes, subsidies and imperfect knowledge.

To circumvent monopoly/monopsony problems, it is often necessary to embrace a geographical area sufficiently large for the market price to be governed by the actions of a relatively large number of demanders and suppliers. However, the larger the area in which rights are transferable, the greater the potential adverse external effects on third parties (see below). So the price of reducing market failure emanating from the dominance of individual traders may be more market failure from externalities.

Voluntary trading may ignore the interests of third parties, and these also are typically expressed in terms of changes in return flows, security of supplies, groundwater levels and quality dimensions. To deal with such problems:

1. Water laws may be enacted to permit compensation or transfer modification if damage is proved.
2. A relevant water agency could be made responsible for identifying third-party effects (thus monitoring and having the power to modify or even veto any given proposed transfer).
3. The party applying for a transfer could be obliged to demonstrate that other parties will not be damaged.

Western states in the United States provide examples of all these practices, although the most efficient procedures seem to be administrative ones where state agencies play a major role in identifying or developing evidence concerning injury to third parties, as in New Mexico (Howe, Schurmeier and Shaw, 1986).

Some transfer externalities may impose not on identifiable third parties but on generalized 'public interest' and environmental values. This is because water produces public as well as private services; examples of the former are the aesthetic pleasure derived from streams of high-quality water and from the wildlife habitat often provided by watercourses. Clearly, water transfers may deleteriously affect these public goods outputs, thus providing yet another example of market failure.

In the United States literature, it is suggested that upholders of environmental interests (state and local governments, amenity groups) should have access to rights markets and the financial and legal ability to bid for water rights on an equal basis with established users. In this way, environmental values can be incorporated into market decisions and prices. In Colorado, Nebraska, Montana and Idaho, the state already has the power to purchase rights. In theory, this resolution of the problem seems attractive, but in practice serious problems are posed: can the financial base of amenity groups correctly reflect the public's evaluation of environmental values (a free-rider problem)? Do not the political and fiscal problems of local governments make it difficult to conceive of the community interest being successfully and accurately represented in the market place by a money bid for water rights?

In Australia, the public goods concern has been different; it is that a free market in transferable water entitlements in irrigation could leave some districts with no economically viable farming, thus leading to other (supplying) enterprises and local communities suffering large income losses. This poses large issues of regional, social and planning policy, which, at the end of the day, local and central governments will have to resolve. Australian transfer schemes have favoured the resolution of such issues through the relevant state agency maintaining the power of veto over potential transfers (Australian Water Resources Council, 1986).

Licence Markets in Britain?

Recently, discussion in Britain concerning the feasibility of abstraction licences being made marketable has increased – Department of the Environment (1992) and Department of the Environment (1995) – especially in the context of the situation in which an existing licence-holder has a lower value in use for the abstraction than a new (and rejected) licence application. So could markets work here? Rees *et al*, (1993) considered this issue. They highlighted practical problems in the implementation of permit markets (especially issues concerning return flows and other third-party effects, and trades between 'sleepers' and active abstractors serving to exacerbate scarcity), and established that only irrigators would be likely to engage in significant trading in South-East England. They therefore recommended a limited experimental scheme, restricted to agricultural abstractors and thus avoiding both potential monopoly problems deriving from water company participation and the return-flow location issue.

CONCLUSION

It will be clear from the above demand forecasts and evidence that demand-management has an increasing role to play in the resolution of the world's growing freshwater problems. Within demand-management, moreover, a switch towards pricing is foreseen. A full consideration of the parallel need to manage the demands for direct discharges would have served to reinforce this conclusion.

Does that mean that the same set of policy tools are capable of ensuring sustainable development as far as water resources are concerned – which is taken to mean the requirement that each succeeding generation should inherit a non-declining (capital) stock of water resources, in both the quantitative and qualitative dimensions (Dubourg, 1993)? The answer must be a definite yes, for the pricing principles and rules developed in earlier sections for quantities (which may be extended to encompass direct discharges to watercourses) will always suffice to achieve 'sustainable pricing' as long as an element is included to cover the costs of any quantitative or qualitative resource depletion. Note, however, that volumetric charging founded on opportunity costs is not a requirement for quantity and quality sustainability. In principle, command-and-control systems can always ensure sustainability, given effective enforcement of the regulations. However, as Dubourg has argued, the objective of policy should be that of *efficient* sustainability – sustainability at least cost – and that does require a leading role for pricing.

It is therefore concluded that, for the most part, moves towards the measurement and economic pricing of water services mean that economic, financial, environmental (including sustainability) and equity interests are all simultaneously pursued. In any major policy shift, however, there are bound to be winners and losers, and there is therefore a particular need to consider seriously how to deal with any extra hardship which would otherwise have to be borne by those already on or within the margins of poverty. As has been seen, the sensitive design of tariffs can help to solve such problems.

The transition to water as an economic resource will not be an easy one for an industry, much of whose intellectual equipment is still rooted in supply-side concerns. The real irony, however, is that a proper consideration of demands and demand-management now provides the only hope of supplying water services of sustainable quantity and quality into the long-term future.

REFERENCES

Achttienribbe, G E (1993) 'Household water consumption in The Netherlands', *Aqua*, Vol 42, No 6, pp 347–50

Australian Water Resources Council (1986) 'Proceedings of the Joint AWRC-AAES Seminar on Transferable Water Rights', AWRC Conference Series No 12, Australian Government Publishing Service, Canberra

BGW (1990) 'Water Supply Policies in Germany', paper given by Bundesverband der deutschen Gas und Wasserwirtschaft, mimeo, London Conference on Water Availability, Quality and Cost

BGW (1993) *Wasserstatistik*, BGW, Bonn

Binnie, C J A (1992) 'Demand management, tariffs and metering', mimeo, Institution of Water and Environmental Management, London

CPRE (1991) *Water on Demand? The Case for Demand-management in Water Charging Policy*, Council for the Protection of Rural England, London

CPRE (1993) *Water for Life: Strategies for Sustainable Water Resource Management*, Council for the Protection of Rural England, London

Dansk Vandteknisk Forening (1993) 'Vandforyningsstatistik 1992', DVF *et al*, mimeo, Copenhagen

Department of the Environment (1985) *Joint Study of Water Metering: Report of the Steering Group*, HMSO, London

Department of the Environment (1992) *Using Water Wisely, A Consultation Paper*, DoE and Welsh Office, London

Department of the Environment (1993) *Water Metering Trials – Final Report*, Department of the Environment, London

Department of the Environment (1995) *Water Conservation – Government Action*, DoE and the Welsh Office, London and Cardiff

Dubourg, W R (1993) 'Water and water quality', in Pearce, D (ed) *Blueprint 3: Measuring Sustainable Development*, Earthscan, London

Dubourg, W R (1994) 'Water', note prepared for CSERGE/Green College seminar on environmental taxation, CSERGE, University College London, London, pp 64–76

Ernst and Young (1992) *1992 Water Rate Survey*, Ernst and Young, New York

ESRI (1994) *Waste Water Services: Charging Industry the Capital Cost*, The Economic and Social Research Institute, Dublin

Herrington, P R (1996) *Climate Change and the Demand for Water*, HMSO, London

Howe, C W, Schurmeier, D R and Shaw, W D (1986) 'Innovative Approaches to Water Allocation', *Water Resources Research*, Vol 22, No 4, pp 222–41

Institute of Fiscal Studies (1993) *The Distributional Effects of Different Methods of Charging Households for Water and Sewerage Services*, Office of Water Services, Birmingham

IWSA (1990) 'Future Water Demand', Papers given at 1990 Workshop of the International Water Supply Association in Basle, IWSA, Zurich

James, D (1993) 'Using Economic Instruments for Meeting Environmental Objectives: Australia's Experience', research paper prepared for the Australian Department of the Environment, Sport and Territories, Ecoservices Pty Ltd, Canberra

Muller, J and Scheele, V (1993) 'Pricing water-comparison of costs in European water services', paper given to *Financial Times* European Water Industry Conference, London

NRA (1992) *Water Resources Development Strategy: A Discussion Document*, National Rivers Authority, Bristol

NRA (1994) *Water: Nature's Precious Resource*, HMSO, London

OECD (1987) *Pricing of Water Services*, Organization of Economic Cooperation and Development, Paris

OECD (1989a) *Water Resource Management*, Organization of Economic Cooperation and Development, Paris

OECD (1989b) *Economic Instruments for Environmental Protection*, Organization of Economic Cooperation and Development, Paris

OFWAT (1990) *Paying for Water: A Consultation Paper*, Office of Water Services, Birmingham

Pigram, J J (1993) 'Property rights and water markets in Australia: an evolutionary process toward institutional reform', *Water Resources Research*, Vol 29, No 4, pp 1313–19

Postel, S (1992) *The Last Oasis: Facing Water Scarcity*, Earthscan, London

Rees, J et al (1993) *Economics of Water Resource Management*, Note 128, National Rivers Authority, Bristol

RSPB (1995) *Water Wise: The RSPB's proposals for using water wisely*, Royal Society for the Protection of Birds, Sandyford

Scott, S (1995) Personal communication, September

Tate, D M (1990) *Water Demand Management in Canada: A State-of-the-Art Review*, Environment Canada, Ottawa

United Nations (1991) *Legislative and Economic Approaches to Water Demand Management*, United Nations, New York

United Nations (1992) 'Integrated urban water resources management', paper given by Peter Rogers to Dublin International Conference on Water and the Environment, mimeo

Water Research Centre (1994) *The Effects of Metered Charging on Customer Demands for Water from 1 April 1989 to 31 March 1993*, Report No UC2072, Water Research Centre, Medmenham, Buckinghamshire (available in OFWAT library, Birmingham)

Winpenny, J (1994) *Managing Water as an Economic Resource*, Routledge, London

Chapter 14

TOWARDS IMPLEMENTATION REALITIES

Judith Rees

INTRODUCTION

In the previous chapter, Paul Herrington has argued the case for water to be regarded as an economic good, with prices for both raw water and treated supplies set 'properly' to reflect the long-run marginal costs (including the environmental costs) of provision. Such arguments are not, of course, new; it is now over 40 years since the seminal work by Hirshleifer, De Haven and Milliman (1960) highlighted the deficiencies of the supply-fix approach to water-resources management and advocated demand management through the use of economically efficient pricing policies. The economic logic of this case is compelling. There is no doubt that water services have typically been underpriced, and those demanding additional supplies have been able to neglect the full costs of their actions.

Today, environmental taxes and full-cost prices have acquired something of a 'moral' status, as forces to correct the past unsustainable abuse and overuse of environmental resources. However, it should not be forgotten that their use is strongly rooted in the concept of economic efficiency. As Bromley (1991) has pointed out: 'efficiency as an objective truth rule is so much a part of the ideology of economics that few seem to recognize its ideological character' (p205). Efficiency need have nothing to do with equity and social justice; nor need it be compatible with environmental ethics or with the values of those seeking to protect traditional economic systems and the communities which depend upon them. 'Proper' water pricing, which maximizes the total value in use of water over time, will not necessarily also ensure that all consumers are able to satisfy their basic needs and maintain their livelihoods. Any moves to introduce market instruments, with prices set to approximate long-run marginal costs, would involve major redistributions of real income and welfare. This means that it is always easier to support economic incentives in the abstract than it is to devise specific pricing or taxation schemes that are politically and socially acceptable.

It has also to be stressed that there are considerable doubts about the ability of proper prices and environmental taxes actually to achieve the desired responses within a reasonable time scale when they are implemented on their own. Such prices and taxes would have to operate in a highly complex, interrelated and imperfect economic world. This world is not peopled by rational 'economic men' who respond dutifully to the correct price signals. Rather, water users have their responses constrained by their past investment decisions, imperfect knowledge and non-profit (utility) maximizing goals. The ability of end-water users to change their patterns of water use and waste-water disposal into more sustainable forms is also partially determined by other actors. The behaviour of the private monopoly water companies is obviously critical, and so too are the decisions of planners and developers on building design, urban form, the location of permitted development and urban densities, all of which affect water use, leakage levels and the potential for waste-water reuse.

Regulation in the water sector has to occur within a complex regulatory environment and the outcomes will be affected by regulation in other economic sectors and policy domains. Water use and waste-water disposal are not just subject to regulation (direct and indirect) by various public sector agencies, but also by the nature of the markets for agricultural and manufactured products and by social forces, which affect consumption norms and public attitudes. In judging the potential effectiveness and acceptability of 'proper' prices and environmental taxes, it is essential to take account of the context within which they would operate. The likelihood is that they will need to be accompanied by measures which ameliorate their redistributive impact, lower the behavioural and informational barriers to response, change developer and planning decisions, shift the profit incentives of the water companies, and reduce pressures within product markets for water-intensive production.

In this chapter attention will be focused on the formidable barriers to implementing anything approaching economically 'ideal' market instruments in the water-supply sector. First, consideration will be given to the use of long-run marginal cost pricing in the networked supply services. Getting prices right in the 'treated' water sector is critical since the water companies are responsible for 80 per cent of all resource-relevant abstractions of water from the natural environment (excluding abstractions from tidal waters and those subject to 100 per cent return flow). Secondly, attention will be paid to the practical, behavioural and political constraints involved in establishing and implementing the 'proper' pricing of raw-water abstraction. Finally, and by way of a conclusion, discussion will centre briefly on the package of regulatory and economic measures that are likely to be needed if water use is to be shifted over time to meet sustainable development criteria. Throughout, the focus will be on England and Wales, but the issues and principles involved have a much wider applicability.

PRICING, EQUITY AND ACCEPTABILITY

Price Rises

The wholesale introduction of long-run marginal cost (LRMC) pricing for water supplies and waste-water disposal represents a major policy shift. It may well be the case that over the long term, LRMC pricing would reduce the need for high-cost supply-expansion schemes and the costly post-generation treatment of waste water. Moreover, in theory it could, indeed, act to ensure that available supply and quality resources are allocated between users over space and time in ways which maximize the total value in use. However, such potential advantages cannot disguise the facts that in the immediate future, supply and disposal prices would increase dramatically and the distribution of provision costs would shift markedly. The political and public acceptability of both the price rises and incidence effects is at best dubious, particularly given the price rises experienced by water customers over the recent past and the widespread public mistrust of the monopolistic water companies.

As Table 14.1 shows in nominal terms, households have seen their water service bills rise by between 50 and 150 per cent from 1989 to 1995 and sewerage bills have increased by 52–122 per cent over the same period. Although real-term rises (minus inflation) have been significantly less (averaging 39 per cent for water and 37 per cent for sewerage), it is the absolute levels of increase which are perceived by customers. Water services have traditionally been a minimal element in total household bills, but by 1995 this was no longer the case, particularly for low-income families. Single pensioners and single parents on income support can pay as much as 9 per cent of their disposable income (after housing costs) on water and sewerage services in high-cost areas (Ofwat, 1993a). Since the relatively poor inevitably spend a much higher proportion of their disposable incomes on basic water services, the recent price rises have had a regressive effect.

A substantial proportion of customers associate these price rises with privatization, the enhanced profitability of the water companies, dividend payments to shareholders and directors' salaries. The capital investments undertaken by the companies and improvements in some aspects of customer service (Ofwat, 1995a) are at best imperfectly perceived. Customer attitudes towards the water industry have undoubtedly changed; they are much less willing to accept what they see as system failures, are less prepared to cooperate with the companies in reducing consumption during drought periods, and are increasingly resistant to the notion that the companies should be able to restrict their usage by imposing hosepipe bans. Such attitude changes were clearly seen over the dry, hot summer of 1995; many customers reacted with hostility to the idea that their increased demands were to blame for shortages and they saw it as the function of commercial companies to meet all legitimate supply requirements (including garden watering). These reactions will inevitably be important to future attempts to make demand-management more central to water planning. Somewhat ironically, the 'commodification' of water has made it less acceptable to introduce regulatory restrictions on

Table 14.1 *Household bills for unmeasured water and sewerage, 1989–95*

Water and Sewerage Companies	% increase water	% increase sewerage
Anglian Water Services Ltd	93.8	52.2
Dwr Cymru Cyfyngedig	69.8	78.4
North-West Water Ltd	65.4	64.0
Northumbrian Water Ltd	68.9	80.3
Severn-Trent Water Ltd	69.7	67.7
South-West Water Services Ltd	89.5	122.4
Southern Water Services Ltd	65.3	58.4
Thames Water Utilities Ltd	55.9	67.4
Wessex Water Services Ltd	67.9	57.1
Yorkshire Water Services Ltd	53.7	61.3
Water only Companies		
Highest % rises		
Tendring Hundred	149.4	
North Surrey	102.3	
Lowest % rises		
Chester Waterworks	49.1	
Portsmouth	52.5	

Source: Ofwat, *Water and Sewerage Bills 1994–95*

use, yet demand-management through pricing is also often viewed with suspicion as a mechanism to enhance further company profits.

The Periodic Review of Prices

In 1994 the Director General of Water Services took the first opportunity available to him to conduct a comprehensive review of water-service prices. Affordability and the willingness of customers to pay higher bills for improved services (including environmental improvements) were important considerations in the review. As early as 1992 it had become clear that the water-price escalator would continue inextricably upwards if customers were expected to pay for the numerous environmental improvements proposed by European and national quality regulators (Ofwat, 1992). Market plans published by the companies in 1993 suggested that average water and sewerage prices would need to increase by 6 per cent per annum (plus inflation) in every year from 1995 to 2000; this national average disguised the fact that in some parts of the country (in the South and South-West, for example) real price rises of 8–10 per cent were projected. Market research conducted for Ofwat and the water companies clearly showed that customers were generally resistant to further price rises and the government came to the view that it would be politically unacceptable to allow price increases to continue to escalate to pay for environmental improvements. 'It is not possible for the improvement of the water environment to have an absolute priority. Improvement must also proceed at a rate which those who have to pay will consider bearable' (Department of the Environment, 1993, p 3). National quality regulators were 'advised' to moderate their demands and not to request improvements in excess of European Union requirements. This political judgement on the importance of affordability has clear relevance for the acceptability of proposals to introduce 'proper' pricing and/or environmental taxation.

The Impact of LRMC Pricing

The magnitude of the price rises which would occur if LRMC principles were used cannot be overstressed. Both the original water price limits established by the government in 1989, and those set during the periodic review, have been calculated using costs which are far below the current cost of replacing water company assets and far below LRMC. In the recent review, for example, the capital base of the companies was set at the average market value of shares during the first 200 days following privatization. It is estimated that these capital values are approximately ten times less than current cost asset values. Moreover, it is now being recognized that the marginal costs of providing new water supplies will increase markedly in the next decade or so because the period of low cost source extraction is now at an end. The impact of shifting water-service prices to reflect the forward-looking costs required for economic efficiency would be dramatic. Even greater price rises would occur if the charges levied on the water companies for raw-water abstraction and sewage-works discharges were based not, as at present, on administrative cost recovery, but on some form of long-run environmental damage or damage-avoidance costs.

It is also relevant to note that moves towards LRMC pricing would act to increase water-utility profits since marginal costs exceed average accounting costs. Profits are already perceived to be unacceptably high as the current debates over a windfall tax on the utilities and a sliding-scale (profit-sharing with customers) price regulation demonstrate. 'Excess' profits could, of course, be removed by taxation and, if the Treasury dropped its traditional objections to the earmarking of revenue, the resulting funds could be employed to ease the impact of the price rises. Grants, for example, could be provided to install in-house and in-factory water-reuse systems or to create hardship funds for low-income households. Additionally, LRMC pricing could be accompanied by regulations requiring companies to 'recycle' profits into lifeline tariffs or into proactive conservation schemes, such as planned water-reuse projects, the development of dual-quality supply systems or the large-scale retrofitting of water-efficient equipment (Rees and Williams, 1993). However, attitudes within government would need to change markedly to allow profit tax hypothecation and the increasingly intrusive regulation of company behaviour.

Metering

It goes without saying that all discussion of 'proper' LRMC pricing remains academic until customers receive a measured supply and are charged on a unit-consumption basis. With any annual charge systems, whether they are linked to rateable values, property tax bands or numbers of residents, customers pay for a service; the marginal unit price for water is zero and there are no incentives to economy. Although the proportion of metered properties has risen steadily over the last five years (7 per cent of households and 75.6 per cent of commercial/industrial concerns are now metered, compared with 2.6 per cent and 66.4 per cent respectively in 1991–1992), it remains the case that 75 per cent of all potable water delivered by the companies is supplied on an unmeasured basis (Water Services Association, 1995).

Any attempt to introduce universal metering would be prohibitively expensive. Internal meter installation into existing properties would cost an estimated £165 per property, the more common external meter some £200, to which must be added additional operating costs of approximately £13 per annum (Ofwat, 1995b). Such costs, which ultimately have to be borne by customers, can only be justified, economically and socially, where metering is the cheapest (in economic and environmental terms) method of maintaining the supply/demand balance. These conditions will apply already in resource short areas where incremental supply costs are high. In addition, there are opportunities to install meters at low cost when new properties are being constructed or where companies are undertaking repair and maintenance work on supply pipes, and further transfers to unit pricing will occur as some customers take up optional metering offers. However, on current predictions, it is highly unlikely that the proportion of metered domestic properties would exceed 25 per cent by the year 2010 and 33 per cent by 2015. Even this level of meter adoption will critically depend on the outcomes of a conflicting set of regulatory, political, social and financial pressures being exerted on the water companies. It is worth noting at this point that, despite its commitment to the use of economic incentives as a means of promoting greater efficiency in water use, the Conservative Government has recently re-endorsed the view that the companies should be responsible for determining the most appropriate charging regimes for their customers, and have rejected making metering schemes mandatory (Department of the Environment, 1995).

Traditionally in Britain, water professionals have opposed metering and there are a significant number of companies with managements who remain unconvinced that cost savings through delayed-capacity construction will result. Some see it as far too risky to rely on metering to balance supply and demand, particularly given the length of time taken to get major capacity-enhancement schemes approved and built; public reaction to shortages in the summer of 1995 have, if anything, strengthened such risk-averse attitudes. Many managers regard metering as an administratively costly charging method, which increases billing complaints, produces a less certain revenue stream and has the 'disadvantage' of allowing customers to pay in arrears. Some companies maintain that their costs are essentially fixed, in which case metering, if it reduces consumption, will merely increase unit costs, while option metering will reduce revenue, as only those likely to benefit financially will opt to be charged on a volume basis. Where such attitudes prevail, only limited progress has been made towards increasing the number of measured properties. There are still companies (Dwr Cymru, Northumbrian, York and Portsmouth, for example) that do not apply measured charges even in new properties (although meter boxes may be installed), and many others have embarked on opportunistic metering only as a result of pressure from the regulators.

Regulatory pressure on the companies to extend metering has been quite intense over the last five years. The National Rivers Authority (from 1 April 1996 part of the Environment Agency) 'supports selective domestic metering with an appropriate tariff, in areas where water resources are stressed... where appropriate consideration has not been given to the introduction of selective metering, the EA will not grant licences for new sources' (NRA, 1992). Although the NRA undoubtedly has considerable bargaining power when new licences are required, the ultimate decision will be political since companies have a right of appeal against licence refusal to the Secretary of State. The Director General of Water Services has also argued the case for selective metering and has made it clear that the companies will need to investigate fully the relative costs and benefits of metering before the need for expenditure on new supplies is accepted as allowable under the price-review process (Ofwat, 1993b). In addition, the companies have been 'encouraged' to adopt more reasonably priced and flexible meter-option schemes and to balance their measured and unmeasured tariffs, so ending the common practice of charging metered customers more for the same service. With the passage of the 1995 Environment Act, a further lever on company behaviour has been introduced through the duty (enforceable by the Director General) to promote the efficient use of water supplied to their customers. However, what this duty will mean in practice remains to be seen; certainly the government makes it clear that 'the duty should not allow water undertakers to impose additional requirements for the efficient use of water on their customers' (DoE, 1995).

On the other hand, company decision-makers are not immune to pressure from a significant and vocal body of opinion that opposes compulsory metering. The reasons for such opposition vary greatly: ideological rejection of rationing by price for essential water services; concern that unit charging will exacerbate water poverty and public health problems; antagonism towards the fact of compulsion involved in metering programmes; arguments that selective and opportunistic metering is unfair since all customers are no longer treated in the same way; and fears that metering will simply increase water prices and monopoly profits. Advocates of metering can and do question the logic of treating water services any differently from essential food, heat and shelter, which are already unit priced. They can also produce evidence indicating that concerns over public health and the welfare of the majority of low-income customers are greatly exaggerated, and it is comparatively simple to show that existing unmeasured charges are also unfair. None of these arguments have done much to change the views of the entrenched opposition to the measure, and fears over health and the impact on socially disadvantaged groups have been given salience as bodies such as the National Consumer Council, the Environmental Health Officers Association and Save the Children (1996) have added their voices to the debate.

The opposition has also been aided by well-publicized cases where large families, and those with medical conditions requiring the use of large quantities of water, have faced major charge increases as a result of metering. Insufficient attention was paid to the incidence effects of metering prior to its introduction. While it is a low-cost option to install meters in new housing, failure to ensure also that such housing is designed for water efficiency creates predictable problems. These were amply demonstrated on a new local authority housing estate in Sheffield which contained a high proportion of low income families with young children: such families had, in practice, very limited opportunities to save water without compromising hygiene standards. Metering became embedded in the debate over water privatization and appeared to vindicate the fears of those who saw private monopoly as incompatible with social responsibility.

Customer and political hostility to metering is very variable spatially. Some companies have been able to proceed with selective programmes with little opposition and indeed with general customer support, but others have felt it necessary to move away from compulsory metering and unit charging of existing customers. This has even been the case for companies in relatively resource-short areas and for those committed to measured charges as the preferred charging method to replace rateable values. Anglian Water, for example, have modified their universal metering plans to avoid compulsion. Meter boxes will continue to be installed, but customers can choose to remain on rateable value (RV) charges and those compulsorily metered in the past can opt not to pay on a measured basis; only when metered properties change hands will measured charges be enforced. Similarly, Mid Southern is installing meter boxes in Alton, but is allowing existing householders to remain on the unmeasured charging system. Yorkshire Water has gone one stage further by announcing its intention to give even the occupiers of a new property a choice over the charging method and will allow all those previously compulsorily metered to revert from measured charges. Other companies, most notably the North West, were also inclined to move away from all forms of compulsory metering, but the drought of 1995–96 has prompted further policy reappraisals.

Both the fact that the drought clearly revealed areas where supply-safety margins were inadequate, and increasing customer resistance to hosepipe bans, have encouraged some companies to bring forward capacity-enhancement plans. Where such plans require new or revised abstraction licences, the views of the NRA have considerable force. Furthermore, evidence is clearly emerging that the upsurge in demand experienced over last summer was heavily associated with higher rateable value properties with relatively large gardens. The potency of metering as a curb on such peak use is demonstrated in Figure 14.1. By comparing metered and unmeasured districts with broadly similar socio-economic and property characteristics, Folkestone and Dover Water Services have shown that unit charging acts to dampen down considerably fluctuations in the peak-to-average use ratio, with peak use less than 20 per cent above the average. By contrast, in unmeasured, relatively affluent properties peak use rose to twice the average; only in unmeasured retirement flats, where clearly there is limited demand for garden watering, was there no surge in peak use.

Since most water infrastructure is designed to meet peak demand, there is considerable force to the argument that unmeasured charging systems benefit the relatively affluent, whose peak use is subsidized by customers

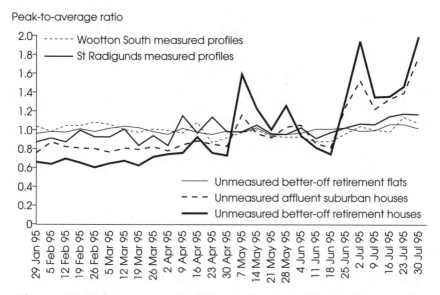

Peak-to-average ratio

Figure 14.1 *Peak to Average Use Ratios: Folkestone and Dover Water Services*

in properties with no or small gardens. Some companies have already announced plans to refocus their compulsory metering programme to target properties with swimming pools – for instance, South-East Water – and to make metering a condition of garden sprinkler use – eg, Severn-Trent. Such targeting not only has the advantage of putting meters into properties where potential water savings are greatest, but it also reduces the political hostility aroused when poor large families are metered compulsorily. However, even these schemes will only prove acceptable to customers where they understand the reality of local resource limits, appreciate the costs involved in capacity-development and transfer schemes and are reasonably convinced that the companies are also playing their part in saving water by minimizing pipeline leakage. These conditions by no means apply in all regions of the country.

Constraints on the Response to Price Signals

Even when households and businesses are metered, there are important informational and financial barriers which can restrict the customer's ability to respond to price signals. Although recent price rises have undoubtedly made industrial and commercial concerns more water aware, studies still suggest that companies frequently lack the economic and technical information necessary to make effective water-conservation decisions. Moreover, some firms are constrained from undertaking major water-saving projects by difficulties in raising the necessary investment funds. Likewise, in domestic properties, there is the legacy of existing water fittings, appliances and hot-water systems, relatively few of which have been designed with water efficiency in mind. Many householders would simply be unable to raise the capital for replacements, even if it was in their long-term financial interests to do so. When new equipment is purchased and new water systems installed, customer choice may still be subject to informational, capital availability and regulatory constraints. Exceptionally few homes, for example, are built to incorporate 'grey water' systems, which allow bath water to be used in toilets, despite the fact that such systems can reduce consumption by up to 30 per cent. Washing-machines that use less water are typically the more expensive brands (*Which?*, January 1996, p 39). Government regulations can also fail to promote water efficiency; the fitting of dual-flush toilets in domestic property has been banned since January 1993; the British Standard WC cistern has a minimum flush volume which effectively excludes from the market lower-use models which are already available overseas. Furthermore, the Water Byelaws, last changed ten years ago, prescribe maximum water-use volumes for appliances well in excess of those employed in the most water-efficient models.

For the most part, the water companies and the government have taken a passive role in ensuring that those in metered premises can respond effectively and speedily to price signals. Indeed, there has been some suggestion that once measured charges are levied, the water companies have little interest in promoting conservation; they increase their revenue by selling water not by encouraging water saving. The Department of the Environment (1995) has conceded that:

> In most circumstances there is no incentive for the companies actively to promote economy in the use of water by, for example, educating non-household customers about the benefits of water saving devices and enabling them to benefit from economy in their use of water.

The new duty to promote water efficiency may lead companies to adopt the more proactive approach to conservation which is now beginning to be employed elsewhere in the world, but much will depend on how this duty is interpreted and enforced.

Several water-supply authorities in the United States have recognized that they have a role 'to show commercial, industrial and institutional customers that increased water efficiency makes good business sense' and to help clear 'the hurdles to implementation' (McGrath and Pinkham, 1990). Such help includes conducting water audits for firms, developing best-practice manuals and providing financial incentives for the installation of water efficient technology. Likewise, efforts have been made, in California and Massachusetts for example, to allow domestic customers to save water through retrofit programmes (toilets and showers are replaced with water-efficient models), conservation advice and appliance inspection services, and water-bill rebates for customers installing low-volume toilets and shower heads (Rees and Williams, 1993; National Rivers Authority, 1995). Such schemes are important not simply because they speed the achievement of water economy objectives, but also because they reduce the social and business costs of shifting water-use behaviour and thus help to 'buy' political acceptability for demand-management.

PRICING RAW-WATER ABSTRACTIONS

The Current Position

Although both the government and the National Rivers Authority have strongly endorsed unit charging by the water companies to promote efficiency and economy, they have been much less ready to ensure that their own abstraction-charging scheme is designed to provide significant incentives for conservation and the efficient allocation of available resources between users. The Department of the Environment acknowledged in 1992 that abstraction charges 'do not bear any relationship to the full costs imposed by particular abstractions, including the costs imposed on the environment' (DoE, 1992, p 24), but the new national charging scheme introduced in April 1993 did not set incentive charges and is unable to fulfil any significant demand-management functions. The reasons for this are not hard to find; it is politically difficult to achieve acceptability for measures which will increase supply costs or water companies, industry and agriculture, will have redistributive effects, and will effectively increase the government's 'tax' take at a time when lessening the 'burden' of government is an important slogan.

As Paul Herrington has pointed out in Chapter 13, the statutory constraints on the NRA are such that they can only recover the costs which have been properly charged to the Water Resources Account. As the Authority has very little funding to invest in major resource projects, this account is dominated by administrative, resource-monitoring, planning and enforcement expenditure, which it is conceded means that 'the water itself is effectively a free good' (National Rivers Authority, 1995, p 49).

What limited potential there is under such a cost-recovery constraint to get some charges up to incentive levels was, however, negated by an NRA Board decision to minimize the shift in the incidence of charges between abstractor classes; political acceptability is as important in raw-water pricing as it is in the treated water sector. The result is that charges are levied on some abstractions which have a negligible impact on resources, so giving less scope for setting unit prices high enough to influence abstractor behaviour in cases where significant resource costs are imposed (Rees et al, 1993). For example, there is little justification for charging abstractors the same unit price irrespective of whether the water comes from a stressed aquifer or from areas where there are problems with rising groundwater levels. Likewise, the use of the same seasonal weighting factor for the whole country fails to take account of the spatially variable impact of summer abstractions. In addition, the practice of using purpose of abstraction as a surrogate for consumptive loss/return flow levels gives no incentive for industrialists or the water companies to reduce the proportion of water 'lost' in the use system or to return waste-water flows to locations where they can contribute to resource availability; they stay in the same charging group irrespective of what they do.

Although the NRA policy of levying charges on authorized volumes (except for a proportion of irrigation water) rather than on actual abstractions is justified theoretically, it reduces conservation incentives under real-world conditions. This arises because many abstractors are unwilling to relinquish or even reduce an authorization. The water companies, for instance, regard a licence as part of their asset portfolio and would certainly not give part of it up without considerable compensation, particularly given uncertainty over the availability of (and conditions attached to) new licences in the future. Therefore, once the availability charge has been paid, the real unit price of raw water becomes zero and no incentives are provided for the introduction of water-efficient practices or increased leakage detection efforts. Similarly, irrigation abstractors are highly unwilling to relinquish licences, since their existence can markedly increase land values – in the most extreme cases by up to 90 per cent where soils are sandy. Although irrigators normally pay half their charges on actual abstractions, such charges in effect only come into force during dry periods when the financial benefits of irrigating far outweigh the marginal costs involved. Under such conditions, the NRA cannot make use of the economic instruments to cope with low-flow conditions; abstractors continue to take suppliers up to their authorizations, irrespective of the impact of their use – until, that is, drought orders can be obtained.

Future Prospects

There is little prospect of any government, however committed to the long-term sustainability of the water environment, agreeing to implement an abstraction-charging scheme which even approximates to the prescriptions for efficiency. If long-run river-flow enhancement costs were employed as the charging base, abstractors in the southern and eastern parts of England would face charges at least 10–20 times higher than at present, and in some areas an increase approaching 100-fold would be likely. Given the high proportion of resource-relevant abstractions accounted for by the water companies, they would bear the brunt of such increases. However, the situation becomes complicated by the relationship between the NRA and the water companies in the development, ownership and control of flow-management assets. Water-resource management is often achieved through the indirect use of physical capital assets owned by the private companies. Most, but not all, new flow-enhancement schemes take the form of joint ventures between the NRA and the companies; in effect, other abstractors and increased flows in the rivers themselves are able to 'ride on the back' of projects funded primarily for public water-supply purposes. In principle, it would be possible to institute a market-like arrangement whereby the NRA used its abstraction charges to pay the companies for the use of their flow-regulation assets, or alternatively, the NRA could own and manage the assets, so in effect becoming a bulk supply authority. The practical and political difficulties involved in such scenarios are not, however, trivial.

What is certain is that moves to long-run full-cost pricing for raw water would markedly increase costs for many of the supply companies. Under present regulatory conditions, the Director General of Water Services would have little option but to allow at least a significant proportion of these costs to be reflected in future treated water prices. In other words, all the problems of public acceptability and affordability discussed earlier apply with equal force for debates over optimum abstraction charges.

Industrial and agricultural abstractors would also not passively accept the prospect of major rises in raw-water prices, which could have a significant impact on their financial viability and competitiveness. Most available evidence suggests that industrial demands for raw water are relatively inelastic in the short-to-medium term. While it is undoubtedly the case that these results are partially explained by the typically low abstraction charges, it cannot be assumed that prices set at incentive levels would automatically cause demands to be elastic. Short-run elasticities for mains water are also relatively low and, of course, treated water prices are not trivial. There are many explanations for constrained response. Most obviously, firms have a massive stock of investment capital tied up in plant and equipment, designed and employed on the basis of low-cost water. Small and medium-sized firms (SMEs), in particular, have constraints imposed by the cost and limited availability of investment capital, and many firms have poor information about water-saving opportunities and the costs involved.

Although some measures may be taken to reduce obvious water wastage in the short run, major investments in water-efficient technologies will normally only take place when plant and equipment are being replaced or modified to meet new product specifications, to improve energy efficiency or to comply with waste disposal or safety regulations. This being the case, many firms need not suffer long-term financial disbenefits as a result of increased abstraction charges, although clearly, running costs will rise before economies in use are made. From a politically pragmatic point of view, it is relevant to note that the marginal cost of achieving water savings varies greatly between individual firms and across industry groups. This means that there will be incidence effects associated with any raw-water price rises; who the losers are and how influential they are will inevitably have an input into political decision processes. In addition, the acceptability of 'proper' pricing will be affected by the speed with which price increases are phased in and by the package of measures introduced to ameliorate both the short-run cost rises and the incidence effects. If charge hypothecation is allowed, it would be possible to link the introduction of incentive prices with redistributive charges, loans or grants and to help overcome the information constraints by providing water auditing and technical advice services. In other words, the regulator could adopt a more proactive approach to resource management rather than simply allowing market forces, with all their imperfections, to rule.

Herrington is undoubtedly correct in pointing out the difficulties some farming communities would experience following the introduction of the 'efficient' pricing of irrigation water. There is now a body of evidence which suggests that even at current water-price levels, a signficant proportion (between 30–50 per cent) of irrigated agriculture is not a profitable activity over the long term, when the real opportunity costs of capital invested in equipment and storage facilities are taken into account (Hinton and Varvarigos, 1990; Rees *et al*, 1993). On the other hand, in the Anglian region where irrigators are clustered, irrigation demand has been increasing by 4 per cent per annum and is projected to account for 34 per cent of the regions' additional water requirements by the year 2021. Much of the increased demand is for the intensive production of soft fruit and vegetables, where returns to irrigation are high and where it is increasingly common for supermarkets and food processors to require irrigation to allow quality specifications to be met. The economically logical thing to do would be to meet this demand growth by reallocating available water resources from currently uneconomic irrigators.

Such a reallocation theoretically could be achieved by incentive pricing, but there is no guarantee that farmer response would occur at the required speed. Given the sunk nature of investment costs and the negligible resale value of irrigation equipment, the short-term response to pricing might be limited, particularly as irrigation is used for non-profit maximizing reasons – namely, the reduction of risk and uncertainty. It is also important that under current licensing arrangements, farmers have an incentive to hold on to a 'permanent' licence even if they have abandoned irrigated agriculture; in other words, the licensed quantity is not available for reallocation. This arises because the existence of a licence enhances land values. Somewhat ironically, the more discussion there is of future water scarcity and the effects of global warming, the greater the perceived value of the licence itself.

Under these conditions it may well be the case that tradable permits could be a more appropriate reallocative instrument. Permits impose no costs on existing abstractors – indeed, they are given a potentially valuable *de facto* property right, which they can sell if it is profitable to do so. This feature is not only likely to increase the political acceptability of resource reallocation, but it also reduces the immediate social costs involved and certainly distances the 'government' from blame as the distributive consequences of reallocation emerge over time. As an environmental regulator, however, the NRA will need to be circumspect in its use of trading. Changes in the point of abstraction and any transfers of supplies between catchments could have significant environmental implications. Trades could exacerbate scarcity problems if under-utilized licences are sold; the reallocation of supplies from uses with high-return flow rates to consumptive purposes will reduce resource availabilities; transfers to more intensive forms of agriculture could compound the problems of pollution from fertilizers and pesticides; and, finally, marketable permits yield no revenue for the resource manager. This last point is important because, without a significant revenue source, any flow-enhancement projects, regulatory monitoring and advisory services or public-education programmes will be subject to the financial restrictions and uncertainties inherent in the annual public expenditure round.

CONCLUSION

A Resource Management Package

The government has 'identified the need for adequate water resources to meet consumers' needs, and managing and meeting demand for water, as key areas for environmental sustainability in the United Kingdom over the next 20 years' (Department of the Environment, 1994). While the environmentally aware will probably associate such statements with demand-management strategies, it would certainly not be evident to many of the general public why there is a need to focus attention on *controlling* their consumption rather than *meeting* their requirements. Britain as a whole is relatively well endowed with water resources. More storage and transfer schemes could be constructed to even out supply-and-demand imbalances; much greater levels of reuse are possible since relatively little water is consumed by use; and desalination remains the ultimate technofix option. From a simple supply-availability perspective, a renewable and reusable resource like water is not physically scarce. More can be supplied at a price, with this price being payable in direct-provision cost terms and through environmental change. Whether this price should be paid and, if so, by whom are, of course, quite different matters.

For many water customers the message of scarcity is a denial of their perception of plenty (with floods and water flowing 'wastefully' to sea) and their knowledge of technical possibilities; if needs cannot be met, water undertakers have not done enough to invest in additional supplies and to reduce pipeline leakage. Following privatization, this line of argument ends with monopolists putting profits before customers and matters become complicated by ideology, political point scoring and ethical arguments about water as a universal service (Ernst, 1994).

The process of water commodification only began in 1973 following the creation of the Regional Water Authorities and the removal of public subsidies. Were 'proper' prices to be introduced in the near future, a truly remarkable transformation would have occurred from water as an essential service, with costs recouped from those who are most able to pay, to water as a commodity available only to the extent that people are willing and able to pay the full costs (including environmental costs) involved. Indeed, it is the very speed of this change which makes it extremely doubtful whether the introduction of fully efficient pricing could be sustained economically, socially or politically. The short-run costs of the change, the extent of the welfare redistributions involved and the highly complex regulatory issues raised by private monopoly involvement in collecting resource depletion or sustainable development 'taxes' must all play important roles in determining public and political acceptability.

This does not mean that economic instruments can have no role to play in shifting water-using behaviour into more economically and environmentally sustainable forms, but that their introduction will need to be phased in and they will need to be accompanied by a package of measures designed to ameliorate socially and politically unacceptable impacts. The package could include:

- *Direct regulations*, building regulations, water by-laws, mandatory standards for water fittings and consumer durables – such measures would all help customers to respond to price and limit the effect of the price rises on bills.
- *Planning measures*, which are designed over the long term to minimize the scope for pipeline leakage, reduce supply pipe pressures, enable sequential water reuse and limit increases in water demand in high-cost or environmentally sensitive areas.
- *Subsidies*, the use of grants, loans or charge rebates to ease the capital availability constraints on investments in water-efficient

technologies.
- *Welfare payments;* the affordability problems for poor, large families are already acute; increased benefit payments and/or lifeline tariffs would be needed to ameliorate such problems.
- *Compensation payments,* which are designed to 'bribe' existing abstraction licence holders to trade in their authorizations; these could occur within the context of a marketable permit system.
- *Auditing and information services* to overcome the considerable informational barriers to price response.
- *Retrofitting incentives or requirements* to promote the use of water-efficient fittings in existing property.
- *The adaptation of price-control regulation* to redistribute the profits from LRMC pricing to ameliorate water poverty and help customers to reduce their bills by saving water, and to give companies incentives to conserve rather than to sell water.

The above list is by no means definitive and many of the measures are politically contentious, particularly given the government's concerns to reduce the burdens of regulation, curb public expenditure and allow market forces to rule. In 1992 the consultation document 'Using Water Wisely' was published, in which a whole range of 'practical ways of making efficient use of water resources' was mooted. After protracted consideration of the results of consultation, in 1995 the government set out its policy with a list of actions and, just as important, non-decisions (DoE, 1995). This document clearly demonstrates the tensions between a commitment to sustainable development and a reluctance to increase regulation over private sector concerns. Statements abound about what the government has decided not to do – it 'does not at present propose to set mandatory leakage targets', 'does not intend to provide financial support for the installation of showers in existing property' or 'to make grants available to replace existing WCs'. Instead, there is much reliance on encouraging manufacturers to provide information about water consumption, on allowing customers and companies to decide whether recycling or leakage control is an economic proposition and on issuing guidance to local authorities and housing associations on water-efficient housing.

All policy decisions result from complex trade-offs between incompatible goals and interests; water resources policy is no exception. Sustainable resource development could undoubtedly be achieved through efficient pricing and market forces; but for them to play such a role, it is necessary to confront now the very real social, political and institutional barriers to change.

REFERENCES

Bromley, D W (1991) *Environment and Economy: Property Rights and Public Policy,* Basil Blackwell, Oxford

Department of the Environmental/Welsh Office (1992) *Using Water Wisely – A Consultation Paper,* Department of the Environment, London

Department of the Environment/Welsh Office (1993) *Water Charges: The Quality Framework*, Department of the Environment, London

Department of the Environment (1994) *Sustainable Development – the UK Strategy*, Cm2426, HMSO, London

Department of the Environment/Welsh Office (1995) *Water Conservation, Government Action*, Department of the Environment, London

Ernst, J (1994) *Whose Utility? The Social Impact of Public Utility Privatization*, Open University Press, Milton Keynes

Folkestone and Dover Water Service (1995) *The Impact of Metering on Peak Water Use*, Folkestone and Dover Water Service, Dover. Reprinted in the Ofwat Annual Report 1995/96

Hinton, L and Varvarigos, P (1990) *Observations on the economic performance of irrigation*, Agricultural Economics Unit, Dept of Land Economy, University of Cambridge, Cambridge

Hirshleifer, J, De Haven J P, and Milliman, J W (1960) *Water Supply: Economics, Technology and Policy*, University of Chicago Press, Chicago

McGrath, L and Pinkham, M (1990) 'Demand management for industry: clearing the hurdles to implementation', *Annual Conference Proceedings*, American Water Works Association, Washington, DC

National Rivers Authority (1992) *Managing the Drought and Water Resources*, Board Statement, National Rivers Authority, Bristol

National Rivers Authority (1995) *Saving Water: the NRA's approach to water conservation and demand management*, National Rivers Authority, Bristol

Ofwat (1992) *The cost of quality: a strategic assessment of the prospects for future water bills*, Office of Water Services, Birmingham

Ofwat (1993a) *Paying for quality: the political perspective*, Office of Water Services, Birmingham

Ofwat (1993b) *Paying for growth*, Office of Water Services, Birmingham

Ofwat (1995a) *1994–5 Report on levels of service for the water industry in England and Wales*, Office of Water Services, Birmingham

Ofwat (1995b) *1995–6 Report on tariff structure and charges*, Office of Water Services, Birmingham

Rees, J *et al* (1993, publically released 1995) *Economics of Water Resources Management*, Technical Report PR/248/4/A, and R&D Note 128, National Rivers Authority, Bristol

Rees, J and Williams, S (1993) *Water for life: strategies for sustainable water resources management*, Council for the Protection of Rural England, London

Save the Children (1995) *The impact of water metering on low-income families*, Save the Children, London

Water Services Association (1995) *Waterfacts 1995*, Water Services Association, London

Chapter 15

THE UK LANDFILL TAX

Jane Powell and Amelia Craighill

EMERGENCE OF THE LANDFILL TAX

In the early 1990s, the UK Government committed itself to encouraging waste minimization, promoting recycling and energy recovery from waste, increasing standards for waste disposal and reducing litter (Environmental Protection Act (EPA), 1990; HM Government, 1990). Integrated Pollution Control (IPC) was to be used to promote waste minimization and a recycling target was set requiring 25 per cent of household waste to be recycled by the year 2000 (50 per cent of the estimated 50 per cent recyclable content of household waste). This policy was nominally given added impetus by the broad commitment of local authorities to Local Agenda 21. In the context of sustainable waste management, Local Agenda 21 called upon local authorities to decrease their dependence on landfill disposal of waste, and to prioritise the reduction of consumption, followed by minimizing the generation of waste, reuse, recycling, recovery of energy, and finally disposal to properly engineered landfills.

A recycling credit scheme was also introduced in April 1992, whereby waste-disposal authorities are obliged to pass on savings in landfill costs to collection authorities, from the collection of household waste for recycling (Turner and Brisson, 1995). The intention of these measures was to move waste disposal up the waste hierarchy, thus supporting sustainable waste management. By increasing the cost of landfill disposal relative to waste minimization and recycling, the latter would become more financially viable. However, the government was aware that such regulatory measures alone could not tip the balance. On the recommendation of the Advisory Committee on Business and the Environment (ACBE), the government initi-

BOX 15.1 THE WASTE MANAGEMENT HIERARCHY

1. Reduction	Reducing the production of waste to the minimum consistent with economic sustainability.
2. Reuse	Putting objects back into use – for example, reusing glass bottles.
3. Recovery	*Recycling:* putting materials back into use – for example, reusing the glass from bottles. *Composting:* processing organic waste to produce a soil conditioner or growing medium. *Energy:* burning waste and recovering the energy, or collecting methane from the decomposition of waste in landfill sites.
4. Disposal	Incineration or landfill without energy recovery. The emphasis must be on ensuring that disposal is environmentally sound.

Source: Department of the Environment, 1995

ated research into landfill pricing and the use of economic instruments (Turner and Brisson, 1995).

To this end, Environmental Resources Ltd were commissioned to examine a range of economic instruments, including raw material and product charges, deposit/refund schemes, waste collection and disposal charges, tradable recycling targets, taxes and subsidies. The report concluded that economic instruments, particularly the collection of disposal charges, would be an efficient means by which to internalize the externalities of waste disposal, and reduce the amount of waste going to landfill through increased recycling and/or waste minimization (Environmental Resources Limited, 1992).

A second report (Coopers and Lybrand, 1993) focused on the present and likely future costs of waste disposal, and identified the main factors affecting the choice of disposal route. It also developed and evaluated options for a landfill tax and its potential consequences. Coopers and Lybrand concluded that a tax could be justified as it would reflect the wider environmental costs of landfill, would promote recycling and waste minimization, and would bring UK landfill costs into line with those of other EU countries. A weight-based tax was deemed to be the most practical, simple and equitable option.

Coopers and Lybrand also identified possible impacts of the tax, which included an increase in landfill costs of 37 per cent – 135 per cent by the year 2000 (to £11–£47/tonne) due to tighter planning controls, a reduction in waste-requiring disposal, and fewer competitors after the forcing out of smaller operators. They also considered that incineration would stabilize at £20–£25/tonne, becoming more competitive compared with landfill. In the short term, Coopers and Lybrand thought that the quantity of waste going to landfill was unlikely to be significantly affected, although in the longer term there was likely to be a shift towards incineration. Even if a tax was set at £20/tonne it was expected to have little effect on recycling, which was only anticipated to reach 12 per cent by the year 2000.

Following on from this research, the Centre for Social and Economic Research on the Global Environment (CSERGE), Warren Spring Laboratory and Economics for the Environment Consultancy (EFTEC) were commissioned to investigate and quantify the externalities of landfill and incineration (CSERGE *et al*, 1993). They were required to provide an economic valuation of the externalities and to discuss how these values relate to the proposed landfill tax. The externalities identified were disamenity effects, air emissions that contribute to global warming, conventional air pollutants (SOx , NOx, particulates), airborne toxic substances from incinerators, leachate from landfill sites, and pollution and accidents associated with road transport. In terms of external benefits, displaced pollution was included in the valuation. This occurs when the energy recovered from waste displaces energy generated by coal (the least efficient type of electricity-generating power stations) and thus also displaces the associated gaseous emissions.

The CSERGE report (CSERGE *et al*, 1993) distinguishes between variable and fixed externalities. Variable externalities, such as gaseous emissions, can be related directly to the quantity of waste disposed – eg, carbon-dioxide emissions per tonne of waste incinerated – while fixed externalities, although broadly affected by the quantity of waste involved, are more influenced by the existence of a waste facility – eg, the smell from a landfill site. Owing to time and data constraints, CSERGE were unable to value the respective disamenities of landfill and incineration and thus concentrated on the variable externalities. If disamenity effects could have been ascertained, their value could be added to the landfill tax, and an incineration tax could also be applied. An incineration tax is considered unlikely, however, as strict emission standards may mean that some of the existing incinerators will have to close down, and planning controls and public opposition hinder the construction of new plants (Turner and Brisson, 1995). The CSERGE report concludes that the external cost of landfill sites with energy recovery is £1–£2/tonne, and without energy recovery £3.5–£4.2/tonne, and that new incinerators have net external benefits of £2–£4/tonne. This gives a difference of £3–£8/tonne, broadly consistent with a landfill tax of £5–£8/tonne (CSERGE *et al*, 1993).

CONSULTATION

The proposal to introduce a new tax on waste disposed to landfill was announced in the Budget of November 1994. To take effect in 1996, the new tax is to be collected by HM Customs & Excise. In March 1995 detailed proposals for the landfill tax were unveiled and a consultation paper released. Unusually, the widely distributed landfill-tax consultation paper gave the waste industry, user groups, environmental organizations and other interested parties the opportunity to comment on and shape the new tax.

The stated objectives of the new landfill tax are:

- To ensure that landfill waste disposal is properly priced, which will promote greater efficiency in the waste-management market and in the economy as a whole; and
- To apply the 'polluter-pays' principle and promote a more sustainable approach to waste management in which we produce less waste, and reuse or recover value from more waste.

(HM Customs & Excise, 1995a)

The overall aim of the new tax is to increase the proportion of waste managed by the techniques towards the top of the hierarchy of waste-management options. The tax also demonstrates the government's commitment to using economic instruments as a means of achieving environmental objectives (HM Customs & Excise, 1995a). It represents a first move by the government to transfer taxation away from labour and profits to pollution and resource use.

The initial proposal outlined in the consultation paper was for an *ad valorem* tax of between 30 and 50 per cent on the disposal price paid, to be applied from 1 October 1996. An *ad valorem* tax was recommended on the basis that it would provide a straightforward proxy for the environmental impacts of landfill disposal. By charging in proportion to the costs of land-fill disposal, the argument followed that it would result in a higher tax for more 'difficult' wastes, which are more expensive to dispose of (and lower for inert waste), and higher where land is scarcest and the impact on communities is greatest. The compliance costs of an *ad valorem* tax were also considered to be lower than a weight-based tax, and evasion easier to detect (HM Customs & Excise, 1995a). Based on an estimate of 100 million tonnes of waste disposed to landfill in England and Wales each year at a cost of £10/tonne, an *ad valorem* tax rate of 50 per cent would raise £500 million, while a 30 per cent tax rate would raise £300 million per year.

The reasons given for HM Customs & Excise to take responsibility for the tax are their experience with indirect taxes and their existing links with the industry via VAT (Romanski, 1995). As the tax is not intended to impose additional costs on business overall, the government proposes to use the income to offset the impact of the new tax by making reductions in employers' National Insurance Contributions (to be applied to all businesses, not just those dealing with waste) (HM Customs & Excise, 1995a). The landfill tax would pay for a 0.2 per cent cut in National Insurance Contributions (ENDS 242, 1995), possibly aimed at the lower end of the salary scale (Romanski, 1995). There would also be the potential for landfill operators to obtain tax rebates by making payments to the proposed 'Environmental Trusts'.

Environmental Trusts

As the levy on landfill disposal is to be applied in the form of a tax, and collected by HM Customs & Excise, it cannot be hypothecated according to Treasury rules. By way of a compromise, environmental trusts form part of the proposal (HM Customs & Excise, 1995a), to be funded by voluntary payments from landfill site operators, who would receive a 90 per cent tax rebate, but would have to contribute the remaining 10 per cent themselves.

The environmental trusts are intended as 'private sector', non-profit making, distributing bodies, administered by trustees. They will be responsible for the disbursement of the funds to approved areas, such as the restoration of old landfill sites where the liability for the site is unclear, and research and development of more sustainable waste-management techniques, especially involving those at the higher end of the waste hierarchy. The trusts are to be constituted so that the disbursement of funds is not controlled or influenced by those making payments to the trusts (HM Customs & Excise, 1995b). The rebate for contributions to trusts will be limited to £90 million per year (Dudding, 1995).

RESPONSE TO THE CONSULTATION PAPER

HM Customs & Excise issued 6,500 copies of the landfill consultation paper and received 720 responses (HM Customs & Excise, 1995c). The majority of the replies generally supported the introduction of a landfill tax, with CSERGE (1995) commenting that it provided a 'double dividend' in terms of environmental controls and reductions in other forms of taxation which reduce the incentive to work and enterprise. The Building Employers Confederation (1995), however, had 'profound misgivings' and some members of the waste industry saw no technological, financial or moral justification as to why landfill is 'bad' (Confederation of British Industry (CBI), 1995). The CBI also object to the tax on the grounds of reduced competitiveness (CBI, 1995).

Although initially intended to provide a means of internalizing the externalities arising from landfill disposal, it has also been argued that the government has since abandoned any pretence of doing this with any precision (ENDS No 242, 1995). Instead, the tax is being seen now as more of a revenue-raising exercise. Friends of the Earth, although supporting the shift of tax from labour, capital and profits on to pollution and waste, view work on assessing externalities as flawed. Although they accept that market instruments have a place in regulating the market, they do not consider that they should be used to internalize externalities (Stupples, 1995).

The waste-management company Biffa Waste Services recently commissioned a MORI poll into awareness and opinions regarding the landfill tax among local authorities and industry (Biffa, 1995). The results indicated that current awareness of the landfill tax and its consequences is low among private companies (26 per cent of environmental managers were aware), but local authorities are much better informed (95 per cent of chief environmental officers). The main concern of the respondents in this poll, and of those who responded directly to the consultation paper, was the introduction of an *ad valorem* tax.

Ad Valorem versus Weight-Based Landfill Tax

The *ad valorem* tax came up against much opposition, with most landfill businesses favouring a weight-based tax on environmental, revenue-raising and administrative grounds (HM Customs & Excise, 1995b). Supporters of a weight-based tax include the Government's Advisory Committee on Business and the Environment (ACBE); Royal Commission on Environmental Pollution; Confederation of British Industry (CBI); Engineering Employers Federation (EEF); Construction Industry Council; National Association of Waste Disposal Contractors (NAWDC); waste-management businesses; Local Authority Recycling Advisory Committee (LARAC); the Centre for Social and Economic Research on the Global Environment (CSERGE, 1995); and Friends of the Earth (FoE) (ENDS No 246, 1995). CSERGE (1995) considers that *ad valorem* charges do not reflect properly landfill externalities, and the tax is explicitly stated to serve this purpose. The Building Employers Confederation are one of the few organizations that support the *ad valorem* tax. This is because construction waste currently is accepted free or at a low fee at landfill sites where it is used for the construction of access roads and as a cover material.

Numerous problems with the *ad valorem* system have been identified, including an increase in the price differentials between sites and the diversion of wastes away from engineered sites towards the cheaper sites which have less environmental engineering measures (ACBE, 1995a; Construction Industry Council (CIC), 1995; UK Waste, 1995). An *ad valorem* landfill tax would also act to increase the existing price differentials between sites, particularly as VAT is to be levied on the tax in addition to the disposal price. This would penalize expensive sites which have higher environmental standards, thus increasing the potential for environmental pollution and encouraging the transport of wastes over long distances (ACBE, 1995a; CIC, 1995). This has been acknowledged by HM Customs & Excise (Romanski, 1995).

The movement of wastes to cheaper sites would also act directly against government policy to raise landfill standards and promote regional self-sufficiency in waste disposal (UK Waste, 1995), and also would reduce revenues to the Treasury. Furthermore, if hazardous wastes are attracted to cheaper co-disposal sites, their operators will require more household waste for its attenuating properties, and may have to be prepared to reduce prices charged for household waste (ENDS No 242, 1995).

A weight-based tax would result in lower price differentials, the revenue would be more predictable, and, with calibrated weighbridges, there would be less scope for fraud and evasion (UK Waste, 1995). However, HM Customs & Excise (1995) believe that verifying a weight-based tax would be more difficult than an *ad valorem* tax. Many organizations, including the Royal Commission on Environmental Pollution and the Association of County Councils, maintain that the likelihood of evasion, even with a weight-based tax, is high (Biffa, 1995).

It is difficult to gauge exactly how high this likelihood is. There is fairly comprehensive legislation in place to prevent disposal at other than regulated landfill sites, although this does not entirely prevent fly-tipping from occurring. With an *ad valorem* tax, there would be a possibility that waste would be disposed of illegally at lower price-banded sites, or into sites which are not licensed to receive the higher price-banded wastes (Hewitt, 1995). The latter problems are avoided with the weight-based tax, although waste-disposal methods will need to be adequately policed after the imposition of the tax. Hewitt (1995) considers that the tax should not be seen as a substitute for regulation and enforcement, and that the new Environment Agency will have a vital role to play in ensuring that regulation is applied effectively and fairly.

One objection to a weight-based tax is the current lack of weighbridges at landfill sites. About 500 will be required (out of 4000 landfills), at a cost of £20,000 each (HM Customs & Excise, 1995). The waste industry considers that the cost of providing weighbridges is not significant (ACBE, 1995b), and the Construction Industry Council point out that small operators with no weighbridge could either use public weighbridges or measure waste by volume and then use pre-set conversion rates to convert it to tonnages (CIC, 1995). Biffa (1995) consider that operators who cannot afford to invest in a weighbridge would have limited capacity to meet their environmental responsibilities, and that mergers of small waste-management companies into larger ones would be environmentally beneficial.

Furthermore, the installation of weighbridges would help to prevent fraud and further the much-needed collation of waste statistics in the UK, which has been a government policy for many years (UK Waste, 1995). It is a requirement under the Waste Management Licensing Regulations (1994) 'to provide and use weighing facilities or use equivalent measurement systems'. This data collation would also be useful for statistics linked to the UK returns for the European Environment Agency. The weight-based tax would also avoid the loss of revenue likely when charges are shifted towards collection and transport in operators with composite bills (UK Waste, 1995).

Although a uniform tax would keep the administrative costs down, it would not provide an incentive to improve standards or reduce environmental impacts (Brisson, 1994). UK Waste (1995) claims that inadequate regulation is damaging the business of high-standard landfills, and they want waste regulation authorities to review licences held by older landfills. They hope for an allowance under the landfill tax for better sites and suggest a banded tax which would reflect the level of environmental protection (UK Waste, 1995). However, this would be difficult to devise and administer. What would happen if, for example, a usually good site had a leak, and why should a complex, engineered site have a tax advantage over a more simply engineered one, if the geology of the latter does not require it (ENDS No 242, 1995)?

An alternative is a banded weight based tax which relates to the type of waste. The construction industry strongly recommends a system of two tax bands, while other organizations (ACBE, CIC, LARAC and CBI) support a three-band system, the highest tax rate being applied to special or hazardous wastes. LARAC suggest that a third tax rate would have given more incentive for the treatment and reduction of special waste (Cooper LARAC, personal communication). All propose a lower rate for inert waste on the grounds that its disposal produces far less externalities than from non-inert waste (ACBE, 1995a; Cooper (LARAC), personal communication). Inert waste could attract a lower tax under a weight-based banded tax than an *ad valorem* tax, although this may not always be the case.

Alternatively, a high tax on the landfill disposal of construction and demolition waste should reduce the demand for primary materials, the mining of which often causes considerable environmental damage. If there is a single tax-band, large construction firms would tend to move inert material between projects and use it for landscaping (leading to the large-scale storage and transport of soil and rubble). Smaller firms would have to bear the tax or fly tip (Building Employers Confederation, 1995).

It is recognized that some industrial groups have made considerable progress in developing recycling and it is considered counter-productive to impose an unfair burden of tax on recycling residues (ACBE, 1995a). The British Metals Federation and the British Secondary Metals Association are seeking exemptions for wastes arising from recycling (ENDS No 246, 1995), and the Energy from Waste Association has asked for exemption from incinerator ash on the grounds that it comes from using waste further up the waste-disposal hierarchy (Biffa, 1995). CIC believes that in-house disposal sites should be excluded from the proposed landfill tax (CIC, 1995).

In order to achieve the necessary shift in the economics of waste-management options, ACBE (1995a) propose an average £8/tonne tax rising to £12/tonne. LARAC suggests a doubling of the tax rates after two years and FoE want the tax set at £30/tonne to provide a strong incentive to recycling. There is concern that a low level of tax would simply be 'lost' in a discounting process by landfill operators, and that movement up the waste-management hierarchy will only be achieved if the level of tax is significant and is progressively increased (Hewitt, 1995).

Environmental Trusts

Most respondents, such as ACBE and the CBI, agree with the principle of environmental trusts, but many question their purpose and structure, and whether there will be sufficient support for them – for instance, Stupples, 1995; Wiseman and Garlick, 1995. The Construction Industry Council (1995) does not support small, locally based environmental trusts because of the problems concerning the administration and supervision of the funds raised. However, UK Waste (1995) specifically recommended that the trust funds should be used to support local projects in the area of the contributing landfills.

There are a significant number of organizations which have expressed doubts about the environmental trusts, and call for more information about their accountability (Royal Commission on Environmental Pollution) or even see them as a 'dubious complication' (West Yorkshire Waste Management; Biffa, 1995). Among those organizations which do support them, there is some dislike of the idea of a clean-up fund for abandoned sites, as it would appear to be providing a subsidy for those who have walked away from their liabilities (Stupples, 1995). It is considered that the fund should only apply to sites 'orphaned' before the tax comes into force, and for research and development into new waste-management practices (ACBE, 1995a; UK Waste, 1995).

There are bound to be conflicting suggestions concerning how revenue raised by an environmental tax should be used. From the perspective of the Treasury, the most simple way is to absorb it into central funds, and allow it to feed through into lower general taxes, lower net borrowing, or both

(Spackman, 1995); see also Chapter 3 of this volume. However, there are pressures to use the revenue to finance environmental protection. The Treasury argue that this case is not a strong one, because any measures worth taking would have been *more* worthwhile before the tax, which is itself designed to reduce environmental impacts. The main advantage for some kind of hypothecation, as is argued by Michael Spackman in Chapter 3, lies in increasing the acceptability of the tax.

Nevertheless, there is considerable support for part of the funds raised to be paid into a central pool to be spent on the development of waste-management areas at the higher end of the waste hierarchy. Areas of particular interest were the promotion of waste minimization (ACBE), investments in recycling and reuse infrastructure, the promotion of environmental purchasing (Recycling Advisory Group), and for general education, training and public awareness (ACBE, 1995a). This could be administered by the new Environment Agency (by whom the Department of the Environment originally favoured the tax to be collected). Finally, there is concern that the 90 per cent rebate will not encourage enough payments to the trusts, and a 100 per cent rebate is proposed by NAWDC (ENDS No 246, 1995) and FoE (Stupples, 1995).

The CBI argue that reducing National Insurance Contributions could favour labour-intensive industries at the expense of others, such as the chemical industry, and they emphasize the need to ensure that the overall tax burden on businesses is not increased (CBI, 1995). There is also doubt that the reduction in employers' National Insurance Contributions will significantly reduce the landfill tax burden on small businesses (Wiseman and Garlick, 1995; CIC, 1995). HM Customs & Excise (1995c) report that 70 per cent of respondents to the consultation paper did not favour the link between the landfill tax and the reduction in National Insurance Contributions, many preferring instead that the money be used more directly to further the environmental aims of the tax. However, many of these respondents are large producers of wastes, and are likely to be net losers. More general businesses, and trade associations, including the CBI, support the proposal (HM Customs & Excise, 1995c).

The MORI poll conducted for Biffa (1995) found that those contacted considered that the landfill tax will make many companies worse off financially. Both companies and local authorities indicate that they will increase the cost of their products and services to make up the shortfall. Increased recycling was also cited by both groups. Industry also mentioned waste reduction and treatment, and local authorities intend to increase council tax and to look to central government for help (Biffa, 1995).

Jenkinson (1995) comments that the landfill tax will impose a heavy burden on local authorities in the UK, of an additional £54 million to £90 million per year (at tax rates of 30 per cent and 50 per cent respectively). As council tax only generates about 20 per cent of local authority income, the extra expenditure has serious implications for their spending profiles (Jenkinson, 1995). If no rebates are given to account for the landfill tax, then savings will have to be made in other areas of an already overstretched budget. The reduction in National Insurance Contributions will go some way to offset the financial burden of the landfill tax, but will not completely outweigh it. Finally, it is argued that most recycling schemes cost more to operate than they attract in revenue or waste-disposal savings (Jenkinson, 1995), and that it would be appropriate for central government to provide some assistance in this area.

Problems with Composite Bills

Currently, there may be a very low or no landfill charge where the landfill operator and user are the same, such as a power-generating company or a local authority (UK Waste, 1995; Wiseman and Garlick, 1995). Alternatively, composite bills may arise, when waste-disposal contracts include the collection and transport of waste in addition to disposal. In these cases, it has been suggested that landfill disposal could have an 'open market value' set by law, based on the average cost of landfill in the UK. This would entail additional compliance costs in calculating the charge and in maintaining records to demonstrate that the apportionment of the charge is reasonable (HM Customs & Excise, 1995). However, this system could distort wide regional variations and thus would not be equitable (CBI, 1995). Another alternative would be to have different 'open market values' for different regions, or different types of waste sites (ENDS No 242, 1995).

However, the results of 'open market prices' are unpredictable (CBI, 1995), as landfill businesses could change their pricing policies to take maximum advantage of the situation with regard to a separate landfill disposal fee or an overall charge with collection and transport. A further problem occurs when void space is paid for in advance, usually charged at a lower rate. This could result in lower landfill tax revenues (UK Waste, 1995). A weight-based system would avoid these problems as the tax would be linked to the weighbridge ticket which would form part of the waste-management audit trail (ACBE, 1995a).

Other Problems with a Landfill Tax in Principle

There is some question as to whether the landfill tax will really lead to significant increases in recycling and waste minimization (Brisson, 1994). According to Coopers and Lybrand (1993), even a £20/tonne tax would lead to only 12 per cent recycling, but there would be a greater swing to incineration. However, this was disputed by the DoE which considers that there will be greater diversion to the options higher up the waste hierarchy, particularly for industrial and commercial wastes that are cheaper to recycle than household waste (Turner and Brisson, 1995). In the MORI poll commissioned by Biffa (1995) 20 per cent of environmental managers and local authorities thought they would increase recycling in response to the landfill tax, and 16 per cent of companies thought they would reduce waste production. Certainly the prospect of the landfill tax, plus the considerable recent increase in the value of waste paper, has stimulated paper recycling, particularly for good-quality office paper. Recycling of other materials could be boosted if recycling projects were subsidized by tax revenues, which is still a possibility with funds from the environmental trusts (UK Waste, 1995).

However, favouring recycling over landfill does nothing to develop the essential markets needed for successfully completing the cycle and creating demand for recycled materials. Also, even if the landfill tax is passed on in higher council tax bills, householders will have no real incentive to reduce the amount they generate, as there is no marginal pricing of waste. It is considered important that regulations allow the tax to be passed back down the contractual chain to the waste producer. Ensuring that the tax is itemized on invoices would increase the awareness of the waste producer (ACBE, 1995a; CBI, 1995). However, in the details released in the 1995 Budget, it was stated that there will be no requirement to show the amount of landfill tax being charged on the invoice (although operators will be allowed to do so) in order to fit in with existing invoicing procedures (HM Customs & Excise, 1995d).

The CBI (1995) stress the importance of maintaining international competitiveness, and that the tax should not be allowed to reduce the UK's natural advantage in having land suitable for landfill. Wiseman and Garlick (1995) also question whether international competitiveness will be affected by the landfill tax, and express concern that the tax will fall disproportionately on small operators. They also remark that some operators may bear part of the costs themselves, so defeating the object of the tax.

The Building Employers Confederation (1995) fear that while major construction companies will pay the landfill tax, their competitors, the cowboy operators, will fly-tip at will and the chances of their being caught are small. Several other groups (such as the Association of County Councils, the National Recycling Forum and the Water Services Association) also believe that there is a high risk of fly-tipping (Biffa, 1995), and this concern was one voiced by many of the respondents to the consultation paper (HM Customs & Excise, 1995c). The possibility of increased fly-tipping is acknowledged by HM Customs & Excise (Romanski, 1995), but they remarked that in the future, fly-tipping could be regarded as tax evasion and therefore subject to HM Customs & Excise penalties in addition to environmental fines. The CBI (1995) argue that there must be increased government action against fly-tipping, but that fly-tipped waste should not incur the tax when another company clears it and takes it to landfill.

Another area of debate concerns liquid waste. Some respondents consider that the landfill tax provides an opportunity to phase out the co-disposal of liquid wastes in favour of environmentally preferable methods of treatment and disposal. The liquid-waste market is highly competitive, with an increasing number of water companies using sewage-treatment works as alternatives to co-disposal sites. A tax of 50 per cent, or even 30 per cent, would result in much less liquid waste going to landfill and more to treatment plants. This could be an environmentally better option than co-disposal, provided the aquatic environment is protected. Some inorganic and organic liquid wastes may be spread on agricultural land, and there is concern about the increased potential for soil and water contamination (ENDS No 242, 1995).

The impact of the landfill tax on the clean-up of contaminated land was also of interest to several respondents. The tax may encourage the clean-up of contaminated land *in situ*, in order to avoid paying tax on contaminated soil disposed to landfill, and thus increase research on *in situ* remediation techniques. Much industrial waste is disposed of under short-term contracts, and these should react quickly to the tax (ENDS No 242, 1995). However, on some sites where there is contamination from heavy metals, tar and oil, the clean-up technology either is not available or is not considered effective enough for housing redevelopments. The imposition of a landfill tax on projects to clean up heavily contaminated inner-city sites could make them non-viable (Building Employers Confederation, 1995; CBI, 1995). Biffa (1995) calls for an outright ban on the landfill disposal of some substances, including fluorescent lamps, certain types of batteries, pesticides and insecticides, because many landfill operators are unable to charge for the full economic cost of future environmental clean-ups.

COMPARISON WITH OTHER EU COUNTRIES

Five EU countries – Denmark, France, Germany, Belgium and The Netherlands – have landfill taxes, all banded weight-based schemes (UK Waste, 1995), which are seen as a way of raising revenue, while promoting waste reduction, recycling and incineration (Brisson, 1994). The cost per tonne varies between £1 and £20.67 (see Table 15.1).

Table 15.1 *Landfill taxes in Europe*

Country	Waste type	Cost (£/ tonne)
Denmark	All	£20.67
France	Municipal	£2.50
	Industrial, hazardous	£5–8
Germany	Industrial, hazardous	£10–41
Belgium (Flanders)	Municipal	£1–3
	Industrial, hazardous	£0.60–7
The Netherlands	All	£10.50

Source: UK Waste, 1995

In France, about 50 per cent of household waste is disposed to landfill sites, many of which are illegal sites (established prior to the imposition of the tax) (Fernandez and Tuddenham, 1995). The landfill tax was created under the 1992 Waste Disposal Act, as one component of a comprehensive waste-management policy, and entered into force on 1 April 1993. The landfill tax was intended to encourage regional self-sufficiency in waste disposal and to achieve increased environmental protection, and it was seen as an application of the polluter-pays principle. It is one of France's first attempts at using a fiscal instrument to increase environmental protection. The tax applies to household waste (and commercial waste which can be assimilated to household waste), but special waste is exempt from the tax, as are in-house landfills used by companies to dispose of their own waste.

The tax is imposed on about 6500 landfill sites, of which 500 are authorized and 6000 are illegal (Fernandez and Tuddenham, 1995). The tax is weight-based, set at 20 FF per tonne of waste, with an additional 50 per cent increase when the waste comes from outside the area (designated by the waste-disposal plan). The tax is expected to raise 350–400 million FF per year, to finance the Modernization Fund for Waste Management (MFWM), administered by ADEME, the French Environmental Protection Agency. Thus, the tax is hypothecated. In return for its exemption, industry also contributes a total of 15 million FF to this fund. The MFWM aims to give financial aid to develop and install innovative waste-treatment technologies, to give grants to local authorities for facilities, to help finance the upgrading of landfill sites, to abolish the illegal sites and to restore contaminated land. The ADEME are also responsible for the verification and collection of the tax, which they are entitled to readjust (Fernandez and Tuddenham, 1995).

It is the French government's intention that the landfill tax should run until the year 2002, after which there will be no direct disposal to landfill, and only final waste will be received. To achieve this, 160 treatment or recycling facilities will be required to ensure that the waste is made inert, stabilized or solidified. Landfill-operating standards will also be tightened and enforced. However, the money in the fund is low relative to its aims, and the target of 2002 may be optimistic unless additional funding can be secured. In France, the landfill tax exists as an effective means of raising revenue for related activities, while promoting waste reduction, recycling and incineration. However, the tax rate may need to be increased to be a more effective deterrent (Fernandez and Tuddenham, 1995).

In Denmark, a waste tax is paid on all waste being incinerated or landfilled. The householders often pay the fee simultaneously with other local authority charges (such as water supply and sewerage), but it must be specified (Danish Environmental Protection Agency (EPA), 1995). The landfill tax is weight-based and applies to virtually all waste, although inert soil used for covering landfills is exempt. It amounts to 195 DKK per tonne, a rate of 78–130 per cent of the disposal fee. The aims of the waste charges, in common with the landfill taxes of France and the UK, are to reduce the total quantity of waste produced and to increase the quantity being reused and recycled. In contrast to France and the UK, Denmark aims to reduce the quantity of waste being both landfilled and incinerated, although the incineration tax is lower than that for landfill (160 DKK/tonne), reflecting the preference for incineration and its position higher in the waste management hierarchy (Danish EPA, 1995).

The tax rates have been increased from 40 DKK/tonne in 1987, and are set to rise to 285 DKK/tonne for landfill disposal in 1997. The Danish Environmental Protection Agency (1995) report that there have been few examples of illegal disposal that could be directly related to the waste charge, largely because of the close monitoring of waste disposal in Denmark. Although the full effects are still uncertain, the waste charge has contributed to an increase in waste being reused or recycled from 35 per cent in 1985 to 50 per cent in 1993, and the proportion of demolition waste being recycled has increased from 12 per cent to 82 per cent during the same period (Danish EPA, 1995). The tax revenue is not hypothecated, although the Danish Government states a desire that it should fund environmental causes (UK Waste, 1995).

In Germany, there is no countrywide landfill tax, but generators of industrial and hazardous waste have to pay landfill disposal taxes in some states. The revenue is not hypothecated, although Germany's government does allow for hypothecation. Similarly, in The Netherlands, the funds from the landfill tax go directly to the Ministry of Finance, and the tax is applied across the country to all wastes. In the Flanders region of Belgium, there is a landfill tax which is banded according to the type of waste being disposed; again, this is collected as part of general revenue (UK Waste, 1995).

RECENT DEVELOPMENTS

On 2 August 1995, the Chancellor announced that the *ad valorem* landfill tax had been dropped in favour of a weight-based tax, a move welcomed by almost all of the respondents to the consultation paper. The tax rates, announced by the Chancellor in his Budget speech on 28 November 1995 (HM Customs & Excise, 1995d), are to be levied at a standard rate of £7/tonne, and a lower rate of tax, which will apply to 'inactive' waste, of £2/tonne. 'Inactive' waste is waste that does not give off methane, and has been defined as that which 'does not physically or chemically react, biodegrade or adversely affect other matter with which it comes into contact in a way likely to give rise to environmental pollution' (HM Customs & Excise, 1995e).

HM Customs & Excise has since announced a consultation exercise concerning the scope of the lower rate of landfill tax, linked to a proposed national waste-classification system. It is intended that all wastes falling within category one of this system should be liable to the lower tax rate. These are:

> ...uncontaminated, naturally occurring rocks, soils, silt and dredgings; uncontaminated glass, ceramics and concrete; and unused, uncontaminated moulding sands, clay absorbents, other mineral absorbents, man-made mineral fibres (including glass fibres), silica, mica and abrasives.
>
> *(HM Customs & Excise, 1995e)*

After consultation, this will be finalized with the introduction of the classification scheme on 1 April 1996.

The announcement that there will be two tax bands has been welcomed by the construction and landfill industries. However, the Building Employers Confederation would still prefer that demolition and construction wastes be made exempt as their materials are often used as cover and for landfill engineering. Some controversy surrounds the definition of soil as 'inactive' (ENDS No 247, 1995), as it will generate methane if it is contaminated with organic material. The Building Employers Confederation also calls for a commitment from the government to increase the tax rates in future years, which the government seems willing to consider. Only by progressively increasing the financial impact on producers disposing waste to landfill, will the tax provide any real incentive for the minimization and diversion of waste, making alternative means of disposal viable (Hewitt, 1995).

Local authorities, meanwhile, are pressing the DoE to allow their participation in the on-going discussions (ENDS No 247, 1995). In particular, this is with regard to the environmental trusts, which local authorities believe they have the expertise and local connections to assist in achieving their objectives (Jenkinson, 1995). The structure of the environmental trusts has yet to be finalized, and conditions applying to the contribution and rebates scheme will be contained in secondary legislation, on which there will be further consultation in 1996 (HM Customs & Excise, 1995e).

CONCLUSION

The introduction of a landfill tax will provide a first step towards an integrated, sustainable waste-management system in the UK. It will provide the means for both producers and consumers to pay the full environmental cost of the disposal of their waste to landfill. However, there is some evidence to show that the tax will not achieve its aims, particularly in the minimization and recycling of domestic waste. The tax will focus the attention on industrial and commercial waste producers who will be aware of the source of the increased costs, particularly if the tax is itemized on their waste-disposal invoice. For a medium-to-large organization, the cost of the landfill tax may well be sufficient to stimulate the introduction of waste minimization and recycling schemes. The general belief of the larger waste-management corporations appears to be that there will be a shift towards providing an integrated service of waste reduction, recycling, treatment and final disposal, but that inevitably this will mean the demise of smaller landfill companies which have less funding and a narrower approach.

The amount the general public pays for waste disposal is not related to the quantity of waste they produce, but is a notional average amount that is included in the council taxes. They are unlikely, therefore, to reduce the quantity of waste they throw away unless the local authority introduces a kerbside charging system based on volume or weight of mixed waste, as has been introduced in Seattle. It would seem that the landfill tax will be more effective in achieving its aim of moving the management of industrial and commercial waste up the waste hierarchy than achieving this for domestic waste.

A further problem that the landfill tax does not address is the stimulation of the markets for secondary materials so that the recycling cycle can be completed. There is no purpose in diverting 'waste' from landfill if there is no demand for recycled materials and products. Hopefully, this is one of the issues that the new environmental trusts will tackle.

REFERENCES

ACBE (1995a) *Response to the Government's Consultation on a Landfill Tax*, Advisory Committee on Business and the Environment, London

ACBE (1995b) 'Coopers and Lybrand Landfill Tax Seminar', London

Biffa (1995) *Industry. The proposed Landfill Tax and its implications: the likely effect on business and the environment*, Biffa Waste Services, Buckinghamshire

Brisson, I (1994) 'A possible landfill levy in the UK: economic incentives for reducing waste to landfill', in Gillies, A (ed) *Making Budgets Green: Leading Practices in Taxation and Subsidy Reform*, International Institute for Sustainable Development, Winnipeg, pp 40–1

Building Employers Confederation (1995) 'Response to the Landfill Tax', Consultation Paper, Building Employers Confederation, London

Confederation of British Industry (1995) 'Landfill Tax: a consultation paper – the business perspective', Confederation of British Industry, London

Construction Industry Council (1995) 'Briefing papers, response to the Landfill Tax', consultation paper, Construction Industry Council, London

Coopers and Lybrand (1993) *Landfill costs and prices: correcting possible market distortions*, HMSO, London

CSERGE (1995) 'Comments on the Landfill Tax', consultative paper, Centre for Social and Economic Research on the Global Environment, University College London and University of East Anglia, London and Norwich

CSERGE, Warren Spring Laboratory and EFTEC (1993) 'Externalities from Landfill and Incineration', HMSO, London

Danish Environmental Protection Agency (1995) 'The Danish Waste Charge Act', summary provided by the Danish EPA, Division for Industrial Waste, Copenhagen

Department of the Environment (1995) *A Waste Strategy for England and Wales*, consultation draft, Department of the Environment, London

Dudding, R (1995) 'Department of the Environment', Paper given at Coopers and Lybrand Landfill Tax Seminar, London

ENDS No 242 (March 1995) Environmental Data Services, London, pp 15–7

ENDS No 246 (July 1995) Environmental Data Services, London, pp 21–3

ENDS No 247 (August 1995) Environmental Data Services, London, p 32

Environmental Resources Ltd (1992) *Economic Instruments and Recovery of Resources from Waste*, HMSO, London

Fernandez, V and Tuddenham, M (1995) 'The Landfill Tax in France', in Gale, R, Barg, S and Gillies, A (eds) *Green Budget Reform: An International Casebook of Leading Practices*, Earthscan, London, pp 209–17

Hewitt, R (1995) 'The Landfill Tax and its consequences', paper presented at the IBC and University of East Anglia conference on Environmental Economic Instruments, 6 November, Royal Lancaster Hotel, London

HM Customs & Excise (1995a) 'Landfill Tax', a consultation paper, London

HM Customs & Excise (1995b) 'Chancellor strengthens landfill tax', press release, 2 August, London

HM Customs & Excise (1995c) 'Landfill Tax', report on responses received to consultation paper, September, London

HM Customs & Excise (1995d) 'Budget 1995: Landfill Tax', press release, 28 November, London

HM Customs & Excise (1995e) 'Landfill Tax: Consultation on scope of lower rate of tax for inactive waste', press release, 15 December, London

HM Government (1990) *This Common Inheritance: Britain's Environmental Strategy*, Cmnd 1200, HMSO, London

Jenkinson, S T (1995) 'Should local authorities be subject to a landfill levy', paper presented at the IBC and University of East Anglia conference on Environmental Economic Instruments, 6 November, Royal Lancaster Hotel, London

Romanski, C (1995) 'HM Customs & Excise', paper given at Coopers and Lybrand Landfill Tax Seminar, London

Spackman, M (1995) 'A Government Perspective – Why Tax?', paper presented at the IBC and University of East Anglia conference on Environmental Economic Instruments, 6 November, Royal Lancaster Hotel, London

Stupples, L (1995) 'Friends of the Earth', paper given at Coopers and Lybrand Landfill Tax Seminar, 12 May, London

Turner, R K and Brisson, I (1995) 'A possible landfill levy in the UK: economic incentives for reducing waste to landfill', in Gale, R, Barg, S and Gillies, A (eds) *Green Budget Reform: An International Casebook of Leading Practices*, Earthscan, London, pp 191–201

UK Waste (1995) *Response to the Government's consultation document on landfill tax*, UK Waste Management Ltd, Buckinghamshire

Wiseman, H and Garlick, D (1995) 'A tax blot on the landscape?', *Wastes Management*, April, pp 54–5

C h a p t e r 1 6

THE BRITISH COLUMBIA SUSTAINABILITY FUND

Jon O'Riordan

INTRODUCTION

In British Columbia, like all other Canadian provinces, discharges to the environment must be approved under the Waste Management Act (1982). Statutory approvals are provided either through a waste-management permit or a regulation covering a class of discharges. Currently, there are some 4000 permits, ranging from small operations such as asphalt plants to large industrial complexes such as pulpmills and the Cominco lead smelter at Trail.

In 1987, the government introduced its first waste-management fee regulation. This regulation established both an application fee and an annual fee. The latter was based on three factors: the type of discharge (air, effluent or solid discharge), the permittee's industrial classification and the capacity of production. Maximum fees were capped at $24,000 for air emissions, $18,000 for effluent and $12,000 for solid-waste discharges. The total amount collected under the regulation amounted to $4 million annually, which was an approximate estimate of the costs of administering the waste-management permit system in 1987. In this sense, the scheme was an environmental charge, as outlined by Michael Spackman and Jean-Philippe Barde in Chapters 3 and 11 respectively, not an environmental tax.

MARKET-BASED INCENTIVES

In 1992, the government introduced the concept of market-based incentives to the waste-permit fee regulation, substantially changing its character and impact. The 1987 regulation was not based on any direct parameters that might affect environmental quality – namely, the volume or the concentration of the amounts discharged. Nor was there an incentive to reduce discharges, especially once the cap on fees had been reached. Further, the costs of administering the permit fee system had risen significantly with the increased emphasis on enforcement and compliance monitoring, quality-control systems to check an analytical laboratory which monitored the data, and the more complex administration of permit applications. All of this was promoted by the growing public concern for environmental protection in the late 1980s and early 1990s. By 1992, the total costs of administering the permit fee and regulations issued under the Waste Management Act had risen to $15 million annually, $11 million more than five years previously.

The new permit fee system, introduced in 1992, was based on the principles of equity, economic incentive and cost recovery. First, annual fees are now based on the quantity and quality of discharges to the environment. Under the 1987 regulation, two municipalities discharging the same amount of effluent would be charged the same, regardless of the quality of this effluent.

Under the 1992 regulation, the municipalities with tertiary treatment are charged significantly less than those discharging primary treated wastes, assuming a similar volume of discharges. Similarly, pulpmills are no longer capped at fixed limits, but are charged according to the amount of discharge and the quality of effluent. As a result, discharge fees for many pulpmills rose by a factor of ten, from around $40,000 per year to over $400,000 per year.

The fees applied to the quality of effluent are based on the environmental objectives for each type of discharge. By policy, the government has established environmental objectives for a range of discharge types, such as pulpmill effluents, air emission, municipal-waste discharges, and a range of industrial types such as mining and smelting. These objectives provide guidance to the actual permitted amounts allowed in each waste-management permit. Generally, the objectives cannot be exceeded in the permit, but more stringent discharge levels can be required for sensitive environments.

The annual fees are thus based on the relative impact of a pollutant on the environment as established in these objectives. For example, sulphur-dioxide emissions are charged at a fee of $2.10/tonne, while fluorides are charged $108/tonne. Similarly, suspended solids in pulpmill effluent are charged $2.20/tonne, while organic chlorines are charged $44.00/tonne. The actual parameter fees are currently based on an arbitrary system, as the overall fee-cap under the regulation has been set at $15 million to recover administrative costs. Consequently, all unit fees for quantity and quality have to be calibrated such that this cap is not exceeded. Thus we see a form of differentiated environmental change that seeks to ensure a political promise that it cannot be regarded as a tax.

REACTIONS OF INDUSTRY AND STAKEHOLDERS

The current fee structure has changed behaviour only on the margin.

Generally, annual fees are still a small fraction of the total cost of industrial or municipal budgets. Many permittees adjusted their permits to lower the maximum allowable discharge (on which the fees are based) to the actual discharge based on monitoring systems. Some smaller operations, for which annual fees represented a large proportion of costs, did make major adjustments to their production processes. But most permittees lowered their discharges only in response to a number of regulations introduced by government over the past five years – notably, dramatic reductions in liquid-effluent discharges from pulpmills, phase-out of smoky industrial wood waste-incinerators and tightened controls on municipal waste-treatment plants. Indeed, many permittees complained that the fees were just another tax that reduced their ability to finance new technology for pollution prevention demanded by these new regulations.

Following extensive consultation on the introduction of the fees in 1992, and more recently to review further changes to the fee regulation, most permittees have accepted the fees as being equitably based and have supported additional measures to spread the burden of the fees across all discharges. Some of the proposed changes include:

- *Greenhouse gas discharge fees.* As part of its commitment to the climate convention, British Columbia has pledged to stabilize its greenhouse gas emissions at 1990 levels by the year 2000. Permit and regulatory fees are to be applied to significant greenhouse gas emissions over the next couple of years, amounting to an additional $10 million per year from these sources.
- *Changing pollution rating factors.* Pollution rating factors reflect the toxicity of one pollutant relative to others. With improved scientific understanding of the health and environmental effects of various pollutants, the pollution rating factor will be adjusted for a range of parameters. The fee-per-tonne will similarly be increased. These changes are particularly targeted at water pollutants that threaten aquatic life and air emissions that affect public health. There also remain some caps on specific pollutants to avoid an undue burden being imposed on specialized waste dischargers, such as heavy metals from the province's few metallurgical producers. These caps would be raised or eliminated.
- *Actual vs permitted discharges.* Credit will be considered for dischargers who lower their daily/annual level of discharge, even though they maintain their permitted levels to cover emergency situations. This approach works only where permittees have continuous monitoring technology.
- *Incentives.* Fees will be reduced to encourage pollution prevention planning, such as reuse of waste, discharge to ground rather than water and recycling.

FUTURE DEVELOPMENTS

British Columbia Environment has found that it requires a mix of command-and-control techniques, plus economic instruments, to pursue its policies of waste reduction and pollution prevention. This policy mix includes regulations, such as the elimination of organo-chlorines in pulp-mill effluent by 2002, phase-out of wood-waste incinerators in populated areas by 1997, and recent regulations to introduce cleaner auto fuels and low-to-zero emission vehicles into the market by 2001. These measures have resulted significantly in job creation and secondary markets, as in more refined paper products, medium-density fibre-board plants to utilize wood waste, and new refining capability.

The province has also introduced user pay-levies on lead-acid batteries ($5.00) and tyres ($3.00) which have led to a complete reuse and recycling of these products over the past five years. In addition, produce stewardship incentives have been or are being negotiated for used oil, paint, household hazardous waste, pesticides, and beverage and plastic containers to require the generator of products to be responsible for their disposal or reuse. These negotiations are backed up by regulations to ensure that all producers conform.

Permit fees will continue to evolve as a key component of this policy mix. In addition to the proposed change noted above, fees will have to be more broadly applied to the increasing number of discharges administered by regulation. New pollution-prevention plans are being negotiated on a pilot basis with seven large-scale industrial complexes. These plans are integrated pollution-control analyses that consider, simultaneously, all types of discharge but also look at energy flows, production processes and opportunities for reusing 'wastes' as by-products to minimize discharges to the environment.

As these plans are developed for all major permittees over the next five years, the government will be faced with an interesting dilemma. If discharges decrease significantly, so should permit fees, yet these are being seen increasingly as a required source of revenue to fund government programmes. Then the real genesis of this policy – cost-recovery of administrative services or an incentive to improve environment protection – will have to be faced.

EDITORIAL CONCLUSION

This manuscript is being completed in a period of unusual electoral sensitivity among the political parties in the UK. The Government has a slender majority of one that could be cut by an untimely illness or death, or suicidal tendencies among its warring backbenchers. The nation faces possibly the longest pre-election campaign in recent history. This is not a time for thoughtful public discussion on ecotaxation, or, indeed, on any form of taxation. The leaders are anxiously reigning in any unscripted voice of a Cabinet or Shadow Cabinet minister to ensure that any hint of a taxation debate is killed before the second soundbite is uttered. So we cannot expect any meaningful political discussion on this whole arena of policy for at least 18 months, and probably longer.

Yet the contributions to this book have all concluded that both the deployment of economic instruments to control demand, to improve efficiency, to redirect waste, and to restrain depletion of reusable resources, with the use of revenue for environmentally and socially directed purposes, are legitimate and practicable actions that are popular and necessary. Ecotaxation is now irreversibly part of the modern political and economic scene. Increasingly, the use of the revenues for a variety of employment and social justice-related reasons is becoming more commonplace.

Revolutions of this kind come slowly, usually by modest experiment, and sensibly without fanfare. There is little point in proclaiming the significance of a set of initiatives that are bound to succeed and fail in almost equal measure until we understand better the social and political ramifications of both charging and redistributing. The world of non-sustainable growth has clothed itself in a web of intricately interconnecting prices, subsidies and taxes that cannot easily or simply be reconstructed towards sustainable development without much trial and error.

So it should not be surprising that ecological tax reform will take time and will not be promoted with much political relish in the foreseeable future. It presents a large and slow-moving target at which its many critics may direct their fire. It also contains a host of contradictions. The 'double dividend' may be illusory, unless pre-existing distorting subsidies, upon which many electrally significant stakeholders depend, are decoupled and dismantled as the new taxes are introduced. Try doing that in an uneasy coalition government or within 18 months of a general election. Any environmentally directed taxation can be used to meet so many objectives that it is in danger of being hopelessly confused as to its purpose. And, as any ecotax proves successful, so the source of revenue, so vital for its wider effectiveness, diminishes. The consequence is either to squeeze up the rate or to widen the net, meanwhile staving off pleas for preferential exemption.

The overall conclusion of this series of essays is that ecotaxation is a concept and a practice whose time has come. The reasons lie more with the prevailing spirit of letting markets work, no matter how imperfect, of encouraging deregulation generally, and of taxing by means other than striking at income and savings, than with a will to move towards sustainable development. The spectre of an uncontrollable welfare state and an increasingly costly ageing population adds to the drive to shift the burden of social payments on to individuals according to need and to means. But shifting the burden of social costs on to private pockets does not reduce the burden. The ultimate dilemma is that ecotaxation is another package of payments whose objective is to lower the cost of the transition to sustainable development in the most efficient and fair manner possible. That fairness aspect will have to be made more explicit. The fact that burdens, which heretofore fell on the poor and the vulnerable without troubling the rich, will now have to be shouldered by the better-off will prove one of the great tests for ecotaxation. In a democracy, the rich may not tolerate the change, yet to stand by and create greater inequality in the name of sustainability is a contradiction in objectives.

This conundrum reveals that the transition to sustainable development will tell us more about how we collectively value the civilities of justice and democracy than it will tell us about our concern for the planet. If this is true, then fine-tuning Pigouvian taxes is a luxury that may fill academic papers but will not assist in the outcome. Identifying the new vista of gainers and losers would be a better academic pastime. And finding ways to allow the hypothecational part of ecotaxation to enable a more tolerant and compassionate democracy to work should be the task for us all in the foreseeable future. Right now there is a ferment of academic and political activity around the future of regulation, of taxation, of the welfare state, of education and of constitutional reform. For the most part, those struggling with such issues are working in a vacuum when it comes to the sustainability transition. So the most urgent test is to find clever, and at times devious, ways to ensure that sustainability in its various guises clothes these discussions with its own visions for planetary survival.

INDEX